The Adventures of a
Victorian Con Woman

'Them as has money and no brains is made for
them as has brains and no money'*

* Mary Braddon, 1835–1914, novelist.

The Adventures of a Victorian Con Woman

The Life and Crimes of Mrs Gordon Baillie

Mick Davis and David Lassman

PEN & SWORD HISTORY

First published in Great Britain in 2020 by
Pen & Sword History
An imprint of
Pen & Sword Books Ltd
Yorkshire – Philadelphia

ISBN 978 1 52676 486 7

A CIP catalogue record for this book is
available from the British Library.

Typeset by Mac Style
Printed and bound in the UK by TJ Books Ltd,
Padstow, Cornwall.

Pen & Sword Books Limited incorporates the imprints of Atlas,
Archaeology, Aviation, Discovery, Family History, Fiction, History,
Maritime, Military, Military Classics, Politics, Select, Transport,
True Crime, Air World, Frontline Publishing, Leo Cooper, Remember
When, Seaforth Publishing, The Praetorian Press, Wharncliffe
Local History, Wharncliffe Transport, Wharncliffe True Crime
and White Owl.

For a complete list of Pen & Sword titles please contact

PEN & SWORD BOOKS LIMITED
47 Church Street, Barnsley, South Yorkshire, S70 2AS, England
E-mail: enquiries@pen-and-sword.co.uk
Website: www.pen-and-sword.co.uk

Or

PEN AND SWORD BOOKS
1950 Lawrence Rd, Havertown, PA 19083, USA
E-mail: Uspen-and-sword@casematepublishers.com
Website: www.penandswordbooks.com

Contents

Introduction

The advantages and limitations of writing biography are summed up brilliantly by the Australian academic John Barnes:

'The ways in which the individual sees himself and the society to which he belongs can never be fully known to future generations; but a biographer can know a great many more facts about the relationships and attitudes that are relevant to his subject's life than his subject ever did. The biographer knows the outcome, knows how the individual life ends, and how it appears in retrospect. With all this factual knowledge, however, the biographer still cannot feel the flow of consciousness – in which the sense of the past is simultaneously present in the hopes and fears for the future – as his subject felt it.'[*]

Few female criminals can have had so much media coverage in their lifetime and made so little impact on the writings of modern historians of crime. A mention of her name in a book containing the history of the Fulham Women's Refuge, discovered while doing the research for a previous collaboration – *The Awful Killing of Sarah Watts: A Story of Confessions, Acquittals and Jailbreaks* (a book about an infamous child murder from the 1850s) – led the authors to recover what they could of her amazing life.[**] Mystery surrounds every aspect of her life-long criminal career, and her motivations are as obscure as her fate. Even her 'real' name is open to question: records have not survived, and despite the use of over forty aliases during her campaign she seems not to have used that of either of her natural parents. In the main we have referred to her throughout the book as 'Annie' because, apart from her later legal adoption of the name 'Gordon Baillie', this is the one she used consistently throughout her life.

It was the *Newcastle Chronicle* that called her the 'Napoleon of Crime', but her career was best summed by the *Aberdeen Evening Express* of 5 March 1888 during the press campaign against her three months before she was arrested:

---

[*] Barnes, 2006.
[**] Feret, p.127.

'The story of Mrs Gordon Baillie is stranger than anything to be met with in the field of fiction. That a woman so illiterate as to be unable even to spell or write her own, or her chosen names & aliases, should for 20 years have managed to impose upon the sharpest and most intelligent people in every English-speaking community in Europe would, if written in a novel, be pronounced as impossible, improbable or ultra-sensational. It is no wonder that she should succeed in defrauding the worlds of religion, philanthropy and political agitation because these have been the fields on which vulgar rascality have practiced with success in all time. There are many who boast of driving a coach and pair through acts of Parliament, but there are few who can for a lifetime defy the law and live as the saying goes, "like a fighting cock" off the spoils. Born into the midst of direst poverty how has she learned her arts and manners? – such characters are born not made. Had she possessed the higher mental qualities which go to make up dramatic genius she may have been the greatest actress of her age.'

What can we hope to know about the motivation and aspirations of Mrs Gordon Baillie? She carried out acts of great ingenuity and daring, trying to fool the world into believing that she was something she was not, a project so obviously doomed to failure at times as to call her sanity into question. She surrounded herself with the trappings of wealth and taste: art, furnishings, champagne, beautiful houses, servants and an ever-available carriage and pair. But were these the aim of a life of subterfuge, or were they just the props in the stage set of her life? No sooner had she swindled some valuable article from some tradesman than she took it to the pawn shop; they meant little compared to the thrill of acquiring them. Even her children, for which it appears she had some affection, were passed off to others at every opportunity before they too disappeared without trace.

Could her upbringing have contributed towards her behaviour? Did poverty, illegitimacy, the lack of a name to call her own or a broken heart give rise to the need to escape to wealth, legitimacy, social standing and acclaim? It seems probable that she had a genetic disposition towards compulsive behaviour. Like an alcoholic who has never touched alcohol, the addiction is there from birth – hard-wired into the system and requiring only for that potential to meet favourable circumstances for it to dominate. If addiction can be defined as the compulsion to engage continually in activities despite any negative impact on an ability to function like others, then this would apply to Annie. She found salvation at first amongst the local evangelical Christians before moving on to the international stage, and even at the height of her fame and physical wellbeing she avoided paying the most trifling sums at great risk to her liberty, reputation and the success of her more ambitious schemes. Her condition required repeated small fixes, and with Annie the addiction was all-consuming – marriage, children, financial security, great houses and works of art, physical attractiveness and charisma were all subordinate to the thrill of the next crime, mere tools in the game. Annie could easily have married into great riches or used her intelligence to acquire wealth legitimately, but that was not the aim. The crime was an end in itself. No matter how big or how small, it fed a compulsion that is still little understood today. Ultimately she is perhaps more to be pitied than condemned.

This is not a small book, but there is without a doubt far more to her life than has been discovered so far and more to it than will ever be known. This was acknowledged in her own lifetime, not least by Inspector Marshall, at the end of her 'career' at the Old Bailey:

> 'Space does not allow here to mention a fiftieth of the extraordinary and audacious stories of her exploits or a tithe of the accomplishments and graces with which she carried all before her.'

One of the hopes behind publication is that more stories will emerge – the lives of four of her children are totally unknown from their early teens or before, yet they must have left some trace and may have descendants living today.

Mick Davis & David Lassman, July 2020

Part I

1848–1872

Chapter 1

Origins
(1848–68)

In the mid-nineteenth century, Peterhead was a small fishing port in the Scottish county of Aberdeenshire, sited on the easternmost point of the mainland and facing the North Sea. It had once been a popular therapeutic spa town, but the excessive building boom that this success provoked spoiled the sparkling waters, while the growth of its fishing industry meant that the grand houses were divided into ever smaller units and the elegant town became run down. At the time our story begins, most of its inhabitants were involved in the herring industry; immense quantities of which were exported to the Baltic ports.

Running roughly from east to west in the town, and close to the port, stands Maiden Street; parallel rows of two-storey fishermen's cottages built with large blocks of the local brown stone. Standing out among these was a slightly larger building, number forty-seven, which nestled between the stone and coal yards, close to the lime sheds. The house had long since been divided into single rooms and a Captain Mackie had just left his room there to move out to Fraserburgh, where he took up the position of harbour master. The next occupant was Katherine Reid, known to all as Kate. She had been born in 1820, the daughter of James Reid, a carter from Longside, Aberdeen, and his wife Anne Gibson. Kate is shown in the 1841 census with seven others of about the same age, working as a servant on a farm at Wester Barnyards, Peterhead. By 1847 she was in the employ of another local tenant farmer, John Newbond, in the same capacity, at his farm in Invereddie, Longside. Master and servant soon became lovers, but when she became pregnant with her third child, Newbond threw her out. At first he denied paternity, despite Kate having been his mistress for some time, and implicated 'other parties' who frequented the farm, though few doubted that he was the father. Kate found temporary employment on a nearby farm at Bogend, Longside, before taking the room in Maiden Street as the time of her confinement drew near. Kate gave birth to a daughter, whom she named Annie, on 21 February 1848, and soon after took her to stay with the baby's grandfather, James Reid, who lived at Ugie Street in the north of the town. She found work 'tramping fish meal' in the holds of ships, then an important export from Peterhead, and helping to store corn and meal in granaries, before returning to work in the fields at harvest time.

An unnamed acquaintance of the Newbond family described Annie as having been brought up 'in the purlieus about the Roanheads and across the damnation gutter', an expression, the informant claims, that 'could only be understood by those who knew the ideas of caste held by the dwellers on each side of the gutter'; in other words, she was born on the 'wrong side of the tracks'. Annie's baptism was not recorded in the register maintained by the Episcopal Church at Peterhead because, according to press reports, a 'strange incumbent' was officiating for a time in place of the regular one. The ceremony is alleged to have taken place about six months after the birth, although there are no entries recorded between April and November 1848; just three blank spaces left for names that were never entered. If Annie had been determined to lead a life of deception from the moment of her birth, she could not have planned it better: there is no mention of her in any official church records and there are stories of a dispute with one of the incumbents who left the job, taking some of the parish records with him and destroying them. Years later, when her age became an important issue, the police had to obtain the sworn testimony of two unnamed 'witnesses to the birth and baptism'. Birth certificates did not become an official requirement in Scotland until 1855.

The first official mention of Annie comes from the 1851 census. On 30 March that year, Katherine Reid, 29, and Annie Newbond, aged 2, are listed as living in a small granite-built cottage in North Street, located just around the corner from James Reid's house in Ugie Street; there is no mention of her other children. Why she gave her daughter the name of the estranged father, rather than her own, is not known – perhaps to embarrass him into admitting paternity or possibly as an act of spite. It is interesting that the woman who later operated under at least forty aliases never had an officially registered name of her own – in all likelihood she was never baptised. To add to this air of mystery, the census gives her name as Newbond, her mother's name was Reid and she was brought up as Sutherland. No wonder she found it easy to adopt and discard names at will later in life.

Annie's paternal family, the Newbonds – sometimes written as Newbound or Newbone – have an interesting connection with alternative identities. In 1790, an Aberdonian named Andrew Shirrefs, known to all as 'Cripple Andy' because he needed the aid of a crutch to get about, published a book entitled *Poems, Chiefly in the Scottish Dialect*. One of the plays in the book was called 'Jamie and Bess', a work described by the 1888 reporter for *The Aberdeen Free*

Press who uncovered this link as 'never rising above respectable mediocrity'. It tells the comic story of two people using false identities to court each other before discovering that they are, in fact, related. The play was first performed in Aberdeen on 12 January 1788, with the two main characters being played by a Mr and Mrs Newbound, who, the reporter claims – quoting an unnamed 'reliable correspondent' – were Annie's grandparents. Their names are printed on the page preceding the play, which shows they must have had some standing in the theatrical world at the time. The famous Scottish poet Robbie Burns met Shirrefs during his third northern tour and noted: 'Met Mr. Shirrefs, author of "Jamie & Bess" – little decrepit body with some abilities.'

It seems that in about 1818 the Newbonds (or Newbounds) had had enough of touring and settled in Peterhead, then still a fashionable bathing resort attracting, amongst others, the Duke and Duchess of Gordon, who were no doubt drawn by the chalybeate springs in the area. The former 'strolling players' settled down to run a pub and stabling establishment, which was notorious for gambling, attracting both local gentry and young ladies of easy virtue. This den of vice lay at the top of Flying Gigs Wynd in Broad Street, where the leading worthies of the town were wont to assemble, and which held a 'Friday Club' – a drinking and card-playing institution for those in the know with money to lose. The premises later became Forbes the Chemist. It is also known that Mr Newbond was at one time manager of the Theatre Royal in Peterhead, which flourished during the town's heyday in the early 1800s. Newbond made a good Falstaff, it was said, and Mrs Newbond was a superior actress, one paper describing her as 'as handsome a woman as ever trod the streets of Peterhead'. It was an attraction which she seems to have put to good use, as another newspaper credited her with having the reputation of easy morals, numerous male companions, and having conceived John (Annie's father) via one of her 'customers' in 1822.

The pub, theatre and gambling den had, unsurprisingly, been very successful, and there was quite a bit of money left when Newbond senior died in 1827. Provost Alexander was the executor of his will and guardian to young John, whom he boarded with a family not far from the town. The census of 1841 shows Annie's future father living at New Seat, Inverugie, Peterhead, and of independent means, in the household of George Paul, presumably a farmer. The likelihood is that the deceased Newbond's estate was controlled by the provost and that the money was used to pay for John's upkeep while he was taught farming. The boy was lame for a long time in his early years, but eventually gathered strength to become a strapping lad of 6 feet who was soon put into his own farm, at Invereddie, Longside, Buchan, Aberdeen. By the census of 1851 he was 28 years old and a tenant farmer of 180 acres under cultivation, with 20 acres of waste moss, employing at least two people on the land and with a household that consisted of five servants (former servant Kate Reid was in the same census, of course, living with 2-year-old Annie in North Street). He was unmarried. Despite these opportunities, it seems that he did not take to hard work, one report describing him as having 'failed in business' while other accounts say he was living 'very fast' and claimed that he was soon taken out of the farm and returned to Peterhead.

The Aberdeen Free Press of March 1888 quotes a childhood friend of Newbond as telling how he had to flee the country after an attempted rape in which the girl he assaulted had her spine injured. She recovered but was considerably deformed, although, as the paper puts it, 'did eventually marry'. It is believed that he moved first to Ireland and then to Newcastle, where he was head of a horse-hiring establishment. Another old friend was reported as having seen him in Newcastle in later years, where he had married a widow who ran an inn at Monkwearmouth, and said that he was, at some point, also living in Sunderland, where he was employed superintending workmen for the local corporation, living comfortably and doing well for himself. Other reports indicate that he died soon after this time.

Whatever the truth about John Newbond's final years, it seems that Annie was fully aware of her parentage. One story has it that she found a copy of a book entitled *The British Herbalist* that Newbond had left to cover a small debt, which she took as a 'keepsake of her father'. Time would show that she had inherited her paternal grandmother's good looks and acting ability, as, ever anxious to improve upon the truth of her own life, she would claim parentage from several high-born sources. During a visit to Peterhead some years later, she mentioned the name of a much-respected farmer, called Bruce, then deceased, in connection with her paternity.

Annie's maternal grandfather, James Reid, was, at the time of her birth, 66 years of age and recorded as living in the same street as his daughter, near its junction with Ugie Street. With him was his second, possibly 'common law' wife, Janet, a domestic servant then aged 59. James died around 1855, sparking a lawsuit between Janet and the family of his first wife, Anne. Despite the hard and uncertain life James Reid had lived, it seems that there was something left worth fighting over – not to mention money for lawyers' bills.

As for Kate Reid, Annie's mother, after leaving seasonal work on the farms and docks she took up regular employment as a washerwoman. Annie would have been about 7 years old at the time. She was the third of her mother's eventual five children – all illegitimate. When the fourth, James, was born in 1859 at Cruden, south of Peterhead, Annie was lodged in the Peterhead poorhouse for a fortnight. Shortly after this time, Kate took up with a local hawker named Bruce Sutherland. He was about ten years her junior and travelled the district with a cart selling crockery. Kate and Annie (who was by now around 11 years old) often travelled with him, during which time it was said that the girl became perfectly familiar with every lane, farm and village in the area. It was in this way that Annie spent her formative years and learned the basics of her future trade; knocking on doors with her stepfather and picking up much of the salesman's patter, while at the same time constantly being told how pretty she was and appreciating the smiles and little treats handed out by the grown-ups. While visiting some of the grand houses she would have also noticed the well-born ladies in their fine clothes and the wonders on display in their homes. She was later to become an excellent horsewoman, and no doubt learnt the basics during this time through driving the cart between customers. It was far from an easy life, and for at least one further winter Annie was placed in the Peterhead poorhouse. Sometime after this she is said to have lived for about two years on a farm in the vicinity of New Maud, about 12 miles west of Peterhead, and it is believed that she received at least part of an education in that district. Annie's young brother James appears later in the story, and apart from another brother named Hamish the fate of her siblings remain unknown – even their names are uncertain; perhaps they didn't all survive childhood. As Annie grew into her teenage years she displayed a strong attraction to evangelical Christianity – either real or assumed – and as 'Miss Sutherland', having taken her stepfather's name, acted as a 'bible woman'. She addressed evangelistic meetings at a building known as 'The Hospital', an old hall at the extreme end of the Roanheads in Peterhead, now long since demolished.

Although born into poverty and illegitimacy, Annie possessed several great advantages over others of her station. All accounts describe her as stunningly attractive, possessed of a phenomenal memory and a fine mimic with a quick wit. Without these, her background would have excluded her from going far in life; perhaps if she had been lucky, she might have caught the eye of a rich man prepared to defy convention and take her as a wife. Alternatively, with her natural abilities she could have tried her hand at becoming an actress – but why confine herself to one stage when the whole world lay before her? She had also inherited a roving spirit, a fierce independence and a determination to make her own way in the world – no matter what the cost.

Chapter 2

A Growing Reputation
(1868–70)

In the mid to late 1860s, Annie, now in her 20s with her widowed mother in tow, headed down the eastern coast of Scotland from Peterhead to Dundee. The city's growth as a successful seaport began in the late twelfth century, and at the time the two women arrived it was experiencing the most prosperous period in its history as the centre of the global jute industry. A demand for cheaper, tough textiles during the earlier decades of the nineteenth century had brought the long, soft, shiny vegetable fibre – which could be spun into coarse, strong threads – to the fore. Dundee mills located on the north bank of the Firth of Tay estuary had rapidly converted from linen to jute, and with the expansion of supporting industries – jute needed to be lubricated with whale oil, for example – a time of inflated prosperity ensued. At the industry's height, the city boasted sixty-two jute mills, employing some 50,000 workers.

Once in Dundee, Annie, with her adopted name of Mary Ann Bruce Sutherland, started teaching Bible classes at a Model Lodging House for females in King Street, located near the dockland area of the city. 'Model', in contrast to 'Common', lodging houses were purposely created to try and improve the lot of the labouring classes and many such places were new-builds, although in this case the building had been the Dundee Royal Infirmary until the mid-1850s. During the time Annie was teaching there, rumour had it that she became associated with an Italian gentleman, who taught her the basics of his language, although nothing further is known about him. From at least April 1869 she was living in Graham Place, off Princes Street, and it was also around this time that her criminal tendencies began to be noticed. She defrauded a few shopkeepers in the town, ordering goods without paying, and as word spread that she was not trustworthy, Annie thought it wise to leave both the vicinity and her mother and live on her own.

At the beginning of 1870, Annie – or Mary Ann Bruce Sutherland – moved around 70 miles back up the eastern coast to Aberdeen. Expensive infrastructure works had caused the city to become bankrupt in the early part of the nineteenth century, but by the latter decades its prosperity had recovered. Among the stories that would emerge from people who came to know Annie at this time is a letter from a Mr W. Christie Crowe, published in the *Edinburgh Evening Despatch* nearly two decades later:

'Mrs Gordon Baillie [the name that Annie would choose later for her career in crime] took a prominent stand in Christian mission work in Aberdeen in about the year 1868 [Mr Crowe's memory seems out by two years]. In the work of evangelistic and cottage meetings, widely carried on at the time, she identified herself, and was recognised, as one of a band of earnest workers. Her stay was short and even then her movements became somewhat mysterious. It was known she was a person without means, but this did not deter her from renting or lodging in an upper-class house near Kittybrewster. To some of us with very sober ideas of grandeur in those days this was nothing less than confounding, and I remember a highly respected gentleman in the city bitterly complaining that she had no more right to live in such a place than he had to occupy the palace of the Duke of Buccleuch. From the house out Calsayseat way she soon afterwards disappeared and nothing more was heard of her. In Aberdeen then, nearly 20 years ago, there appeared the shadow of the desperate events that were to follow. In her personal appearance and captivating manners lay, undoubtedly the evil influence of "Mrs Gordon Baillie".'

W. Christie Crowe 2nd March 1888

The upper-class house that Mr Crowe recollected was in Powis Place, Kittybrewster, to the north of Aberdeen city centre, and Annie engaged an elderly spinster to clean it, telling her that if she needed hot water to get some coals and she would cover the cost, along with that of any food required. A dealer sent up some furniture and the old lady worked heartily to get the place in order. Miss Sutherland (Annie) explained her lack of clothes and personal effects by saying that her mother was to have come with some of her luggage but had let her down. Seeing that her mistress was without even a change of linen, the soft-hearted spinster offered the loan of her Sunday-best underclothing, an offer that was eagerly accepted, despite them having been worn at least once by the giver since being washed. The underwear was never seen again, nor were the pairs of footwear lent to Annie by the poor shopkeeper who lived opposite. Both victims would testify later, however, that their patroness was 'the nicest spoken lady they ever saw'. We do not know if 'Mamma' did let Annie down with the luggage, but whatever the truth, the house was rented and furnished expensively in her mother's name and the two were reunited there at some point, when Kate came to live with her daughter once more.

While residing in Powis Place, the pious Miss Sutherland set up a non-denominational mission school just around the corner in Nelson Street, beside the United Presbyterian Church, and engaged two assistant teachers. Soon she had a large attendance of very young scholars, but they were occupied more in singing and being lectured on religion and morals than they were in receiving a useful education. She made much of her devotion and organized a clothing society, along with mothers' meetings, the latter patronized mainly by elderly females captivated by her eloquence and piety. She professed to be under influential patronage while engaged in these charitable works and this helped her to obtain large amounts of fabric for the seamstresses on credit, while women members paid a small weekly subscription. The whole enterprise seems to have been a front for raising funds so that Annie could feed her increasing appetite for improving her own comfort and social standing – although this is not to say that her little flock didn't benefit as well. Such contrasting behaviour became a regular feature of her life. She once organized a large tea party and invited all the poor urchins of the district. Bread for the feast was supplied by the local baker, who went unpaid, and on another occasion, while at a grocer's shop in Gallowgate, she ordered a number of parcels of tea for distribution amongst the poor. How could a humble grocer not take pity on a pretty young Christian woman dedicated to charitable works who was in such a hurry on her way to visit a 'poor woman, just about to be called away to God' that she had forgotten her purse? The kindly shopkeeper also lent her a pound for her journey which, along with the money for his tea parcels, he never saw again.

Miss Sutherland gave improving advice to her assistants, warning them against the love of finery, jewellery or excessive display in dress, while all the time fleecing tradesmen and those she professed to help of the very same items. The money poured in, charitable deeds were performed but little was actually paid for. She made the best of her caring reputation, borrowing money and obtaining credit to enable her to continue with her 'good works'. In August, along with various other goods, Annie managed to obtain a gold watch and a ring on credit from a jeweller near Union Street, in the city centre, promising to pay 'when the school inspector came round'. The inspector's visit seemed to take a very long time; she returned to the shop to explain that he had still not shown up and borrowed £1 on top, to pay for articles she had purchased 'round the corner' but had again left her purse at home. The poor jeweller did not see her for a considerable time and discussed his concerns with the police, but did not make any official complaint until he heard that other local tradesmen had been conned in the same way. Miss Sutherland was taken to the police station and became most indignant about her treatment. She managed not only to talk her way out of her predicament, but instigated legal action against the watchmaker for slander, indignity and the suffering that he had put her through, claiming £300 in compensation. The case got as far as having time allocated in court, but was dismissed when the aggrieved Miss Sutherland did not appear. The watchmaker won his case by default and was awarded his expenses against her, which were never recovered, nor was the watch or the ring, although she would later repay him the borrowed £1 and a local draper managed to recover £7 that was owed to him.

Common sense would seem to indicate that this way of life was not sustainable in the medium to long term, and as word got around town and more creditors began banging on the door, Annie and her mother had to leave the grand house. Despite 'Miss Sutherland's' surprise and dismay at this turn of events – she publicly expressed shock that her mother should have behaved so badly in not paying the rent and running up such debts – Annie was forced to take common lodgings elsewhere in the town in order to continue her charitable work, first in the Spittal and afterwards in Park Street. By now even the earnest young teachers that followed her began to realize all was not as it seemed and took their leave. She kept in contact with some of them, and they later referred to her as 'yon woman that lived by her wits' and indicated that her letters showed a standard of education far below an ordinary level of scholarship. When the traders of Aberdeen began to press for payment, Annie realized that she had outstayed her welcome and decided to take up some of the offers she had received to preach back in Peterhead, where she was highly thought of as a speaker. In the autumn of 1870, she accepted an invitation from the newly convened branch of the Plymouth Brethren there and began to address their meetings, leading prayers and preaching with great conviction. On the first of her two visits, she stayed in Broad Street with William McLean, a 34-year-old tinsmith and former Baptist whose family owned a rope-making business in the town. Initially he ran the group from his drawing room and eventually became well known as an evangelist in Northern Ireland. During her time back in her home town, Annie spoke freely about her parentage and early connection to Peterhead, showing a perfect familiarity with the area. Writing in later years, McLean said: 'She was the deepest woman I ever met, so sweet and could talk so like a Christian.' He also states that his wife 'found her out' and that she was asked to leave, but gives no further details. It was also noted by several who knew her in the early years that she was a 'splendid mimic'.

While devoting herself to visiting the poor at Roanheads and other slum districts, Annie had her photograph taken in the studio of James Shivas, a fashionable young photographer of Queen Street, and is reported to have fallen desperately in love with him; she later claimed they were engaged. The relationship was broken off when he went to see her in Aberdeen and discovered that her accommodation was merely an attic and not the mansion he had been lead to believe; the affair quickly turning sour once he had the measure of his 'conquest'. It is possible that this man was the young Italian of previous years and that the two stories have become confused, but with the passage of time it is impossible to tell and no further details have emerged. A letter written not long afterwards from a Trade Protection Society, detailing certain of 'Miss Sunderland's' activities in the town, mentions the name of the man to whom she was said to be engaged, but unfortunately this letter seems not to have survived. Whatever the identity of the gentleman, the affair seems to have affected Annie deeply and was put forward in years to come as contributing to her mental state.

Only a few weeks after this visit to Peterhead she returned, taking advantage of a casual invitation given to her for the following summer by one of the people whom she had met at a revivalist meeting. Her hosts retained lively memories of this unexpected second visit, which to their great surprise lasted a fortnight. They professed themselves deceived by her sympathetic manner and appearance of benevolence, and found her airs quite amusing, except towards the end of her somewhat overlong stay. She told them that she had returned to Peterhead partly to make enquiries about property to which she believed herself entitled through her parents, and partly because she was soon going out as a missionary to Rome and was waiting for William Pennefather, the evangelical Anglican mission worker in London, to make arrangements for her. With hindsight, it is not unreasonable to assume that the speed of her return was connected to the enquiries that the police were making in relation to goods that had been ordered and remained unpaid for back in Aberdeen. Be that as it may, she again occupied her time speaking frequently at temperance meetings and devoting herself to visiting the poor, often taking them the greater part of her own dinner, although this great benevolence was normally dispensed at the expense of her indulgent hosts. She professed to be greatly addicted to literature and stated that she wrote poetry in *Good Words*, a religious monthly, under a *nom de plume*. As an amusing example of her habits, her hosts observed she always carried a magazine or something of the sort when she went out. Although she could read and write, her handwriting was not very good, but she knew exactly how to express herself. She did not go to church, declaring that she could never listen to a sermon as she was always thinking for herself and so she stayed at home to read. All things considered, she was generally thought of by her hosts as being of a 'prepossessing appearance, [with] ladylike manners and good education'. They maintained this rosy view of future events would show otherwise.

Whilst in Peterhead, Annie visited a school at St Fergus, about 3 miles to the north-west, and spoke with much indignation of the disgraceful lack of accommodation, which fell far short of that needed for the number of scholars. She took down various details and assured the teacher that she would take up the matter and see that a suitable new school was procured. The teacher came from the same area, and Annie visited her family's farm, sometime after which they received a very kindly letter from her purporting to come from a college in London. There must have been more to the letter than good wishes, as in response they sent her large supplies of chickens and other farm produce, for which they were never paid.

It became Annie's practice for the remainder of her career to gain the confidence of useful people through her charm and charitable acts, and obtain from them letters of introduction to influential contacts elsewhere. Failing this, she would just forge the initial set, using genuine names, and work her way up the social ladder, hoping not to be discovered. She was introduced to some Aberdeen friends of her hosts in Peterhead and later obtained small amounts of money from them, but a more remarkable exploit was that of fleecing members of the police themselves. Annie had made friends with the sister of a Peterhead policeman named Gordon, and from her obtained a letter of introduction to some of his police friends in London. She managed to obtain sums of money from them, presumably to further her good works. Whilst taking tea with her new friend on a particularly cold day, Annie persuaded Miss Gordon to loan her a brand-new cloak, which she promised faithfully to return, though unsurprisingly she never did. When the time came for her to leave, she asked her hosts to lend her £5, which they felt unable to do, and after what must have been an awkward conversation they gave her 10 shillings for her train fare. Such petty and constant pilfering could not go on for long without word getting round, and shortly after Annie had left Peterhead, Provost Alexander received a letter from a Trade Protection Society enquiring about 'Miss Sunderland' and giving several particulars as to her activities in the town – this was the letter that included the name of her alleged former fiancé.

Another person she dropped in on during her visit was her maternal aunt, Janet Strachan (née Reid), the younger sister by three years of Annie's mother. Strachan would later talk at length about their early history to a reporter from the *Aberdeen Free Press* (mother Katy or Catherine Reid was still living at the time of the interview.) The civil case against James Reid's widow, also called Janet, a few years before had resulted in a win for Kate's side, but despite their victory Janet Strachan claims that she returned her own share to Janet Reid. Perhaps this was the family 'property' that Annie had been enquiring about. Kate, it seems, kept her portion, which helped to give rise to a 'split' in the family, but also enabled her and Annie to move from Aberdeen to Dundee. Aunt Janet had no news from her older sister until Annie's visit to see her in 1870. When the reporter asked about her niece's charitable acts, she denied that Annie had ever distributed charity to the poor at Roanheads. According to her it was about this time that she – now around 23 years old – turned her mind to easy money, her mission being to collect alms for herself using a respectable front rather than give money away to the needy. Janet mentions an instance where, seeing that her gold ring was a little worn, her niece offered to take it to a jeweller in order to have it made stronger by adding a bar of gold to it. The aunt speculated that this must have been very hard thing to do, as the ring had still not been returned to her years later – either that or Annie had conveniently 'forgot' to return it. According to the aunt, Annie had told her that an old lady in Dundee had taken a fancy to her and put her in a good school at New Maud, where such refined education had left her unsuited to the sort of manual work her background would dictate. Annie had also learned how her good looks could be used to her advantage and had acquired 'ideas above her station'. It was said that she could not, or would not, in the current phrase, 'black her own boots', and when the old lady died, Annie said that she was left all her clothes and personal property. Despite these claims, there does not seem to have been a school at New Maud until 1896 and it seems that Annie's education was rudimentary at best, as there were many stories in years to come about her poor spelling and grammar, which she covered by employing a secretary.

Having outstayed her welcome in Peterhead, Miss Sutherland used her introductions – real or manufactured – to spend between ten and twelve days in Liverpool, meeting prominent people and getting promises for a grand scheme to introduce continentals to the joys of the Protestant religion. An account in the *Fife Herald*, following a later police report, says she fled to Liverpool to avoid creditors, and then left there for the exact same reason. Meanwhile, an unnamed correspondent to the *Pall Mall Gazette* in 1888 recalls Annie's time in the city:

> 'Mrs Gordon Baillie was then a charming Miss Sutherland Bruce, who was full of a scheme for setting up a girl's school in Rome on Protestant

principles. Her scheme did not sound unreasonable and she seemed by her earnestness and sweet manners a suitable person to undertake it, although she expressed her religious convictions rather oddly. She had a beautiful frank face, deep earnest eyes, a graceful figure, a sweet voice and gentle sympathetic manners. She was soberly but becomingly dressed. I recollect thinking her bonnet was perfection for a pretty woman bent on a sympathetic mission! She made a round of visits to certain rich and generous merchants of Liverpool; and she won them all to her purpose in so far as to collect a considerable – probably large – sum of money.

'She was the guest of relatives of my own near Liverpool during part of the time. She gave me the very faintest indication of some heart sorrow she had had. The tears came into her eyes but she checked them as she alluded to it in a low sad voice. On leaving she gave an address in London where she was not known. She wrote to me from London that she had changed her London address, and was starting for Rome. Tradespeople in Liverpool then began to write to me to know where she was to be found as she had left debts unpaid. Among other things she had purchased a gorgeous sealskin cloak worth perhaps £20 or £30. The next I heard was that she had been seen by a friend of mine driving about Rome in a pretty pony carriage which, with the sealskin cloak, she was enjoying at the expense of the kind Liverpool merchants.

'No school was ever started. It is difficult to set the charming creature down as wholly a swindler. She seems to be one of those strange creatures who appear now and again in society born with a taste for intrigue and roguery, and probably through a lack of all moral sense hardly able to know truth from falsehood.'

As Annie's reputation for untrustworthiness grew along with her creditors throughout Peterhead, Dundee, Aberdeen and Liverpool, it must have been obvious that she would have to set her sights further afield. This search for riches would soon lead her to Europe, New Zealand, Australia and America, but first it was time to try her luck in the richest city on earth. Annie headed for London.

Chapter 3

A Tale of Two Capitals
(1871)

We cannot know for certain how the 23-year-old Annie made the journey from Liverpool to London, but it seems more than likely that she would have completed the 178 or so miles by rail. The option of travelling by road or water was open to her, but given the many advantages steam engines held over rival modes of transport – increased speed being the main one – this must have appealed to her. No doubt she would have literally begged, borrowed or stolen the fare money so as to reach London as quickly as possible, putting as much distance as possible between herself and her most recently acquired creditors in the shortest amount of time.

Liverpool had a strong case for being the birthplace of railways, or at the very least of ushering in the golden age of rail. Although the Stockton to Darlington line opened in 1825, preceding the Liverpool to Manchester one by five years, it was the latter which sparked the 'railway mania' that swept the country throughout the following decades. The Liverpool to Manchester line had come into existence through the frustrations of Manchester cotton mill owners, who were fed up with moving their raw materials from the Liverpool docks by canal and the near-monopoly that the canal owners had over that mode of transport. The businessmen achieved their aims more fully than any of them could ever realize, as not only was their cotton brought successfully from the one place to the other, but soon paying passengers were also being carried. The growth of the railways was startling: in 1838, a decade before Annie was born, the annual number of rail passengers stood at 5.4 million, while just over forty years later, in the year before she travelled to London, it had increased to an incredible 336 million. London had become connected to Birmingham in 1838, making it the first inter-city line (Manchester was then only a town), and two years later, through the Grand Junction, Birmingham was linked to Liverpool.

However Annie made her journey to London, once there she continued to use the name Mary Ann Bruce Sutherland. From the stories of those she met while in the capital, it seems that for the most part she was involved in fund-raising for her trip to the continent, with the aim of starting her school in Rome.

One of the people Annie met in London was an unnamed Baptist minister, who recalled his impression of her:

> 'She made her appearance in this neighbourhood early in 1871 and expressed a desire to be admitted as a member of my church, alleging that she belonged to a Free Church somewhere in Scotland. I immediately requested the certificate of the clergyman, it was however not forthcoming and I declined to receive her into our communion. The members of my church thought I was being too severe and on my devolving the responsibility on them, they elected her. At this time she also became a candidate for mission work in India but by some steps which I cannot trace she soon started the project of education in Rome.'

The minister's initial view proved to be the correct one, as '[we] soon heard of suspicious proceedings in this neighbourhood. She was expelled from our church for dishonesty before she left for Rome or immediately afterwards. She is a most plausible and fascinating woman.'

During her time in London, Annie visited the Colonial and Continental Church Society. In a letter to the *Glasgow Herald* the following year, its secretary recounted:

> 'Her first visit to this office was in June 1871 when she was introduced to me by a lady who had been acting as a bible missionary in Paris and who had only made her acquaintance that morning. Miss Sutherland offered her an engagement as mistress of one of her middle class schools. My friend told me that she had joined in prayer with her and had agreed to provide her with board and lodging and passage to Rome. Miss Sutherland was very chary in answering my questions. I thought her too young for such a position and was not satisfied, especially as I found her at fault about many of the leading people connected with Italian missions. She called in a very nice brougham with a man in livery and her brother, a boy about fourteen, dressed in a handsome suit of grey tweed Highland dress. She betrayed constant ignorance of religious matters both at home and abroad and asked us for introductions to our London bishops.'

We do not know who the 'man in livery' was – possibly a driver whom she had hired with the brougham – while details surrounding her brother's arrival in London also remain unknown. James was then about 14, having been born in 1859, and in a much later letter to a newspaper, the author states:

> 'In age Miss Sutherland's brother would correspond with a Mr James who left Edinburgh two years ago in debt to his landlady Messrs Kennington & Jenner and others. He did evangelical work amongst the poor in the Grassmarket. It seems that her brother James, when he was brought to Edinburgh by Miss Sutherland was in tatters, [but] when he came to us he had on a beautiful Highland dress and carried a silver mounted stick.'

Annie followed up on her lead from Peterhead and called on Miss Gordon's brother; a member of the detective force who was also studying foreign languages. She professed a great interest in Hindustani and convinced him of her intention to go to India as a missionary, whereupon he lent her several valuable books that she promised to return the next day. A week went by and the books had not been returned. Miss Gordon's brother went to her address, and despite her apologies and promises to send them on to him by messenger, he refused to leave the house until his property was returned, which it duly was.

He must have been one of the very few to have escaped with his goods intact. Others who encountered Annie during her London stay were not so fortunate. From one gentleman she obtained £30 to send out an Italian teacher to precede her to the school in Rome, and, as the premises would need to be furnished, she ordered £100 worth of furniture from a cabinet-maker. The goods were shipped to Rome but never paid for, and were eventually sold off to pay the outstanding rent. To help her further fund-raising while in London she somehow managed to obtain a room to use as an office or meeting place in Red Lion Square, off High Holborn. This central London location was near Gray's Inn, one of the four Inns of Court (professional chambers for barristers) in the capital.

During its turbulent history, Red Lion Square was rumoured to be the final resting place of Oliver Cromwell (*sans* head), became a hangout for thieves and vagabonds, and had witnessed a pitched battle between workmen and more than 100 lawyers over its potential development as an exclusive enclave. By the time Annie set up shop in 1871, the lawyers were long defeated and the area had become both fashionable and popular with the professional classes – including solicitors and barristers, along with doctors and wealthy merchants. Notable residents earlier in its existence included Percy Bysshe Shelley's grandfather and John Harrison – inventor of the marine chronometer. By 1822, No. 13 was Headquarters of the Mendicity Society.

According to the 1850 edition of *Hand-book of London: Past and Present*, by Peter Cunningham, 'The society gives meals and money, supplies mill and other work to applicants, investigates begging-letter cases, and apprehends vagrants and imposters. Each meal consists of ten ounces of bread, and one pint of good soup, or a quarter of a pound of cheese.' Cunningham also records that 'the affairs of the Society are administered by a Board of forty-eight managers'. Possibly this was the organization through which Annie acquired her 'office' space, but once again we cannot know for certain.

More recent and influential residents of Red Lion Square were the poet and painter Dante Gabriel Rossetti and textile designer William Morris. Rossetti had earlier belonged to the group of English painters who became known as the Pre-Raphaelite Brotherhood, the group having been founded in the year of Annie's birth: 1848. The group's intention was to reform art and they became the subject of much controversy in 1850, with the original group disbanding soon afterwards. Rossetti then moved into Red Lion Square, No. 17, for a brief six-month spell in 1851. Rossetti met William Morris and Edward Burne-Jones, and from this meeting the furnishings and decorative arts manufacturer and retailer Morris, Marshall, Faulkner & Co. (later to become Morris & Co.) was founded in 1861, with its first headquarters at No. 8 Red Lion Square. This was a mere decade before Annie found temporary residency. Now that she had a place to work from, various lucrative meetings were organized and on one occasion she is alleged to have arranged a gathering in the house of a lady that was attended by a baronet and his daughter, along with various clergymen and several Americans. She opened the meeting with prayer, then delivered a short address which was very well received.

What could be considered her biggest London conquest was an American banker called Robert Bowles, of Bowles Brothers & Co., 449 The Strand. The bank had branches in New York, Geneva and Paris, and was owned by four brothers. Robert ran the London branch, and according to contemporary reports, Annie induced him to send a letter of credit for £100 to Rome to assist in establishing the school and also managed to get him to hand over more than £50 in gold. However, in January of the following year, 1872, the bank ceased trading with debts of £80,000. Three of the brothers fled to America, while Robert was arrested for fraud after 200 debentures – medium to long-term 'instruments' of debt – lodged with them were found to have been illegally transferred to another bank. He was released on bail and the case dragged on through the police court until reaching the Old Bailey in February 1873. As the other brothers were still in America and could not be examined, it was the court's judgment that because it was impossible to decide who had been responsible for what, the case against the remaining brother, Robert, should be dismissed and he was released. However, lack of evidence is not proof of innocence, and it does raise the question of whether Bowles and Annie had devised some mutually beneficial plan, or if their fraudulent doings were simply coincidence.

Whatever the truth behind Annie and Robert's relationship, by the time the bank collapsed in early 1872, Annie had long flown from the capital. After leaving London, instead of going to Rome, she headed back up north, this time to Edinburgh. The city centre between Princes Street and George Street became a major commercial and shopping district, a development partly stimulated by the arrival of the railway in the 1840s. The main consequence of this was that the Old Town became an increasingly dilapidated, overcrowded slum with high mortality rate, although improvements carried out under Lord Provost William Chambers in the decade before Annie's arrival began the area's transformation.

Annie was accompanied on this trip by her brother James and an elderly lady, a Mrs Wilkes, who had some connection to Edinburgh, as had James, who had lived and worked there before going to London. The two women had met at the British Museum while Mrs Wilkes was undertaking research for a theological book that she was writing. Once engaged in conversation, Mrs Wilkes soon succumbed to Annie's charm and agreed to become involved in the foreign school scheme. This new companionship was swiftly exploited, and Mrs Wilkes was probably the woman mentioned in the *Glasgow Herald* article who had introduced Annie to the secretary of the Colonial and Continental Church Society and who had been doing missionary work in Paris. Once arrived in Edinburgh, the trio (Annie, her brother and Mrs Wilkes) checked into a hotel in the West End for two weeks. At the end of this period, however, they were unable to pay their bill, so part of their luggage was detained until payment could be made about a fortnight later. Leaving the hotel, they moved in with a female friend of the ever-useful Mrs Wilkes who lived in a third-floor lodging in St Andrew's Square, in the city's New Town, where they stayed for about three weeks. While at this address, Annie – still introducing herself as 'Miss Sutherland' – called on several leading ministers and laymen, ostensibly to obtain their support and influence on behalf of a scheme, she told them, to support middle-class schools in Italy. Her initial aim was to raise £1,000 for this cause. She recruited mainly amongst the Free and United Presbyterian Churches and managed to convince a number to become more heavily involved, including a Dr Bruce, who became treasurer.

Once Annie had secured what she felt was enough support, she had circulars printed with the names of twenty-two Edinburgh worthies, whom she claimed formed an organization that included an honorary treasurer, secretary, six gentlemen who were part of a 'London Committee' and a London solicitor. In addition to these gentlemen, the Foreign Secretary was a Miss B. Sutherland of Rome and the Home Secretary none other than Mrs Anna Wilkes. The circular stated:

> '[I]t is essential that the rising generation of Italy, the people of the coming time, should receive good moral and religious culture [and] it is high time that those who delight in doing God's work should do so in this instance, when His finger so evidently points the way to that sunny land of His abundant gifts. Italian teachers will be engaged ... and pupil teachers trained in the mother establishment in Rome which will be under the establishment of Miss Bruce Sutherland assisted by other ladies who have volunteered their services.'

Despite this high-minded rhetoric, plentiful donations, increasing social standing and respect from the great and the good for her tireless endeavours, Annie was still unable to forgo the opportunity for continued petty swindling. When gathering support for the Italian scheme she employed one Peter Jackson, a cab man and well-known member of the Carrubbers Close Mission of the Free Church. Upon engaging his services, Annie told him she preferred him over other drivers because of his interest in that mission, but despite spending several days in her service he never received a penny.

Elsewhere in the city she obtained goods whose bills would remain unpaid – from a boot-maker she obtained pairs of boots for herself and brother, and from a high-class clothier a kilt suit ordered for a fictitious relation. She obtained numerous other articles from various tradesmen and businesses around the city. They called at a photographic studio in Princes Street and all had their portraits taken; Annie being taken in five positions. From a grocer she procured a hive of honey, which she presented to one of the gentlemen she hoped would help in her educational work, and from a bookseller in Princes Street she purchased *Flora MacDonald* and *Ballads of Scotland*. She also ran up a bill of nearly £8 for printing and stationary (which no doubt included the circulars). At the same time, and on various well-rehearsed pretences – such as being disappointed in receiving expected monies due to her – she obtained loans of sums varying between £1 and £20 from several ladies and gentlemen, all to be repaid in a 'day or two'; but as usual, none were.

All these nefarious activities and misdemeanours committed by Miss Sunderland were, of course, unknown to Mrs Wilkes and their unnamed host, who was now invited to join them on their trip to Rome. The friend's father forbade it until he had met Annie himself, so they all trooped off to the West Highlands to meet the family. The 'friend' took up the story during an interview years later with the *Dundee Evening Telegraph*:

> 'Everyone in the house was taken with her at first, she could preach, pray and sing beautifully. She sang hymns to perfection, all from memory, never using music or a piano. She lived in our house for about a fortnight but before it was finished we saw that she had no religion and little education. She never attempted to write and I wrote all her letters to the Edinburgh Committee. My father said a child of 10 years could have puzzled her in geography. Despite this she had some remarkable abilities. For instance on the first Sunday she walked 5 miles to church along with the family and when we returned she could repeat all the sermon. She had a wonderful memory. On the following Sunday however she sat in her bedroom with the door locked, and, we suspected, reading a novel. At that time she was a dark handsome woman, but her hair was cut very short as though she had recently been in prison. Towards the end of the fortnight we saw that she could not leave us for want of money. I said to my aunt it would be better to give her what would take her away than have her in the house any longer.'

Realizing that her stay with the Wilkes family was rapidly coming to an end, Annie paid a visit to the Union Bank in town – whose agent was a friend of her host family – and drew out £20 'on representation that she had an account in Edinburgh'. She gave their address as her place of residency and the money was duly handed over. With part of it she hired a carriage and paid off a few small debts before leaving for London the next morning with her brother and Mrs Wilkes. Later that day the family was contacted by their friend at the Union Bank to inform them that Miss Sutherland 'had not a farthing in Edinburgh'. When Mrs Wilkes (now in London) was given this shocking news, she paid the debt to 'prevent further trouble' and probably to avoid the intense embarrassment she must have felt at introducing Annie to her friend and her family. This also put paid to any plans she had of accompanying Annie on the trip to Rome and ended their relationship.

Worse was to follow. Annie had earlier persuaded four ladies to give up their positions as governesses in order to go to Rome with her to teach at the new college, but they too became aware of her true nature when they reached London and would go no further with the scheme. A £1,000 pledge made in Edinburgh and destined for the school never made it into Annie's hands. As had happened so many times before, once she left a place, countless unpaid accounts and bills came to light. Many claims for money were sent to the committee, but she did not visit them on her way to London and left a great deal of debt behind her. Others who had given her gifts felt betrayed or merely embarrassed at being taken in, including an eminent Edinburgh clergyman who had presented her with a quantity of hymn books as a token of esteem.

Despite these setbacks, the tireless fund-raising that Annie had undertaken in London and Edinburgh must have produced many more results than we can now discover, because toward the end of 1871 she left home shores and headed across the English Channel for the continent. All thoughts of India – if there were ever any serious ones – were now gone.

Was her aim just to tour around Europe, have a good time and see what she could loot, or did she genuinely hope to establish schools and then milk them for funds once donations started to arrive? We can only guess at her intentions. Maybe she had no settled plan and would take whatever opportunities arose.

Chapter 4

A European Sojourn
(Dec 1871–Sept 1872)

On Tuesday 19 December 1871, Miss Annie Bruce Sutherland left England, bound for Rome. Mrs Wilkes no longer wanted anything to do with her, and Annie's younger brother James had been sent on ahead with the Italian teacher, using the £30 that she had 'borrowed' from the gentleman in London. Annie made the journey accompanied only by a page boy (or 'buttons') whom she had engaged in the capital, and after crossing the Channel, probably from Dover to Calais, they arrived in Paris around fifteen hours later. While at the railway station in Paris, Annie delved into her repertoire of 'tricks', this time pretending to have lost £20 somewhere in the station. Annie and the page boy – who seems not to have been in on the scam – searched the station for about an hour, but with no luck. Her 'buttons' did not think that there had been a £20 note in the first place, believing that this was merely an attempt to get some gentleman or other to take pity on her and lend her the money. Whether she was successful this time he did not know. After three days in Paris they made for Turin, where they stayed for a night and a day. Annie was so short of ready cash that she went to the British Consul in an attempt to borrow some money so that they could continue to Rome. The consul was unforthcoming, so the 'honour' fell upon another gentleman, on his way from Brighton to Sardinia, to lend her the required amount and the pair arrived in Rome around Christmas Eve.

Despite her lack of money, there seems to have been no expense spared in terms of personal comfort once at her destination. By all accounts Annie rented a beautiful villa on the outskirts of Rome that she called Seven Hills Cottage. She furnished it with the goods from London that were destined for the school. She engaged the services of a carriage, in which she would be driven about all day, meeting the people from whom she hoped to obtain donations.

Once in Rome, and posing as a 'distinguished philanthropist', Annie visited the contacts she had been given introductions to back in England and continued her practice of using these to obtain further ones to prominent

Christians on the pretence of raising funds for the establishment of a children's home and the Protestant seminary for young ladies. At the same time, she claimed that her school plan was under the patronage of Lord Shaftesbury, the politician and social reformer, amongst other worthies, eliciting promises of future support for her schemes. Amongst the people she met in Rome was the Reverend Alexander Williamson of West St Giles, Edinburgh, probably one of her 'introductions' – who was at the time preaching at the single-room Scotch Church there. He would later describe her as a 'rather fascinating lady' who remained behind to talk to him after his first service there at the beginning of 1872. She introduced herself as Miss Bruce Sutherland from Caithness and was accompanied by a boy of around 12 years old that she referred to as her brother, but whom the learned gentleman believed might be her son (although for that to be possible Annie would have only been 12 when she gave birth). The Revd Williamson recalled:

> 'The lady in a most gracious manner thanked me for my sermon and especially for the evangelical doctrines she had heard. She told me that she was in Rome to establish a seminary for young ladies who would be taught English and Protestant Christianity … She talked a good deal about what she would do for the Italian girls and when she got a sufficient number of boarders she was going to bring them to the Scotch Church to sing in the choir. I thought this was very good but (with a quiet smile), I wondered very much how Italian girls could come and sing Scotch psalms. However, that was her look out; she said she was going to teach them. She spoke of Italian as a mellifluous language but I never heard her speak a word of it. [She] took a great position in Rome. She drove about in a carriage with her brother and a young "buttons" in livery whom she had brought from England and who had gold lace around his cap. She was introduced to the very best circles of English society in the city and people spoke of her school as an admirable thing. She engaged a governess before she left England and got her to procure a sealskin jacket for her and although she got the jacket she managed to give the governess the slip, for she had no governess in Rome.'

The reverend and his wife were invited to visit her at the villa, but an acquaintance of the clergyman, a doctor from the north of Scotland who spent every winter in Rome, advised him not to call on her at once but to 'see how things develop'. She was rumoured, he said knowingly, to 'borrow money freely'.

Williamson heeded his friend's advice, and later stated:

'I never called upon her at her villa, but I believe it was a very fine place. She was in the habit of driving out with her fashionable acquaintances and would order the coachman to stop at different bazaars where she wanted to make purchases. She would suddenly remember that she had forgotten her purse and request the loan of ten, fifteen or twenty francs, as the case may be. I told her that a famous Scotch divine (since dead) who came from Caithness was about to visit Rome. She did not however, appear to be pleased with the prospect.'

Her mother and several of her friends back in Peterhead received letters post-marked Rome, but whether it was ever Annie's intention to implement her schemes is impossible to determine. Perhaps she genuinely believed that they would happen but the gap between fantasy and reality was too great, or perhaps her tendency to live life 'to the full' got the better of her and she spent the money before it could be adequately apportioned. Her grand plans were just as likely to have been pretexts for raising money for her own use as for their stated purpose. The fact of the matter is that she did hire staff (even if they didn't make the journey across from England), and indeed, the Italian teacher who had accompanied her brother was now in Rome. Could this be the same teacher who had taught Annie basic Italian during her time in Dundee? We will never know.

What is known is that within six months of arriving in Rome, she could no longer afford to pay the rent on Seven Hills Cottage. The furniture was sold, as was everything else in the house, whether it belonged to her or not. The cash provided some respite, but was not a permanent solution, and many of the local traders to whom she owed money were becoming more than excitable. One butcher, it was said, became so angry he threatened to 'do for her' if his account was not settled immediately, which 'frightened her so much' that she paid it and calmed him down. However, word got around of a young female swindler on the loose and credit became harder to obtain. It was time to move on once again. 'Charm and beauty will only go so far when money is involved,' remarked Williamson. It was time to leave, and this time as well as a change of scene there would be a change of name.

In mid-June 1872, a correspondent writing to the *Peterhead Sentinel* claimed that Annie arrived in Turin under the adopted name of Madam le Baronne de Boorman Stuart (or Stewart, the family name of the Earl of Moray, whom she later claimed was her natural father). Along with the impressive-looking cards in that name that she handed out, there was an equally impressive backstory. She said she was a natural-born American, the widow of a middle-aged French general of distinguished rank and fortune, whom she married when only 16 on the advice of her father. He left her a widow with an honoured name, a handsome income from his vast estates and a good pension from the French government. She had left Paris when the siege by the Prussian army began in late 1870, leaving her two small children behind with her husband's relatives, and had not heard from them for some time.

Back in Rome, it wasn't just Annie's creditors who had been left in the lurch, but also the page boy who had accompanied her across the Channel. With money running low and her brother James again available to run errands, she had no use for another mouth to feed. 'Buttons' could fend for himself, as he would later recount:

> 'She went [from Rome] without paying me my wages or telling me where to go, but some kind gentleman made a subscription for me and I came to England. When in London she used to ride about all day in a carriage which she hired from eleven till about four. She engaged me for two years at five pound per annum and everything found. She bought me a suit of livery with the button "S" for Sutherland. I don't suppose I shall ever get my wages.'

The Reverend Williamson adds a little more detail:

> 'Then she left Rome leaving behind the poor "buttons" whom she had brought from England. The lad of course was in rather a sad plight in a strange land with no means of earning a livelihood. Happily, knowledge of his circumstances came to the ears of several English and Scottish gentlemen staying in Rome and they got up a subscription for him and sent him home.'

Once in Turin, Annie became acquainted with the acting US Consul, and having convinced him of her story she set herself up at the Hotel de Liguria, a first-rate establishment in the city that was popular with English and American tourists. Annie was now 24 years old and at the height of her beauty. In her assumed role she was much pitied and admired by residents and tourists alike, which helped her dupe tradesmen right, left and centre until one of the circle suspected the veracity of her claims. She had adopted a pronounced nasal twang, which he thought was too broad to be natural. The landlord of the hotel sent in his bill to Annie just as an English bishop staying in Turin called upon her and took her out for a drive with his family. When she left his carriage she said that she was going back to the hotel, but never arrived – Madame de Boorman Stuart was no more. This little episode was an unusual departure from Annie's usual *modus operandi*, and is the only occasion we know of that she pretended to be anyone other than the daughter of a Scottish noblewoman.

As her trail of debts grew through the swindling of the city's tradesmen and shopkeepers, Annie moved to Florence, taking with her all the linen and goods that she had obtained from Turin's credulous inhabitants. She stayed firstly at a hotel and then at a *pensione* (lodging house) at No. 9 Rue Castiglione, where she utilized the names of people she had met in Rome; her new friends, of course, knew nothing of the debts she had left behind. She talked a lady resident there into introducing her to her banker, and with her unwitting help obtained a large sum of money, leaving her luggage behind as security – which when examined was found to consist of boxes and suitcases filled with stones and rubbish. Reverend Williamson gave an insight into her time in Florence:

'I next heard that she had turned up in Florence and a lady I know very well there met her at the hotel in which she was staying. From this lady I learned that on one occasion Miss Bruce Sutherland asked her to accompany her to her bankers. The lady who was going out for a walk, assented quite as readily to go in that direction as any other and together they walked to the bank. In Florence of course banking business is done very differently from here. The two ladies were ushered into a room hung around with fine pictures and while Miss Sutherland was doing their business with the banker my friend, not wishing naturally to come within earshot of the conversation moved around the room examining the paintings until the transaction was completed. Sometime afterwards this lady had occasion to call herself upon the banker to get some money on her own account, and in the course of conversation the banker remarked, "Did you know the lady with whom you called the last time you were here?" "No," she replied, "I had only called in with her as we walked out together." "Well I gave her several hundred francs, partly because I saw you, a very respectable lady, with her and I thought it would be alright but I have never heard more of your friend or the money!"'

With funds for once and flushed with success, Annie moved back to Turin intent on pulling the same stunts again, but the embarrassed banker was by now only too aware of her exploits and telegraphed Turin to tip them off. Some reports say that she was arrested and spent some months in a Turin gaol, although nothing has been found to confirm this and several people claiming to know her movements at this time did not mention it.

As her fund-raising tour of the continent was starting to reach the end of its natural life, Annie began her return home via Paris. Upon arrival in the

French capital she met a Mrs Rachel Graham, the wife of Reverend James Graham, minister at Broughty Ferry which, at the time, was a separate burgh to the east of Dundee. She explained to Mrs Graham and her circle that she was deeply engaged in prison reform, visiting hospitals and prisons, reading the *Bible* to the sick and condemned. At the same time, she succeeded in cashing three or four cheques on banks based in London and Scotland, all of which were dishonoured as she held no accounts at any of them. Various hotel bills remained unpaid, and from one warehouse she obtained a sealskin cloak, no doubt to go with her jacket, valued at £16 13s 4d, which with other fashionable items came to a total of £33. If Annie was thinking of going home in the not-too-distant future it was not public knowledge, as she let it be known that she intended to stay in Paris through the winter and send her brother to college there.

Among the many people she met in Paris at this time was a gentleman from Dundee who, in a letter to the local newspaper some time later, stated that he knew her during August and September 1872. As far as he understood, she was engaged in philanthropic work around prisons and came from Forfarshire, where her mother had an estate named 'Lilybank', which ran from Newstyle to Blairgowrie. According to this gentleman, Annie and her brother had been travelling for some time and had been in Egypt – and up the Nile – Palestine and Italy. He also believed her to be fluent in French and Italian. She told him that she had been in Paris for about three weeks, despite the danger and desolation of the city, which was in transition between the previous year's crushing by the French Army of the Paris Commune and the birth-throes of the Third Republic. Annie and her brother drove about all day in a carriage, and both of them were always well dressed. When she left Paris, the correspondent continues, she told the hotel she would be back the following week but would have to leave briefly because she had received a telegram saying that her aunt had died. Before she left, she borrowed £2 from the correspondent's son-in-law. The gentleman correspondent was most surprised to bump into Annie not long afterwards back in Dundee, at the Kinnaird Hall Christian Conference. He mentioned that a lady from whom she had obtained several articles was anxious to see her and Annie promised to write to her, explaining offhandedly that it was 'only a few collars'. It is highly unlikely that the woman ever saw her money.

Annie was now back on home soil, having left a great number of creditors across the Channel in both Italy and France. Whatever plans she had for the future, the consequences of her previous activities were beginning to catch up with her. Annie was destined to spend the next period of her life in her native country, but not in the style that she hoped for.

Chapter 5

The Prodigal Daughter
(Sept–Oct 1872)

Miss Sutherland returned to Dundee in early September 1872. It is an example of the utter recklessness which marked her career that she would return to a town where she was well known, having left less than two years earlier due to her increasing reputation for untrustworthiness. According to a subsequent newspaper report, she had been well known in Dundee three or four years previously when she had worked briefly as a draper's assistant in Murraygate, and during this latest stay she bumped into her former employer in Reform Street. He asked how she was getting on, to which she replied 'A1'. It seems that nothing went missing during her employment there – or nothing that was noticed!

It is possible that she believed at this early stage that she could talk her way out of any legal action over her debts by claiming that they were just that – civil debts that she fully intended to repay once her situation improved. Her beauty, charm and pious life would help to smooth the way and disarm any doubters.

Kate, her widowed mother, was still in the town, living at 58 Kemback Street, but Annie forsook this humble abode and took up temporary residence at The Waverley Temperance Hotel while she conducted a search for 'more suitable' accommodation. The various agents that she contacted were asked if they could find her a house of 'only ten rooms' as she was going to get her mother to come and live with her. The story goes that she narrowly missed out on obtaining possession of the most aristocratic property in the neighbourhood.

Annie was never short of stories to tell her eager listeners, many of which could well have been true or at least half-truths: at one time she lived with her mother near the 'Ferry', at another time it was her aunt; she and her mother had lived at Forfar; she had a wealthy uncle and a brother in the navy, whose half-pay she was in the habit of drawing; and of course she had charge of a scholastic institution in Rome – and so it went on.

Amongst her differing accounts of how she obtained a living, the one used most frequently was the missionary school in Rome, which she claimed provided her with a salary of £150 per year. This would have been the hardest for any doubters to disprove, and it must have been quite easy for her to embroider her recent experiences. She caused lively interest as she narrated her philanthropic efforts in visiting prisons and reformatories on the continent, speaking with much conviction and knowledge. She delighted in telling anyone who would listen how she had met the Pope and kissed his ring. Annie made herself particularly conspicuous at a Christian Conference held in the town, where she was observed with a pencil and notebook, as though taking notes for some publication or private study.

Annie allied herself with the Organization of Good Templars, a group committed to alcoholic abstinence and organized as a sort of secret society like the freemasons – doubtless the conspiratorial element appealed to her. Annie went along one evening to a lodge meeting in Broughty Ferry to which the public were admitted. She so impressed everyone with her enthusiastic evangelism that she was invited by the chairman to address the meeting. She did so and, rather cleverly, corrected an error into which the chairman had fallen when he said that she was not a Good Templar. She replied that in fact she was a Good Templar, but was only eight days old. This statement from 'Sister Sutherland' secured the cordial approbation of the meeting and she proceeded to speak about a recent local incident in what was characterized by several who heard her as a 'fluent style'. The story Annie told was that she and another lady were coming down Whale Lane, a less-than-salubrious avenue of warehouses well known in Dundee as a place of drunks and tramps, when she observed what she thought was a bundle of rags. Upon examination this turned out to be a poor ragged urchin boy asleep by the road. Annie asked his story and submitted him to a cross-examination worthy of a QC. Finding him unwavering in his testimony, she took him to his home to see if his piteous tale was true. She had the meeting spellbound as she depicted in emotional language the scene of suffering, squalor and misery that she beheld there. All this misery was due, of course, to the demon drink – Annie knew her audience!

Annie claimed that she was anxious to learn some foreign languages – Italian in particular – and arranged with a teacher in Broughty Ferry for lessons. Drawing forth her purse at their first meeting, she asked if she should pay 'just now', and was told that would not be necessary. Sensing a soft target, she returned once more and obtained a loan – but did not visit again.

On the last day of September, she left The Waverley and moved into Whitfield Cottage in Pitkerro Road, located about halfway between the city centre and Broughty Ferry, which she had been renting and attempting to furnish for several weeks. She installed her mother and brother Hamish, and then continued with her own inimitable style of fraud and deceit, including borrowing money from Mrs Graham, now returned from Paris. She finally succeeded in furnishing the house at the expense of local traders. She seems to have become a little uncertain about how things would work out, or maybe it was just another ruse, as she put her affairs in the hands of a solicitor, Mr Mackay, instructing him to negotiate a settlement with her creditors. Either way, he seems to have believed in her and for a while tried to put her debts in order; but the inevitable happened and he ended up becoming one of them.

One correspondent to a local paper, known only as 'Mr N', describes meeting Annie during this time. He recounted how a 'shabbily dressed female' presented herself as Miss Sutherland from Wick and claimed to know a reverend doctor of the town who had directed her to his door. The reason for this was a deep and loving friendship that had supposedly existed between Annie's mother and a relative of the correspondent. Despite certain misgivings, Miss Sutherland was received with all due hospitality – her high-flown talk and endearingly flippant manner drowning all suspicions. She told how she had come all the way from Greenock that very day on urgent business, and that she and her mother had a large dressmaking, millinery and boarding establishment in Glasgow, with boarders who included a university professor and a German student. She addressed herself to the listener as if they had been intimate friends all their lives, and the correspondent and his wife were so completely under her spell that a bed was aired and prepared for her, with everything provided to make her comfortable and happy overnight.

Mr N continued in his letter that he was astonished at her knowledge of the many influential citizens of Dundee and surroundings, particularly those considered the most charitable. She claimed to be on intimate terms with the Bishop of Brechin and announced that she was to call on him first thing in the morning. One thing that did strike them as strange was that she had nothing with her to indicate she had been travelling. She left to 'visit the bishop' and returned in time for dinner, but now with a new silk umbrella and articles of dress of a very fashionable kind, along with a new purse and bag upon her arm. When it was time to say goodbye, she told them she was off to Arbroath and may not see them again. She was bidden a very affectionate farewell and seemed to be very grateful for the kindness that had been shown. Annie left them an address in Douglas Street, Blythswood Square, Glasgow, and departed.

To the great surprise of Mr N and his wife, Annie returned about a week later, saying that she had now rented a house in Broughty Ferry at £70 per year and invited them to see her. During the nineteenth century, with the rise of the area's reputation as the jute industry's global centre, this former fishing and whaling village had become a haven for wealthy jute barons, who built luxury villas in the suburb. As a result, Broughty Ferry was known during this period as the 'richest square mile in Europe'.

Mr N happened to mention that he knew someone who was looking for a position in the stationery line, and Annie replied that she was well acquainted with the stationery firm of T. Nelson & Sons in Edinburgh and immediately offered to write to them about a situation for him. When this offer was declined, she changed tack and mentioned her friendship with a gentleman who had similar contacts in Reform Street. Mr N said he was perfectly acquainted with that person, at which she seemed frightened and changed the subject, continuing with her seemingly unstoppable patter. This time they did not invite her to stay the night and she left pretty late in the evening, but that was not the last they were to see of her:

'She called again two nights thereafter but would not come into the house. She wanted to see [me] "just for a moment". I went to the door and although the lobby was in darkness I could plainly perceive she was very much agitated. She said she had a coach hire to pay and would take it very kindly if I would just make her the loan of the very small sum of 10/-. I declined to do so as it struck me forcibly the sum wanted did not square well with the residence at Broughty Ferry of the annual rent of £70. She came down to 7/6d then to 5/- and lastly 2/6d! Still I held out against her most bland entreaties and sure promises of being refunded in the space of two days. I thought I would however make a compromise, and offered to pay her fare to the Ferry and curiosity lead me to offer my company as far as Arbroath station which she hastily declined. She pocketed the fare to the Ferry; promised to pay it back in two days, shook hands cordially, bade an adieu and disappeared into the darkness and drizzling rain; I have not opened my eyes upon her lovely face since.'

It seems from this episode that Annie was seriously down on her luck– almost openly begging for small change – but she soon perked up. A watchmaker she had known, and from whom she had obtained several pieces previously, was asked to supply a watch of value. Annie explained a little about her finances and told him about her £150 salary, which would enable her to set up regular payments. The jeweller told her that if she was right about her financial affairs she was living far above her income, and offered to help add up her debts and show how little her reckless spending would leave from her salary. It was obvious, he explained, that she could not come from a holiday tour of Rome to Broughty Ferry and live as she was on what she earned. 'She became penitent and a tear fell gently from her eye,' recalled the watchmaker – but she still walked out of his shop with the watch!

Her *modus operandi*, then as ever, was to hire a pony and phaeton in Dundee and travel around to the various shops, placing her orders; the grand-looking carriage serving to put the tradesmen off their guard. Drapers, grocers, boot-makers, all received her custom. She ordered a piano for the cottage and had her photograph taken for a '*carte-de-visit*'. With her continued behaviour of purchasing furniture and other goods without paying, she once more created a stir among the shopkeepers in Dundee and Broughty Ferry, although not everyone was taken in. A linen draper whom she tried to take for a considerable sum had a feeling something was not right and thought of a clever ruse to determine the truth. She was in his shop ordering material quite lavishly, and he began to add on 1/- or 2/- per yard extra to the ordinary price of the goods. Annie was unfazed by this, however, and continued to place more orders. Needless to say, the required items were not delivered.

Another story goes that mother and daughter stayed in Graham Place, almost opposite the police station. A correspondent stated that:

> 'The mother was a devout hard-working Highland woman who could hardly speak English. I remember hearing an incident about Mary Ann Bruce when she was about 24 years of age while she was living there. I heard of her having done one of the cleverest things that have come under my notice. She was due several people money and one day she met a man in the street to whom she owed a pound. He stopped and I believe said "Well Mary Ann I must at once have my pound" to which she replied "I have not got your pound but you will get it." She asked him to wait a minute while she went into a shop nearby. I believe that she had never seen the shopkeeper before but after a few minutes she came out with a pound and handed it to the creditor, how she managed to wheedle it out of a stranger I cannot say but I thought at the time it was remarkably clever.'

Due to the way in which the late nineteenth-century banking system worked at this time, fraud was easy to commit and very common. One regular method was for the prospective fraudster to obtain references, real or contrived, and appear at the chosen bank, impressing the manager with confidence and talk of great sums to come. A convincing amount of money would be deposited, and a cheque book issued. Cheques were a sign of respectability to any tradesman eager for a sale, bearing as they did the name of old and established companies; if such a respectable concern thought the customer worthy of its trust, who was the lowly shopkeeper to decline? Goods of say

£20 would be purchased, and with a short but convincing story a cheque for £30 would be presented and accepted, the balance of £10 being handed over in cash to the customer, along with the purchases. With goods and cash secured, it was back into the carriage and off to the next shop. By the time the cheques were returned as 'no effects' or 'insufficient funds', the small amount that had been initially deposited with the bank had been withdrawn, leaving only a few shillings, the goods had been sold and the fraudster had moved on to the next town. The secret of continued and successful fraud of this kind is, of course, for the fraudster to keep moving – something Annie seemed curiously reluctant to do. It is amazing that she managed to get away with anything at all in Dundee, given her previous behaviour in the town.

Whatever her thoughts were on evading the long arm of the law, if she had any at all, the net was closing in. It seems that the Dundee tradesmen were a little sharper than their counterparts elsewhere. Many simply made their way out to the cottage at Whitfield to repossess their goods, but others took a harder line and put their cases into the hands of the public prosecutor.

The final nail in the coffin of this stage of Annie's career came on Saturday 12 October 1872, when the weekly *Dundee Courier* published an article under the damning headline: 'A Wholesale Female Swindler in Dundee'. The article contained frightening details of her recent activities:

'Within the past few days a female swindler possessing more than ordinary "dodging" powers has been plying her art in Dundee and neighbourhood. Her dupes are generally of the shopkeeper class, but several private families in town have also been honoured with a visit from her ladyship. Her modus operandi seems to be as follows:- Having entered a provision store, (a most common practice of hers), she in a most dignified manner proceeds to order a long list of groceries which the shopkeeper, believing her to be a new customer, is very active in supplying. All at once however she discovers on opening her purse that she is "short" by perhaps 10/- of the cost of provisions but states to the unsuspecting shopkeeper that she will send her servant along in the evening with the balance. In this arrangement the shopkeeper almost invariably acquiesces. It is needless to say that neither the "lady" nor her servant ever put in an appearance and within a day or two the shopkeeper discovers that he has seen the last of his new customer.

'No later than Thursday last her ladyship visited the shop of a painter and decorator in town and as usual success crowned her proceedings. Having wished the master "Good Day" she desired him to send a couple of men out to her cottage at – – – (a non-existent place) in order to have it painted. The master told her that her requests would be acceded to at once. Before leaving however, the usual statement was made that, having to purchase a great deal of goods her money had almost run dry and she would be obliged for the loan of £1 which she would return on the painting of the cottage being completed. Such a request made by a lady of such apparently very high standing, the gentleman could not think of refusing and another victim was added to the long list.

'What tends to make the statements of the lady all the more true is the religious turn which her ladyship invariably gives to the conversation. She very often tells her dupes that she has been attending the Dundee Christian Conference and she was delighted at the large attendances, being confident that much good would accrue therefrom. This swindler is supposed to be the woman who succeeded in defrauding a large number of shopkeepers here three years ago in much the same way as she is doing at present. At that time on the representation that her "mamma" was to call and pay it she succeeded in obtaining a lady's watch from a watchmaker in town. Wonder has been expressed that the police authorities have never had any complaints lodged against this woman. We believe that although many would gladly lodge a charge against her, yet, rather than be annoyed with the matter they continue silent and so the swindler remains undetected.

'This was the case with the "pipe" swindlers who, in the shape of foreign sailors visited us last spring. In order that shopkeepers may be on their guard against her ladyship we may state that she is stated to be a tall thin woman, [with] a pale countenance, apparently about 25 years of age. Her get up is of the "swell of the period" style and she talks English very well with a rather northern accent.'

Annie was arrested at 11 o'clock at night on Tuesday 15 October 1872, at Whitfield Cottage, Dundee. Before being led away, she had the forethought to pick up two volumes of a novel to while away the hours of waiting at the turnkey's office. Upon arrival she was described as a very respectable and handsome lady of middle height with very delicately formed features. She was dressed wholly in black – black straw hat trimmed with velvet and silk ribbons and a black feather; heavy black sealskin jacket and a black dress with a white collar and black tie and a white embroidered petticoat. She held a white handkerchief in her right hand and had a scarlet muffler hanging over her left arm and kid gloves.

If the return to Dundee raised questions about her judgement, then her arrest multiplied these. The newspaper report detailing the 'Wholesale

Female Swindler' had appeared a full three days before her arrest. Did she not read the papers? Was it not obviously time to use her 'more than ordinary dodging powers', obtain a third-class ticket to London and lie low until the heat died down? To give her the benefit of some common sense though, it was just possible that she naively assumed that her various frauds would never be linked together and that she could play the 'dizzy blonde' and charm her way out of the situation, passing most activities off as civil debt.

On the day after Annie was taken into custody, she was examined by Sheriff Cheyne before being committed to prison. She acted and spoke with remarkable coolness, calmly stating she had done nothing wrong, denying she had ever obtained goods without paying for them and even denouncing some of her creditors for demanding payment for their goods while others had 'behaved like perfect gentlemen'.

The Dundee *People's Journal* of 2 November 1872 reported that the court had agreed to accept bail of £40 for the 'liberation' of Mary Ann Bruce Sutherland, 'who was recently apprehended on certain charges of swindling', but it seems that such an amount could not be raised and so she remained in prison until a date for her trial could be set. During her time on remand she retained the 'ideas above her station' that she had acquired and maintained the persona of someone of higher status. She had taken offence at the prison rules, refusing to take exercise in the courtyard along with the others. One of the local magistrates visited her and tried to talk her round, to which she replied: 'What! With these persons? Oh dear No!' Her charm worked on him as it had on so many others, and she was allowed to exercise alone. Having won that point, she pushed her luck and complained about the lack of literature available. The prison library contained one-and-a-half books: a treatise on cookery, which under the circumstances was not particularly useful, and the first part of a history of Scotland. This point she also won, and more literature was provided. The books stayed, but she was eventually compelled to take her turn with 'these persons'. While on remand, her photograph was taken, at the request of the prison authorities, by John Wanless of Dundee, and she was described in prison records as 'slightly pockmarked and bearing a mole on the left side of the neck'; an observation that was to have dire consequences for her in years to come.

Chapter 6

A Bad Press
(Oct–Nov 1872)

While Annie was in prison on remand and the case was being prepared, the local press had a field day printing stories and rumours about her; all the accounts outlined so far appeared in print for all to read between her arrest in October and trial in December. As well as the letter to the *Glasgow Herald* mentioned previously, a London Baptist minister who had met Annie recalled his experience of her:

'She made her appearance in this neighbourhood early in 1871 and expressed a desire to be admitted as a member of my church, alleging that she belonged to a Free Church somewhere in Scotland. I immediately requested the certificate of the clergyman, it was however not forthcoming and I declined to receive her into our communion. The members of my church thought I was being too severe and on my devolving the responsibility on them, they elected her. At this time she also became a candidate for mission work in India but by some steps which I cannot trace she soon started the project of education in Rome. We soon heard of suspicious proceedings in this neighbourhood. She was expelled from our church for dishonesty before she left for Rome or immediately afterwards. She is a most plausible and fascinating woman. I sincerely hope your Scottish Judges will not let her loose upon society for some time to come.'

Another letter-writer to the newspapers, the gentleman who had met Annie in Paris during the last period of her stay in the summer of 1872 and then again in Dundee, claimed that he had always been suspicious of her. He stated he had written to her old hotel in Paris – the 'Hotel Londres and New York' at the Place du Harve – shortly after Annie was arrested, and had enclosed several newspaper cuttings of her exploits.

The hotel proprietor's reply found its way into print:

'She stayed at our house as part of Mr Cook's party to Italy so I had every confidence in her. On the day previous to her departure she asked me whether I would cash a cheque upon the Bank of Scotland where she was well known. I said I would but was much surprised, as upon leaving – pretending to have received a telegram which no one saw – she asked me for a leaf of notepaper and in great haste wrote me a cheque for £15.6s. When I presented the cheque to the banker who happened to know me, it struck him that he must have been done also as she had called on him with the recommendation of some honourable person for cashing a cheque for £14 which she said was to pay her hotel bill! Since then a good many people had called for the money for goods she had bought. One was a bill of £50, another banker was done for £10 and yet another for a similar amount. The matter is now in the hands of the police.'

Another useful contact that she had made was the eminent English physician Sir John Ross Cormack, who, according to the Revd Williamson, did not care much for her and thought she was 'one of those strong minded women that are going to reform the world'. He sent the following letter, dated 26 November 1872, from 7 Rue d'Agnesseau, Paris, upon hearing of her arrest on the Dundee fraud charges, having had a very similar experience:

'I have seen Mr John Arthur, who in consequence of my showing him the paragraph, has written to you, and advised others swindled here by Miss Bruce Sutherland to follow his example. You are likely therefore to hear from Mr Andrews a banker and money changer, the keeper of the New York and London Hotel (Place de Harve) and a dressmaker whose name I forget. The hotel keeper informed me that many trades people were defrauded by the woman and her little boy accomplice. I was no loser by her but she very adroitly came about me in such a way as to lead people to believe she was acquainted with me. She came first of all accompanied by a lady of quiet demeanour and respectable appearance who was I imagine about 40 years of age. Miss Bruce Sutherland represented herself as the friend of Mr Edie the Scottish Consular Chaplain of Paris, on whose suggestion she said she had come to me in the hope that I might be able to procure for her from the Prefect of Police, permission to visit the prisons and penitentiaries for women in this city. She said she had visited similar institutions of Italy and Germany but had failed to gain access to those of Paris. In reply to my enquiries she said that her object in visiting female prisons was the reformation and more judicious punishment of women, a subject which she had much at heart and which she was writing a paper on for the Social Science Association. I believed her and set her down as a strong minded woman teeming with genuine philanthropy and personal vanity.

'She spoke with so genuine a Scottish accent and seemed so earnest in her benevolent purposes that I took some trouble on her behalf, the result of which was permission for her to visit the prisons. She called several times on me in reference to this matter and after her visit to the prisons she came to tell me what she had seen. I have since discovered that she was sent to me by Mr Edie as a friend; that he knew nothing of her except as a casual attendant at his church. I have also ascertained that she spoke of me at the hotel where she lived and to various trades people as being well acquainted with me and with many others of whom she knew absolutely nothing except by adroitly thrusting herself on them as on me for the object of being helped in pretend projects of philanthropy.

'On the day she left Paris she rushed into my consulting room – though my servant tried to prevent her, as I was at the time in the midst of my consultations, and exclaimed that she was in a fearful predicament; a telegram had just arrived saying that her mother was dangerously ill at Lilly Bank in the north of Scotland, that she had not enough money to pay her hotel bill and her journey; that if she waited for money she might never see her mother. Her voice quivered as she spoke and her anguish was still further proved by her tearful eyes. She said that she only required £10 and that Mr Arthur would give her French money for that amount for her cheque on the National Bank of Scotland at Edinburgh if I said that I knew her. I did so by writing a few words on my card. Mr Arthur cashed her cheque for, I think £11. Two or three days afterwards, the lady who called on me with Miss Bruce Sutherland came to ask her address stating that she had left Paris in her debt and had not paid her hotel bill etc. I do not know whether this elderly lady was a confederate or a dupe of the younger. She remained at the hotel some days after Miss BS left. The landlord believed her to be no confederate but simply a casual acquaintance picked up on one of Cook's Continental Tours. A retrospect of my conversations with both ladies leads me to suspect that they were confederate swindlers and that the elder remained in Paris after the younger to observe what I and others did when the swindling tricks came to light. You may use the information I am now giving you in any way you please. I retain the photographs to show the hotel keeper but will return them.'

The Reverend McDougall of the Free Church at Florence also responded to the *Glasgow Herald*, in great depth it has to be said, after reading about the case in the press:

'I very earnestly desire that you should make a thorough exposure of this case as I see by late newspaper paragraphs you are doing. It is one of the most barefaced and ignorant impositions I ever heard of. It will form a most useful warning to our Christian Public to be careful about the parties they trust with their money. It was only last summer that Miss Sutherland put in the "Bruce", and without warrant. She had never been to Italy and I believe speaks neither French nor Italian, indeed, she writes English most ungrammatically. Yet the cleverness of this imposter lies in the circumstance that she really fell on a scheme which begun by proper parties and well carried out might have been very useful. Indeed several parties had spoken of such a scheme and I can safely say that with my 15 years knowledge of Italy had I been a free man and not over head and ears in other works I should have gone in strongly for this very scheme projected by Miss Sutherland.

'The first mention of her name to me was at the United Presbytery of Edinburgh in the Autumn of 1871 and I then learned from Dr – - – that she had taken the liberty of putting his name and that of other eminent and respected men down upon her printed lists of "Edinburgh Committee" although he and others had given no sanction – indeed had not been asked by Miss Sutherland when she called upon these gentlemen. As I was going up to London a few days afterwards I promised to make enquiries and communicate what I could learn from friends. Calling at the offices of the Evangelical Continental Society, 13 Bloomfield Street, Finsbury, London, I found there that Miss B Sutherland was a humbug, knew nobody, had no money, borrowed from the poor but respectable housekeeper and never kept her promise to repay the small sums. The housekeeper had at first taken pity and given Miss Sutherland food from time to time and allowed her to write letters there, and told me how cleverly, from one good and well known gentleman in London she got upon another and from another to a third till she actually had some small uninfluential drawing room meeting. All this and more I let Dr – - – and many other inquirers know, and thought the woman's game was up.

'However, having come on to Florence in October 1871 and gone to Rome soon after, I was dining with Rev Dr Phillip, Jewish missionary in Rome when he asked me casually if I knew a Miss Sutherland who was coming along because a friend of his, Signor Gioia had been engaged by her and was waiting and waiting but no money had come. Of course I knew the whole truth. Dr Phillip and his family opened their mouths wide and thought I was hoaxing them but I got Gioia and all our old friends in Rome put on their guard, and I believe was the means thereby of very considerably limiting her operation in Rome.

'Miss Sutherland travelled out first class and got, for she had always lost her purse, the loan of £10, immediately on entering Italy from a nice young man, the son of a London banker. Arrived at Rome she began her usual career of begging and borrowing from all and sundry, druggists etc. She started a carriage with a smart tiger, took a villa which she called Seven Hills College and furnished it readily enough. The Roman shopkeepers thought she was a person of wealth. She never had but one child at the college. Her prospectus is so full of grammatical blunders that only an ignoramus could have written it. Rome was very crowded with wealthy people last winter and she had a fine field but I cannot say if she got into respectable society there. Funds did not come in, suspicions were awakened, and people rushed to the villa and took back their goods and she made off. I know of one huge fraud she committed there however. She got 3000 francs or £120 from a well-known Roman banker. He was unwilling to give it but his wife like a good Christian, urged him to accommodate a person working in the good cause and so the 3000 francs were given and never seen again.

'It was further ascertained that previous to coming to Italy Miss Sutherland had gone to Liverpool where she engaged a Miss S. to come to Rome and through her she got to know big people in Liverpool, the mayor of the town included and I think had a meeting. Miss S. found out the scoundralism in London and went to every member of the so called committee, to the banker who had nothing at her credit; to the chairman, who knew nothing of Miss Sutherland's antecedents; to the solicitor etc. Of course all these gentlemen were very much ashamed of having been imposed on, especially my good friend Mr JS of the Monthly Tract Society 27 Red Lion Square who actually gave her and her accomplice a room on their premises.

'On the 2nd of May Miss Sutherland had the effrontery to call on me here claiming to be an intimate friend and using the names of several ministers in Edinburgh as her best friends and protectors. By that time I knew she had been publicly turned out of a West End Baptist Church in London and all of her other misdeeds so that you can well believe I talked to her more plainly than I ever did to a human being. She became very white and bit her lip and my wife was inclined to be sorry for her. I acquainted her landlady who she was and all the stall keepers at Mrs Seymour's Bazaar the next day, to give her no credit and to watch their goods as she was going from one to another and I thought she would be foiled here. Alas! One of my bankers gave her 600 Italian lire or £24, which he has never seen again. She swindled him very cleverly. She used my name, said she was deeply interested in evangelistic work, that her boxes were coming from Rome, addressed to his care, (they never came) and that her letters had got mislaid but would doubtless come alright in a day or two when she would return the money. On his suggesting that she draw upon her mother she adroitly and satisfactorily answered, "Well you see my mother is an old lady, knows nothing about business, allows me a certain monthly sum, and would be alarmed if I were to draw on her."

'From Turin I was written to by a friend of her landlady about her wishing to leave her brother, (supposed by many to be her own child) at school in the Waldensian Valleys, near Turin. Thereafter I lost sight of her and was delighted beyond all measure when the report reached me that she was safely ensconced in Dundee Gaol. I see she has only got nine months so you will soon have your hands full with her misdeeds again. The photographs you sent to me which are speaking likenesses, I shall keep as souvenirs. Her eyes and her smile are her two killing features.'

The 600 lire from the bank in Florence was borrowed against a note dated 7 May 1872. The banker explained the situation behind it:

'Miss Sutherland's first acquaintance with us was as a charitable young lady inquiring about the address of the Protestant Orphan Asylum and the Italian Reformatory House of Protection, prisons etc and how to get permits to visit them. After two or three visits of this description she borrowed 300 lire under pretence that her mother must have mistakenly sent her remittance to Rome. A few days later she borrowed another 300 under the pretence that she had not yet had the remittance, and that she had a telegram to come immediately to Turin and join a friend who after spending a few days there would return to Florence with her. She mentioned the name of Mr McDougall and several others as intimate friends and played the religious and charitable lady perfectly.'

Annie was to be defended by a Mr Archibald Paul, who was so annoyed by the effects that all the stories about his client might have on her case that he wrote to the press himself:

'Miss Bruce Sutherland. Sir, I observe that Mr Henry Miller, Messenger-At-Arms, and designing himself of the Guardian Society's Offices, Glasgow, has written a long letter to you and your contemporary in condemnation of this unfortunate young woman who is on the very eve of being tried by a local jury in Dundee. It may be a very good way for Mr Miller advertising his, "Guardian Offices" to the public or of recording his own feats of arms, but certainly it is the most unmanly and ill-timed letter which could possibly be written to the public. It is not for me here to say a single word about Miss Sutherland's guilt or innocence; suffice it to say that she courts her trial now approaching and relies upon the jury deciding the case upon the evidence to be laid before them and not upon the wild and uncalled for letters and articles which have from time to time appeared in newspapers and which the accused has had no opportunity of answering.'

Paul certainly had a point, as all the press coverage was highly prejudicial, making a fair trial very unlikely, in a way that would be unthinkable today. The Henry Miller mentioned by Paul belonged to the Glasgow and West of Scotland Guardian Society for the Protection of Trade. He seems to have been a self-righteous busybody and head of a protection society for local businesses that largely orchestrated the press campaign, as well as distributing photographs of Annie and her brother to its members and local tradesmen. Effective though Miller's activities may have been within his peer group, they were written about in less than glowing terms by the local papers, who described him as 'a most voluminous correspondent', 'wandering in a confused way from the particular to the general', and when it came to their prey, 'denouncing them heartily for their own and their dupe's good'.

An example of the danger of taking Miller's stories at face value occurred in a report on the case published by the *Oban Times* in its edition of 3 November 1872. Recalling the time that Annie was planning her European tour, the newspaper printed a detailed account, credited to Miller, which described how in August 1871 Miss Sutherland was accompanied by 'an elderly female having a ladylike exterior who went by the name of Mrs Anna Wilkes'. Mrs Wilkes, they implied, was a party to staying at a hotel without paying and lending her name to a bogus circular designed to raise funds for the school in Italy – in fact she was named as the 'Home Secretary' of the campaign on the leaflet. The story was also carried by other papers, but a few weeks later the *Oban Times* felt compelled to print the following:

'We stated that the result of enquiries made and published by Mr Henry Miller of the Glasgow Guardian Society into a case in which the names of Mrs Anna Wilkes and Miss MA Sutherland were associated, commenced with their joint endeavours in regard to a scheme for promoting education in Italy and ended with the information that the latter lady had been taken into custody on a charge of purchasing goods without the means of paying for them. Since then Mrs Anna Wilkes has informed us very fully with regard to her connection with Miss Sutherland. She assures us that, with ample guarantees of Miss Sutherland's respectability she entered upon the philanthropic work in company with other persons whose names she has mentioned – well known for high character and position in society; that at Miss Sutherland's request she introduced the subject to her solicitor; that she advanced funds for the expedition to Scotland and subsequently, having reason to believe that she had been deceived, disconnected herself from the work and obtained the services of an accountant to make the separation more complete. Mrs Wilkes asserts that she left no bills unpaid in Scotland, and that she received no subscriptions.

'It appears to us that Mrs Wilkes' statements are thoroughly trustworthy and that she has been unjustly treated in the report of the Guardian Society of Glasgow. For our own part we regret extremely having made reference to their unfavourable view of her association in this affair and trust that this expression of our deliberate opinion may be as widely circulated as the report upon which our remarks were based.'

This was not the first time that the object of Miller's campaigns had fought back. Earlier in the year, in June 1872, the publisher of *Gibbs Penny Guide-Books*, Mr James Gibb, was intending to open a branch of his business in Glasgow when his business activities were attacked in Miller's journal. Gibb responded: 'It does appear to me that the society of which he is the secretary and manager is established for the destruction of trade instead of the protection of it, as a trial in a Court of Justice will perhaps someday show.'

Whatever the general opinion of Miller, the fact remained that huge swaths of column inches – containing truths, half-truths, untruths and rumours – were in print and there for all to see, and the damage had been done. What mattered for the prisoner sitting in her cell awaiting trial was that those who would pass judgement on her in the courtroom had presence of mind enough not to be swayed so easily.

Chapter 7

The Trial
(Dec 1872)

On Friday 6 December 1872, Annie was placed before Sheriff Cheyne at the Sheriff's' Court, Dundee. Prosecuting counsel was Mr Dunbar and she was again defended by Mr Archibald Paul. She was arraigned on seventeen charges, as follows:

Mary Ann Bruce or Sutherland, having formed a fraudulent and felonious purpose of obtaining the goods and money of others upon false pretences and appropriating the same to her own uses and purposes:-

1. Did on one or more occasions in the month of April 1869 employ Andrew Smith Geddes, tailor, of King Street, Dundee, to make a jacket, vest, and kilt for a boy and send the articles, which the accused received, to her then residence in Graham Place, Dundee, representing that she would pay for the same within three weeks but which she did not intend to pay.
2. Did on the 10th of November 1869 induce DS Kerr, partner of the firm Kerr & Smith Watchmakers, Dundee, to supply her with a gold watch at the price of £4.10s. of which she paid 10s. falsely and fraudulently pretending that she would pay the remainder in monthly instalments of £1 each which she never intended to pay.
3. On the 11th of December 1869 the accused did induce Margaret Robertson or Davidson, milliner of Reform St, Dundee, to supply her with a jacket and send it to her residence in Graham Place, representing that she would pay the same in the latter part of that day but appropriated to her own use without intending to pay.
4. On one or more occasions between the 16th and 21st September 1872 the said Mary Ann Bruce Sutherland did within the premises of Constitution Road, Dundee, possessed by Robert Nicoll cabinet maker, request him or his clerk to supply her with and send to her cottage at Whitfield Cottage near Dundee a sofa, six mahogany chairs, six birch chairs, six cane chairs, three mattresses, an easy chair, a table, and three and a half yards or thereby of floor cloth

representing that her mother had money in the bank and that she would pay for the articles by the end of the month. Having received the articles to the value of £26.11s.6d she did not pay or intend to pay for the same.

5. In the month of September 1872 she induced Isabella Ireland assistant to William Ireland, hardware merchant of Union Street, Dundee, to supply her with a gold finger ring saying that she would pay for the same within a few days but failed to do so.

6. On September 20th 1872 she requested Archibald McLaggan manager to James Dickie, wire worker of Barrack Street, Dundee to send a bird's cage valued at 15s.6d. to her stables in King Street representing that she would pay for it in a few days, but failed to do so.

7. On Monday 23rd September 1872 within or near the shop of Andrew Dougan, ironmonger, of Bank Street, Dundee did request John Stewart to supply her with two coal scuttles, four mats, six ivory tea knives, six dinner knives and forks, six tea spoons, a coffee pot, a kettle, a knife board and two sugar boxes and to send the same to the stables in King Street representing that she would pay for the items a few days after.

8. On Monday 23rd September 1872 within the shop of Burns and McCrostie drapers in Church Street, Dundee the accused did request John Marshall salesman to supply her with a table cloth and represent that she would pay for it in the latter part of the same day.

9. On one or more occasions in the month of September 1872 within the shop at Nethergate possessed by Alexander McIntosh carver and gilder she did request four pictures to be framed valued at £3.13s. and sent to her at the stables in King Street when completed, saying that she would pay within a day or two. She received them without paying.

10. On the 25th of September 1872 at the shop of George Wylie Howie, a watchmaker of King Street, Dundee, she did take a gold watch to 'show her mother' with a view to purchasing it but neither paid or returned it.

11. On the 2nd of October 1872 within the manse of Rev. James Graham at Albert Road, Broughty Ferry she did request Graham Mitchell or Rachel his wife to lend her the sum of £2 and said that she would return it within a day or so which she did not.

12. On the 7th of October 1872 she did from the shop of Helen Webster Thomsen in Gray Street, Broughty Ferry receive two pairs

of boots and one pair of slippers on credit saying that she had the money at the bank of Mr Methven at Broughty Ferry but when she had called to draw it he had been out.

13. On 7th October she did borrow £1 from Peter Young a surgeon saying that she would repay it in a day or so but didn't.

14. On the same day above she borrowed £1 from Peter Robinson a cabinet maker of Hilltown promising to repay it the same day but didn't.

15. On the same day she borrowed 10s. from RTM Allan a hairdresser in Queen St, Broughty Ferry.

16. On the same day she induced William Shepherd the manager of GH & G Nichol ironmongers of Gray Street, Broughty Ferry to lend her £1 promising to repay it in a day or so but didn't.

17. On Wednesday 9th of October 1872 at the hotel in Reform Street, Dundee possessed by Jessie Crawford or Lamb widow and hotel keeper she did borrow £1 promising to repay it in a day or so but didn't.

'Miss Sutherland' – Annie – was asked to plead, and replied: 'I am not guilty of fraud.'

The case was adjourned until Thursday 19 December 1872.

* * *

On the appointed day the court was crowded as Mary Ann Bruce Sutherland was placed in the dock before Sheriffs Heriot and Cheyne. She pleaded not guilty to each count in turn and sat with the utmost composure, not seeming in the slightest way dejected. A reporter described her appearance:

'She was respectably dressed in a black dress and a dark brown sealskin jacket. Her hat was of black straw trimmed with velvet and feathers and on her neck she wore a collar with a pure white silk neckerchief. Kid gloves of a dark green colour were on her hands and linen bands covered her wrists. She was holding a pink silk shawl in her hands. In appearance she could be described as "prepossessing". Her face was naturally pale more mild than sharp in expression manifesting considerable self-possession and coolness. Her features are round and comparatively short, her cheekbones are high and the nose and mouth, though somewhat small are well formed. Her eyes are black and mild in expression.'

Mr Dunbar opened the case for the prosecution. The first witness was David Salmon Kerr, a Dundee watchmaker, who stated that 'Sutherland' had called at his shop in November 1869 to pick up a gold watch that had been ordered previously. Kerr had 'done things' for her before and she had 'always played honourably'. She had claimed she was a teacher who could not pay the full amount at once, but paid 10 shillings and promised to pay the remaining £4 in monthly instalments. Kerr told the court:

> 'She never called at my shop till after 3 years and I didn't see her again until last October when I met her by chance in Seagate and asked for the £4 ... she seemed surprised that her mother had not paid it and again promised to pay but did not. I heard that she was leaving town and went around to her house, she was not in but her mother said that she knew nothing about a gold watch.'

Sutherland claimed the watch had been given as a present to her cousin, a Miss Jessie Robertson, at a local school, but enquiries by Inspector Aiken showed that there was no such person at the school. Although she had cousins, none could be traced named Robertson.

David Godfrey of the Waverley Temperance Hotel, Dundee, then gave evidence to say that she had stayed at his hotel from 5–30 September 1872. She said that she was from Edinburgh, but had been in Rome for some time and had left her mother there. Sutherland claimed that her mother had been left a small estate and that she was here to sort out the affairs. Later her mother and brother arrived, and they moved out to Whitfield Cottage. Godfrey had a lot of trouble in getting the bill paid and had to threaten the accused. She returned later and had dinner with her mother and brother at a cost of 4/6d, which was never paid. She left her umbrella as a pledge, but it proved worthless.

Robert Warden, the next witness, said he had supplied the prisoner with over £25 worth of furniture from Nicoll's furniture shop on 17 September, which she said was for her mother. The furniture was delivered to Whitfield Cottage but not paid for. Her reason for not paying at once was that they had just bought the house, which had taken all their money. Mr Nicoll had read something in the papers that caused him to call at the cottage and take back all his furniture. He saw the prisoner's mother there and asked about her supposed annuity. Mrs Sutherland replied that the only annuity she had was her hands. Warden continued that he had many creditors who had promised to pay but had not done so, which was common practice in Dundee, provoking laughter in the court.

Isabella Ireland then deposed that Miss Sutherland had obtained a ring from her hardware shop the previous September, which was worth about 25 shillings, and had not paid for it. When questioned later, Sutherland expressed surprise that the account had not been settled and referred her to Mr Mackay, her solicitor.

The prosecution witnesses kept coming and the case against Annie grew. The manager of James Dickie, a wireworker's shop, stated Annie had ordered a bird cage and had it sent to Robertson's stables in King Street, where she kept her carriage, but she never returned to pay for it. In September she called at the premises of Alexander McIntosh, carver and gilder, and ordered four pictures, asking for them to be framed for her. 'I delivered these to Robertson's stables and there learned that her carriage was only a hired one,' recounted Mr McIntosh. 'She brought in a painting of The College of Rome to be framed but did not pay so I kept it. I went to her cottage at Whitfield and took back the pictures.' Meanwhile, a Mr Howie said that Sutherland had taken a gold watch on approval to show her mother. She did not return to pay for it, so he went to her house to reclaim it and was told to send his claim to Mr Mackay, her solicitor. He later retrieved the watch from her mother. 'The hue and cry was out about Miss Sutherland before I got the watch back and everyone was after their goods,' he said. Finally, on 4 October 1872, Miss Sutherland called at the shop of Peter Robinson of Hilltown, a cabinet maker, and selected articles worth around £8 or £9 and asked him to look out for a second-hand phaeton as the one she had was too small. Miss Sutherland then pulled one of her favourite strokes: she had to attend a 'meeting of ladies' that evening, at which there was to be a presentation and a subscription raised, she explained, but she had come out without any money. Could she possibly borrow £1 until tomorrow, when she would come in and settle the whole account? He lent her the money and she offered an IOU, but Robinson said that it wasn't worth it. She didn't return until sometime later, when she asked for the goods to be sent to her cottage: '[S]he made various representations in order to induce me to send the goods but I began to suspect that things were not right and didn't do so.' The £1 was never repaid.

One local newspaper described Annie's appearance in court:

'With a nose of proportions that would have pleased Napoleon, a chin whose development, and lips whose mould and compression bespoke strength of character and firmness of purpose, she sat and eyed attentively each witness that mounted the box to pour forth his or her tale against her – watched each witness with a keenness of glance that betokened she was taking the deepest interest in her case, her lips, which she bit now and again twitching as each new story unfolded. Here is a woman whose career is far from an everyday one, even in the annals of crime. Considering her lady-like manners; her carriage and deportment; the softness of her voice and her continual readiness to use it everywhere, not only to her own advantage but to enlighten and gratify those she conversed with, her coolness and self-possession, we need not wonder though she was more than a match for the vast majority for those on whom she had designs. From her travels on the continent she had become well informed and entered freely into conversation with whomever she came into contact, and considering how far she is from the ordinary style of the "rogue and vagabond", and remembering the general principles on which shopkeepers and others do business in this country, it would often have savoured of suspiciousness more than enough, if not of insult, to have called in question her honour or good intentions.

'Still, it does seem remarkable that her career of fraud was not cut short long before this by some of her friends more discerning than another or by some unlucky accident. The story of her doings in Aberdeen and Dundee, in the south of Scotland, in Rome and in Paris opens up a field for speculation as to how it [could] have gone on for as long as it did and also the motives that could have animated her in many of her transactions. If some of these are examined from a professional criminal's point of view, the wisdom of them will not be very apparent. The taking of a house in the immediate vicinity of Dundee and furnishing it in the grotesque manner in which it was furnished – the walls hung round and round with pictures while the rooms were uncarpeted might be held as some reason for the hypothesis that she is tinged with insanity, that her mind is not in a healthy and normal condition. The amount of sheer nerve required to go through all she has done is something marvellous to contemplate. But if Miss Sutherland is afflicted by a species of insanity no one will deny that there is wondrous method in her madness.'

The prosecution then called Annie's mother, under the name of Catherine Sutherland, a widow of Cotton Road, Dundee, to give evidence about the watch. She informed the court:

'The prisoner is my daughter. She is aged 25 years. She was employed as an evening teacher in the Model Lodging House in Dundee and she kept a school at Rosebank for a short time. She left Dundee three years ago and went to London ([in] 1869). I had letters from Rome written by her. She returned to this quarter about the beginning of September last. During her absence I was residing at Kemback Street, Dundee. I was neither at Rome or any other place with her. When she came back she took up quarters at Godfrey's Waverley Hotel and at the end of the month went out to Whitfield. I went with her. I never authorised her to purchase furniture for the house. I did not authorise her to get a gold watch for me, nor a gold ring. I had no money in the bank in September or October last neither had I any annuity. I supported myself by the labour of my hands.

'I did not buy a house last September. My daughter had a gold watch before she left Scotland but she did not tell me where she had got it. I never promised to pay for that watch neither did the prisoner ever give it to me. She took the watch away with her to the best of my knowledge. I saw another watch in the possession of my daughter last September. She did not tell me where she got it. I believed it was the one she had taken away with her. I never authorised my daughter to get a watch from Mr Howie to show me. I got a watch from my daughter to pawn and I did pawn it for £2. I gave her the money and also some more. When I pawned the watch I understood it was the one she had when she left Scotland as she said nothing to the contrary. Sometime after my daughter's apprehension I learned that the watch belonged to Mr Howie. I redeemed the watch and gave it to Mr Howie.'

More prosecution witnesses followed. Rachel Mitchell or Graham, wife of Reverend James Graham of Broughty Ferry, stated she met Annie for the first time in Paris, where they stayed at the same hotel: 'We agreed to meet up back in Broughty Ferry which we did in September and October, she borrowed £2 from me for some things she had bought, she said she had money in the bank but could not get it without her mother's signature. She never repaid it.' Helen Thomsen stated she had sold the prisoner footwear to the value of 19 shillings and 6 pence that was never paid, but had never had any dealings with Miss Sutherland's mother. Peter Young, a surgeon of Wellington Street, Dundee, told the court that the defendant called at his house to borrow £1, as she had a lady to see that evening to whom she owed 50 shillings and she was £1 short. He said she insisted on writing an IOU, which at first he did not want, but 'she forced it upon me saying that it was more business-like. I called in to get the debt repaid and met her mother and I asked her about all the stories in the press. She claimed that there was another Miss Sutherland doing this and not her daughter.'

Another witness from whom Annie had borrowed £1 was Walter Shepherd, manager of an ironmonger's at Broughty Ferry. Once more, the loan was never repaid, nor was there payment for £3 worth of goods that she had ordered, though these were eventually recovered.

The penultimate prosecution witness was a Mr Allen, a perfumer also of Broughty Ferry. He had first met the prisoner at a revival meeting three or four years ago but had not seen her again until September, when she called at his shop and borrowed 10 shillings from him. She said she had been engaged in missionary work in Rome and was employed by Miss Annie Macpherson, the well-known evangelistic community worker in London. Allen also accompanied her to a Good Templar mission, which she addressed, and she again promised to repay the loan but never did. 'I wrote to Miss Macpherson,' said Mr Allen, 'as I suspected that some of the statements she made about that lady were untrue. Miss Macpherson had never heard of her.'

The prosecution then stated that it did not consider it necessary to go into several of the other charges – numbers 1, 3, 7, 8 and 17 – and declared the prosecution case closed except for Mr Aitken, who had been an inspector of police in Peterhead and was now inspector of the poor. He was called as a witness to disprove Annie's claim, made upon arrest, that she was a simple school teacher at St Fergus.

After the prosecution had finished stating its case, Annie's solicitor, Peter Mackay, whom she had hired to sort out her debts, was called to the witness stand and made the following statement:

'The prisoner called on me and at her instigation I inserted an advertisement in the newspapers calling upon those to whom she was indebted to send in their claims. The prisoner was apprehended before the advertisement appeared. The prisoner had asked me to raise an action of damages for defamation of character against the newspapers, contained in articles published by them. She called to see a proof of the advertisement and called several times after that. The articles contained stories about two ladies going about the town and swindling. I made very little enquiry into the matter but the prisoner in my opinion is charged with a deal too much. I was not satisfied with the inquiry I had made and therefore did not raise an action of damages. I visited the house in which the prisoner lived as I was suspicious about her. I then found that she had been telling me untruths. Afterwards I found that she had employed Mr Paul as her agent. None of the accounts due by the prisoner handed to me have been paid and she did not give me money to pay them. Had I been in possession of £15 or £20 which the prisoner claimed she was to get when she called on me I could have cleared her debt. My own expenses were paid.'

A statement by Annie herself, dated 15 October 1872, was then read out to the court, in which she denied all charges against her:

'I am aged 23 years. I am unmarried and reside at Whitfield Cottage near Dundee. I know Mr Howie, watchmaker in King Street, Dundee. I was in his shop some weeks ago, paying him a small sum for some repairs he had done for us, when we began talking about the price of his gold watches. After some more conversation I told him I would not think any more about purchasing a watch on that day. He pressed me however, to take one and show it to my mother, saying, if we did not want it I could return it. I took it away and went back on the evening of the next day and told him we would keep it provided he would give us till the term, that is Martinmas to pay for it. His answer was "Certainly; whenever is convenient to do so." I thought no more about the matter till I met Mr Howie on the street. He said he was just coming to call on me as in consequence of something he had heard he wanted immediate payment. I told him I would call on him in the evening and give him either his money or the watch.

'Accordingly, I called upon him and stated, which was the fact, that I had put all my matters in the hands of Mr Mackay, solicitor here, to whom he should apply. I told him at the same time that he might still have the watch if he wished but would rather prefer to keep it as I had made a present of it. He said very well and I went away on the understanding that he was to call on Mr Mackay. I admit my liability for the debt and deny that there is any imposition on my part. I presented the watch to my mother and she has it.

'With reference to the charge of obtaining £2 from Mrs Graham by false pretence, I have to state that I lived in the same hotel with her and her husband on the continent this summer and I had been at school with some of her relations; that she had invited me to visit her and that finding myself in Broughty Ferry about the beginning of this month with only £3 in my purse to meet an account of £5 which I had to pay. I called on Mrs Graham and asked her if she could oblige me with a loan of £2, which she gave me and which I intend to repay. I did not make any false representations to her to induce her to give me the money, and in particular I did not tell her that my mother or myself had money in the bank at Broughty Ferry. All I said to her was that it was too far to go back to Whitfield to get the money.

'I paid the five pounds to Mr Forbes, [of] Murraygate, Dundee on the same day, the receipt is with Mr Mackay. With regard to the boots and slippers which I am said to have got from Mrs Thomson in the Ferry by false pretences, I admit having got such articles but I entirely deny that I made any false pretences. The boots were for my brother, Hamish Reid Sutherland who was in the shop when the purchase was made. I said nothing to Mrs Thompson about having money in any bank or about Mr Methven; in point of fact I do not know any person by the name of Methven and have no money in any bank in the country. All that was said about payment was that I asked Mrs Thomson, "Will it do to pay them on Friday?", on which day I intend to be in the Ferry, [and] she said "Yes." I did not go down to the Ferry on the following Friday and did not pay the account. It is still unpaid and has I believe, been handed by Mrs Thomson to Mr Mackay.

'I admit ordering a suit of boys' clothes for my brother from Mr Geddes in King Street, Dundee in April 1869. The suit was sent home to Graham Place where we were then residing. I never doubted that the account had been sent in and settled by my mother. I have met Mr Geddes repeatedly since and he never said anything about it.

'I was at the time a teacher at Rosebank School, Dundee, of which Mr Smith was the master. I also admit getting a watch from Mr Overgate. The watch was for my cousin Jessie Robertson, then a teacher at Miss Edwards School in Bucklemaker Wynd, Dundee, but who now has a school at St Fergus, Aberdeenshire. She was in the shop with me when we went about it, but I did not tell Mr Kerr that it was for her and he put it down to me, I daresay as he knew me. It was to be paid for in monthly instalments and I think I took two of these to him from my cousin before I went abroad, which I think I did about a month afterwards. I supposed till I met Mr Kerr on the street the other day it had been paid.

'I got about £20 worth of furniture from Mr Nicoll, cabinetmaker, Dundee sometime last month. I told him I could not pay for them just yet and he took my bill for the price which is not yet due. I forget the day which it is due but it is about the end of this month.

'I admit having got a gold ring with "Mizpah" (Lord Watch Over Me) on it from Miss Ireland, Union Street, Dundee in September last. It was too dear and I meant to return it. In the interval I had given it to Mr Smith of Broughty Ferry as a pattern for a similar one for a woman named Allan who lives beside me at Whitfield.

'About the same time I bought the ring I bought a bird cage from a man in Barrack Street. I told him to send in the account but he never did. I also admit to having got some things from Mr Dougan, ironmonger in Barrack Street on 23rd September. I told him I could not pay the account until the middle of October and the things were sent in on that footing.

'I also admit getting 3 photographs from Mr McIntosh, [of] Nethergate. I certainly had every intention of paying for them. I also admit some weeks ago having borrowed four shillings from Miss Lowden, [of] Reform Street. I tendered her a half sovereign in payment 3 or 4 days after I got the loan but she had no change and said I could pay another time.

'I also admit borrowing a pound from Dr Young, a pound from Dr Robinson and 10 shillings from Mr Allan of Broughty Ferry. Nothing was said about payment of any of these loans and they would have been paid by this time if I had not been apprehended. As to the pound alleged to have been borrowed from the manager of Messrs Nicoll, Broughty Ferry, I understood my mother had paid for it. I think Mrs Burness advanced me some money but she has clothes of greater value belonging to me in her possession. With reference to the pound borrowed from Mr Robinson I wish to explain that he said he would put it in the account.

'I have been for the last two years and nine months, superintendent or foreign secretary of some schools in Italy and I am only at home at present on a holiday. The salary is about one hundred pounds per year.

'All of which is the truth.'

*   *   *

Once Annie had outlined the only defence open to her, that she was a young teacher who had got into debt when things became too much for her and had always intended to pay what she owed, the jury retired at 4.30 pm. They returned at 5.00 pm to ask for guidance. Could they only find the prisoner guilty if they were convinced that she *never* intended to pay for the goods? Sheriff Heriot explained that if they were convinced Annie had obtained the goods without intending to pay for them, then she was guilty of fraud. If they thought she intended to pay for the items, they could give her the benefit of the doubt.

At 5.15 pm the jury returned with its verdict. They found by a majority that Annie was guilty of the following counts: No. 4, Mr Nicoll the cabinet maker; No. 10, Mr Howie and the gold watch; No. 12, Helen Thompson and the boots; and No. 14, borrowing a £1 from Mr Robinson the cabinet maker. The jury put in a recommendation for mercy.

Annie had done well under the circumstances, but the weight of evidence was too strong, the press campaign must have had its effect and she had no one to speak up for her. Annie would probably have got away with count No. 10, the gold watch, if her mother had backed up her story, which she could have done quite easily without any detrimental effect to herself, but maybe they did not have an opportunity to get their stories straight before the trial. In all probability her mother had no idea which answer would be most beneficial to her daughter, so she did the only thing she felt she could do – she told the truth. Having said that, it seems that there was not much love lost between them. They could not even agree over her age – both getting it wrong, as at the time of the trial Annie was, in fact, 24 years old.

Sheriff Heriot, in passing sentence, said he was considering her previous good character, her youth and the fact she had already done two months on remand. Given the nature of the offences, however, which were of public importance, he could not pass a sentence of less than nine months, a very harsh one considering the total amounts involved and the jury's recommendation. Heriot must surely have heard the rumours and read the papers, believing that there was for more to her activities than those before the court, and sentenced accordingly.

Annie was led to the cells before being taken off to Perth Penitentiary. Beyond turning very white, she showed no signs of discomfort at the verdict and subsequent sentence, leaving the dock with the same cool and composed air she had shown throughout the trial. Even at this early stage of what was to become an incredible career of deceit spanning decades, all concerned were fascinated by her and recognized there was something very special about her. The following day, the *Dundee Courier* reported:

'In her career she has shown an ability and an energy worthy of a better cause than hers, and of a better fate than that which has overtaken her. With her moral nature what it should have been, her intellectual parts, her courage, her resource and indomitable will, what they have proved to be, she would had she found her proper sphere, been an ornament to her sex and even an honour to the race. To look at her yesterday as she sat in the dock between two helmeted policemen was a study, as her career of imposture and crime is a study of no little interest.'

Even her entry into prison was not to pass without comment. As well as the often-admired 'sealskin jacket lined with ermine', she had with her 'a travelling trunk, marvellously constructed, a mechanical curiosity, containing innumerable drawers arranged for the reception of female finery'.

Reflecting on the case some time later, an unnamed correspondent to the *Aberdeen Press* noted that:

> 'When in Dundee she so mesmerised the local magistrates that none of them would convict her of swindling; and she had to be brought in front of the Sheriff before she was sent to prison. The late Provost said to me, "Well sir, I cannot believe, even after the sheriff has convicted her that Miss Sutherland is guilty of deliberate swindling." When she gave orders to tradesmen "all over the shop", and when she was at last convicted, even some of the heaviest creditors refused to believe that she intended to cheat them out of their money ... she must be awarded the distinguished credit of one of the most remarkable female characters of this or any other age.'

Whatever fascination Annie held for people, the truth was that she had been found guilty of committing fraud and sent to prison for it. The curtain had fallen on the first act of what would turn out to be a most extraordinary career of deceit over the following decade and a half.

Part II

1873–1884

Chapter 8

The Willing Victim (1873–75)

There are no records of how Annie spent her time in prison. She may have found her time inside reasonably easy; her poverty-stricken origins would have enabled her to understand and mingle with the other inmates if she had wanted to, dropping her aristocratic pretentions while keeping up her religious and charitable front. This was not the route she chose; she had perfected the art and act of a gentlewoman, and that was how she intended to continue.

Meanwhile, the Glasgow Guardian Society held its annual meeting in mid-March 1873 and, undeterred by the Mrs Wilkes affair, congratulated itself on helping to bring to justice 'one of the most audacious cases of systematic fraud which has come under consideration … her career may well be said to be unprecedented'.

As the date of her release from prison drew near, Annie was in correspondence with a Dundee gentleman who had promised to help her. *The Dundee Advertiser* obtained some of her letters to 'a well-known philanthropic gentleman' and published one of them, dated Perth, 3 September 1873:

'My Dear Sir, I trust your good nature has covered what your good sense saw in my not writing as agreed. If it is any excuse my visit to Dundee was indeed painful – more than I can express; but you know that my burden is not for a day, or for a year, but for life, and I must learn to bear it calmly, silently. Nevertheless it is a profitable and sweet necessity to be cast on the naked arm of God. I hope you do not think me insensible to the great kindness you have shown me. Words are poor but accept my thanks and believe me ever to remain,
'Yours very respectfully, Annie D Bruce Sutherland.'

Sadly, this rather odd note lacks details of its recipient, but is doubtless to one of the people she was hoping to use once her sentence was completed. Whilst she was inside, the press continued its fascination with her. One newspaper published a letter from a Broughty Ferry resident:

'Mary Ann Bruce Sutherland is still well remembered in Broughty Ferry where she victimised many of the shopkeepers and others. She was styled the "Lady Swindler" and it was her doings here that led to her conviction for fraud. Having hired a pony and phaeton, she drove around the shops, the appearance of the phaeton completely putting the merchants off their guard. When receiving the goods the story that she invariably told was that she had "forgot her purse". In this way she succeeded in attiring herself in a fashionable and valuable sealskin jacket obtained from one of the leading drapery firms in Dundee.'

Annie was released from Perth Penitentiary on Thursday 18 September 1873 and, despite the crushing setback of a criminal conviction and time in a harsh prison, was still determined to pursue her chosen career. Prison was no deterrent – anything but: the months in Perth Gaol had given her time to think and plan. Mary Ann Bruce Sutherland, the pious schoolmistress and daughter of a washerwoman, would be consigned to history. The new 'persona' must be bigger, bolder and centre stage, and with this in mind Annie Ogilvie Bruce was born, a well-bred lady of the Highland aristocracy who, with a little refinement, emerged as the disenfranchised, possibly illegitimate daughter of the Earl of Moray, and if that family chose to deny any connection … well, they would, wouldn't they!

As with most of the names Annie used throughout her life, this new one contained some connection to her past. She nearly always kept the name of Annie, and now simply dropped her stepfather's surname, Sutherland, off the end and became Miss Bruce. The origin of the Ogilvie part is not known, but she would surely have had her reasons for adopting it. Her head teeming with schemes and ideas, she had first to find somewhere to stay while putting her new plans into practice, so took lodgings at South Methven Street, Perth, a mere mile from the prison gates. Years later, after all and sundry had come to know Annie by the name of Mrs Gordon Baillie, a reporter from the *Dundee Courier* tracked down her old landlady:

'At first the old lady was by no means inclined to be communicative, and responded to the question whether it was the fact that "Mrs Gordon Baillie" had ever found shelter under her roof by requesting to be informed who had had the hardihood to couple her name with such a woman? However, on being assured that the secret was known only to a few, and that there was no fear of her name being coupled with such a person she consented to tell all she knew about the adventuress.

"Well," [remarked the old lady], "it is fully fifteen years, I think since she lodged with me.

"'A rap came to my door one afternoon and upon going to answer the call I saw what I took to be a well-dressed good looking young lady, who judging from her eyes had evidently been weeping. She said she had just been seeing a friend off to America, [and] she engaged a single room.'"

"'Do you know what means she had when she came to you?'" [the reporter inquired.]

"'Oh yes she had money, for she paid a week's rent forehanded.'"

"'How did she spend her time?'"

"'Mostly in reading and writing. In fact she wrote so much that I fancied she was writing a novel. She was quiet, reserved and ladylike in her manner. No one visited her except Mr Graham a Methodist minister who has long since left Perth. Mr Graham sometimes visited along with his sister and the three have more than once had tea together in the same room. Mr Graham and his niece frequently walked out with her, and she occasionally dined with them.'"

"'By the way what name did the woman give?'"

"'She told me her name was Miss Bruce and that she belonged to the north, she was with me two or three weeks, and I sent her about her business.'"

"'How was that?'"

"'A few days after she came to reside with me a gentleman called upon her, who I was led to understand had something to do with Lord Kinnaird's Estate. Miss Bruce told me so. Miss Bruce and the gentleman went away together for the ostensible purpose of visiting the Kinnaird estate. She remained away about a week. A few days after she left I was surprised to learn that my, "lady lodger" had been in the Penitentiary. After being away about a week, as I have said, she returned to my house and I was "a taken" when I saw her. Coming into the room she smilingly extended her hand to me but I drew back and declined to shake hands with her.

"'You did not tell me you had been in the 'Penny!'" I said to her.

"'No but what harm will that do you?" she replied.

"'Well you cannot remain another night here," I said.

"'I may tell you it was night when she came back. I insisted that she should leave my house at once and she did so.

"'Do you know whether she left Perth when you turned her out of your house?" [the reporter asked.]

"'I know she did not leave town at that time because I met her several times on the street during the next few weeks. She wore a veil over her face but I never showed that I knew her. I believe she resided in the north east part of the town".

"'Did you get any explanation from the reverend Mr Graham as to his acquaintance with Miss Bruce?"

"'I called upon him afterwards and complained of having such a woman foisted upon me. It was because Mr & Mrs Graham came about her that I considered her a highly respectable person."

"'Was Mr Graham astonished when you told him that you had learned that she had been in the penitentiary?"

"'Well he didn't seem to think that I was justified in turning her out of my house."

"'When you read the reports in the newspapers did you recognise in 'Mrs Gordon Baillie' your former lady lodger, Miss Bruce?"

"'Oh yes I saw it was her. Just last night my daughter, after reading an account of her doings, remarked that she would not for all the world that anyone should know that that woman has ever lodged with us."

'I hinted that the connection was certainly not one to be proud of,' [the reporter continued,] 'and assured the old lady as I took my departure that I would respect her wishes as to the suppressing of her name. Mr Graham the Methodist minister referred to was only three years in Perth altogether. All attempts to trace Miss Bruce's movements during the remainder of her brief stay in Perth have proved unavailing. It does not appear that she left behind her in the fair city any of those touching reminders in the form of unpaid bills with which she was so lavish.'

It is likely that Annie and her mother became permanently estranged after the trial, which is hardly surprising as she had sought to use Kate as an excuse for many of her actions, and the old lady does not appear in the story again.

According to Annie's later accounts, it was around this time that she became acquainted with Sir Richard Duckworth King, of 2 Chesterfield Street, Mayfair, and her life changed forever. King, the son of Vice Admiral Sir Richard King, was born in 1804. After Eton he entered the British Army in 1822 and achieved the honorary rank of major, before retiring on half-pay. He succeeded to the baronetcy in 1834 and married two years later. Unfortunately, his wife died within a year and he never remarried. His life seems to have been pretty quiet and not much has been discovered about him – probably as there was nothing much *to* discover. He was for some time a director of Provident Life Insurance and seems to have spent a large part of his life at home amongst his retainers in Mayfair, visiting his club and generally enjoying his money.

How and under what circumstances he met Annie is not known. Possibly it was through the church or theatre, or maybe he was involved in certain philanthropic work. What is known for sure is that when they met, Sir Richard was in his mid-60s and very rich, while Miss Bruce was in her mid-20s and had nothing but her wit, beauty and determination. Whatever the circumstances surrounding their first meeting, accounts agree that he became completely besotted with her, offering her his 'hand and heart'. Despite the age difference, it is quite possible that they became lovers for a while; both were single and had a great deal in common – namely Sir Richard's money. Whatever their arrangement was, he soon became her benefactor, admirer and protector.

Years later, in an attempt to prise the two of them apart and protect the family fortune, his immediate relations portrayed him as a doddery old fool preyed upon by a cunning woman – which he may have eventually become, but he was certainly competent enough to give evidence to the court in 1876 and make payments to a married woman for a child he acknowledged as his a few years after that. Sir Richard obviously had other lovers, and it is perhaps reasonable to assume Annie did as well. Very little has been discovered of her activities from the end of 1873 until the spring of 1875, but it is possible that she spent this time with Sir Richard, spending his money, learning the ways of the aristocracy and grooming him for a role that was to last for the next ten years.

One account of her activities during the tourist season of 1874 has surfaced, however. It seemed 'Miss Bruce' arrived one evening at Inverness by the Caledonian Canal steamer, having just completed what was known as the 'Royal Route' from Glasgow to Oban. She was accompanied by a maid, who at once called a cab for 'my lady', and together they drove off towards the town. In passing a pleasantly situated cottage, Miss Bruce's eye was drawn to a sign advertising 'lodgings'. The cab was stopped, entry demanded, and before the lady of the house had time to discuss terms, Miss Bruce and her maid had settled down and ordered tea. Miss Bruce became for a time the landlady's constant companion. The courteous manners and ladylike bearing of her visitor won her admiration, and she was soon introduced to several friends. Sometime after Annie had taken her leave, the landlady accepted an offer of marriage. Miss Bruce had left an address and had made such a favourable impression on her former host that she was invited to the ceremony, which she quickly accepted. At the marriage service she conducted herself with the dignity befitting the role that she had rehearsed so often, and delighted all with her affable manners and interesting reminiscences of travel in foreign parts.

Annie still professed a great interest in religious matters, and during her earlier visit she had made the acquaintance of several gentlemen of position in Inverness. Such was the impression that she made among them that when she left, she did so with the 'good wishes of all'. During her current stay she became the guest of a gentleman whose acquaintance she had made in connection with some religious services on her former visit. She drove about freely and went to the length of entertaining several of these new gentlemen friends to a sumptuous meal at one of the principal hotels. Her visit had now lasted for several weeks and she showed no sign of leaving. When at last she took her departure it was much to the relief of her host, who was known as a pious and single man.

By June of 1875 Annie was living in Rutland Street, Edinburgh, a short street of pleasant Georgian townhouses, almost certainly rented for her by Sir Richard King. During her time there she made a point of seeking out a young theatrical correspondent who, in his own words, 'enjoyed nothing better than to see a good play miserably acted by a band of amateurs, as it gave me the opportunity of airing my "exuberant verbosity" and slating the performers all round'. He took his next 'opportunity' during a performance by student actors of Ellen Wood's *East Lynne*, with the result that 'sundry vows of vengeance were communicated to me which made me feel rather shaky for a night or two as I had been mauled once before'.

One morning, shortly after the review had appeared, he received a note asking him to call at an address in Rutland Street. Feeling rather apprehensive, he armed himself with a stout stick and went around there. He was shown into the drawing room, where he met a middle-aged lady who took him upstairs. There, in the well-furnished drawing room, he was greeted by a number of ladies enjoying afternoon tea. His confidence returned as he saw no six feet dramatic amateur actors amongst them, but, still clinging to his stick, he was offered tea by the most attractive of the group and the purpose of the summons was explained.

The host was a playwright who told him that she thought him to be 'the greatest dramatic critic of the day' and was much amused by his review of the student production. She had written a play, she explained, on the life of Flora MacDonald, which she wanted help in producing for the stage. She had obtained his name from a theatrical literature shop in Greenside that he was known to frequent. He was so impressed by her appearance, the sweet frank face, musical voice, sparkling brown eyes, lithe graceful figure, jet black hair cut short and her flattery of him that, in his words, 'I would have promised her anything and was quite entranced by the little sorceress.'

The critic's name was George Stronach, and captivated by the beautiful playwright he soon called again, although the promised manuscript of Flora MacDonald was not forthcoming, 'to my disappointment as I longed to give her work a somewhat more favourable criticism than the one I had passed on the university comedians'. Despite this, they agreed to meet again and on the next occasion, at her suggestion, went to the Princess's Theatre to see a performance of *Giroflé-Girofla* – a comic opera written by Charles Lecoq, performed, according to our critic, by a 'first rate company' that included Henry Corri, Catherine Lewis and an operatic tenor named Mr Knight Aston. Stronach continues:

> 'With Mr Knight Aston, I could see early in the play, her ladyship was vastly impressed and she badgered me with questions – much to our neighbour's disgust – as to what I knew about him. She went into rapture over his voice and figure as he gave a very weak version, I thought, of 'My Father is a Banker Old', but perhaps I was beginning to feel the green-eyed monster working his way through my heart.'

Mr Knight Aston was part of a provincial tour with Mrs W. H. Liston's London Opera Company that had opened in Birmingham on 12 April 1875 and reached Edinburgh on Monday 21 June, where they played for six nights. Despite Stronach's disappointment at being used to facilitate Annie's ogling of another man, they became friends and returned to the same opera every other night. He bumped into her one afternoon in town and made the jocular remark: 'Girofle tonight Miss Bruce?' 'No,' she replied, 'I'm going to Roslin and you are coming with me.'

At 4 o'clock that afternoon, she drove them both the seven miles to the chapel in a steady drizzle. The young critic later recalled:

> 'It was rather a melancholy drive, as her ladyship was not in a communicative mood and when her temper was up the best thing to do was to let her have her own way. She seemed to be forming some of those wicked plots which her active brain was ever hatching ... during the walk through the chapel she became quite lively, the poor boy guide had to submit to a ton of chaff from the irreverent beauty as he read out the Latin epitaphs with his stick always a yard in front of the word.
>
> '[After tea at the hotel] ... on the way back she had a little cry and took me into her confidence – that she was the daughter of a Scotch peer from whom she received a handsome allowance which would cease if she went upon the stage which she was determined to do. She wanted to make a name for herself in the world's history. Through the agency of

the *Edinburgh Evening Despatch* she has achieved this more successfully than she bargained for in 1875. I was also interested to know that she wrote for *The Saturday Review*, although I must acknowledge my surprise some days afterwards to get a letter from her with the day of the week spelt "Saterday". My faith in the bone-fides of reviewers who could not spell the name of their own journal waxed rather faint. I was asked to interview 3 students who annoyed her by hanging out signals to her from their rooms at the back of the square. Another serious problem she had was that of a young clergyman staying in the same home who would persist in sending up love letters to her, placed in the toes of her boots after the servant had brushed them. These ministerial amatory epistles – several of which I have beside me – were certainly worthy of this original post office. During her stay in Rutland Street our lady gave a splendid dance at which there was a delightful mixture of folks who knew nothing of each other. I wonder if the confectioner was ever paid for the excellent banquet he provided on the occasion? She did everything in fine style as well she might. A rather severe illness cut short further visits to Rutland Street but she kept me plied with heaps of letters, (with the Bruce crest) and books (wonderfully annotated) – everything I wanted except the manuscript of Flora Macdonald.

'Thoroughly done up I took a run down to Dumfriesshire to stay with some friends. [Stronach was convalescing at Beattock about 60 miles south of Edinburgh.] This was on a Friday and on the Saturday as I was sitting at dinner, I was handed a telegram which about knocked me over. It ran "Leaving by two train. Meet me at station. Bruce". This was a startler as there was no accommodation for her and the elderly friend of our first interview who acted as her "companion" in the house where I was comfortably lodged. And what explanation was I to make to my friends for the appearance of this new star in the Dumfriesshire heavens? It had to be done however and there was another farm not far off where I was assured they would be glad to receive her. I was rather doubtful of this but jumping into a trap I went off to the station to await her ladyship. On the train drawing up the silly old lady threw out a travelling basket which upset and displayed on the platform a grand array of broken glasses and bottles. Miss Bruce let the "old stupid" as she called her have a warm ten minutes of it for her pains.

'For my sake perhaps she received a hearty welcome and as she could suit herself in any company –in castle or cottage – she became in a couple of days the most popular member of the household. Not content with the turn out belonging to the farmer she engaged a splendid machine and a spirited horse from Dumfries and we cut a decided dash in the neighbourhood when she whipped up the animal and sent him at racing speed along the road. Although she was an excellent driver, she was occasionally not very particular about what she drove over in the course of her travels as on one occasion she went right across a pack of hounds. How the huntsman did swear over her but she kissed her hand to them and drove on.

'The time passed merrily enough. She displayed her horsemanship – I my want of it, causing her more amusement than it did me. I initiated her into the mysteries of fly fishing and assisted her ashore when she slipped into the stream and got in over her shoe tops. She didn't care a bit, however for the contretemps, but took off her stockings and fished on until they were dry. On these outings we were occasionally accompanied by a fire eating half-pay Major T whose head was completely turned by the "little devil" as he once styled her. During all this time I had not the faintest suspicion that "adventuress" was the proper description of this fascinating creature.

'Whatever she purchased in my company on our visits to Dumfries and elsewhere she paid for and her apparent generosity on many occasions could not but deceive one. For instance in Rutland Street she once called in from the street a little Italian boy with his monkey. For a quarter of an hour she kept up or cleverly pretended to keep up with the conversation in Italian which she said she could speak fluently although she could not write a word of it. She loaded the boy with fruit and presented him with 5s when he was leaving the house. I thought this was terrible extravagance but she decided the lesson in Italian was worth the money. She was totally ignorant of French or German and she could neither sing or play the piano. I made painful, or rather pleasing, efforts to teach her the melodies of Knight Aston's songs but the failure was complete, she had no ear for music. As for her bad spelling she cleverly concealed it by equally vile writing or the convenient alternative of telegrams which she made use of to an extravagant extent. She never tired of repeating Shelley's *Epipsychidion* and was a "powerful declaimer in blank verse".

'But to return to our pastoral life and the incidents – not forgetting our visit to Dumfries on a market day. My bliss was to be of short duration as it was fated that I should mortally offend her. She was seated on a swing in the garden one fine morning with the family admiringly looking on as I sent her flying through the air. Even when she insisted in getting off I let her have the full benefit of the excitement which she didn't seem to appreciate as highly as her audience whose faces changed from smiles to broad grins. The reason was at once obvious, the fine "Flaxmanesque bust" eulogised by the writer in the *Court and Society Review* and of which I had serious suspicions, was gradually dropping down and disappearing from view! Something in the interior had given way. For this grave offence I was banished from her company after a stormy little scene.

'This was a Thursday, [and] on the Saturday I had an engagement for lunch with a gentleman, a widower who owns one of the most charming little estates in Dumfriesshire. We were in the smoking room when my friend called my attention to a carriage coming up the avenue with a Highlander in full dress sitting behind – for I forgot to mention that Miss Bruce never travelled without a good-looking rival of John Brown. I saw at once who our visitor was and felt annoyed at her cheek and told my friend that I would not see her but hurried down the steps in a state of virtuous indignation. She opened out on me for intending to leave without bidding her good bye, a very lame excuse I thought for her supreme impudence in driving up to the home of a total stranger. She was not invited to step upstairs and my lady drove away in very doleful dumps.'

George Stronach was not the only person Annie cultivated during her time in Edinburgh. An unnamed 'Edinburgh Lady' would later tell a local newspaper the story of how a Miss Bruce knocked on her door one day in May 1875, bringing with her some fancy needlework which she wanted to sell in order to help the poor people of the district. Annie had obviously done her homework and had chosen her target with care. The two ladies got talking, and it emerged that Miss Bruce knew all about the Edinburgh Lady's marriage, when and where it had taken place, the birth dates of her children and many small incidents in her life. On the following day Annie returned, accompanied by an old lady whom she described as her chaperone. The pair became firm friends and she visited at least twice a week over the next few weeks, frequently staying to dinner and making herself quite at home, while enjoying the company of the children to whom she presented costly toys. At some time in this period Annie expressed a desire to have her photograph taken with the oldest boy, but her host was afterwards glad that she did not consent to this being done.

It was also during this period that upon learning that the lady's husband had a spirited grey horse and several carriages, Annie lost no time in communicating her fondness for 'handling the ribbons'. She suggested a brake carriage, and this was agreed, on the understanding that the coachman should be allowed to occupy the seat of the vehicle, but Annie drove at such an incredible speed that the poor man was terrified.

The Edinburgh Lady and her husband were present at a supper Annie gave in Rutland Street, during which she was led in by Dr Mapleson, the late physician to George IV. Shortly after, Miss Bruce informed her host she was to proceed to a country house near Lochmaben, in Dumfriesshire, where she intended to stay for some time, and in return for the hospitality shown her she wished her host to visit along with her children as guests. The Edinburgh Lady continues the story:

'After Miss Bruce had been away for a while she came back to Edinburgh and unexpectedly called on me one morning saying that she had not got her usual remittance from her lawyers in London [and] asked whether I could give the loan of a few pounds. I did not happen to have the amount she wanted but my husband loaned her £15 or £16. Miss Bruce stated that she would refund the money when I next came to visit her. Shortly afterwards we took the train to Lochmaben where she met us at the stables in charge of a handsome trap to which a thoroughbred Arab pony was harnessed.

'A gillie in full Highland costume was in attendance and we drove down to the farmhouse where Miss Bruce was staying. There was also a gentleman of independent means who had been living at the place before Miss Bruce's arrival. It later transpired that he had lent Miss Bruce a considerable sum which he recovered after some difficulty. My children and I were most hospitably entertained and held picnics everywhere. Through the landlords several of the lairds invited us to attend high tea parties which we did, Miss Bruce being a great favourite wherever we went. Among the places we visited were Dumfries and Castle Douglas where one day boating on the lock Miss Bruce nearly upset the craft in which we were seated. I stayed with my host for three weeks and every night we played whist being joined in the game by the gentleman to whom I have referred. Miss Bruce never took part in it, she never gave a reason but lay on the couch pretending to read a novel. She never turned over any leaves and I am satisfied that she never read any, [as] occasionally I could see the page was turned upside down. I began to be concerned about being repaid the sum I had lent her because, believing that I was about to get it back, I took less money from home with me then otherwise I would've done.

'At length I asked her about it and she completely changed her demeanour towards me saying, "I will get your money tomorrow."

Tomorrow came but not the money. I asked her time after time but she always had a plausible excuse. The gentlemen visitor at the farmhouse invariably accompanied us on our journeys. Once she made a trip to Dumfries with a sealskin jacket and came back without it looking very dejected as if something was annoying her and I made up my mind that something had gone wrong. I cannot say exactly what first aroused my suspicion but I eventually asked once more for the money to which she replied, "I did not get it from you, I got it from your husband and when I go to Edinburgh I shall give it to him." To that I said in the hope of being successful, "But I did not bring much money with me and I now require the money in order to pay what I owe." She replied that I was her guest and had nothing to pay. For some days I did not mention the matter again. One day we went to all the trip without the gillie and on this occasion and Miss Bruce herself attended to the wants of a pony, she washed the animal's bruised knees in a business like fashion and bound them with a handkerchief.

'On another occasion we attended the Operetta House in Waterloo Place and two young men who sat behind us were so charmed with Miss Bruce that they wished to be introduced to her but I cannot remember whether the desire was gratified. I remember another occasion during a visit to Dumfriesshire when she went about for several days wearing a widow's weeds. She often aired her so-called knowledge of the Italian language and declared that she could read [the Italian poet] Tasso from the original. While we were at Lochmaben there was a quarrel between her [and her] elderly chaperone, a nice quiet lady who shortly after left for London. One other Lochmaben incident was that while she was absent one day a delicate looking lady between 20 and 30 called at the farmhouse requesting to see her [and] in the course of [a] brief interview she said that Miss Bruce had been very kind [to] her while in Moffat. Afterwards we were inclined to think that the lady was no other than a detective officer in disguise.

'Before leaving the farmhouse that day I asked the landlady to have my account ready and this was waiting for me in an envelope lying on the mantelpiece. When Miss Bruce saw it she asked why the landlady was writing to me. I replied that it was my account for staying here, [and she said,] "Oh! But you're my guest! You have nothing to pay her." "Well," I rejoined, "we came as your guests but we do not leave such." She afterwards looked daggers at me. Later on while I was walking in the garden before engaging in the usual game of whist I saw Miss Bruce pacing the drawing-room [in] a very distressed state of mind. I imagined there was something wrong. She was talking to the gillie. As I intended leaving for home the next morning I asked once more for my money and she seemed greatly annoyed at me for insisting that I was to pay the landlady. She said she would give me my money tomorrow then closed the door. The table of the room was littered with accounts and letters. She turned on me and said, "What do you mean by snubbing me?" I replied, "I don't snub you, but you are not what I thought you were." She thereupon grabbed my arm – this was about one or two in the morning – and forced me down on the couch and said, "What do you mean?" I said nothing more than that things are not what I should like or what they ought to be. I became very frightened that she would not let me out. At that moment there was a knock on the window and when I asked her what it was she said it was only some of the hands after the female servants. I said, "Open the door this moment!" I then went towards the door screaming. The members of the household were awakened by my screams and Miss Bruce was obliged to let me out. When half way upstairs I almost fainted.

'Next morning I was determined to leave for Edinburgh and at the breakfast table in the presence of the household I asked Miss Bruce for my money and when I was engaged in packing in my room she came with the money that I had lent her which I afterwards learnt was borrowed from the gentleman visitor. Miss Bruce drove me to the station and on the way made every possible attempt to restore friendship. She said she would come to Edinburgh and see me but I told her that she need not do so. Shortly after my return the gentleman visitor called on me inquiring after her whereabouts. Miss Bruce got to know where I had my dresses made and as she particularly fancied a cloth dress which I had, she wrote to the tailor who made it and using my name she gave an order for a dress of the same kind to be supplied. The order was not complied with as I'd taken steps to put the tailor on his guard as I did to others in the city. We learned that Miss Bruce incurred debts in Edinburgh to the extent of some hundreds of pounds and continued to travel about in a carriage with a flunky behind her, again forgetting her purse and dodging her bills, [and] it is reported that one jeweller in Edinburgh alone lost in the region £200. Another thing I shall say is that the gillie was afterwards put in taking charge of the sticks and wardrobes of visitors to the Royal Scottish Academy were I met and spoke to him.'

These two tales from the same period in Annie's life show different sides to her character. On the one hand she was at pains to keep Stronach on her side and keen to impress him with her wealth, social skills, horsemanship and social standing, while at the farmhouse matters seemed to deteriorate in front of the Edinburgh Lady and Major T as she appeared distressed and bad-tempered with a 'table full of accounts and letters'. As always there were problems over money.

The unfortunate 'wardrobe malfunction' in front of Stronach and the others also seems to have affected her deeply and may have added fuel to her serious spat with the Edinburgh Lady. Having fallen out with her hosts and guests in both properties, she made her way back to Edinburgh, as did the others in their own time. We hear nothing more from the Edinburgh Lady, but a later report claims that Major T. was very keen to recover his loan, which was still outstanding. Hearing that she was in London, he obtained her address and went to confront her – whereupon she pointed a pistol at his head, although eventually the situation calmed down and the sum was repaid. Life at Rutland Street had now turned sour, with mounting debts and numerous rumours flying around her small circle of friends after the Dumfriesshire episode. Stronach still had much to say: 'I saw her once again in Edinburgh when she asked me for some London introductions which I gladly gave her as I considered she would do them credit. One of these was to my editorial friend who wrote that he would soon cure my "Scotch Lassie" of the theatrical fever'.

It was now October 1875, and amongst Stronach's list of contacts was his 'editorial friend', Joseph Hatton, a well-known novelist, journalist and editor of *The Sunday Times*. Hatton had received an exciting account from his Scottish friend of this lady of 'rare courage and feminine loveliness'; the letters were accompanied by photographs of an attractive aristocratic young woman, and it was obvious to Hatton that Stronach was in love with her. She appeared to be a lady of birth and wealth, an orphan and of age, who was intent upon a career on the London stage come what may. The Edinburgh journalist asked only that he give her help and guidance when called upon. In due course the woman to whom Hatton referred to in print, for some reason best known to himself, as 'Miss Ogilvie Westerne', arrived and did not disappoint. She spoke with a slight Scotch accent, was splendidly dressed and seemed quite innocent of London life. She spent some time being tutored by the American actor and elocutionist Hermann Vezin, before deciding that she wanted to write. 'I have not come to London to act,' she declared, 'I have been in the habit of writing for the press. I have a diploma as a practitioner in one of the Scotch hospitals. I have studied politics. I have written a play; and so you see I have a good many irons in the fire. What I want to do first is buy a newspaper.'

Somewhat shocked by this statement of youthful confidence and ambition, Hatton asked her if she had a large fortune.

'Yes,' she replied, smiling.

'Then you had better have a theatre as well as a newspaper if you are anxious to get your troubles over quickly,' he said to her, half in jest. She rose to the bait and with obvious irritation shot back at him:

> 'You think you are talking to the inexperienced girl described by your Edinburgh correspondent! Let me undeceive you; I have been my own mistress almost since I was a child and have had a long career of work; I have invested money in many strange ventures and never lost any; and when you talk sarcastically of my having a theatre you don't dream that before six months are over my head I shall a have a newspaper and a theatre. I can afford it!'

With her sheer nerve beginning to earn his respect, he asked her if she had agents or solicitors to whom she could turn for advice.

> 'No, no, I never ask their advice; I simply tell them what I wish. I want you to advise me and if you will let me know of any good newspaper in the market for sale I will buy it, and although I would not hurt your feelings for the world, I shall ask you to make it a business matter between us.'

Hatton made it plain he would have no part in an enterprise that would be a source of serious anxiety to someone who had been asked merely to advise, and continued: 'Can you guess how much money has been invested in the little journal in the office of which you are now sitting? Twenty thousand pounds, and I would sell it for a couple of thousand this moment – but not to you!'

She smiled and thanked him for being so frank, but begged him to understand that she did indeed have the money for both newspaper and theatre, but first she would need a clever businessman and a secretary to assist her. Hatton recalled: 'She looked at me with a fascinating glance and I confess I began to admire the brave, daring Scotch beauty.'

The following week, Annie called again, drawing up in a carriage and pair attended by obsequious flunkeys. She confessed to being in need of help. She had taken rooms in a house where the proprietor had gained some influence over her by opening her mail, and through the making of serious enquiries had discovered she owed money 'in the north'. Miss Westerne felt it was time to 'come clean' and 'tell the truth': she was in fact the illegitimate daughter of the Earl of Moray, with an estate in Scotland which provided a considerable income paid quarterly by the Earl's agents:

'I am extravagant, I have always been accustomed to buy everything I like. The accounts are only a few hundred pounds and my agents will pay them but the quarter is not up and don't you think that it is a very shameful thing for this man to try to get money out of me by spying? I have already lent him a hundred pounds, what ought I to do?'

Hatton gave her a letter of introduction to an eminent solicitor who put a stop to the prying landlord, whereupon she announced that she was to stay in London, take a house and send for her Scottish servants. A few days later, a house agent wrote to Hatton asking if she was a responsible person, and he replied telling them the little he knew and referred them to her agents. Realizing that she had few, if any, friends in London, Hatton introduced Annie to his wife, and the two ladies soon became good friends and could often be seen driving along together in the carriage and pair that Miss Westerne had the use of and which she was believed to own. In this way she succeeded in getting to know numerous tradespeople to whom the journalist and his family were known, and who believed such an introduction to be quite satisfactory. According to Hatton's account, his wife and Westerne went to the theatre together, but Mrs Hatton was not favourably impressed with her companion's manners and explained as much to her husband.

Before long, Annie moved into a house very close to the Hattons at 11 St James Terrace, Regents Park, St John's Wood, and there is an amusing story told of her arrival. She called in to enquire about the rent, with her carriage at the door, and suddenly became concerned about the safety of a 'relic' that she had with her, and with the landlord's assistance brought in a large crate which she placed in the hall. It was a heraldic window, she claimed, from her grandfather's Highland castle. Exactly what this stage prop was supposed to contribute to the proceedings is unclear, but both parties were eventually satisfied and she moved in with her maids and housekeepers, footmen, secretary, horses, carriages and dogs.

During her time in London, Annie and George Stronach kept up their correspondence, as he later related:

'I had numerous epistles from her in London thanking me for the assistance I had given her and inviting me up to town, but my ardour was completely cooled by this time. I heard that she had furnished a large house of 3 or 4 floors and I speculated on the cost of such an experiment. Then one day in *The Scotsman* I came across an advertisement:

Wanted: the address of Miss Annie Ogilvie Bruce of Rutland Street.

'I sent a reply asking the purpose for which the information was wanted. Miss Bruce had "let in" a Princes Street jeweller to the amount of £200 and her bill was still unpaid. The firm knew nothing of her whereabouts. I at once wrote to my London friends to put them on the alert as the jeweller acquainted me with the fact that innumerable tradesmen whose names they gave me had been done in the same fashion. Among the worst cases was that of a poor milliner and dressmaker who had just started business. I was not surprised when my folks in the south refused to believe me. They said I must be mad. Alright, I said to myself, somebody will be madder in a week or two I bet.

'About this time a lady looking over an album in my house came upon the charmer's photograph and asked me how I came to know Miss Sunderland. "Miss Bruce is that lady's name," I said and then the whole of her Dundee career was narrated as well as her doings at a hotel in the north where this lady was staying at the time and where a large bill was still owing. My sisters' faces were a study on that occasion. Later on it came to my knowledge that my heroine had taken a shooting lodge at Moniack near Beauly and had succeeded in leaving without the payment of rent. Several large heavy boxes lying at the station were embargoed by the landlord but their fair owner, driven over in a smart dogcart, managed to step into the London train at another station on the line. The landlord rejoiced at the thought of the silver plate he had laid hold of, alas for the confidence of man, the contents were bricks and straw.'

Hatton received the unwelcome news about his new lady friend's true identity with great alarm, and was not prepared to accept the accusations without at least giving Miss Westerne an opportunity of explanation. He went to visit her immediately, showed her the letter he had just received and asked for an explanation.

'Come with me, my dear sir!' she said. 'Come at once, my carriage is at the door. I will explain, but I beg of you to come to my house!'

They arrived at her lodgings and Hatton was shown what Annie claimed was a bundle of love letters from his friend George, couched in the warmest terms and offering marriage. 'I refused him only this week, as you see and he has sworn to be revenged, and this is his method. What do you think of a man who can be so base'?

After this final exchange, Stronach declared he and Hatton were no longer on speaking terms. Stronach's final comment on his former friend was: 'As for the confiding editor who took it for granted that the bundle of letters showed to him contained an offer of my hand and heart to the accomplished lady who was driving his wife about London in her brougham, he was the greatest disbeliever of the lot. He was highly indignant at my presumption.'

Hatton was satisfied with her explanation and despatched a rather sharp note to his Edinburgh friend. However, doubts lingered and grew as gossip began to circulate. Stronach sent him the advertisement in which the lady was 'wanted'. Hatton did some digging and wrote asking for references to her agents and solicitors, adding that until they were received he would prefer it if she did not call on him again. She replied with a 'dignified' note saying that 'she would not trespass further upon my courtesy; and that someday I should know her better and when we met in society I should no doubt apologise for suspecting her'. Shortly after this came letters from tradespeople, to whom Hatton's name had been given as a reference. He wrote once more asking her not to use his name, on pain of legal proceedings. She retorted scornfully and agreed not to mention him. Hatton continues:

'I did myself the honour of cutting her dead and cautioning everybody against her. But she was so handsome, she looked so happy, she drove such splendid cattle, she spoke Italian so fluently and become so popular with tradespeople and local visitors that I began to think I had made a mistake, though I was content to walk in the shadow of my neighbour's magnificence.'

Some weeks later, with the truth becoming ever more apparent, Hatton wrote in despair to Stronach: 'My Dear S. What am my to-do? Miss B has run up tremendous accounts with all my tradesmen who can't get a penny out of her. Yours H.'

Stronach replied: 'My Dear H. I told you what to do six weeks ago and you gave me no thanks for the information. Do what you like now. Yours S.'

After this final exchange Stronach declared he and Hatton were no longer on speaking terms. Despite what must have been quite devastating revelations, as time passed he reflected rather fondly upon his time with her:

'Such were a few of my experiences of Mrs Gordon Baillie. I wish I had known of her recent appearance in Edinburgh when I might have called in to enquire after that long neglected manuscript of Flora Macdonald. My only regret is that she did not postpone for a few days her return to London as I had an engagement to meet her at dinner the following week. She was certainly a charming woman and a perfect lady in manners and appearance. The tableau would have been worth an instantaneous photograph as would have been another scene between the "Crofter's Friend" and my younger brother in Australia, (who knew her well in the old days), now, [1888] editor of the largest circulation weekly in Sydney.

'She was certainly a charming woman and a perfect lady in manners and appearance. Men and women who came under her influence were simply magnetised; the attraction seemed to be irresistible. Many a quiet laugh I have when I read her letters, over the days when my fellow clerks used to chaff me unmercifully over my acquaintance with the "dashing Bruce", and wonder to myself why I should have been called upon to act as escort to so talented a lady. I have given these puzzles up long ago as one of these puzzles that no plain looking fellow can ever solve. I enjoyed the fun while it lasted and as she never borrowed money from me the amusement has cost me nothing but my time which was of little value in those days. A lady friend who spent several days with her assures me that our heroine slept of nights, "like a top". I know she always appeared to breakfast in the mornings as fresh as a lark. Her room was described as a curious conglomeration of soda water bottles, clothing, powder puffs and writing materials – all mixed up in inexorable confusion. She would occasionally favour my friend with a *"pas seul"* [solo dance] on her return from riding – madly executed in her riding trousers, minus the skirt. The dance I am assured was thoroughly original.'

In all probability, Annie tracked Stronach down initially hoping to use the theatre critic as an introduction to Knight Aston, with the ruse of her non-existent play as bait. Possibly she had heard about the dynamic operatic tenor from one of her lady friends or had seen him somewhere before. To attend the opera a young lady needed a companion, and who better than a theatre critic? Finding him intelligent and companionable, she encouraged the relationship and maybe the brief friendship became real as well as convenient. When things in Edinburgh became too hot, his country retreat provided a very useful bolthole to escape her creditors and she took the opportunity for a few weeks' holiday in Dumfriesshire with a pleasant and witty escort. Even with the passage of years, it does not seem to have occurred to our worldly wise critic that he was being used from the start, but as he indicates he probably wouldn't have minded anyway. Annie's own memory of their time together, however, was rather different, as we shall see.

When Annie moved into St James Terrace she had little or no furniture, so she made the acquaintance of one Joseph Brown, a dyer and well-known money lender of 332 Camden Road, Camden Town. She represented herself as an authoress and a lady of the literary profession (she told the local baker she was a correspondent for the *Weekly Despatch*). Brown was not a man to be trifled with, having appeared often in the civil courts pursuing various defaulters with some enthusiasm. He would lend money – often very large sums – on what were known as 'bills of sale'. The borrower would 'sell' a few of their possessions, often furniture, to Brown for an agreed sum, but retain possession and use of the items until the sum had been repaid plus interest. It was a criminal offence for the borrower to sell or dispose of the goods until the loan was repaid. Interest rates often amounted to 200–450 per cent.

Annie obtained an initial £200 from Joseph Brown in March 1876, eventually managing to increase this to the then vast sum of £1,900. With this she furnished the house and set herself up in some comfort, but no amount of money could ever be enough for her and despite Hatton's wishful thinking and doubts about his doubts, 'Miss Westerne' carried on in her inimitable way – 'Buying everything everywhere; spoiling the Egyptians of the West End of pictures jewellery, silks, satins, cabinets and goods of the costliest kind – as fast as they were delivered to the front door they disappeared out the back.'

Annie's extravagance and escalating debts were to cause her greater problems than usual the following year.

Chapter 9

A Scottish Retreat
(1876)

As Annie settled into life at St James Terrace she began once more to assemble a team around her, which she financed through a combination of fraud and money from Sir Richard Duckworth King. One of her new companions was a Mrs Kate Miller, who Annie claimed had been recommended by Charles Wyndham, a well-known actor who specialized in comedies and popular melodramas. In 1875 he became manager of the Criterion Theatre in London's West End and produced a long series of plays in which he took the leading part, the first of these being *The Great Divorce Case*, which opened on 15 April 1876. It is very likely he would have known Knight Aston, and probably got to know Annie through him. Mrs Miller was introduced as the widow of an army officer who had once been in good circumstances.

Another of the posts to be filled at the beginning of 1876 was that of secretary, for which Annie engaged an Irishman called Thomas Henry Leigh Toler. Toler was about 50 years old and, according to some accounts, a one-time draper's assistant from Dublin. Information on his early years are sparse, but under the name Thomas Henry le Toler he was declared bankrupt in 1851, when he was a shopkeeper in Wicklow, after which he became an agent for The Prudential Mutual Assurance Investment and Loan Association of Dame Street, Dublin. He continued in this capacity for at least another couple of years, as well as acting as secretary of The Dublin Association for the Protection of Trade, which operated from the same address. The insurance company eventually became the Prudential we know today, but the Dublin Association broke up shortly after Toler resigned in 1854, amidst much acrimony. There is no record of Toler being convicted of any offence while in Dublin, but he was again made bankrupt in 1867, when he was described as being 'not in any business'.

From around March 1874, Toler was employed by William Henry Woods, an accountant of 111 Cheapside, London, as his corresponding clerk. He left on 18 February 1876 to take up the position as Annie's secretary, but how and where they first met is not known. It is just conceivable that

Annie's account of his engagement, after replying to her advertisement for a secretary, was genuine. He was never arrested or charged with any offence in conjunction with her, and all his later legal troubles seem to have begun once their relationship ended. In whatever way it came about, Toler was taken on and moved into St James Terrace as Annie's secretary and correspondent in charge of her business affairs. Annie introduced him to Sir Richard King that same year, and over the next nine months Toler claimed that he paid out between £5,000 and £8,000 of King's money on her behalf, and he had receipts to prove it. He also grumbled that he had not received his salary and was due the sum of £90.

True to form, Annie did not keep up the payments on her loan from Joseph Brown, and when he called around to St James Terrace in August, to see about his money, she wasn't there, and nor was his money – in the shape of the furniture which had secured the loan. Asking around, and after 'some communications', Brown was told Miss Bruce had gone to Inverness and was in the process of raising a mortgage upon her estates in Scotland, but that there was some delay with the Scottish lawyers. Brown was furious; he fired up Mr Maynard, his solicitor, and the pair set off northwards in pursuit of his assets.

In the summer of 1876, Miss Annie Ogilvie Bruce rented a country retreat in the beautiful countryside around Inverness. According to some reports this was Moniack Castle, a large sixteenth-century tower house, but in fact it was the more modest although still very imposing Easter Moniack House near Beauly. With the property came its shooting rights for 'the season', and Annie agreed to take it from 22 August 1876 until May 1877 for a total of £300. She moved there with her team and a great deal of Mr Brown's furniture. The likelihood is that she intended to host shooting parties as a way of raising funds and meeting some influential people.

Upon arriving in Inverness, Brown and Maynard got straight to work. Being told that Miss Bruce was indeed in town, they decided to walk through the shopping area to see if they could find her. They soon came across Henry Toler, accompanied by the object of her admiration from the Scottish theatre, Mr Knight Aston. Brown reported:

'I collared Mr Toler. He trembled and offered to shake my hand. I expressed my opinion of him, which was not favourable and was very strongly put. Toler offered to find Miss Bruce for me if I would let him go and I told him that if he would not take me to where she was I would give him a "good hiding". We went up the street together. I kept hold of him by the arm and walked up to the High Street where I saw

Mrs Miller, [Miss Bruce's lady companion], on the High Street. She saw me and ran into a shop, I ran after her and there I saw Miss Bruce. I said, "Come out here, you swindler; I want you!" She ran out of the shop saying, "For God's sake don't expose me." I told her she had stolen my goods and that I had come down to put her in custody. She said, "No, we are alright." I told her that she had pawned some and stolen others. Toler then came and begged that we would go into The Peacock; the four of us went into a room and had a rather stormy meeting, – so much so that the people came up two or three times on account of the noise.'

Things calmed down enough for the party to move on to Moniack, and remarkably Brown and his solicitor stayed the night. The next morning, Brown and Toler went for a walk to talk things through and, working on the principle the best way to cover up a lie is to tell an even bigger one, Toler explained that Miss Bruce was mortgaging some of her vast estates in the north and mentioned the names of a few of the lawyers in Inverness who were involved in the transaction. The problem, explained Toler, was that they were unable to find any document to confirm Miss Bruce's birth date, and also needed a declaration that she was unmarried to progress things. Miss Bruce was not short of funds in general; far from it, she had received money from a gentleman who had given her £5,000 in the last few months, but things were just a little tight at the moment. There were a few more angry meetings, but ultimately agreement was reached that Miss Bruce would return to London, taking the furniture with her. Annie's later comment on the situation is telling. She admitted that Mr Brown did come to see her on business and that they had been in dispute, but she added: 'Why, they say Brown advanced me £1,900 under the belief that I was a gifted authoress! Well now, you go and try to get Brown to advance money on that authority – that's all!'

She makes a good point. Brown was a hard businessman and it is unlikely that her furniture was worth £1,900. Whatever the truth of the matter, furniture was only one of Annie's problems. She seems to have put her time in Scotland to good use. Sparkling wines were ordered from one firm, groceries and provisions from another, and roasts from tradesmen in Inverness and Beauly, while the leading millenary and drapery establishments in the area were called upon to furnish the best arraignments to adorn the lady. She won the admiration of a clergyman of the Free Church at Inverness, who had spent time in Canada, and it was whispered abroad that he had made her acquaintance in that Dominion and knew her to be immensely wealthy. All were ready to supply her every want. She was a frequent visitor to Inverness, to which she drove in a neat little pony and phaeton, making calls on her friends and ordering fresh supplies for her establishment. At Moniack, Miss Bruce lived a fashionable and apparently enjoyable life. She prided herself on her Highland ancestors and showing her admiration of the manners and customs of those among whom she had taken up her abode. On special occasions she donned the kilt and philabeg with Glengarry bonnet and crest. The Northern Meeting, the great fashionable gathering of the year in the North, was close at hand, and it was confidently expected Miss Annie Ogilvie Bruce would figure there as one of the leaders of society. So confident was she of securing entry to this select assembly that she ordered a most gorgeous outfit for the occasion. But it seems that the stewards were a canny lot, as it was said that 'she might as well have endeavoured to attend the Queen's drawing-room', and her attempt failed. The story goes that the dress stayed in the bag in which it was sent to her, unused and unpaid for.

Annie was not to be outdone. A grand dog show was to be held under the patronage of the nobility of the North, and on the opening day she entered the lists with a beautiful Maltese dog named Babee and carried off the third prize. She drove home in triumph, but ugly rumours began to circulate. It was said she had not paid the entry money for her exhibit and that the secretary had had to deduct the amount from the prize money. Meanwhile, shopkeepers were beginning to get uneasy, her fascination was beginning to wear off and people were starting to make enquiries. In the end, several summonses were issued, and the messenger-at-arms paid her a visit. Miss Bruce received him cordially and invited him to take refreshment while pointing out the quality of her furnishings, assuring him that matters would soon be set right as she was expecting some wealthy friends from London.

Several Inverness tradesmen in Union Street, High Street and Church Street had lively recollections of her time there. In one case she had obtained the business card of a wine merchant and presented it to a supplier giving an order, which was at once supplied. According to one later report, 'Miss Bruce is still liable for the amount – some £10.' Another case involved a well-known manufacturing firm of Highland tweeds. Miss Bruce introduced herself as the lessee of the shootings at Moniack and readily obtained a Tam o' Shanter bonnet. She was so delighted with her purchase, as it suited her dress and knickerbocker suit, that she went back for another. This was in the autumn of 1876, and although the account only amounted to £1 14/- it remained unpaid. Several drapery and millenary establishments were owed large amounts. In one case, a major firm of provision merchants in Union Street was asked to supply several items, but suspecting something was wrong, the firm insisted on payment of the account and got clear. Several others also insisted upon cleared cheques before the orders were attended to, and in this way kept their books free from the name of Miss Ogilvie Bruce.

Despite all the jollifications, the rent had not been paid, the wolves were at the door and yet another speedy flight seemed in order. One story goes that she dressed herself in a gentleman's outfit to appear as a Cockney tourist and made her way downstairs to escape, but was seen by the cook who recognized her and demanded her wages. Despite the rather absurd insistence that 'she' was Miss Bruce's brother, the cook was not to be easily fobbed off and so received payment before letting her leave. Annie made her way to Beauly and hired a carriage and pair without being recognized before doubling back and catching a train south at Culloden.

Annie's own account of these events, given in a long interview to a journalist from the *Edinburgh Evening Despatch* more than a decade later, is unsurprisingly quite different. She explained she was not at Moniack Castle at all but had rented the smaller Easter Moniack – which was true, as previously noted – but took no furniture from London as the place was fully furnished: adverts in the local papers before and after her tenure offered 'The Mansion House of Easter Moniack' with rooms that are 'large and airy, and comfortably furnished with shooting close at hand, stables, coach house and double kennels'. The house was regularly let by its owners the Frasers, an ancient Scottish family, and available annually from Whitsunday. To add weight to her statement, there is no indication that the main castle was ever available for rent. Her second point was untrue – she did bring furniture from London, and obviously so, in the light of future events. But it begs the question: why *did* she go to all that trouble and expense of shipping furniture from London to Inverness, to a house advertised as already furnished, and one that she was only renting for a few months? She had not given up the place at St James Terrace, so presumably she would have moved the furniture back again had events not taken the turn they did.

It is also interesting to note that Knight Aston was with her when Brown arrived. His list of engagements shows him in Scotland at the time: Glasgow on 20 August and Edinburgh the next day. He has no other recorded dates until mid-October, when he appears at the Criterion Theatre back in London. His presence at the house does not, of course, mean that he and Annie were now co-habiting, and it may well be that he was merely visiting and quite possibly returned to London shortly thereafter. Annie also states in the in-depth interview with the journalist that she left Moniack when she received word Aston was dangerously ill, which would fit in well with his absence from theatre bills throughout September and most of October.

In this interview, Annie also has a tirade against the newspapers and their reporters:

'It just shows how little they know of the real facts. They speak a great deal about "sparkling wines" and general extravagance. As a fact I lived very quietly. What is the meaning of this? "Sparkling wines were ordered from one firm, groceries and provisions from another, while the leading millinery and drapery establishments were called upon to furnish the best raiment to adorn the lady." What do they mean? Is it simply that I purchased food & clothing? What manner of man is it that is childish enough to write to the papers about that? I presume I could not live on the bricks of Easter Moniack, or dress in sheep skins; and the best of the thing is that I never had an article of dress – not so much as a handkerchief from any Inverness tradesman. I took with me all the dress I require, I simply had provisions from Inverness. Oh! the smallness of the thing is perfectly appalling. How in the name of reason do you suppose I would have duped Inverness tradesmen if I had been doing the same thing in 1874, as it is said. Here I am back in '76 and, if the report was to be believed, getting unlimited credit from the same class of people whose old bills were unpaid! More than that; many of the Inverness people with whom I dealt continued to supply me in London, but I didn't get unlimited credit, I got what I wanted, just the usual thing and I had no need to ask for more.

'As for my "flight" from Moniack, there was no flight. What had I to fly for? The paper says I left a train of tradesmen's bills and small debt summonses as a slight memorial. I don't know how to contain myself at that. It is utterly, disgracefully false. We have inserted notice after notice in the papers asking for outstanding accounts and the only Inverness bill which can be heard of is a miserable 24 shillings for Tam O'Shanters. That is absolutely all. This lying is mean, mean. I can't find words to describe it. Debts! Why don't the creditors send their bills then? That is the only way of getting at the bottom of the affair satisfactorily.

'Besides, the Inverness people continued – some of them – to supply me with certain goods. They knew my address and it certainly isn't the usual thing for tradesmen to keep back their bills. Why didn't – why don't – they send them? If there are debts the men to whom they are due must be a queer set. There are no debts and the only item of this Moniack charge which has any truth in it is the overlooked account for Scotch bonnets. It is shameful! And to a woman too! It is sufficient to drive one mad – or cynical for life. To think that there are so many cowards in the world!

'I left rather earlier than I had intended – for the simple reason that I received word that my future husband Mr Whyte was dangerously ill. But I did not leave hurriedly, or even at a few hours' notice – it was a matter of days. I took with me a few boxes containing necessary dresses and other clothing and Mrs Millar and Toler remained behind to pack up all the rest of my belongings and to hand over the house to Mrs Fraser's representative. I did hear something after about a squabble between Toler and Mrs Fraser's solicitor. What may be at the bottom of it I can't say. Perhaps Toler perpetrated some fraud – he may have done for all I know. Otherwise I can't account in any way for the outcry concerning Inverness.'

As to the allegation that she escaped in a man's clothing, Mrs Baillie 'burst into a hearty laugh' and replied: 'Now just take a fair look at me. Do you think it possible that I could pass as man. Oh fancy me dressed like that. The man that wrote the paragraph must be a perfect genius. Fetch him to London and we'll try and start him with a society paper.'

She also had a few words to say about the alleged 'dog exhibition' incident: 'Oh, I am said to have exhibited a Maltese dog at an Inverness show! I never had a Maltese dog to exhibit – it is sheer invention. But I wish I had one now. If I had I'd call him Snyder.'

When the interviewer asked why, she continued:

'Oh! It's just a joke. You see I am so many people according to these reports that I can scarce recognise myself. It reminds me of Rip Van Winkle. You remember how Rip went around all his friends after the twenty years sleep and could not find anyone who knew him. "If my dog Snyder was here he would know me." Well poor me! I have not even a Snyder.' [This was a somewhat strange assertion, as Rip's dog was called Wolf.]

The *Edinburgh Evening Despatch* had given Annie a fair chance to reply to her critics and had published her account in some detail, but Percy Frost, her 'husband' at this later date, sent a most indignant letter following its publication, complaining that it had been abridged in such a way as to make it 'disgracefully unfair'. The editor had the final word:

'We have afforded the person calling herself Mrs Gordon Baillie every latitude to meet that charges brought against her and now that she has told her story – or as much of it as she chooses to speak and we to print – we have no hesitation in saying it is a tissue of misrepresentations, concealments, and evasions and that it amply confirms our former declarations that the woman is a designing and unscrupulous adventuress.'

Not everyone was so set against her. One of her neighbours during this period had much to say in her favour. She knew her as Miss Bruce and described her as an angel of charity to the poor, sick and unfortunate, to whom no one ever applied for assistance in vain when she had some money. When she didn't have funds she would give away anything pawnable that came to hand. She had also had two good offers of marriage from men of means who would have set her up for life, but gave her heart to an opera singer.

Meanwhile, things seemed to be going to plan with the furniture and move back to London. It was loaded up and ready to be transported back to the capital, but, furious at being given the slip and loss of her rent, Mrs Fraser, the proprietress of Moniack, seized the goods while they were in transit, in lieu of the £300 rent still owing. In the ordinary course of events the furniture and effects would have been taken to auction, advertised for sale and sold, with the money used to cover her loss, but now it was Joseph Brown's turn to act. He managed to stop the auction by claiming that the goods were, in fact, his, and then took the matter to court.

The case of Joseph Brown of 5 Brecknock Road, Camden Town, versus Mrs Jane Ann Fraser of Rebeg Cottage, Kirkhill, was heard before Sheriff Blair at Inverness Sheriff Court in June 1877. In his evidence, Brown claimed Miss Bruce had been introduced to him as an authoress and he had advanced her £1,900 worth of credit, with which she purchased the furniture and other items. She had claimed to be the daughter of the Earl of Moray and owner of the estate of Boleskine* in Scotland, upon which she was raising money, but the transaction was being held up by lawyers; once that had been sorted out, she would be able to repay what was owed. Mrs Fraser, in turn, alleged that Brown and Annie had 'colluded' against her and come to some arrangement between themselves regarding the goods and their return to London. They almost certainly had, although not necessarily in the way Mrs Fraser thought. The court found against Fraser and Brown won his case, as it was decided that he had first claim on the goods.

With judgement in Brown's favour, it was ordered that, with the exception of about thirty named items – which included silver-backed brushes, an oyster

---

* Boleskine is an estate and manor house on the south east side of Loch Ness, famous for being the home of Aleister Crowley and then Jimmy Page of Led Zeppelin. Legend has it that it was built on the site of an ancient church which burnt down, killing all its inhabitants. After Crowley, one of its owners committed suicide in there and it passed through various hands until being seriously damaged by fire in 2015. It remains a ruin, and according to its owners is unlikely to be rebuilt. Sadly, it seems that Annie had no real connection to it at all.

knife, a map of Scotland, an egg whisk, an inkstand and a few chamber pots, presumably all belonging to Moniack House but swept up in the general clear out – everything was to be returned to Brown by 20 December or £300 was to be paid to him in default. Yet this was not to be the end of the matter. Fraser launched an appeal and the case rumbled on through several hearings until it was heard in front of Sheriff Ivory (who appears later in the story) at Inverness on 4 December 1877. The appeal was then dismissed and the goods had now to be returned by 16 March 1878, with Brown's expenses totalling £102 7/- to be paid by Fraser. The unfortunate owner of Moniack had finally lost.

In another twist, it emerged Annie had entered into an agreement with a Mr Wain on 7 January 1876 over certain items in the London house, and when she defaulted on the payments, these were made the subject of a court order by the Sheriff of Middlesex. On 1 April 1876, bankruptcy proceedings were begun against 'Annie Ogilvie Bruce, spinster and authoress' of 11 St James Terrace, Regents Park. Brown stepped in and paid off the outstanding amount so that all the items could remain in the house and the bankruptcy proceedings were stopped. Presumably Brown's payment formed part of the £1,900 loan he had advanced, and he was expecting a decent rate of return on his outlay. The fate of Mr Brown's large loan is not known, but it can be assumed it was satisfied in some way as he was not a man to let a sum like that go. In all probability it was Sir Richard King who was the loser in the end.

One further story from that summer of 1876 has it that Annie had also agreed to rent a house about 14 miles away from Moniack, in the village of Fortrose, as it had long been her practice to have, where possible, more than one address. This was to be let through an established firm of solicitors in Inverness. As she was driving there in her carriage, she saw two fine horses at the side of the road, in the minister's glebe, and asked his reverence to sell one of them. After some haggling a deal was struck, but fortunately the animal was never delivered. On another visit to the place, she was accompanied by the sister of an Inverness Free Church minister, whom she introduced as a friend. She was very communicative and familiar, talking about her estates in different parts of the country and making many enquiries about the local clergy. The owner of the house had her suspicions about the new tenant, so she and her husband went to see the agent, who assured them that everything was fine and that Miss Bruce was perfectly good. Agreement was reached to rent the house for £30 per month, but Annie never took up residence, probably due to her unexpected return to London. Legal proceedings were taken out against her, resulting in the owner paying out £40 in fees but getting nothing in return.

Chapter 10

The Road to Matrimony
(1876)

The past few months had been pretty hectic for the inhabitants of St James Terrace. Joseph Brown's intervention had spoiled the party in Inverness but the little team seemed to be intact, cooking up whatever schemes and scams took their fancy and milking Sir Richard for whatever they could get. However, there was now a fourth member of the party, and part of the job of the other three must have been to keep him as unaware of their day-to-day activities as possible. Annie was in love.

Thomas White was born in 1844 in Aston, Birmingham, the son of William Allen White, a railway guard, and Ann Aston. According to the census of 1851, the family was living at 35 St James Place, Aston, and Thomas, aged 7, had a brother and three sisters living with him. By the next census, in 1861, he and his family had moved to 77 Ashted Row, Birmingham. The 17-year-old's occupation was given as 'apprentice'. Presumably he was receiving musical training at this time, as when asked in 1890 how his musical career began, he replied:

> 'I come from an old musical family, my grandfather was one of the founders of the Birmingham Festival Choral Society and was for many years its conductor. When I was 10 years old I sang before the Queen, it was at the opening of the Aston Hall and Park to the public. I had to sing solo in a kind of hymn "Now pray we for our country" as the Queen came into the chapel with the Prince Consort and the Duke of Cambridge, [and] she put her hand up to stop the others from coming in and when I had finished she asked if the little boy would repeat the solo and I did so.'

The relatives he talked about were almost certainly on his mother's side. In the census of 1871, his parents are still in the same house, while next door was a Mary Aston, aged 38, a single woman and a 'teacher of music'. Ten years previously, another 'Mary Aston' is listed in the same parish as a 44-year old Professor of Music and daughter of John Aston, 78, retired, who was, in all probability, the 'conducting grandfather'. However young Thomas White's taste for comic opera came about, on 21 February 1870 he appeared under his first stage name of Aston Whyte at the Victoria Music Hall, Newcastle, as one of four artistes singing 'operatic selections and glees', along with Signor Sanguinetti and his wonderful troupe of performing birds, as well as the celebrated performing dog Toby, from Bailey's Prize Punch and Judy Show, late of the Crystal Palace, Sydenham. Thomas would by now have been 26, and had presumably been performing for some time. A review of the company's month-long tenure in Newcastle described his performance as 'well, and carefully rendered'.

By April of that year (1870) he had joined a professional touring company run by Alfred G. Vance, a clever Cockney actor, singer, songwriter, mimic, comedian, dancer, author, composer, buffo vocalist, manager and blatant self-publicist who, not without justification, styled himself 'The Great Vance'. Vance and his troupe toured the country almost continuously, and in April 1870 Vance's Concert and Operetta Party were appearing at the Drill Hall in Bristol. Top of the bill was a young lady called Miss Mabel Brent, soprano, while near the bottom of the short list was Mr Aston Whyte, the new tenor. His time with Vance's group ended when they had finished at Bristol, and at the start of May a short item in the press announced he had relinquished his place in the troupe due to illness but was now well recovered and available for work. As he didn't rejoin Vance, there would seem to be more to it than a couple of weeks off sick; possibly a blossoming relationship with the young soprano had something to do with it.

Whatever his reasons for leaving, he had not been wasting his time while with the troupe and soon after became engaged to Miss Mabel Elizabeth Brent. The soprano had an interesting pedigree as the daughter of Eliza Travers, a well-known actress and singer at Sadler's Wells. She made one of her first public performances at the age of 14, taking part in an evening concert on behalf of Barnsbury Literary Institute at Myddleton Hall, Islington, in December 1862. Accompanied by her father, J.F. Brent, a government inspector and amateur pianist, she was, by all accounts, well received. Mabel continued to sing in the odd concert at Myddleton Hall and the North London area, not far from the family home. She often sang alongside her mother, and on occasions was accompanied by her father. She soon ventured further afield, taking on engagements around the country, and in March 1870 joined 'The Great Vance', who began that year's annual tour at St James's Hall in Regent Street, London. When she and Aston had appeared on the bill for the Drill Hall in Bristol, it was the first time that they had worked together.

Mabel continued with Vance until around April 1871 and then dropped from sight until August that year, when she was engaged by Henry Leslie, who had just formed a touring group to perform Offenbach's opera *The Princess of Trebizonde*. Her first performance was in Brighton that month, when she appeared on the bill as playing the part of Zanetta.

Aston, as we have seen, had left Vance's troupe more than a year before, in May 1870, and had advertised for work in the trade press during that month. His speciality was a form of comic opera then becoming fashionable – these were French productions translated into English known as 'Opera-Bouffe' and closely associated with Jacques Offenbach and later by Gilbert and Sullivan. Whether he found any employment during the following period is not known, so his appearance in Bristol, while with Vance, is his last recorded appearance under the name Aston Whyte: 18 months later, in November 1871, he had adopted the name Knight Aston. He is included, under his new stage name, as part of a concert party at the Albion Hall, London Wall, on behalf of The City Musical and Elocutionary Society, which took place on 1 December. It is probable he and Mabel got married during this 'resting' period and possibly took an extended honeymoon, but no doubt he would still have needed to earn a living. After that performance in December 1871, there is another year-long break in press reports and Aston does not appear again until singing tenor at the first production of *L'Oeil Creve* at the newly refurbished Opera Comique at The Strand in London, which commenced on 21 October 1872. He now seemed to have secured regular employment, this engagement with the troupe continuing until May 1873, when he joined the London Opera Bouffe Company and began a UK tour which opened on 2 June. By July he was in Plymouth, appearing in Offenbach's *Bridge of Sighs*, with his part 'receiving the loudest applause'.

Mabel stayed on with Henry Leslie's touring company, in the part of Zanetta, until around July 1873, which is possibly when she gave birth to a daughter whom they named Eleanor M. Aston. Aston used his stage name liberally in daily life, as well as professionally, and for whatever reason gave his daughter his stage surname. Nothing else has been discovered about Eleanor, including her birth, nor any record of her parents' marriage; the only proof of her existence is a listing in the 1881 census, when she was 8 years old. At Christmas 1873, Mabel was working at the Standard Theatre and performed in the pantomime *Dick Whittington and his Cat*, in which to some acclaim she played Alice, Dick's love interest, 'to advantage'. It was to be her last role.

A notice in *The Era* for early February announced Miss Mabel Brent was 'now prostrate with typhoid fever and that under the most favourable circumstances it must be some weeks before she will be able to resume her professional duties'. In the end it was not to be, as Mabel died of typhoid, complicated by bronchitis, on 26 February 1874 and was buried in the family grave at Highgate cemetery on 9 March. She was 25 and had been married for only two years.

Aston Knight, her bereaved husband, seemed able to carry on with 'business as usual', as he was included in the cast for Miss Selina Dolaro's *Madam Angot Company* and appeared at the Theatre Royal Nottingham for twelve nights from 13 April, less than two months after his wife's untimely death. This engagement was followed by a tour of provincial theatres in Manchester, Bradford, Liverpool, the Isle of Man, Glasgow, Edinburgh and Brighton, along with frequent returns to London. He continued to traverse the country for the remainder of the year and on through 1875, until meeting Annie under circumstances already described. He had now undoubtedly become one of the best at what he did, as he was accorded excellent reviews whenever he appeared.

How soon after Annie's initial infatuation in June 1875 her courtship with Knight Aston began is not known, but they were together, in whatever arrangement, by August 1876, when his presence was noted at Moniack. On 1 November 1876, Annie married Knight, under his real name of Thomas White, by licence at the Registrar's Office in Marylebone. He described himself as a widower, aged 33, and as a 'musical artist', the son of William Allen White, a man of 'Independent' means. Although in truth his father was a railway guard, he did appear on the electoral roll and owned the house he occupied. As we have seen, it was his mother's side which had the musical talent, and also presumably the money. The renowned opera vocalist was possibly embarrassed by his father's lowly occupation, so 'improved' upon it. It was certainly his mother's maiden name he chose for his career. In all probability Annie had just realized that she was pregnant, and as Aston was booked for a long tour, a quick marriage before his departure was the logical thing to do. It would legitimize the baby, and marriage by licence – rather than waiting for the banns to be read – was quicker and a lot more discrete as there was no chance for anyone to object.

On the marriage certificate both Annie and her father's occupations were left blank, along with her father's name. How she explained this to Aston is an interesting question, although in press reports years later, she was alleged to have claimed her family had threatened to disinherit her if she married a 'common singer', so that was probably her way round it. Marriage gave her another new identity, with all links to her recent past severed, or so she hoped. They gave their address as 11 St James Terrace, Regents Park, and the witnesses were Ruth W. Millar and Lucy Murray. White's daughter Eleanor would have been about 3 at the time.

It is pretty certain Aston knew nothing about Annie's past when they met, and it was unlikely she would have been found out, as there was no obvious connection between the 28-year-old ex-prisoner and con-artist Mary Anne Bruce Sutherland from Peterhead, and beautiful, vivacious and well-off 24-year-old Annie Ogilvie Bruce, who lived in a magnificent house in St James Terrace with her servants and attendants.

Aston was away a lot of the time, wrapped up in his career and his own importance, but how she hid the constant petty frauds and deceptions from him is as big a mystery as why she continued to commit them. It was perhaps all part of the 'thrill'. Her bills, accommodation and staff were paid for by Sir Richard, and she was about to marry a very successful opera singer with a good income. Why try to hide from the bakers' bills? When she met Aston she was already in debt to various local tradesmen, and claimed to them that her debts were to be settled by a 'foreign prince or baronet'. It is also possible that Aston didn't know about King's money: Annie might well have explained that her apparent affluence was due to inherited wealth or just 'money from family'. Although love is blind, Aston was perhaps not the keenest blade in the knife box. With Miller and Toler to cover for their employer, Annie seems to have pulled off the deception remarkably well. There is no evidence to show that Aston was aware of her criminal activities or that he was a party to any of them. At the time of their marriage, Aston was appearing at the Strand Theatre in London with the Carl Rosa Company. He must have begun a trip across the Atlantic almost immediately after his marriage, sailing from Liverpool by steam ship on a journey that would have taken eight to ten days.

Aston made his first appearance in America with Emily Soldene's forty-strong troupe the English Comic Opera Company on 18 November 1876 at the Globe in Boston, Annie's new husband playing the defendant in *Trial by Jury*. This was the second comic opera written by Gilbert and Sullivan, and the performance was a huge success. An appearance in Lecoeq's opera bouffe *La Fille de Madame Angot* shortly after provoked the following rather mixed review: 'Mr Knight Aston proved to be a very good looking, well dressed and agreeable actor who has a good voice but a bad method and sang as well as he could with a slight hoarseness which very likely is the result of the weather.'

The troupe's performances were extremely well received but the trip itself proved to be a catalogue of near disasters. They were booked to appear at the Brooklyn Theatre on 5 December 1876, but as Soldene couldn't stand the place they took an engagement in Rhode Island instead. That night the Brooklyn Theatre burned to the ground with the deaths of around 300 people, many unidentified, in one of the worst fires in American history. Not long after, on 29 December, the troupe was on a train crossing the Ashtabula Bridge. They reached the other side, but the train following only got as far as the middle when the struts gave way and the train plunged into the river, with ninety-two of the 159 passengers killed.

Knight Aston's employer, Emily Soldene, was the founder, leader and principle artiste of the group. She was born in Clerkenwell, London, in 1838 and started her career as a classical singer. Soldene made her first stage appearance in 1862 at around the time that the works of Offenbach were becoming fashionable in London, and it was with this 'opera bouffe' – comic opera with elements of satire and farce – that she found her true vocation, appearing in this role for the first time in 1869 at the Standard Theatre in London. Her singing voice and organizational skills made her an instant success. She realized early on that physical attractiveness was a major element of pulling in the paying public, so selected the most attractive girls and handsome men that she could find to fulfil her roles. Aston and Soldene had known each other for some time, as they were regulars on the London and provincial theatre circuit – he worked with her at the Opera Comique in London's Strand Theatre in February 1876 and was part of her troupe in Edinburgh the following August.

Why Annie didn't leave with her newly acquired husband when the troupe sailed for the American tour is not known – possibly the trip was organized by Soldene well in advance and there was no room for hangers-on – but either by accident or design she was to follow very shortly after. First, however, she had some important shopping to do. Taking her carriage and pair, and accompanied by Mrs Kate Miller, she went to see Mr and Mrs Graham, ladies' outfitters, in Brompton Road and spent £300 on a trousseau. Following this, she called at Westbourne Grove and placed an order for almost £50 worth of baby clothes. The goods were delivered to St John's Wood and remained unpacked, ready to be loaded aboard the ship to New York. None of the goods had been paid for, and as Annie slipped out of the back door and out of the country with the loot, Mrs Miller was answering the front door to the police.

Chapter 11

America!
(1877)

L eaving for America when Annie did proved a very timely move. In January 1877 the Westminster Police Court issued a warrant for her arrest, along with her companion Kate Miller, for fraud, alleging they had swindled goods, in the form of the clothes kindly provided by Mrs Graham. On 24 January, as the police called at St James Terrace, Annie was sailing off to America aboard the SS *Decolia* from Liverpool. It seems odd that Kate didn't go with her – perhaps she had to attend to affairs in London.

In America, the Soldene tour was going well and Aston was receiving great reviews. By the time Annie caught up with him, near the end of February, the group were in St Louis, about 1,000 miles from her arrival port of New York.

Emily Soldene takes up the story:

> 'We played 2 weeks in St Louis where we were joined by Mrs Knight Aston, just out from England, a tall handsome, distinguished looking woman. She brought her husband the most wonderful looking presents; a gold mounted dressing case, a diamond ring, diamond studs, etc etc. I am sorry to say that this magnificent lady turned out to be the notorious Mrs Gordon Baillie, who escaping from London, (with much spoil) left her faithful servant to suffer three years "hard" in her stead. The presents were part of the loot.'

All true enough apart from the sentence of her 'faithful servant', whose fate was somewhat different, as we shall see.

Despite the troupe's professional successes, the series of barely believable disasters still followed in their wake. On 28 April 1877, the night after they checked out of the Grand Southern Hotel, the building burnt down with the loss of around a dozen lives. When they arrived in Galveston, Texas, Aston was convinced that his luck had run out: he woke to find their hotel full of smoke and rushed about raising the alarm, only to find the smoke was coming from a burning timber truck outside and pouring in through an open window!

It is unlikely that Annie accompanied her husband on the lengthy trips, and as her pregnancy advanced she would probably have preferred the comfort of New York and possibly the opportunity to visit some of those wonderful new department stores. Aston, of course, had to keep to the gruelling schedule, and was conveniently out of the way. On Monday 30 April 1877, the troupe opened for a week in Philadelphia. The initial reception was mixed, with Aston being described gnomically as having 'made a declaration of dramatic independence that eschewed all precedent', but before long their reviews, and his in particular, were excellent and he was being billed as one of Soldene's 'principle members', excelling in his role as Bluebeard. The troupe's last performance on this American tour was at Baldwin's Theatre, San Francisco, on 15 July 1877 and this time reviews overall were poor, except for Aston, who was again 'excellent'. The troupe had been booked to appear for six weeks at the Union Square, New York, from 6 August, but decided instead to leave the country. What went wrong is unclear, but it seemed all was not well between Aston and Emily Soldene. One newspaper report stated: 'Knight Aston the tenor to whom CA Chizzola and Emily Soldene are indebted in $3,000 of borrowed money, got out attachments against their luggage going to Australia.'

From San Francisco, Soldene and her company sailed on the SS *Zealandia* to Auckland for a tour of New Zealand and Australia. Aston did not go with them. Perhaps he never intended to, or maybe he changed his mind when they argued over money. Whatever the reason, it must have been around this time that his daughter Gabrielle, who became known as 'Snowie', was born in New York. Her exact date of birth is unknown as the city did not record births before 1880.

It was not long after this that Aston and Annie, along with their new baby daughter, decided to strike out on their own. A report in the *New York Herald* of September 1877 described Aston as the '*late* first tenor of the Soldene Troupe' and stated that Mrs Aston's 'Our Drawing Room' party would start a tour of the Eastern States and Canada the next week, performing an original musical comedy called *Cupid's Conquest*, especially written for them by Julian Magnus. The company was reported to include Miss Blanche Gordon and Mr Tom Whiffen, along with 'The well-known tenor' Mr Knight Aston. Apparently, 'Mrs Aston's speciality is a brief lecture, with illustrations, on prominent social topics'! If this strange hybrid venture ever got off the ground it must have been very short-lived and certainly did not trouble the critics, although there was perhaps another reason for this endeavour not being pursued – Annie was now pregnant with their second child. The pair remained in New York and Aston gave a Thanksgiving charity performance at St Celia's Church for the benefit of the church that November.

In a bizarre newspaper article, published in March 1878, Aston is alleged to have been offered engagements by Max Strakosch, the Bohemia-born impresario, but declined, saying that he had a highly sensitive stomach and would not be able to sing duets with American soprano Clara Louise Kellogg due to her strong onion breath, which 'would have the same effect on him as sea-sickness would have on a able bodied man'. The article continued that he, Aston, took the steamer back to Europe before she could vent her wrath. Ms Kellogg was not the only one with something to vent, it seemed, as an article in the English newspaper *The Illustrated Sporting & Dramatic News* for May 1878, presumably published soon after the couple left the US, contained the statement: 'Numerous creditors are anxiously inquiring the whereabouts of Knight Aston's wife.'

While Annie and Aston were singing and shopping their way around the US, the former's companion, Kate Miller, a 'fashionably dressed' woman described as a housekeeper and widow, aged 40 and of good education, appeared at Westminster Police Court on Tuesday 30 January 1877. She was charged with conspiring to obtain, and obtaining, goods by false pretences. Also charged, but unfortunately absent, was a Miss or Mrs Bruce, both being residents of St James Terrace, St John's Wood. The main charge was that they had defrauded Mrs Ann Graham, a draper, of 102 Brompton Road. It was alleged that at the beginning of that month, Miss Bruce and Miss Miller had gone into the shop and ordered a black silk dress, along with several other articles. The pair claimed to be in receipt of significant incomes, Miller receiving £80 per quarter, while Miss Bruce claimed further to be the daughter of an earl with large estates in Scotland. One of them had returned on several occasions and ordered a great many more things, some of which were for Miss Bruce's forthcoming wedding. The goods were to be delivered to the house in St James Terrace and paid for on delivery. Mrs Graham had visited the house and, seeing that it was beautifully furnished and that all seemed to be in order, complied with the request. Fabrics and clothing to the value of about £400 had been ordered, of which around half had been delivered. Despite the agreement, no money had been collected.

Later in the month, the trusting Mrs Graham called at the house again to ask if she might have payment, but was told that nothing could be paid immediately and someone would call in and settle the bill on the following Monday. On the appointed day she received a telegram saying that Mrs Miller would call round on the Tuesday, which she did, but only to say that Miss Bruce was out of town for ten to twelve days but would pay half of the money 'without fail' upon her return. In the meantime, Mrs Graham was beginning to hear rumours which led her to believe 'Miss Bruce' was not all she appeared. She was already married, people said, and the furnishings that had so impressed her when she visited were, in fact, the property of Joseph Brown.

Now highly suspicious, and unconvinced by the debtor's excuses, Mrs Graham called once more and this time Miller told her that Miss Bruce was abroad, as she was unable to stay in the house because 'there were so many people after her', which doesn't really sound like the words of a co-conspirator. Graham collected what articles she could find in the property, but left a petticoat and a paletot or fitted jacket which Miller had been wearing. The witness stated in court that she believed Miller had done all she could to help find Miss Bruce and recover some of the items, and that when she called on the last occasion she had found 'scores of tradesmen deploring their losses'.

Another charge that Annie and Kate faced involved an order of baby linen to the value of £47/10/- from Cox, Sons and Stafford, silk mercers, of 63 Westbourne Grove. The order had been delivered but not paid for, so John Stafford and his partner went around to the house to demand payment. Arriving at lunchtime, they were still there at nine in the evening when they heard a carriage draw up and saw that Miss Bruce was in it. Instead of Bruce coming into the house, Mrs Miller entered the carriage and the pair drove off. The next witness in the case was Miss Florence Palmer, an assistant to the firm, who proved the delivery of the goods. The facts were accepted by the defence, who claimed there was no intention to defraud, merely a promise to pay on delivery that was not complied with. It appeared that Miss Bruce had a cheque for £300 on her when asked for the money, but sadly nothing smaller.

There were also other cases. Mr C. Mortimer Bonner, a stationer of Albany Street, had supplied despatch boxes, jewel case, opera glasses and other items amounting to £39, which remained unpaid. It was alleged on this occasion that Kate Miller had posed as Miss Bruce's aunt, and having spotted an envelope on the table with the crest of Mrs Graham Smith, a lady of position in Piccadilly and Brighton, claimed that they knew her well, though Miller was quite adamant in denying this at an earlier hearing.

Despite the absence of the main defendant, the court proceedings went ahead. Thomas Toler was called as a witness, still declaring himself to be a 'member of the Irish bar'. He was not implicated in any wrongdoing, and despite checks revealing that the Irish courts had no barrister by that name, was allowed to give evidence. Toler explained that he managed the affairs of

Miss Bruce as her secretary and correspondent, and when asked about the arrangements at St James Terrace, he said that Mrs Miller was not paid a wage but received free board and he was of the opinion she was in receipt of 'small donations' and articles of clothing. Toler stated that he also boarded at the house and repeated his claim he was still owed his salary of more than £90 and that during a period of eight or nine months in 1876 he had paid out between five and six thousand pounds on behalf of Miss Bruce, who he firmly believed to be the daughter of the Earl of Moray. He added that he knew Miss Bruce had been contemplating bankruptcy on or about 17 December of the previous year, and his evidence was largely in line with the explanations given to Joseph Brown the previous summer at Moniack Castle.

In the absence of Miss Bruce, those left behind were desperately trying to cover the debts. Reports in the press stated that the creditors 'had been referred to a gentleman, but when he was consulted on the matter he said he had lent Miss Bruce £5,000 in the last 12 months and could lend no more in the same year'. The 'gentleman' is not named, but was almost certainly Sir Richard Duckworth King, whose role in these affairs will be explained later.

Kate Miller gave evidence to say that she had been living with Miss Bruce since July 1877 as her housekeeper and companion, although Toler said it was May. The prosecution was anxious to prove that the story of the forthcoming wedding was untrue, which would have gone towards denting the credibility of the defendants, though it is hard see what practical difference this would have made to the charge. Toler stated that he knew Miss Bruce to have been married to Knight Aston since the previous November. Miller covered the accusation that the marriage had already taken place by saying that Bruce had only married in a registrar's office and was intending to have a proper church ceremony in public so that it would be announced in *The Times*. The 'second wedding' story was probably true. Annie was pregnant with Aston's child and he was about to spend some months touring America. The 'the eve of departure' register office ceremony was to guard against the child being born illegitimately while Aston was away.

Annie stocked up on baby clothes, a wedding trousseau and expensive gifts for Aston, which she took with her when she went to join him. It was not Annie's style to do things by halves, and a full church wedding may well have been in mind for the coming months in America. In mid-February the case was adjourned due to the 'absence of necessary witnesses'. Mr Brown, who had at last received some satisfaction for his well-travelled furniture, was 'ill' and his evidence was needed to prove the goods in the house belonged to him and not to Miss Bruce. This is odd. Brown was no stranger to the courts and would have had to be in a bad way not to have made it into the witness box to seek revenge on those who had wronged him. It is likely there was more to his role in the whole affair than he wanted to reveal in court. As we have seen, before the intervention of Mrs Fraser, Brown and Annie had reached an agreement whereby the goods were to be returned to London. The presumption must be that the furniture was back at St James Terrace and was now being paid for in some way –the last thing Brown would want to do was rock the boat by giving evidence against her. At the same time, the prosecution was short of someone who could give evidence as to Ms Bruce's marital state and could not find Lucy Murray, a witness at Annie's wedding. The second witness was Ruth W. Millar, who may or may not have been the person in the dock, or at least connected to her in some way.

Bail was applied for on the grounds that even though Miss Bruce was extraordinarily extravagant, she did not have access to large sums of money and in any event, Mrs Miller was only her confidant and companion and therefore could not be held to account in the matter. Miller's solicitor seemed to weaken her case somewhat by revealing that his client had 'even effected a compromise with Madam Graham by offering her an IOU for the goods' – which had been accepted – hardly the actions of a mere servant who could 'not be held to account'. Bail was initially opposed by the prosecution, but was eventually set by Mr Lushington, the magistrate, at the impossibly high sum of £300 – two sureties of £150 each – and to nobody's surprise Kate Miller was carted back to prison.

The final Westminster committal hearing was held at the end of February. Mr Woolrych, the magistrate on this occasion, was not convinced that the affair at the stationers constituted false pretences and the charge was dismissed, along with that of the baby clothes from Westbourne Grove and other lesser matters. Enquiries into the whereabouts of Miss Bruce continued without success, and the case was dragging on and running out of steam. Nevertheless, the magistrate was satisfied there was a case to answer regarding the main charge of defrauding Mrs Graham, so Kate Miller was committed for trial at the Central Criminal Court – The Old Bailey. She made her first appearance on 5 March 1877 on the single charge of 'Unlawfully conspiring together with another person to cheat and defraud James Graham of a quantity of silk goods and other articles'. Miss Bruce was still at large and the case was postponed again, with the prisoner returned to custody. Mrs Miller appeared for the final time on 9 April, but as Ms Annie Ogilvie Bruce could still not be found, the court decided it had had enough: in the court record, 'Bills Ignored delivered by Proclamation' appeared next to her and Annie's names and she was released.

Like others associated with Annie's criminal career, Kate Miller seems to have no traceable past or future. The witness's name on the marriage certificate is almost certainly Ruth W. Millar and not Kate Miller. Was she merely a housekeeper employed for a few months, the widow of an army officer fallen on hard times, or was she more deeply involved? The trial never reached a stage where she had to account for herself, and her defence, via her solicitor, never expressed any shock or animosity towards her supposed employer for leading her into crime and then running off and leaving her to face the music. It seems Kate, Ruth or whoever she was remained loyal to the end and made herself scarce as soon as she was released from the courtroom.

While the happy couple – Annie and Aston – were enjoying the delights of comic opera in America, and Miller was enjoying her freedom, Annie's 'private secretary', Lee Toler, was conducting a little 'play' of his own. This involved him going around to all the local tradesmen and asking them to contribute towards his fare to America so he could go and confront her about their unpaid bills, representing himself to them as having been as badly conned as they had. It seems, however, that none of them took up this tempting offer.

Chapter 12

Mrs Ogilvie-Whyte
(1878–83)

Knight Aston had left the Soldene Troupe when they departed for New Zealand in July 1877, after touring with them for around sixteen months. When he eventually left the US, in April the following year, he did not return to London immediately but went to Milan, where he studied under San Giovanni and Francesco Lamperti while engaged as Rigoletto in Verdi's opera of that name at the D'Alverme Theatre. Perhaps understandably, he does not mention Annie in any of his later interviews, so there is no clue as to whether she went with him, but it is likely that she returned to London to face the fallout from the Miller case and to organize their domestic arrangements. They had a young daughter and Annie was, of course, pregnant with their second child, due in November, to be named Ada Mary Whyte. Her second pregnancy may account for them giving up the idea of the touring company and returning to Europe.

The grand house at St James Terrace was now long gone, and rumour of her return to London had got around. She was traced by an irate tradesman to a drawing room apartment in Mornington Crescent, Camden Town, and after banging on her door and demanding the £13 he was owed, he received a promise that she would pay him within a week if he said nothing to the other tradesmen to whom she was in debt. He agreed, but Annie moved on before the time was up. He managed to track her down once more to a place in Richmond and threatened to tell all the shops in the area of her character unless he was paid. Again, she promised the man his money but disappeared without paying; this time he was unable to find her and heard nothing more until he read about her in the papers, many years later.

The ever-present question is how much did her husband, Knight Aston, know or suspect about his wife's activities? Did they have massive rows over it, or was he so wrapped up in his own career he didn't notice? Whatever the truth, he must surely have been made aware of the raid on their house, the arrest of Kate Miller and the linking of his wife's name, and therefore his own, to a fraud approaching £400. The offences occurred in the early part of January, after he had left for the US, but there had been detailed reports in *The Times* and the London papers. He was a well-known figure within the entertainment world, and if the search for 'Miss Bruce' was connected to Mrs Whyte, such a scandal would have caused intense embarrassment. All his friends, and many who had come to hear him sing, would be aware of the 'affair'. The fine new clothes Annie had taken to America to greet her husband, the presents she took for him and the very clothes his new-born baby was wearing were the result of that same swindle. As we have seen, the case petered out in April, but the damage was done. It is possible that unless he was in communication with friends in England, Aston knew nothing about it, or alternatively he spent the few months in Italy to keep out of the way until things died down. Years later, when asked to comment on the press details of the case and other debts run up at that time, Annie gave a very different version to the one told in court, passing the blame on to others, which may have been the same story she fed to Aston, either in America or upon his return:

> 'I had no idea until after I came back from America of the transactions Miller had carried on. She was very extravagant and just went to the shops ordering whatever she wanted without giving a moment's thought as to where the money was to come from. I don't like to say too much against her, for although she used my name freely, as you know, and did me a great deal of harm she behaved well enough to me in many ways. Of course it is dreadfully unfortunate that her name should appear in connection with mine; but I had no debts then – they were hers and I simply ask for accounts. If I owe anything then let the bill be sent in.'

It is difficult to see from this account what transactions Annie is referring to. The goods obtained before she left involved both her and Kate in attendance, and it was only a few days after she left that Miller was arrested and remanded in prison for three months, before fading from the scene. Maybe she was just trying to muddy the waters.

In this later account, Annie also went on to outline what she called the 'doings of Toler'. When she left for America to join her husband, Toler, according to Annie, having realized that he would get no more work from her, formed a 'very pretty little plot'. With the aid of Mrs Miller, Annie claimed, he drew up a long list of tradesman's accounts:

> '[A]s he knew that Sir Richard King was an intimate friend of mine and one who thought much of my welfare he went to Sir Richard and

said, "These are the debts due by Miss Bruce and if we don't get them squared she will be brought back from America". Sir Richard believed the scoundrel and got into a state of anxiety, ultimately he gave Toler £5,000 to try and square up the matter.

'I never heard until I came back from America which was in ten months' time. So as soon as Sir Richard heard that I was back he called upon me, produced the list of supposed debts and utterly prostrated me with astonishment. I told him at once that he had been swindled and he soon saw it himself. We consulted our solicitors who advised us to let the matter alone. They said, and it was quite true, that if we took it up we should only send good money after bad, that the case would necessarily bring up the fact that Kate Miller had been my maid and had conducted her frauds from my house, that though I was quite able to clear myself from all complicity with Miller it would only create a *cause celebre* and do us no good. Then Sir Richard was getting very old and was frightened of bother and I on my part had no desire I can assure you to become a notoriety in connection with such a matter. We finally decided to let the affair drop.'

As for Toler, Annie stated that he often used her name in frauds. For one thing, she said, 'he wrote a letter purporting to be on my behalf to the Scottish distillers with whom I had had dealings asking that certain goods should be forwarded. But the distillers suspected something and communicated with me.'

To be fair to both Toler and Miller, they had been left to carry the can somewhat when Annie left for America, and were possibly unsure whether she was coming back. Miller was, of course, in prison and Toler simply turned the situation to his advantage. He was now 52 years old and unemployed. He kept his address at 3 Plowden Buildings, Temple, and began working with a man named William John Gentle Barrett, who was described as an accountant of 25 Kynaston Road, Stoke Newington, and a former member of the Stock Exchange who had defaulted. As noted previously, Toler had been introduced to Sir Richard King the previous year and was used to dealing with Annie's finances; therefore, her story about Toler obtaining money from King on the pretence of paying her debts makes perfect sense.

Toler put the money to good use. In 1877, he and Barrett formed a company called the British Association for the Facility of Commerce, with himself as manager and Barrett as secretary. The pair took on beautifully furnished offices at 30–31 New Bridge Street, Blackfriars. The stated aim of the company was to collect debts and supply information to the trustees of client companies as to the solvency of those with which they dealt, as well as make enquiries relating to traders, to ensure the payment of rents, guarantee the integrity of clerks and acts of a similar nature. For this, clients would pay an annual subscription. But the whole organization was a sham, used mainly for the cashing of bogus cheques. They realized that it would take more than a posh office and shiny new furniture to impress potential clients and give the impression of a thriving business, so they took on staff who, it emerged later, had nothing to do all day apart from the odd bit of filing – 'three of us to do five minutes' work', as one of them put it later. Toler and Barrett were arrested in March 1879 and charged with conspiring to obtain various sums of money from a number of people by way of deception, mainly passing cheques for amounts they knew could not be met and having no intention of paying the amount owing.

In an interview years later, Annie stated that a letter from Sir Richard King was found in Toler's pocket when he was searched. As a result of enquiries about it she was put on notice to the effect that she might be required to give evidence in court as a witness at Toler's trial at the police court, although in the end was 'heartily glad' she was not required.

After the preliminary hearing at the Mansion House, during which Sir Richard King himself gave evidence, Toler and Barrett were committed for trial at the Old Bailey in April 1879, and on this occasion Sir Richard's appearance was excused. King's doctor said that his patient was now 75 years old, was suffering from an acute attack of bronchitis and was therefore unable to attend without risk to his life. He issued a statement, which was read to the court, stating that he had known Toler for the past three years, having been introduced to him as secretary to Miss Bruce, and that he was owed between £800 and £900 – money advanced to Toler during the past two years. He had been given cheques in return, but none of them had been honoured.

Toler made a long speech in his own defence, went through each charge in detail and denied all knowledge of any frauds committed by Barrett. On 5 May, Toler and Barrett were convicted, and after the former asked the judge if he could appeal on the grounds of misdirection, each received five years' penal servitude for obtaining money by false pretences.

Interviewed some time later, Annie gave her version of events in which she sought to distance herself from Toler:

'He got to know in some way or other that I wanted a secretary and applied to me. He gave out that he was an Irish barrister and came with several letters of recommendation and ultimately I took him into my service. He was the deceiver now. Didn't Blackie say I would have deceived the devil if I deceived him? Well Blackie should just have known Toler. I was completely taken in – as you will hear. He was such a nice old man, with a long white beard – the very quintessence of respectability – that I never for a moment suspected what he was capable of doing. Oh! The fraud!'

After his release from prison, she claimed that Toler came to her in rags, begging. Despite her later self-serving opinions of him, it seems that Toler was only looking out for himself. He said nothing against her during the Miller trial, and had their roles been reversed she would have undoubtedly done the same to him – or worse. In 1888, when the interview with her was conducted, Toler's reputation was already destroyed and he was an old man in the middle of his second five-year term of imprisonment. Nothing Annie said about him could therefore cause him much harm. As regards Kate Miller, Annie seemed to retain some fondness for her:

'There is a word more I should like to say about Mrs Miller. She wasn't so bad as was made out. Doubtless she was fearfully careless about money matters. She was vain and all that, but she was the tool of Toler. He it was without a shadow of error who had her arrested and that, mind you was after he had used her in every way possible for his evil ends. She was the victim of Toler's schemes. I am sorry for her. She was poor and allowed Toler to lead her into lurches where he left her and turned her accuser. He was a villain, that man!'

If true, this conspiracy between Toler and Miller must have been carried on behind Annie's back. After her release in April 1877, Kate, or Ruth W. Miller – if that was indeed her name – loyal servant and widow of an army officer, is not heard of again.

At some point, flushed with Aston's success in America, Annie tried her luck with G.R. Sims, the well-known novelist, dramatist and journalist, who, on the face of it seemed a good target. Sims wrote extensively about the plight of the poor and women's suffrage, as well as being fond of a drink and no stranger to the gaming tables. Also, as luck would have it, he had written a comic opera that was being performed at the Royalty Theatre in London. Sims himself takes up the story:

'She came to me one day in Gower Street, calling herself Mrs Knight Aston with a long rigmarole about the great success her husband had made in comic opera in Australia and offered me £500 for the Australian right of "The Merry Duchess". I didn't like the lady's manner. She talked too big, and her tongue went at such a rate that it was difficult for me to get a word in edgeways. I saw at once that she was not a desirable customer and politely choked her off; but she returned to the attack and called again and again. She was a rather fascinating woman in her manner and her appearance was good but she always gave herself away after she had been talking for the first 5 minutes. At last, to get rid of her I gave her a note to take to my solicitor authorising him to draw an agreement on the payment of the £500. As soon as she had taken the note I sent one on to him by hand, warning him that I did not like the lady's style and that I thought she wanted to get the mss [manuscripts] and score for purposes of her own. I told him to see the colour of her money, not in a cheque but in Bank of England notes before he went to any trouble in the matter. After one interview we heard no more from her.'

With the Miller affair's inconclusive outcome having pretty much faded from memory, Knight Aston returned from Italy and prepared to face his public once more. He rejoined the Soldene Troupe – presumably whatever differences there had been between artiste and troupe leader had now been settled. The Soldene Troupe had recently returned from Australia and opened on 16 September with *Genevieve de Brabant* at The Alhambra in Leicester Square. Aston joined the cast on 9 November 1878, a couple of weeks before Ada Mary – his second daughter by Annie – was born. It was his first appearance at that theatre. He was now aged 27 and took the title role of Paquillo in Offenbach's opera *La Perichole*. Perhaps fearful that his heavily pregnant wife might still be the subject of police attention – because of all the terrible things Toler and Miller had done in her name – Annie moved out of London for the birth.

In November 1878, Annie rented a furnished villa of eight rooms named 'Ferndell', in the hamlet of Clynder on the banks of Gare Loch in the parish of Roseneath, West Dunbartonshire. The owner was a widow, Mrs James Robertson, who lived in Glasgow. Annie was accompanied by a 'gentleman who passed as her husband', and on Friday 22 November 1878, she was attended by Dr McKenzie of Kilcreggan while she gave birth to their second child, a daughter who was named Ada Mary Ogilvie-Bruce. Eighteen days later, on 10 December, she registered the birth at Roseneath, giving the father's name as Thomas Ogilvie-Whyte, who was described as a 'merchant'. Her own name she gave as Annie Ogilvie-Whyte, formerly Miss Ogilvie. She is alleged to have expressed 'great disappointment that it was not a son to heir an estate which she had frequently talked about owning in the Highlands near Oban'.

Annie, Gabrielle and baby Ada lived quietly at the address but in good style, managing with just one servant. Mrs Ogilvie-Whyte was described by a lady who met her frequently during her stay as 'a woman with a conspicuous figure which having seen one could never forget. She was stout, good-looking, of ruddy complexion and always seen in a fancy white dress with a grey "Ulster" down to her heels. Free and open in manners, a fine conversationalist and altogether a wonderful woman.' The lady continued that she was in the habit of getting jewellery and other articles sent to her from Glasgow on approbation, and sometimes these did not meet her high standards. One Glasgow firm sent to London to obtain a fine dressing case for her but never received payment, even though she seemed to have plenty of money. A local gentleman who had been invited to dine with them states that in the evening her husband sang several songs, accompanied himself on the piano and was obviously a professional. A tailor in Greenock supplied him with several suits for his stage appearances, and was still looking for payment after they had left.

After a week or so, Aston left Annie and their daughters at the cottage and returned to London. She told the locals that he had gone to his shooting lodge for a few weeks, but their servant claimed that he had left after a row over money, which does have a ring of truth. He was back at The Alhambra on 24 November in *La Perichole*, two days after Ada's birth, and did not return. The source continues that initially they seemed to have plenty of money and paid their way, but 'no one could get money out of the gentleman's hands', whereas Mrs Ogilvie-Whyte always seemed to be in funds. Annie stayed for another month or so after Aston left, but by the beginning of 1879 her creditors had begun to demand their money and one local trader managed to seize a large travelling trunk in payment of one debt, although this was swallowed up in expenses and ultimately he got nothing.

Annie and her servant, along with the girls, left when things became too hot, after giving just one day's notice, and she was subsequently found to owe money in Glasgow, Greenock, Garelochhead and Helensborough, as well as to the local people in Clynder. The rent, remained unpaid, as did Dr McKenzie's account.

Whether Aston was aware of the details entered on Ada's birth certificate is not known, although there is, of course, no law against giving a child whatever surname the parents desire. The occupation of 'merchant' probably sounded better than 'singer', even though Aston was an internationally acknowledged operatic tenor approaching the top of his profession. Another possibility is that Annie was covering her tracks, as had she put down the father's occupation as 'operatic tenor' or such-like, the pair might be more easily traced by the creditors that she unquestionably intended to leave behind. The 'Whyte' with a 'y' instead of an 'i' was a spelling that he had adopted before he met Annie. The double-barrelled Ogilvie-Bruce was probably just a snobbish affectation and another false trail.

In 1879, the couple were living at 7 South Moulton Street, Grosvenor Square, London, as Mr and Mrs Knight-Aston, with a country house at Heath Lodge, Pinner. Aston was pretty much a regular fixture on the London stage from the end of 1878, but there are signs that not all was well at home. A strange report in the stage paper *The Era* tells of Aston being taken to Westminster County Court by his coachman, a Mr Drake, for the sum of £4/3s/6d. It emerged that Drake had been in Aston's service for some time, but was summarily dismissed on 26 December 1879 without his wages being paid or any reason for his dismissal being given. He had driven Aston from his country residence to The Alhambra on the previous evening, with no complaint being made. Aston's case was that Drake had mistreated the horses under his care and had been driving whilst in an unfit state, and the 'trifling sum', which referred to his unpaid wages, had been withheld as a matter of principle. Judgement was given in March 1880 in Drake's favour for the reduced amount of £1/14/6d.

Despite these strange events, Aston's career was going from strength to strength and he was asked by W.S. Gilbert to stand in for John Power, the tenor, when the latter was taken ill. He recalled:

> 'The D'Oyley Carte employed me to play Ralph Rackstraw [in Gilbert & Sullivan's *HMS Pinafore*]. Gilbert, who stage manages his pieces wanted me to do this, that, and the other – he is very fussy. I said, "I think I know sufficient of the stage to make the character myself. If I fail I will alter the part and play precisely your lines." Well he was so satisfied with the performance that he declared my conception of Ralph Rackstraw was better than his own. Gilbert arranges all his stage business and wants everyone to act just as if they were figures on a chessboard.'

Annie's activities immediately after her return to London are not known, and it is probable that she was just living quietly and looking after her young family. It wasn't too long, however, before she felt able to return to 'work', and during her time at South Moulton Street she is alleged to have duped a Miss Nelson, of 23 Great Portland Street, out of a valuable diamond and emerald necklace. The victim reported the theft at the Marlborough Street Police Court, but this was not proceeded with due to 'the clever manner in which the fraud was committed'. The victim was very probably Mary Nelson, a hotel proprietor.

Annie and Aston may have been having their problems, but it seems that they were not totally estranged, as their fourth and last child, Allen Bruce Whyte, was conceived in or around January 1881. The following month a newspaper called *The Penny Illustrated* carried a short piece in its gossip column about how one of its reporters had spotted a story in a suburban paper. It concerned a well-known actor at a London theatre being summoned by his laundress for the sum of 14 shillings, which it described as 'contemptible', as the actor was in receipt of a good salary. No name was mentioned, but immediately below it was another item saying that: 'Mr Knight Aston is still at the Strand and sings and acts as well as ever in *Olivette*' – a fairly pointless comment within a gossip column, unless the two were supposed to be linked in the mind of the reader. Another sign that things were not all well within the Aston family occurs in the census return for 3 April 1881, which shows Knight Aston, aged 31, a married vocal artist, living at 7 Gower Street, Finsbury, as a lodger, with his 8-year-old daughter Eleanor M. Aston. A pleasant enough address, but where was Annie, their other children, servants and the coachman driving in from their country house in Pinner?

In June 1881, a furnished house called 'Stoneydown' at Walthamstow, with 5 acres of ground, was advertised for rent by a Mr Edward H. Harding of 3 Gordon Square, Bloomsbury. He and his nephew, John Ashford, held the lease on the house, saying a portion of the furniture might also be available, but that some of it was of family interest and not included. Mrs Whyte – Annie – went to see it in a very dashing carriage and introduced herself. Upon hearing of his family and the furniture, she became friendly and discussed her own background as he showed her around the house. She explained that her maiden name was Hope-Johnstone and she was connected to the Earl of Aberdeen. Her marriage settlement, she claimed, was £1,000 per year, and Sir Frederick Johnstone, a friend of the Prince of Wales, was the trustee.

Annie explained that her husband, although called Whyte, was an operatic singer performing under the name of Knight Aston at the Strand Theatre and that he was the proprietor of the comic opera *Olivette*, which was being successfully performed there at the time. She said he was, in reality, 'Baron Aston' of Birmingham and there was a lawsuit then pending by which he hoped to get possession of his estates, after which the family might become reconciled. She told Mr Harding that she had a large house in Pinner which she let for £500 per year and asked him to not mention Sir Frederick Johnstone, because of family dissatisfaction with her having married a singer, but that she had other references she would supply. They were using the name

Whyte, she explained, to conceal their identity, as their friends would object to a connection to the stage and her husband was 'not exactly a knight but he ought to be a baron if only he could get his rights'.

On her next visit, a few days later, she was accompanied by a gentleman and her three daughters in a fine carriage: presumably the party included Aston's daughter, Eleanor. The man was introduced as her husband, Mr Whyte, and referred to as Tom. He said very little, but wore an eye glass and said merely 'yes' or 'no' to her observations. They both looked over the place and agreed to take it for the remaining eleven years of the lease at £85 per annum, along with some of the furniture as it 'would be a pity to pick the house to pieces'. Mrs Whyte also agreed to keep on the servants at the house. The lease was to be in Mr Whyte's name and the matter was put in the hands of solicitors Chilcocks of St Martin's Lane. The contents were valued at £200, and included a cow and 5 acres of land. An inventory was taken, and the lease was signed on 20 July 1881.

It might be thought that anyone who would let a house when confronted with a story like that deserves all they get, but let the house Mr Harding did – and with predictable results. There is nothing to show that Aston was a party to all the absurd family history stories and claims of references obtainable from highly placed people, as this was done on her first visit before he saw the place. His reported monosyllabic replies to her questions perhaps indicate that he did not have much interest and was merely following his wife's lead. The move may have been one final attempt at a reconciliation, but more probably, as she was now six months pregnant, Aston was just seeing her through the birth and providing a home for the children. He was, or had up until a few weeks before, been living in lodgings alone with his daughter, and had been absent from the stage at the Strand Theatre since 10 June.

Their last child together, and only son, was born on 10 September 1881 at Stoneydown, and registered as Allen Bruce Whyte on 21 October. Aston was back on stage at the Strand Theatre by 4 October. If he had any hopes of his wife settling down with the enlarged family, turning over a new leaf and mending her profligate ways, they were soon to be dashed. Mrs Whyte was at pains to strike up a friendly relationship with her new landlord and his family, and expressed great interest in the good dress sense of Harding's mother, remarking that she supposed she paid for her fine items as she got them, just as she did herself. On the contrary, explained the helpful landlord, she had an account, and then gave the charming young lady the name and address of the shop which, of course, soon resulted in a large unpaid bill – one among several others in the Walthamstow area. The Astons lived there for about six months, during which time there were numerous reports of disgraceful behaviour in the house, with quarrelling and fighting. Harding had travelled down from Reading in response to a letter received from his nephew about the tenant's behaviour. It seems from magistrates' court transcripts, years later, that John Ashford had stayed at the house himself for four or five weeks, but could not remain because of the behaviour of Mrs Whyte. Before he left, Ashford noticed some articles not included in the inventory, including a clock and table cover, had been taken away and 'some plausible excuse made to Mr Harding'. Mrs Whyte had also agreed to look after a large brass banner for the landlord, but this too was no longer there.

After she had been at Stoneydown for a few months, Mrs Whyte had a dispute with a cabman which caused her details to be published in the papers, and she was summoned to appear at Mansion House Police Court for 'bilking' the driver over his fare. A Mr St. Aubyn appeared as solicitor in support of the complainant, but it seems that Annie had other plans and simply did not turn up on the day, although what ultimately became of the matter is not known. Unfortunately, the publicity attending the proceedings caused her whereabouts to be betrayed to a firm of solicitors in the City, who had had previous dealings with her, and resulted in the seizure of what remained of the furniture in the house.

The pair had only paid rent for the first three months, and when Harding called round 'in a furious rage' to collect the arrears he noticed that items of his furniture was missing and threatened to call the police immediately. Several of her previous creditors had tracked her down and carried off the furniture as payment. Mrs Whyte went down on her knees and begged him not to say anything, as she would get the money from her solicitor in Birmingham immediately, and Harding was eventually induced to leave. By the time he had discovered that the solicitor mentioned did not exist, the birds had flown and he was left £360 short. Annie or Aston had sold several items of the 'missing' furniture to Mr Attenborough, a pawnbroker in Chancery Lane, for £350, while the rest had indeed been seized by creditors. The house was emptied, whilst the cow, which had cost £25, had gone for £15 about a fortnight after they moved in. In the end, Harding received only £70 of the rent and £70 on account for the furniture. The servants hadn't been paid, and one had even been offered the tennis net and balls in lieu of wages! The lease was recovered after some difficulty, and Harding believed she had moved to Brook Street or South Moulton Street, but that 'she had told so many lies that he could hardly remember'.

There is no information about what Aston was doing during his time away from *Olivette* in the Strand, but a short mention in the theatrical newspaper *The Era* in June 1881 noted that a Monsieur Guillaume Loredan was showing great versatility in Knight Aston's role. He was back in October, but on 17 December the same paper noted that Mr Knight Aston was 'so indisposed that he has been compelled to relinquish his professional labours and will spend the winter in Nice'. The relationship between Annie and Aston had now broken down irretrievably, and presumably he wintered alone. In an interview years later, he said that he had to give up the part due to rheumatic fever and rheumatic gout.

In the early part of 1882, he signed up with Messrs Dunning, Wallace & Co., who had just taken out new leases on the Opera House in Melbourne, Australia. Knight Aston, described as late of 'The Alhambra, Globe, and Strand theatres (having played the original Valentine in *Olivette*)', was one of the first to agree to join the new company as its organizers scoured London and Paris for suitable talent for the new season, due to commence on 2 September. Aston arranged to set sail for the other side of the world; possibly he took Eleanor with him, though there is no further record of her in either country. Whether Annie knew he was going or whether he just crept away is not known, but it was certainly a life-changing move for all of them and he was not to return to England for twenty years.

John Wallace – one of the directors and manager of the new company – Aston and the rest of the troupe boarded the SS *John Elder* from London on 1 July and made their way to Melbourne via Plymouth. Also on board was Sir Henry Parkes, Premier of New South Wales, returning after a few months' break. The ship's crew and passengers were undoubtedly delighted to find themselves in the company of a group of opera singers, and were entertained during the voyage – probably being the first to hear something of the five new comic operas Wallace was taking with him. He and the troupe arrived in Melbourne on 14 August 1882.

Meanwhile, things seemed not to be going well for Annie back at home. According to a later investigation, carried out by an Inspector Marshall, a conviction in the name of Mary Ann Appely Bruce was recorded on 19 December 1882. This was for fraud, on which there was a sentence of nine months' hard labour. Nothing has been found relating to this case in existing records, but as it came from Marshall himself (who plays a major role later in the story) and went unchallenged at the time it came to light, it can be assumed to be true. There are no records of the date of arrest, but as cases can often take months to get to court, Annie could have been arrested some time before Aston left and this may have provided the final push he needed to make the break.

If Annie did serve more time in prison, she would have been released in the summer of 1883 and would, to all intents and purposes, have found herself to be single again. Whether this is what she wanted is a matter of conjecture, and one report claimed she was making enquiries about Aston in London, of persons connected with Australia, saying he had deserted her. Whatever her feelings, his departure enabled her to give free rein to her chosen career. There is no record of what happened to her three children while she was in prison, or subsequently, but there are stories about her using a number of aliases around this time, including that of Mrs William Maitland of 5 Duchess Street, Portland Place, Mrs Lee Toler, Mrs Melville Whyte and Mrs Henry, adopting the names of people close to her. However, details are sketchy and rely on later newspaper reports that do not give dates or circumstances behind the various names. She spoke to tradesmen again of a 'foreign prince' and a 'baronet' who were supporting her schemes and would settle her bills, and it is reported she still lived in luxury, with private secretaries, butlers and a magnificent retinue. In addition to any other of her little ventures, Sir Richard King's money was still available. It is stated she returned to London in August 1883, presumably from prison, and as 'Mrs Whyte' rented 15 York Terrace, Regents Park. She is said to have left owing large sums, after using the furniture as fuel, so perhaps it took a while for the funds to start flowing again. With the new aliases came new addresses, and she is reported to have occupied 11 Portsea Place, Connaught Square, as Mrs Annie Ogilvie White, whilst also keeping a place at 84 Cromwell Road, Bayswater, and sometime later at 4 Bryanston Street, near Portman Square. The latter was the property of two unsuspecting maiden ladies who never saw a penny in rent, and it is here that she is believed to have used the name Gordon Baillie for the first time. Under the name of Ayrd Whyte, she produced several pieces of poetry, one of which was the mercifully short piece entitled 'Aujourd'hui' (meaning 'Today'):

> Cold blows the wind across the mountain;
> Faded are the lilies by the way;
> No ki's song, all silent is the fountain – Tis today!

Even the authorship of her poems is in doubt, as another story states that she was once the guest of an authoress, also named Whyte, who lived in South Kensington. It seemed they met on a bus, and having begun talking they got on so well that Annie was invited to her house and stayed for three days. When she left she 'accidentally' took away the manuscripts of poems which found their way into print under a different name.

In one scam, given by the press as an example of her *modus operandi* during this period, she was alleged to have persuaded a woman to trust her with £300 to invest in a company she claimed would yield around 25 per cent interest.

Once the victim parted with her money, Annie found a better use for it: when asked to account for the funds later, she produced a letter signed by her victim stating that she had voluntarily lent Mrs Gordon Baillie the money for a term of years without conditions. Annie had dictated the document, saying it was only a form and was needed in case the stockbroker should ask whether the money was her own. 'The shares are very much sought after,' Annie had explained, 'you couldn't get them yourself, but sign this and I will get them for you.'

Another of Mrs Gordon Baillie's London landladies during this period was Madam Mott, a Frenchwoman who lived in Southampton Street on the Strand. In place of rent she received pawn tickets, which she was told were of great value, but when she came to collect on them, she was told by the pawnbroker they were 'special contract' tickets that had already expired.

In 1883, Annie became the acquaintance of an old lady calling herself La Comtesse de Bronte who resided in considerable comfort, first at Foley Street, then Langham Street and finally at 83 Mortimer Street, all within central London. It seems that this lady owned a large quantity of jewellery and received an allowance from the Countess of Aberdeen, who was a known political radical. The countess was married to Lord Aberdeen, a Liberal peer, and supported women's rights as well as education classes for servants and, interestingly, a scheme to sponsor young women who wished to emigrate to Canada and the colonies. Unsurprisingly, Annie and the rich old Comtesse became close. According to the source, Annie 'espoused the cause of the Nihilists and induced the Comtesse to become the president of a shadowy Nihilist Society', though why nihilists would want a president, let alone a countess in the role, is not explained. Presumably this introduction took place sometime after November 1884, when she met Percy Frost, who moved in such circles.

The countess is also part of the strange story of how Annie came to adopt the name Gordon Baillie. The countess had a dog named Gordon, which was the family name of the Earl of Aberdeen, whose mother's family name was Baillie. Many of Annie's other aliases and false names had at least some basis in fact, bearing in mind she never had a name of her own, but the one by which history has come to know her seems to have no connection with anything else in her life and this explanation is as good as any other, linking her to the Scottish aristocracy that she imitated so well.

The first recorded use of the Gordon Baillie name comes in a short report in the *Aberdeen Free Press* of January 1884, when Annie donated 150 blankets to the Skye crofters, 'with which island Mrs Gordon Baillie *has for some years* identified herself', indicating the name predates her meeting the countess by some time, so perhaps this story has as much foundation in fact as the many other accounts of herself. Whatever the truth might be, the relationship between Annie and the countess didn't end well. Annie took a fancy to several paintings belonging to de Bronte and bought them off her with a cheque for £70. The cheque bounced, and Annie and a male friend took her out to dinner to explain. The next morning the Comtesse became ill, and after lingering on for a week was found dead on the floor of her room, and it was reported that 'the doctor was able to certify that she had died from an apoplectic fit, and an inquest was not held'. There is possibly more to this tale than meets the eye. During a legal argument over the estate of Annie's benefactor, Sir Richard Duckworth King, in 1889, the names of a number of people who had claims on him and to whom he had given money were mentioned in court; amongst them was 'a lady who said she was the last of the Nelsons, and who called herself the Baroness Bronte'. Also mentioned, immediately after, was 'Miss Bruce afterwards Mrs Aston White, now known as Mrs Gordon Baillie serving a term of penal servitude'.

Chapter 13

Theatrical Aspirations
(1884)

On New Year's Day 1884, an organization known as The London Association for the Protection of Trade published a report on a Miss Ogilvie Bruce in its monthly newsletter. Her signature was prominently displayed on its front page, and inside there was an article on various frauds being carried out by a woman who used the names of Mrs White, Miss Bruce and T. Henry, alias Teller. The article stated that numerous enquiries had been received by the society from pianoforte manufacturers, chemists and other businesses from whom she ordered goods. Amongst the addresses she used were 59 York Terrace, York Gate, and 30 Liverpool Street, King's Cross. The latter proved to be the address of Mr Toller, who was lodging there, and who had sent out letters ordering goods signed 'T. Henry'. In previous issues the newsletter had also carried reports of the activities of a Toller White, Mrs A. White and Miss Annie Ogilvie Bruce, but they do not seem yet to have linked their 'quarry' to either Mary Ann Bruce Sutherland or the emerging Mrs Gordon Baillie.

The London Association had been formed in London's West End in 1842 as a mutual support group for London businesses. They held weekly meetings, where they exchanged views on current questions of commercial interest, asked advice of one another regarding the credit of customers, related experiences with swindlers and named bad debtors. Membership was strict and only by the recommendation of two existing members, which was then voted on by the entire membership during quarterly meetings. This procedure aimed to ensure any information was trustworthy, while withholding information or sharing it with non-members was a reason for expulsion. By the end of the century, branches and imitators had spread throughout the country and beyond.

For Annie, in the guise of Mrs Whyte, no sum was too small to go unpaid, and given her comfortable circumstances – courtesy of Sir Richard – her behaviour seemed at times deranged. In February 1884, for example, she was ordered to appear before the magistrate at Mansion House Police Court to answer charges of more unpaid cab fares. One paper reported:

'A lady, it appeared, entered a hansom cab and was driven about to several places after which she got out and coolly walked away. The unsuspecting driver waited for some time and subsequently inquired after his fare at each of the houses where she had stopped. In every instance he was informed she was Mrs White of 29 [sic] York Terrace, Regents Park. A summons was taken out, but the official of the court failed to serve it, even though he spent half an hour knocking and ringing at the door. After watching at a little distance, he saw a woman go up to the door and followed her, she said she was Mrs White's servant, but he could get nothing out of her except that he was to put the summons in the letterbox. This was done but the lady neither appeared nor sent any answer to the court. It was asserted that she had for a considerable time pursued a similar system of "bilking" cabmen. A warrant was applied for, but Sir Andrew Lusk wished servicing of the summons to be tried again, promising that if the mysterious Mrs White did not attend on that occasion, he would take serious steps to bring her to book.'

It seemed that the repeated summonses for unpaid fares was beginning to have some effect on her – although not a deterrent one and certainly not one worthy of her showing up in person. The week after the non-appearance at Mansion House Police Court, Mrs Annie White of 59 York Terrace was ordered to appear at Marlborough Street by James Mills, driver of cab no.8567. This was for unlawfully refusing to pay two sums of 7/6d and 2/6d, for the hire of his cab on 4 and 5 March 1884. The court was told that the defendant made a habit of avoiding fares, 'by different subterfuges', and had described herself at various times as the wife of a colonel, an artist or a wealthy farmer. At the hearing, a woman stepped forward and stated that she knew Mrs White and that she would pay the money owed to Mills. The unnamed 'defendant's representative' was ordered to pay the cab fares of 10/- plus a fine of 5/- and 4/- costs. It was also stated in court that Mrs White had been summoned to attend at least half a dozen police courts for non-payment of cab fares, and that she had employed solicitors to appear for her. Her dislike of paying cabmen must have cost her a considerable sum of money – assuming of course that she paid the solicitors. The mysterious debt payer was not named. Was she the servant whom an agent of the court had spoken to while attempting to serve a previous summons, a secret benefactor or Annie herself, unable to resist a bit of theatre? Whoever she was, there was little doubt that such repeated offences over a small area and time period could only have one result, if continued, and Annie was lucky not to have been arrested and charged with multiple offences. Her motives for the repetition of such trivial con tricks are difficult to understand, but could not have been financial. Perhaps the best explanation is that it was thrill-seeking, pure and simple. The bigger, long-term frauds and con tricks were fine for occupying the mind and perhaps filling the purse, but maybe her addiction to excitement sometimes required a more immediate fix.

Press reports covering 1884 credit her with working with a woman called Heath in raising money by false cheques on Messrs Ransom & Co.'s Bank, as well as working briefly from 11 York Road in Brighton and defrauding many people in the town, although nothing else has been uncovered about this 'Brighton connection'. Annie was moving around a great deal at this time and also still using the name of Mrs Maitland; she gave her address as 56 Welbeck Street and a house in Harley Street, owned by a Mrs Trejardo.

Annie's pretentions towards the more socially acceptable forms of acting resurfaced in June 1884, when the following advert was placed in stage paper *The Era*:

MRS GORDON BAILLIE
Provincial & American Tours
Ladies and Gentlemen desirous of visiting the United States and
Australia should address
Wm. Maitland, 52 Regent Street

The following also appeared in *The Era* in its 13 September 1884 edition:

MRS GORDON BAILLIE
And her COMEDY DRAMA COMPANY.
On account of her recent accident
Mrs Gordon Baillie has been compelled
To cancel all English Engagements.
American Tour will commence in December,
With Australia to follow.
Address all communications to
GILBERT TATE, Toole's Theatre, London

In September 1884, Annie took on the services of Tom Russell as her secretary. Presumably she paid him, albeit with Sir Richard's money, as he had nothing but nice things to say about her in later years, although exactly what his duties were are unclear. There are reports that Toler returned to the fold after his sentence for fraud, but nothing has been found to substantiate this – and Annie strongly denied it in a later interview, as we shall see. With so much going on, Annie felt the need for yet more staff and placed an advert for a 'lady secretary' on the front page of the London *Morning Post* in autumn

1884. The advertisement was answered by an experienced woman from St Leonards-on-Sea, who turned up at the house in Upper Brook Street rather earlier than the appointed time and was shown into the dining room by the housemaid. She found the house very opulently decorated and furnished, and during the couple of hours she was kept waiting observed a very busy place with constant comings and goings, which she assumed were other potential applicants being interviewed. Eventually Mrs Gordon Baillie's voice was heard ordering tea for the schoolroom, followed by the pattering of tiny feet scampering up the stairs and, at last, the lady of the house entered the room: '[D]ressed in the most exquisite taste, in the richest of walking costumes of a soft grey shade, Mrs Gordon Baillie posed gracefully on a chair opposite me, offering a thousand apologies.'

'My babies insisted on my taking them to the pantomime … they are having tea now with their governess. After being so long here you must require some refreshment. Bring some Champagne,' she said to the housekeeper.

'It is not come ma'am,' replied the housekeeper.

'Then bring some Canti. You like Canti?'

The wine arrived and Mrs Gordon Baillie was again called away by one of the servants. The hopeful interviewee pondered the strange wording of the advertisement, which included the phrase 'exceptional advantages to be enjoyed in consideration of which a small premium would be required', but this unusual clause was not referred to by either side throughout the interview, which was described as follows:

'Do you think that you should like to be my secretary?' asked the lady after some pleasantries.

'It is impossible to reply until I hear something of the duties required. I purposely refrained from giving you any particulars about myself or troubling you with questions which could all be answered in an interview,' answered the interviewee.

'It was the brevity of your reply, and the practical tone of it which made me set aside your note as the first to be answered out of the six selected from the 100 replies I received. Such things too, some of them. I have had a young Irishman as my secretary the last year. It has been a help to him and he has been a great assistance to me, but now all my friends are crying out that it would be much better for me to have a lady of middle age, especially as I shall be constantly travelling about. You understand that it will look better for I am a young woman still, and the world may talk.'

'It is wonderful that it has not done so already.'

'Well it is perhaps; but this gentleman is only 21 – quite a youth.'

The interviewee asked how many hours a day she would be required to write for and was told:

'I am rather erratic, my best work is generally done around midnight. I never dine till eight o'clock, sometimes later. Generally I begin work at eleven and go on until 4 in the morning. I then sleep until 11 when I have my breakfast. In many ways I feel that a lady who would come to my house at any hour I required her would suit me better. If you are fond of travelling and change there would be plenty of it. You would have to be prepared to hear me say in the evening, "Tomorrow we must start for the Antipodes" or for Germany or New York as the case may be. I certainly intend to lecture in America and I would not go about alone.'

'What would be the subject of your lectures?'

'Always the same, the crofters, are you interested in them?'

'In the question certainly, but ...

'Now don't tell me you are not anxious to see their grievances redressed!' Annie interrupted. 'As my name tells you I am Scotch. It is a good old name and family so my husband retained it. If you are much in London you must have often heard of me. I am quite a public character in reference to the poor crofters.'

Embarrassed by the fact she had never heard of her prospective employer, the woman explained that: 'I live generally in the country and suppose I ought to be ashamed to confess I have not heard of your enthusiastic efforts on behalf of these people. It is strange too because I am very much in rapport with people who interest themselves in all great social movements.'

'The apathy of the government is a disgrace and scandal to the nation,' observed Annie.

'Something must be allowed on the score of patriotism.'

'Well you – you are English of course. Have you ever been to Scotland?'

Annie explained that she had estates in the Highlands and in Staffordshire, where she would leave her children with the governess when she went abroad. She then asked the lady if she was fond of work.

'Yes, but not during the night; only at reasonable hours.'

Things were not going too well. Annie said she wanted someone who could originate as well as take dictation: 'Nobody else would be able to help me. I must have a woman with brains. No mere dilettante who would like to sit in dressing gown and slippers over the fire would be of any use to me.'

'I should think you would scarcely find any but a girl fond of rush and excitement who would fall in with all you propose,' the interviewee replied.

'And without brains which I'm sure you possess.'

'Girls distance women nowadays,' the woman observed, 'but as you say you wish for protection – or friends wish it for you – that purpose would hardly be served by engaging a young lady.'

'No, besides I feel sure I should like you.'

Perhaps because the interviewee did not appear flattered by the remark, Annie added: 'It may be better for me to have a lady not quite so ...'

'Pray say old, for at middle age it is absurd to pose as a young woman and you will excuse my remarking that as you have told me nothing definite as to my duties or your plans it seems useless discussing the matter further. Probably, you will fix on one of the ladies waiting to see you.'

The interviewee recalled: 'At this Mrs Gordon Baillie smiled for she saw that I did not accept her ruse of having an unusual number of visitors.'

Then Annie added, 'I feel that I have treated you very badly but will you call here again or shall I go to see you?' Finding her companion did not respond, she continued: 'Perhaps it would be better for me to write. You shall have a long letter with full particulars. Then can you can let me know what you think. Goodbye.' Annie then extended her hand and said: 'We shall soon meet again I hope. But I may tell you that before all things I wish to make a career for myself.'

'Of course, no letter came. Mrs Gordon Baillie could have given utterance to no words that would so thoroughly have set the seal to my opinion concerning her,' the potential secretary later recounted, 'but there was not a ring of truth in her voice despite the beauty and fascination of her manner.'

A correspondent to *The Globe* newspaper, calling himself 'A Lookee-On', also recalled meeting Annie – Mrs Gordon Baillie – during this period:

'[S]he came to a West-End boarding house where I was with some friends. We speedily came to the conclusion that she was an adventuress and a rather vulgar one. She was a handsome woman, somewhat bold in manner and decidedly under-bred. She was getting up a theatrical company to go the colonies. Her children did not live with her but occasionally visited her and I remember how lovely these poor little mortals were. After a few weeks sojourn at the house she was requested to leave at once as it was discovered that some of her antecedents were known, [and] she left without one word of protest.'

Sadly, there are no further details. There is also uncertainty as to whether she was living at 29 or 59 York Terrace; possibly she spent time at both. At least one of her stays was of short duration, taken under the name of Ayrd White, and her tenure ended with three men taking possession on behalf of the people who had supplied the furniture.

From October to December 1884, advertisements were placed in the theatrical newspaper, *The Stage*:

MRS GORDON BAILLIE

Australian and American Tour

(Via Cape Town)

Will commence early in January next.

Address

Gilbert Tate

Embankment Chambers, Charing Cross, London

Like previous attempts at appearing on stage or forming her own touring troupe, nothing seems to have come of it. Possibly nothing was intended to come of it, as she may have been hoping to raise funds and pocket the proceeds. Possibly she felt she had a future on the stage and hoped to impress Aston with her success, in the hope of winning him back or prove she could form and run a touring company where he could not. Whatever the purpose, she seems to have convinced George Rignold, a well-regarded actor and soon to be theatre owner and manager in Australia, of her scheme. She told him she was putting together a magnificent theatrical company that was to tour the world for two years. She agreed to engage him and his brother Bill to write plays for her at £50 per week, and he thought he was on to a good thing. Sometime later though, an acquaintance asked him who she was, as she was claiming that she knew him well. The actor replied:

> 'Bothered if I know. All I know is she engaged us for some visionary company which never came to anything. I believe there was the devil of a row with some fellow who wrote a play which she wouldn't accept. I saw her the other day and asked her how things were coming along and she said that owing to her absorbing interest in the crofter scheme she had to let the dramatic undertaking stand for a while – I think it's likely to stand for a considerable while!'

In November 1884, Annie went so far as to rent the Imperial Theatre with Captain Disney Roebuck, saying that she intended to appear herself as Lady Clancarty, the lead role in an historical romance of that name by dramatist Tom Taylor. Her performance never reached the stage, and Roebuck was both out of pocket and furious. He had also put money into advertising her 'Cape and American Tour' with Gilbert Tate, a dramatic agent, which she constantly postponed while away in Skye. An advert in *The Stage* towards the end of that year announced that the tour would commence in the following January, but upon her return from the Scottish Isles she cancelled the whole thing. On 20 December 1884, she sent the following for inclusion in *The Era*:

CAPTAIN DISNEY ROEBUCK
Mrs Gordon Baillie's Cape and Australian Tour.
This lady writes:-
4 Bryanston Street, Portman Square. December 17th 1884
Concerning her Cape Tour, as that has been postponed indefinitely, all matters connected with it are also postponed.
Captain Disney Roebuck, permanent address, 102, Piccadilly, London
W.

Roebuck had had enough, and went so far as to bring a claim against Annie for the £150 he had lost, but he died while on business in South Africa in March 1885 and the action therefore was discontinued.

Over the previous few months, a new life had begun to materialize for Annie, ripe with possibilities of excitement and enrichment far beyond those of the stage. The plight of the crofters in the Scottish Highlands was becoming desperate: it was a cause to which Annie professed a passionate belief and one which was to change her life forever.

Part III

1884–1888

Chapter 14

The Skye Crofters & the Revolt of 1884

The Isle of Skye is the largest and northernmost of the major islands in the Inner Hebrides of Scotland. The island's peninsulas radiate out from a mountainous centre, dominated by the Cuillins, the rocky slopes that provide some of the most dramatic mountain scenery in the country. Historically, many of the Scottish Highlanders had made a living from trading kelp, a large brown seaweed which when dried and burned produced sodium carbonate. This product had several industrial uses, including the manufacture of gunpowder, and was in great demand during the wars with France. The tenants not involved in either tilling the land or fishing made a basic living from this, but as ever it was the landlords who grew rich. The war ended in 1815, and peace – combined with cheaper sources of calcium carbonate mined elsewhere – meant demand fell away, with devastating effects on local communities, many of whom were reduced to living on shellfish, with others forced into begging or crime.

Between 1841 and 1881, the population of Skye dropped from 23,000 to 16,800, and by the 1880s many of the indigenous people of the islands and highlands had been 'cleared' from large expanses of their ancestral lands, with large numbers of them having emigrated to North America. Of those who did not emigrate, many were crammed into crofting townships on very small areas of land, where they were subject to abuse and exploitation by their landlords. Many others lacked even crofts of their own, becoming cottars or squatters on the crofts of their neighbours. Landlords turned most of the land over to use as sheep farms, hunting parks and deer forests. In addition, during the 1880s, the Highlands and Islands were still trying to recover from having been ravaged by the potato famine of the mid-nineteenth century. On top of all this, wool prices collapsed, sheep farmers 'profits and landlords' rentals fell back sharply from the heights they reached in the 1860s and early 1870s, and poor harvests throughout 1881 and 1882 plunged the crofting population to a level reminiscent of the earlier great potato famine.

Things came to a head in April 1882, when, to add to numerous other woes, the tenants of Braes, an area near Portree, faced eviction. Lord MacDonald, owner of the land, called in the sheriff, who was sent from Portree to evict crofters who were protesting at their treatment by withholding rents and allowing their sheep to feed off his private lands. The sheriff was met on the road by an angry mob, who forced him to burn the eviction notices, while his assistant was assaulted by a crowd of boys who poured 'certain domestic utensils fully charged' over his head. The officers beat a hasty retreat. It was great fun and a small victory for the crofters, but nonetheless, the law had been broken and the authorities felt compelled to react.

Sheriff William Ivory appealed for help to the Glasgow police force, who sent forty men to assist. They marched towards the scene of the trouble, but were met by 100 men, women and children amid heavy rain and howling winds. They had managed to arrest five people within the first twenty minutes, when all hell broke loose. Stones were thrown, and as boulders darkened the sky, the police charged with drawn batons. Many on both sides were injured and the situation became very dangerous, with attack followed by counterattack, until the constables managed to break through with their prisoners still restrained. The incident became known as 'The Battle of the Braes'. When tried, the five prisoners were found guilty of assault and given small fines, which were promptly paid by a hastily formed defence committee, and they were carried home as heroes. A stand had been made and the country began to take notice. In terms of gaining the sympathy of the public, the crofters were protesting effectively, with rent strikes and land raids gaining support. The weather made their plight even more difficult, and on 1 October 1882, after prolonged rain in August and September, came a severe southerly gale which destroyed the unharvested grain and damaged or destroyed their fishing boats, nets and fishing gear.

Fighting on the side of the Skye crofters was the Land League, an organization that had grown up in response to the continuing unrest. Like similar established groups in Ireland and England, its outlook was broadly socialist. The manifesto of the English organization exclaimed:

'And whereas the appropriation to the few of the land on which and from which the people of England must live is an efficient cause of dullness of trade, lowness of wages, the idleness of men who should be at work, the forcing of women and children to unnatural toil, the depopulation of agricultural districts, the crowding of city slums, the sapping of national strength by forced emigration, the physical and mental deterioration due to unwholesome employment and lodgings, and of the vice and crime that spring from poverty: It is therefore the duty of all Englishmen to secure the restoration of England to its true owners, the people of England'

The Land Leaguers organized collections of money for the crofters to pay the fines and expenses of any of their number who should be arrested, as well as drawing up petitions and encouraging a general climate of opposition to the landowners amongst the inhabitants, with strategic rent strikes and trespassing of their cattle. Aware of all this and still smarting from the humiliation of the 'Battle of the Braes', Sheriff Ivory began to rethink his strategies. Instead of the 24-mile-long treks through rough territory with hails of stones injuring his men, he proposed a naval force, aboard a gunboat, which would have the advantage of surprise and ability to land a large force close to the crofters' homes. The idea of using military force was rejected, but the authorities added it was not for them to determine the mode of transport by which a squad of police officers might effectively be transported. Ivory began to recruit men. He was unable to do so locally, as too many had sympathies with the people they were to be deployed against, so he went to the Lancashire Police Committee. They agreed to help on the condition that every expense was paid by the Scots and every claim for compensation or injury was also met.

Meanwhile, rent strikes, trespass and general anti-landlord activity continued, and the authorities felt compelled to uphold the rule of law before things got completely out of hand. In January 1883, six policemen from Inverness-shire made their way towards Glendale to reinforce the local authorities and pave the way for the serving of summonses on five locals, forbidding them from pasturing their animals on the lord's land and harassing the estate shepherds. They were by met a crowd of about 400, who had been tipped off, and were lucky to survive with merely cuts and bruises. Ivory again appealed to Westminster for an armed force, but was again turned down. To send the military against groups of men armed with sticks and stones did not sit right with Gladstone's Liberal government, even if such a force could be assembled in time. Coupled with this was the feeling that a lot of the unrest was due to the intransigence of the local lairds.

Nonetheless, the crofters of Glendale were treating the place as an autonomous state and this could not possibly be allowed to continue. The Westminster government sent an official, Malcolm MacNeill, to negotiate and explain it's position. A large meeting was held, during which four men were asked to surrender into custody before any negotiations could continue. They were to be charged with 'seizing the grazing lands of the landlords and allowing their own animals to use it', while driving off the landlords' own sheep and cattle, and failing to respond to a summons. As well as this, it was demanded that all crofters' stock be removed from disputed lands. Foremost amongst the crofter leaders was John Macpherson, 'a powerful man, [with] a white beard down to his chest, and a tongue that could cleave oak'. He now stepped forward to explain the crofters' case. There were no fences, he said, to stop animals going 'where they will', and his countrymen had offered to pay a fair rent for the lands but had been refused. They had used the land for thirty-seven years, he continued, and were now being turned from it and the land rented to newcomers.

A brief meeting was held amongst the crofters themselves, and it was agreed that three of the four men requested would surrender to the authorities and put their case before the court. But that was as far as they were prepared to go – and they would go to the court in Edinburgh under their own steam. This was a way of averting more bloodshed and the arrival of the military. The optimists believed the three would be acquitted of wrongdoing, and that once those in authority heard their case there would be an enquiry or Royal Commission into their grievances. When they finally appeared in court, they were immediately granted bail of £100 each and proceedings got underway with arguments back and forth as to the movements of cattle and intimidation of the tenant farmers. It was all in vain. Giving judgement, Lord Shand stressed there was only one point at issue – whether the respondents had committed a breach of the interdict or order of the court granted on 6 July 1882, which prohibited them from 'pasturing, or herding their sheep or cattle on those lands, allowing them to stray, and obstructing, molesting and interfering with the occupiers of the lands or farms'. Unsurprisingly, the four were found to have ignored the order and were therefore in contempt of court; not only that, but attempts to enforce the order had been met with violence and intimidation.

The crofters' hope of claiming the moral high ground, in front of an impartial court, were dashed. Macpherson and the two others were sentenced to two months' imprisonment. They were taken off to Calton prison, and although there was initial discomfort, they were very well treated, with comforftable beds and meals supplied and paid for by the Edinburgh Highland Land Law Reform Association. They had no complaints, but back in Glendale the news of the verdict was met with 'great surprise and deep sorrow', and according to the *Dundee Evening Telegraph*, 'they will carry on the agitation to the bitter end and will never surrender until their grievances are redressed. The sentence of the court has tended to cause the agitation to spread and take a deeper root and hold on the minds of the people.' As a propaganda coup, the crofters and their agitators could not have hoped for a better outcome.

To show its even-handedness and in the hope of diffusing further protest, the government responded in May 1883 with a much-requested commission of enquiry, headed by Francis Napier. With the 'Glendale Martyrs', as they were now known, in their cosy cells and the crofters looking forward to having their grievances heard by Napier's commission, they continued with their rent strike but as a conciliatory gesture drove all their stock off the disputed land at Waterstein. As the 'Glendale Three' were packing their bags for a triumphant return, however, the landowners, with a crass misreading of the situation, issued seventy notices of eviction in response to the continuing rent strike. After a somewhat weak attempt to serve the notices, which was met by an opposition force of 1,000 people, the forces of law and order retreated and sent the orders by registered mail, which was never collected.

The Napier Commission enquiry was thorough, wide-ranging and in-depth, but its recommendations, published in April 1884, fell a long way short of addressing crofters' demands and achieved nothing except a further wave of protests. The earlier demonstrations had been confined largely to Skye, but in 1884 protest action became more widespread and many thousands of crofters became members of the Highland Land League or the Highland Land Law Reform Association, which had been building support amongst exiles and supporters in London. Prominent amongst these were the American socialist philosopher Henry George and Michael Davitt of the Irish Land League, who advocated the nationalization of land. George had recently published a bestseller entitled *Progress & Poverty* and was one of the leading Christian Socialists of his day. Both gentlemen were rumoured to be heading for a tour of Skye in support of the crofters' cause. George made it in February 1884 and was supported by Macpherson in a short series of lectures, advocating land nationalization. Then in April, the Highland Land Reform Association of London asked all those who were prepared to assist the movement to get in touch with them immediately: battle lines were being drawn, rent strikes were spreading and in October that year, 1,000 crofters on the Kilmuir estate joined the strike.

Sheriff Ivory performed the usual ritual of sending a small detachment of policemen into the lion's den, with the predictable result of them being met in Uig by hundreds of crofters and sent scuttling back to Portree. Maybe Ivory was hoping for a more explosive outcome this time to force the government's hand. If so, he needn't have worried about the lack of serious violence. This time the government listened to his appeal. A 'reign of terror' existed on Skye, it was said, and 'the immediate despatch of a gunboat and marines is absolutely necessary to protect the police in protecting property and the persons of lieges on the island'. Reluctantly, Gladstone agreed and 350 troops were landed on Uig, although the government were at pains to stress that they were there only to support the police in their duties. On 15 and 16 November, naval vessels, with merchant ships in support, entered Portree

Bay. In response, Macpherson appealed for calm and negotiation rather than violence and confrontation. The small gunboat *Forester* and the *Lochiel* were joined by the main force aboard HMS *Assistance*, with 350 marines and 100 seamen. The captain of the *Assistance* leapt ashore with gun at the ready and began shooting at the local deer on the moor around Portree. The crofters were apprehensive, shocked, outraged and fearful, but above all they kept their cool. Small parties of redcoats came ashore and marched up and down a little, but were met with a bemused indifference.

This 'circus' was then moved around the island to Dunvegan and Glendale, and the stage was set for two, as yet unknown, players to gravitate towards its centre: a public schoolboy who was a vicar's son with dreams of socialist revolution, and a washer-woman's penniless daughter from the slums of Peterhead, who thought herself a countess and lived accordingly.

Chapter 15

A Worthy Cause
(Nov–Dec 1884)

We will probably now never know what captured Annie's interest in the Scottish crofters' cause, but whatever it was, she was certainly involved in it by the beginning of 1884. As we have seen, Mrs Gordon Baillie had sent 150 pairs of blankets to be distributed amongst the Skye crofters that January. Possibly the romance and adventure of the revolt in her native Scotland struck a chord, or she may have indeed had genuine sympathy with the crofters' plight – bad people sometimes do good things – or she may just have seen a cynical way to collect money from a passionate people, just as she had with the evangelical Christians many years before. Determined to see the situation for herself, she put her theatrical plans aside and arranged to visit the islands, intending to make the cause of the crofters her own and begin one of her most audacious schemes.

On the afternoon of Thursday 20 November 1884, accompanied by her secretary Mr Tom Russell and her maid – whom she referred to as 'auntie' – Annie arrived at the village of Strome to catch the ferry to Portree, Skye's principal town. They found that the boat only ran three times a week, so they would have to wait all night or take the 45-mile-long old coach road via Kyle of Lochalsh. Chosing the latter, after a change of horses they arrived late at the Portree Hotel on Skye, run by Donald MacInnes, a known supporter of the crofters' cause. It was a harsh winter's day and they were almost frozen, but soon revived after a few glasses of toddy and settled in for the night. The next day, Friday 21 November, with a carriage and pair hired from the landlord, they made their way across the island to Dunvegan for an appointment to meet the legendary Glendale Martyr, John Macpherson. When they arrived at their hotel, the small party found themselves in the middle of a scrum of reporters and marines who had also just arrived. Standing out amongst the former was a young, opinionated and heavily moustachioed idealist who had just returned from addressing a meeting with the martyr himself.

Robert Percival 'Percy' Bodley Frost was born on 20 December 1858 at Winchmore Hill, Edmonton, North London, the son of Yorkshire-born John

Dixon Frost, the incumbent of St Paul's Church, Winchmore Hill, and his wife Elizabeth. He went to Marlborough College, an independent Wiltshire boarding school founded in 1843, which specialized in preparing pupils for the Royal Military Academies at Woolwich or Sandhurst; its ethos was anti-commercial and anti-intellectual, fostering and supporting the benefits of Empire and the idea that the British were a 'conquering and imperial race'. Frost was by all accounts a very diligent pupil, who gained a scholarship but for some reason did not take it up. After leaving Marlborough in 1876, he worked for a shipbroker within the City and enjoyed a combined annual income of between £400 and £500, from both that employment and his family, until 1880, when the death of his father provided an inheritance which gave him ample funds.

While at Marlborough he had formed a close association with another pupil, Henry Hyde Champion. Champion's background was different from that of Frost's in that he had been born in Poona, India, the son of Major General James Hyde Champion. It was the custom at the time for officers serving abroad to send their children home to be educated. By his own admission, Champion was not very academic, and after Marlborough he attended the Royal Military Academy at Woolwich before being posted to Afghanistan in 1879, where he caught typhoid and was invalided out of the Army towards the end of 1880.

Whilst Champion was back in London to convalesce, he met up with Frost, who took him through London's East End and showed him the desperate conditions of the poor. With Champion shocked to his core, the pair resolved to do what they could to improve the lot of working people. They spent several months in America in the early 1880s, during which time they discovered the ideas of pioneering socialist Henry George and his newly published work *Progress & Poverty*. An integral part of George's theories was a strong Christian belief, which dovetailed well with Frost and Champion's view of the world and was to guide their political development for years to come. In September 1882, Champion resigned his army commission, ostensibly in disgust over the conduct of the Egyptian War.

The 1881 census for the Frost family home at 30 Woburn Place, Bloomsbury, has 22-year-old Percy living with his widowed mother and three sisters. With family wealth behind him, he did not seem in a rush to carve out a career for himself, and his occupation at this time is given as a clerk within the West India Merchant Office. He passed his Civil Service exams in June 1882. Champion and Frost spent much of their time in each other's company and in the offices of H.M. Hyndman's Social Democratic Federation (SDF), which they joined late in 1882. Their social circle was remarkable.

The physician Havelock Ellis, for example, described them as 'two amiable and noble-spirited young men', while socialist campaigner Hubert Bland remembered Frost as 'a well-dressed, good looking, gentlemanly young man who wrote well and spoke well, and was popular and trusted'. Hours spent in the company of luminaries such as William Morris or George Bernard Shaw would not have been considered unusual, as they were all enthusiastic about the new cause of socialism – one which did not necessarily mean the same thing to each of its adherents.

In April 1883, Frost and Champion, along with several others, formed the Land Reform Union, consisting of around seventy members, with Frost as secretary and Champion as treasurer. On 9 January 1884, Frost wrote a letter to the *Pall Mall Gazette* about American political economist Henry George, as the 'Hon. Secretary of the Land Reform Union' and giving the address as 30 Woburn Place, Frost's family home. One of the Union's main aims was to promote the ideas of their hero Henry George, but ironically, by the time arrangements had been made for him to undertake a lecture tour in England during early 1884, the pair had moved some distance from his ideas and were now closer to those of Karl Marx. Meetings were held at the Communist Club in Tottenham Street, a few doors from the Old Prince of Wales Theatre, in a disused harmonium factory that was home to several radical socialist organizations including the German Socialist Working Man's Club. A reporter from *The Morning Bulletin* described the scene:

'[W]e dive down a narrow brick passage next to a coal shed, cross a small dark yard dimly lit by one gas jet and enter a small lobby. A black bearded man puts his head through an opening and demands our business. We enter our names in a large book and hand the janitor one penny; he gives us a slip of paper which is our credential for the rest of the evening. The premises consisted of a long room with a bar, (unlicensed) about 60 feet long by 18 wide, there are billiard tables, two long dining tables, a kitchen and a skittle alley. The atmosphere is one of sausages, sauerkraut and odorous cheese, [and] a bell rings and we go upstairs and into another long low room with little interest attached to it but it is here that Percy Frost presided when his great friend ex-Captain Henry Hugh Champion delivered his first lecture in London. On the small square platform at the end had stood Liebknecht, Prince Kropotkin, Karl Marx and his daughter Eleanor with her husband Dr Aveling, William Morris, Charles Bradlaugh and many others prominent in the socialist and anarchist movement of that time. ... Its members are all skilled artisans who are receiving the highest wages, their intelligence is high and this is what makes them dangerous.'

In June 1883, Champion and Frost teamed up with J.L. Joynes in order to establish the first of several journals: *Christian Socialist, A Journal for Thoughtful Men*. Frost appealed to its readers to recruit lay churchmen who had been under the 'evil influence of the leaders of the church, saying that socialism was "catholic enough to embrace alike, Christian and Atheist'". The pair soon left the paper, but continued their work with the SDF. They were both now members of its executive council, and the first membership card Champion signed as honorary secretary was that of William Morris. Frost was also secretary of the agitation committee.

The inaugural issue of Federation paper *Justice* appeared on 19 January 1884, and to boost sales in its first year, the unsuspecting public in Fleet Street and the Strand were treated to the sight of Frost, Hyndman, Champion and even William Morris trying to sell copies, with limited success. Frost was a frequent contributor, and in August wrote an article entitled 'Prince & Peasant or round about a royal residence', in which he argued that the royal labourers were very poorly paid and had to walk 4 or 5 miles to and from work, which involved them starting out at 4.00 in the morning and not getting home until 8.00 at night, while their wage was as low as 10s per week.

According to later recollections by Champion, Frost was still living with his mother, who was in receipt of £3,000 a year, with Frost now receiving £800–£900 per year from a family trust. Despite this, it was reported in June 1883 that all his money had gone and he was facing bankruptcy. On Thursday 11 November the following year, Frost boarded the mail train from Euston to Glasgow to report on the troubles in Skye as a representative of the *Pall Mall Gazette* and, covertly for now, the Social-Democratic Federation.

Frost appeared in the Highlands a week or so before Annie, and by then had teamed up with Henry Paget, an artist who was on the staff of *The Illustrated London News* and whose brother, Sidney Paget, found fame illustrating the Sherlock Holmes stories in the *Strand* magazine. They arrived hoping to catch the ferry from Strome to Dunvegan, only to discover there was no daily steamer. They pleaded hard with Sheriff Ivory, who was at the head of the expedition, for a passage on one of the gunboats engaged in the crusade against the crofters. After a while, they talked him round and were invited to travel with him aboard the steamer *Lochiel*, which was transporting the constabulary, Procurator–Fiscal and Chief Constable. It seems that the sheriff had a weakness for seeing his name in the London press, and allowed himself to be moved by the thought of the two young journalists being cut off from reporting the action. No doubt hoping for flattering reports in the newspapers, he granted Frost and his friend a passage on his boat and they sailed for Dunvegan, much to the chagrin of local journalists, who were denied such favouritism and had to either wait until the ferry was running or follow Annie's route overland. The little fleet, consisting of the troopship *'Assistance'* and the gunboat *'Forester'*, as well as the *'Lochiel'*, made its way to a small jetty opposite Colbost and unloaded 100 Royal Marines in three boats, each man with forty rounds of ammunition, fifteen constables and assorted dignitaries.

Once off the boat, Frost congratulated himself on how he had 'wormed official secrets' out of Sheriff Ivory during the trip and how clever the two 'journalists' had been at playing a double role, being hand-in-glove with the sheriff in the evenings and pumping the man for information, while plying him with drinks and encouraging him to treat the local Scottish papers shabbily. This double-dealing lasted for nearly a week, during which time they followed the police and marines as they marched backwards and forwards across Skye, attracting more amusement and derision than fear from the few people they met along the way.

On Friday 21 November 1884, a big meeting of crofters was taking place which was to be addressed by John Macpherson himself, and the authorities had decided a show of strength by a large contingent of armed men from off the island was the best way to deal with the situation. Once assembled, they marched the 4 miles to Glendale, following the well-trodden, boulder-strewn path that had seen the humiliation of their colleagues in the recent past, and then down into the valley of Glendale itself. Among the waiting crowd was a party of local crofters who had just returned from a fishing trip to Kinsale in Ireland, where they had met people in a similar situation to themselves and learned from them about how to fight back.

The meeting, hastily gathered in the traditional way by the sound of horns, was about 700 strong and presided over by Macpherson. It had been planned to take place simultaneously with the march past of the troops. Macpherson addressed the large crowd, inveighing against misrepresentation in the press and declaring the rightness of their cause. He spoke against the *Inverness Chronicle* and *The Scotsman*, which he said had made no use of a statement of facts he had sent to them. He was dismissive of the force of marines and police that would, in a few minutes, pass them, and asked the crowd to be courageous and not afraid because they had never broken the law. He assured his audience that meetings would continue to be held and agitation persisted in, no matter how many policeman or marines the government might send, and then declared that Glendale and Skye men were as loyal as any within Great Britain. A crofter said that he thought the appearance of the warships might be a good thing as it would highlight a cause that they were prepared to die for. Reference was also made to a circular which had appeared in several newspapers, urging crofters to cut telegraph wires and commit similar outrages, but the speaker assured them that this was the concoction of some of the landlords' friends aiming to provoke violence.

With the assembled crowd intent on listening to what Macpherson – the Glendale Martyr – was saying, the redcoats were ignored, and the forces of law and order repaid the compliment in kind, with both sides going about their own business. The redcoats looked on in a rather bemused fashion while the officers congratulated each other on getting an opportunity for the men to stretch their legs, as a week had elapsed since they had been ordered from their barracks at Portsmouth – many having only recently returned from the Sudan. One report declared: 'No one spoke of the crofters. If you had asked one of these town bred tobacco chewing Englishmen what a crofter was, he would have given up the conundrum and asked you to put a simpler one.'

Several speeches were delivered and a resolution passed pledging the meeting to conduct agitation along constitutional lines until redress of the grievances complained of be obtained. As the meeting was nearing its end, Frost asked permission to address the crowd as a delegate of the Land Restoration League. The Martyr readily consented. Wearing a magenta (some say pink!) 'Tam o' Shanter', which 'beamed like a star in the crowd of men dressed in dark blue homespun', Frost outlined his ideas, which were later published in various reports in the local press:

> 'The proceedings were brought to a close by Mr RPB Frost[, a] delegate from the English Land Restoration League, in which he urged continued and persistent agitation within legal limits. He drew a comparison betwixt the rural poor and the poor at the east end of London, where he said, the families were herded together by the avarice of landlords without sufficient space to breathe. Into such places the rural population was being driven by the greed of landlords in the Highlands and he asked them legitimately to resist them. He censored Sir William Harcourt for having organised the present expedition at the instigation of prejudiced landlords and complained of the delay of the government in legislating on the Crofter's Commission report. During the time they were bickering about the franchise and looking for a cry to go to the country with.'

One section of his speech, however, shows the idea of shipping the crofters abroad was by no means agreed policy amongst the radicals at this time:

> 'And now about emigration. They were told that there were too many people in the island. (Cries of, "Not at all!" and cheers.) There were

17,000 people in the island and if they were allowed to cultivate these fertile glens instead of having them turned into preserves for game and sheep forms could it be maintained that they could not raise food for twice the number that was in the island at present? Not only did he say so but every skilled agriculturalist would say the same thing. If any should emigrate it should be those who took what the workers made and did not perform any sort of useful work for the community in return. It was the landlords and not the crofters who should be sent to Manitoba and they would have to do an honest day's work and would be better for it. He then proceeded to quote the commandments saying that the fifth commandment saying honour thy father and thy mother and thy days may be long in the land which the Lord thy God hath given thee. They were husbands and fathers and it was their solemn duty to obey that commandment and get back the land for themselves their wives and their children.

'He elicited a burst of applause when in answer to the argument that the crofters should have patience he said, "You have waited too long already; you have had too much patience."'

As Frost reached the climax of what was described in one paper as 'violent socialistic and seditious speech', the sheriff and the body of marines appeared, and Frost was at last seen in his true colours. Realizing how he had been tricked, Ivory 'gave vent to his feelings in a burst of un-parliamentary language'. Frost was equally mortified to realize that his cover had been blown and that he would lose his official patronage with all his access to the sheriff's plans and attendant jollifications. Unsurprisingly, they were not seen again in each other's presence. As the meeting separated, a considerable number of crofters attached themselves to the rear of the soldiery, following along in mock formation. Frost and his friends returned to Dunvegan, and shortly after 'a waggonette … containing 2 ladies and a gentleman' drew up at the Dunvegan Hotel. Mrs Gordon Baillie, the 'crofters' friend', had arrived.

When Annie and Frost met, there was an immediate attraction that was remarked upon by the other guests and they became, as it was phrased at the time, 'firm friends'. The attraction of Annie for Frost was obvious: a beautiful woman, rich, brave, intelligent and committed to the same cause as himself. For Annie, here was a very handsome man, ten years her junior, from a comfortable middle-class family with a good income and contacts in the Christian community – which she knew from her earlier interactions to be easy prey. He was idealistic and not terribly bright, a rebellious Christian Socialist, naïve and soon to become totally besotted with her, offering the distinct possibility of money, stability and even some fun along the way.

On the following Monday, the 24th, Annie attended another crofters' meeting prior to her interview with Macpherson. A contemporary sketch from *The Illustrated News* shows her addressing the crowd, during which she was subjected, as reports put it, 'to harangues delivered in a language of which she understood not a single syllable'. This is unlikely, as she was as conversant in the many forms of Scots as any of them, it even being said once that her mother could barely speak English. It is perhaps an illustration of how convincing her upper-class impersonations were. After the meeting they made their way to Milovaig, Macpherson's own township, to see for themselves the condition of the people. Macpherson had been informed that a Mrs Gordon Baillie, a friend of the crofters, was coming to see him, but he did not know who she was, so no special preparations had been made for her reception. He was tremendously impressed when he did meet her though, and he showed her around the crofters' houses and introduced her to two poor widows, to whom Annie gave gifts. The party then returned to Macpherson's cottage for tea, where she explained that she was going to set up a ladies' commission in London to send yarn to the Highland women to knit, and that the committee would then sell the articles, although nothing more would be heard of this scheme. The next day, Macpherson and several of his friends called on her at the Dunvegan Hotel and stayed with her until 11 o'clock.

Not long after this meeting, a further six policemen and twenty-five marines were landed at Dunvegan Castle, the *Forester* remained in Loch Dunvegan, and in the course of the afternoon the *Assistance* and *Lochiel* steamed around to Portree to await further orders. Small numbers of police officers were billeted at the main trouble spots throughout northern Skye, with the main force anchored in Portree Bay as reinforcements in case of serious trouble. However, there was to be no insurrection or 'Peterloo Massacre'. The crofters' leaders and Macpherson kept their heads and realized the futility of violence under such circumstances; and besides, the troops could not stay for ever.

With Annie's mission in the Glendale area completed, she returned to the hotel at Portree, turning heads as always, dressed in a brown tweed dress with a heavily furred and tight-fitting brown jacket to match. On her head was a Tam o' Shanter bonnet and she had a red tartan shawl across her shoulders, while her fingers had a profusion of rings and bangles. The little party kept to themselves, dined well and seemed to be involved in a literary venture. Amidst the rumours that circulated amongst the locals was that she was writing a novel, and there was curiosity around her lack of luggage, which only seemed to consist of one small case. During her time in the town, she made a few small purchases and ordered a quantity of cloth to be distributed amongst the poor. When the merchant suggested that he received payment before he sent the goods, she assured him it would be met as soon as the order was fulfilled – it probably goes without saying that he never saw a penny. They attended the local church on Sunday and invited the minister to dine – he was very taken with Annie and her intimate knowledge of the Highlands and its prominent people, whom she seemed to know intimately. Nobody asked about a Mr Gordon Baillie or questioned Percy Frost's frequent attendance.

Annie sat for dinner at the table with the other visitors in the evenings, and even joined the gentleman for their toddy afterwards, sometimes staying up with them until almost midnight. Frost, Annie and her party stayed on for a couple of days, enjoying each other's company. The landlord at Portree did not stint his charges but his large bill was settled handsomely, with Annie only questioning the charge for the upkeep of her horses, which she thought should have been included. Payment was by cheque, which was duly honoured. No doubt it was in her best interest at this juncture not to create a bad reputation for herself, hard though it must have been.

Chapter 16

Recollections
(Nov–Dec 1884)

To those newspapermen who had rushed across to Skye expecting to report on a bloody rebellion, the whole thing must have come as an anti-climax. They had to 'make copy' where they could – hanging around the Portree Hotel. One reporter, styling himself 'One Who has Met Her', would write an article for the *Peterhead Sentinel*, years after the event, in which he gave a detailed account of his impressions:

'Recollections of Mrs Gordon Baillie' by One Who Has Met Her

'It was at the close of November 1884 that I saw her for the first and last time. The "crofter rebellion" which for months had been keeping men's minds busy had just been suppressed. Two gunboats and a troopship had been for several weeks cruising about in Skye waters and six hundred marines were quartered at seditious spots all over the island. The excitement was over, the odd score of newspaper correspondents had with a few exceptions gone away, when one evening it went around the scribes that Mrs Gordon Baillie had sent a sword to John Macpherson the Glendale Martyr. Who she was nobody could tell. That she was a personage of some importance was by everyone taken for granted. That she was a woman of views and was a profound if eccentric sympathiser with the crofters was considered extremely probable from the fact that she had sent a weapon emblematic of heroic defence in a just and noble cause to the crofter leader.

'There was much mystery and absolutely no data to go on as to the woman's personality. All the same the Gordon Baillie (or as some of the reporters made it, Baillie-Gordon) sword story did duty as a three hundred word telegram when copy was getting scarce. The next three days were spent by the newspaper folks in a part of the island some twenty miles distant from their headquarters – Portree – and by the time of their return the much talked of Mrs Gordon Baillie had arrived and taken possession of the Portree Hotel where the press representatives had for three week been putting up. How comic in the light of recent disclosures do the events of that period appear now!

'Poor Donald the proprietor, a particularly "canny Hielanman" with a fine sense of the right side of a shilling, suave, saponaceous and sycophantish to swell travellers, went off his head in the presence of this gorgeous creature. At least we, his newspaper patrons thought so. When we came back after a weary pilgrimage to a far north disturbed township, our erstwhile dining place was held by the enemy. We couldn't have dinner and we were very hungry! Not for a couple of hours we were told, (we thought rather sharply and contemptuously after we had just paid a third large week's bill); they had been given no warning of our coming, else it would have been alright. With many muttered grumbles we were shuffled into an adjoining room where by the aid of a paraffin lamp we set about to write a number of press messages.

'There was but a wooden partition dividing the rooms and through a crack in one of the panels, I saw that our host, genial and soapy, had put his best foot foremost and was striving to regale his illustrious visitor right royally. Tall handsome paraffin lamps we had never seen before had been brought out and the tempered brilliance of their rays fell with a crimson glow on an elaborately spread table, where the snowy cloth, the glittering cutlery and the burnished dish covers vied with the gilt foil of champagne bottles and the prismatic reds and greens of the champagne glasses in making up a pleasing gastronomic picture, doubly pleasing to the eyes of a hungry man. Phew! What a turn up there was to be sure!

'"Lachie" the towzy haired Gaelic speaking waiter was temporarily deposed from office – he was deemed unpresentable before the magnificence of Mrs Gordon Baillie, this splendid lady all the way from London; the host and hostess did the serving themselves; and Lachie the reduced menial, fetched the soup and other viands from the kitchen but never crossed the door. Through the accommodating crack in the panel I could see Mrs Gordon Baillie at the top of the table flanked on the right by an irreproachably dressed young man, abounding in collar, of jet black hair and pasty face, – her private secretary, and on the left by a trim deferential looking creature who smiled skilfully to her cue between the spoonfuls of soup when anything funny was said, her lady's companion. Mine host through possible want of practice, was nervous, red and perspiring, but the meal passed off merrily. The lively chatter and the peals of laughter led always by the lady at the top of the table were incessant. And so we chaffed and waited, the tantalising clatter of knives and forks and the occasional popping of the champagne corks leading a fear to some profanity.

'Full two hours elapsed and we were fed in the little room all by ourselves. It was rather a scratch dinner, but with whetted appetites we were loath to complain of receiving literally the crumbs that fell from the rich man's table. Frequently I have thought with a smile within the last few days of the present imaginings of that desillusoine [*sic*] hotel keeper. Ach Gott, how we were all taken in and done for!

'Might I not write of the disorganisation into which the whole establishment was thrown during the visit of this peerless swell, of how the housemaid strove to catch sly peeps of her from the chinks of bedroom doors in the morning, how the host and hostess held daily Cabinet Council in the bar-parlour to present a diversified menu to please her dainty palette, how the district was requisitioned for tit-bits, how innocent, unoffending fowls were slain, how the best horses were kept ready in the stable to carry her precious person to scenes of misery among her much loved friends the suffering crofters – how in short no effort was spared to secure the goodwill and the distinguished patronage of this errant child of a nomadic Peterhead pork butcher and a Dundee washer wife? Portree is not a great centre of population, yet truly she "painted the town red".

'Three more days had gone and the remnant of the specials went with them. I was left alone, and was idling by the time in the hotel until the Saturday's steamer should arrive from Glasgow to take me to Stornoway. On the previous afternoon the thought struck me that for lack of a better matter I might get a column of copy out of Mrs Gordon Baillie by interviewing her. And so I did. There is no virtue at this time of day in adopting the "I told you so before" attitude. I frankly admit that I was sold, – utterly and completely sold. But I enter as a plea of defence that I am hoodwinked in good company. No one who aspires to a modicum of common sense cares to think of being befooled by an arch imposter, least of all when the schemer is a woman. I seek consolation in the knowledge that some other people not known as simpletons have believed that black was white, as taught by this feminine professor of the sustained sham. I am not sure even that I might not get lost in admiration at the success of the thing, as at the tricks of an accomplished necromancer and cry "Encore", "Bravo" [and] "You did that very well". Both afterwards and at the time I saw her I did have certain suspicions about her. She contradicted herself two or three times on minor details.

'She denied having ever sent the "Glendale Martyr" a sword and a letter. The letter appeared in print in a day or two. Mystery! She had come to Skye to find materials where with to write a book. Many months elapsed, (it was due in January) and it did not come off. Odd! She had four pretty "beybeys" with whom she was very very happy. But her husband, who or what was he? Didn't draw on this point. Lady's maid, later sounded on the same subject, smiled very sweetly and prevaricated. Singular to say the least! She was strong in what might be termed constructive theory, and her plausibility to quote the choice terminology of Professor Blackie, another victim, "would have deceived the Devil". Then the discrepancies in her speech would recur to one's mind, dwell there for a moment and vanish. It came to be a case of saying, "Oh, all these people know her; it's alright". She had a private secretary ergo she must be a real blue[-]blooded aristocrat; only such can afford a luxury like that. The papers now say she can't write. There was the triumph of the art. The completeness of the deception was helped by the excellence and appropriateness of the appointments.

'The disclosures of the past week have recalled to my mind several references made in conversation by this woman which seemed at the time I can remember to lack point or want explanation. The promised book on the crofter question, we know was never published: it is open to grave doubt if a page of it was ever written. On learning, however that I hailed from Aberdeen, this would[-]be novelist appeared struck with an idea. Could I by any means get her some information regarding a great storm that took place on the east coast some thirty or so years ago when a large number of fishermen lost their lives? This was of course to work into the coming volume. I undertook to try, and as a matter of fact sent her some clippings from an old newspaper file bearing on an event she referred to. In this connection she mentioned the name of the Buchan district on the coast of which she gave me to understand the disaster had occurred.

'Did she know that district at all? I asked her. "Slightly – Yes" (chewing the end of a long newly sharpened lead pencil she held in one hand while in the other she held an open book). She knew some friends in Peterhead once but it was long ago. The newspaper clippings were sent in due course from Aberdeen to the address she gave in the hotel, No.4 Bryanston Street, Portman Square, W. I offered to take a note of the name in a pocket book. "No, no; see here" she said and going rapidly to a[n] escritoire at which her lady companion was engaged, she took a sheet of her own notepaper and handed it to me. It looks a small matter but even the stationary used by this woman was suggestive of wealth and of luxurious comfort. It was of the highest quality of handmade note, thick, ribbed and of the antique pattern with frayed uncut edges, the latest freak of the aesthetic fad. At the top of the page above the address was the crest *"Fuimus"* (We Have Been) suggesting to the confiding mind a long line of pedigreed ancestry and the coursing through her veins, if you like, of the blood of a hundred earls. Again I say look at the get up of the article and cease speculating at the silliness of this woman's dupes.

'In the spring of 1885 came a letter to my address with a big portentous envelope and the *Fuimus* crest on the back of it. It was from Mrs Gordon Baillie's private secretary and expressed her thanks for the newspaper cuttings. She was so sorry that owing to her presence in Paris she had not sooner acknowledged the cuttings which she had only got on her return to London. The letter wound up with a very cordial invitation to call on her next time I came to town. Accompanying the note was what purported to be a Christmas card on which were printed some very twaddling verses dedicated to "My Paddy". The card was also illuminated with cupids.

'About the same time the editor of a Highland newspaper showed me a typewritten letter he had received, the author of which, dating from Dublin and signing himself Elihu K. Dielman banteringly twitted my editorial friend with having published an account of Mrs Gordon Baillie's appearances to which the writer was prepared to take some exception. Mr Dielman also explained that Mrs Gordon Baillie was well known in certain circles of Dublin society. I mention the circumstances apropos of the announcement made in the Scotsman's account of our heroine's adventures that one Mr Lee Toler, an Irish barrister, admitted having supplied her with money to the tune of something like £5,000. I leave the point for those to make something of who have the detective instinct strongly developed.

'One other point and I have done. The Mr RPB Frost who is referred to in the "Scotsman" account as the Mr Mathews who accompanied Mrs Gordon Baillie to Melbourne turned up in Skye almost simultaneously with herself. This man was peculiar. A young man of 28–30 years of age and conspicuous by a big black moustache, a pink Tam o' Shanter, and a long Ulster cloak, he came there as the apostle of advanced Radicalism to preach that doctrine to the crofters. Well educated, fluent of speech, self-possessed, and of good address he impressed one in after[-]dinner talks over pipes and liquid refreshment as a type of the professional agitator or platform spouter, cram-full of argument, fallacious or other, where with to demolish political adversaries. In brief he was "Trafalgar

Squarish". During his stay in the island it was noticed that he and Mrs Gordon Baillie became mutually attracted to each other. This was made the subject of some good humoured chaff on the part of Mr Frost's colleagues, who bantered him on his audacity and the success with which he ingratiated himself with the distinguished London lady. These two persons, for the past four years at all events, have been acting in pretty close concert, with what object in view readers can judge for themselves.

'Looking back upon it all now how strange it all seems! Another illustration that truth is stranger than fiction! Several times within the past few days I have felt inclined to tap my forehead as the railway guard taps with a hammer the wheels of the cars after a hundred mile run – just to see if they are quite sound, you know, and no cracks. This shock to one's judgement is horribly unsettling.

'Mrs Gordon Baillie will now go under. The evil star of her histrionic genius (for I believe it was more that than anything else that carried her through) has passed its zenith and has sunk under a cloud from which again it will never emerge. The lessons of her history must make the cynic more cynical, and make us pin our faith to the Philistine proverb, "There's nothing succeeds like success."'

It was on this same visit, a day or so later, on Monday 1 December 1884, that Annie was interviewed at Portree by a special correspondent of the *Aberdeen Press & Journal*. She was described in appreciative detail by its reporter, who was at pains to give details of her appearance and offer some insight into her interest in the crofters:

"Although I belong to, and have been reared among the aristocracy, my sympathies are not with them. I think they have been guilty in too many cases of very great injustice."

'These are the sentiments of Mrs Gordon Baillie a literary lady who has left her mansion in Bryanston Street, Portman Square, London, and has journeyed by quick stages to Skye, to see there with her own eyes the attitude of this dissension[-]racked island, and to weave her impressions into a novel.

'The Skye crofter has recently become the object of the attentions on the part of all kinds of people who regard him as fair game out of which political and social capital may be made. His grievances and wrongs are the fulcrum on which astute propagandists see an opportunity for applying the lever which their power controls, and the resistance to which are the rights of property as recognised by law. And so it is that while some see in the Skye crisis the kernel of a social revolution which may yet grow into a hard nut for some prospective government to crack, others there are who are content to take advantage of the passing storm and make the story of the crofter's daily life the theme of a new book.

'It is a rather odd thing to encounter a woman of fashion in the wilds of this West Highland region, among mud huts, peat bogs, shepherds' cabins, poverty and wretchedness – made more wretched by the dreariness of December – one who has forsaken the haunts of London gaiety even for a few weeks only and who prefers spending a night in a crofter's hut to a "small and early" in a fashionable square and long bleak drives across desolate[-]looking country by night to a night at the opera. Yet so it is. Mrs Gordon Baillie has, she says, profound sympathy with the crofters and the reasons for her coming to Skye are hinted at in the lines just written and in the opening sentences of this letter.

'It was my fortune to meet her in the coffee room of a hotel in the island, where along with a lady companion and a private secretary* she had just put up after returning from Glendale. There she had been visiting the famous John Macpherson and hearing from the lips of him and his fellow crofters a recital of the grievances of which they complain.

'A fine woman! Young, of prepossessing appear, her features yet bore the stamp of mature womanhood. Her lissom figure has just reached that period in life when it begins to show a tendency towards embonpoint. Today its lines are revealed to perfection beneath a crimson dressing-gown the skirt of which is fringed at the foot with point lace. Red silk stockings and natty high[-]heeled shoes with steel buckles complete a toilet as simple as it is effective. The fourth and fifth fingers of her right hand were encrusted with jewelled rings, the gems in which sparkled and gleamed in the firelight as dusk fell and the single bangle on her right wrist played upwards and downwards on a plump and well-turned arm, which a little below the elbow, was framed in the same lace setting as the skirt of the dress.

'Large brown sanguine eyes beamed lustrously from beneath a profusion of fair hair falling in curls over her forehead – eyes that are penetrative and keen for a moment till they have got something to fasten on that amuses the fancy when instantly the corners pucker and a burst of merry laughter is the result. Then they retire to repose in their lair to watch again for their prey. Full neck, delicate chin, sharp

---

* Tom Russell, see Dundee Evening Telegraph 5 March 1888.

The Roanheads, Peterhead. (*From an old postcard*)

Flying Gig Wynd, Peterhead. (*Peterhead town website*)

Peterhead Fish Workers. (*© Gorman family archive, cc-by-sa/2.0*)

The Sherriff Court, Dundee. (*© Bill Nicholls, cc-by-sa/2.0*)

Knight Aston in Boccaccio.
(*From an old print*)

Easter Moniack. (© *Craig Wallace, cc-by-sa/2.0*)

A Phaeton carriage, suitable for a little shopping. (*From an old print*)

Emily Soldene. (*Creative Commons Licence*)

The Isle of Skye. (*Reproduced with permission from the National Library of Scotland*)

Annie addresses the Crofters meeting, November 1884. (*From an old print*)

Annie the time of the 1884 Glendale
Disturbances. (*From an old print*)

The Glendale Martyr. (*From an old photograph*)

John Blackie in around 1870. (*From an old
photograph, Creative Commons*)

Annie in Highland dress, 1880s. (*Wyndham,
published 1929*)

Annie as an Athenian lady at the Prince's Ball, 1885. (*Sketch by Johnson, 1885*)

The 'Heraldic Window' being delivered. (*Cardiff Times*, 1888)

Joseph Bebro, aka Harry Benson, aka Handsome Harry. (*From a contemporary sketch*)

Annie, from a photograph taken in 1887. (*R. Stanley & Co., London*)

Calton Jail, where the crofter women were imprisoned. (*From an old print*)

Detective Inspector Henry Marshall. (*From a courtroom sketch*)

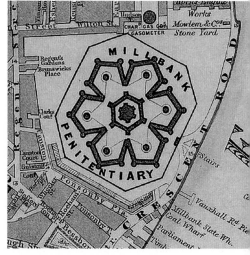

Millbank Prison on the Thames. (*From an old print*)

Fulham Women's Refuge in 1858. (*From an old print*)

17 Talbot Road, North Kensington. (*Author's collection*)

Annie as she appeared in the dock in New York, 1902. (*From a contemporary newspaper*)

Blackwell's Island, New York. (*From an old print, Wikipedia*)

Knight Aston in 1889. (*From a contemporary sketch*)

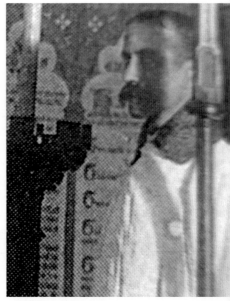

Percy Frost in Italy in the 1920s. (*The only known photograph*)

nose and arched mobile eyebrows complete a countenance the features of which are set in a tawny brown skin indicative of perfect health, the effect in colour being heightened by two pink spots on the cheeks just beneath the cheek bone. The majestic sweep of the yard or so of flowing robe that falls in graceful curves behind the buckled shoe nervously patting the fender, the elbow resting on the marble mantelshelf and supporting the head which is thrown a little to one side, contribute to a pose suggesting, perhaps the unconscious attitudinising of an actress of the stage.

'The shrug of the shoulders and the occasional gleeful child-like clapping of the hands when her sense of humour is touched help to deepen this impression but it wears off during the course of conversation in which strong sympathies and much womanly instinct are betrayed.

'"You represent a Conservative Journal?" She asks rapidly, and apparently jumping to the conclusion that I carry a revolver in my pocket wherewith to kill a crofter.

'"Well more pity for you; all the same we will give you some refreshment." And she fills a glass with refreshment from a decanter on the table.

'"Yes I have come from London to see the crofters in their homes. I am sincerely sorry for them and I'd do anything in my power to help them, but I cannot so what's to be done? I am a woman and not a politician and I cannot see here this business is to end. But this I know, if this crisis continues to grow, and if the landlords press for evictions, there will be bloodshed before 6 months are over."

'"Why do you think so?"

'"Because I have seen enough to make me believe it. I have been in the crofters' houses in Glendale and have studied the demeanour of the inmates and know that they are desperate. I have asked them, supposing you were threatened with eviction?

'"We will fight!" they answered eagerly. "The military cannot remain here for ever and when they leave things will go from bad to worse. I have asked Macpherson what he'd do if he were to be turned out of his house for the part he has taken in this agitation."

'"I'll defend my home even though (pointing to the grate in the fire place) I'll tear that out and use it as a weapon."   -

'"And I believe they are in earnest.

'"What do I think of John Macpherson?

'"John Macpherson is a man who if he had had an education would have made a great statesman, a man with a splendid looking head and of great wisdom; his character and style are reflected in his house. It is unlike the other crofters' houses by which it is surrounded. The little sitting room with the illustrated paper prints on the wall has a wooden floor not like the other miserable hovels I was in where the floor was earthen and upon wet days gets into a state of mud. Why don't these people poor as they are do something to improve the interior of their dwellings!"

'Mrs Baillie tackled but did not solve the problem of the crofters' *vis inertae*.

"'No. My object in coming to Skye is not so much a political one. I want to work the story of the crofter's grievances into a novel. Macpherson would not do altogether for a hero. I am to utilise the story of the big spate of 1877 when the churchyard was washed away and the mansion house at Uig was wrecked by the flood as the basis to workup on. Then I am to bring in the idea that this was an act of Divine providence directed against landlordism – the light in which it was regarded by all the crofters in the island. I shall give lights and shadows to the crofters' life interspersed of course with bits of narrative and description; but the leading theme of the book will be that of a visitation of Providence coming upon the island."*

'In answer to my query as to whether she knew Gaelic, Mrs Baillie said that she was a Scotch woman born in Oban, she understood the language but could not speak it. Nobody, she admitted who did not know Gaelic could understand the tone and catch the spirit of the life of the Celt, and make any book dealing with his habits a success.

"'I hope," she continued, "to help in the averting of public attention on this question and I am confident that it has almost come to a head."

"'Have you observed," she asked after a while, "that I am represented in the newspapers as having sent a sword to John Macpherson?"

'I answered that I had.

"'Well then," she resumed with some animation, "I wish you to give it a public contradiction. The idea! I should like to know why I should give a sword to John Macpherson. I'd sooner think of giving him 5 pounds."

"'But a holograph letter accompanied the sword," I ventured to observe.

---

* This very same story is told in the Aberdeen Press & Journal for 24 November 1884 – she may well have had it open before her as she explained the plot of her novel.

"'Yes indeed I saw the letter," she went on. "It is an illiterate, vulgar piece of work and it is anonymous. As if (contemptuously) a lady would send a letter of that kind.

"'Are you aware that your movements are being observed by the public authorities in Skye?" I asked again

"'My movements? No. Why should they?"

"'You have been credited with sending a sword to the leader of the revolt in Skye, accompanied by a highly inflammatory letter, and you have been associated for the past few days in Glendale with a Land League emissary who has been delivering speeches on behalf of his association to the crofters."

'And here Mrs Gordon Baillie's sense of the ridiculous completely got the better of her. She laughed consumedly at the situation and spoke gleefully of the entertainment she would provide by the recital of this experience to her friends in London on her return from Skye.

'Then, the conversation languishing, the novelist of the Skye crofters placed on the dining table a two-shilling edition of *My Heart's in the Highlands* which she had held open in her hand during the interview and after the usual courtesies I withdrew. Odd isn't it to find such a one as the lady I have been describing seeking in the mud huts of the crofters the raw material where with to make a book. It's another phase of the late rebellion.'

The provenance of the sword remained a puzzle for some time. It was sent to John Macpherson at Glendale with a note dated 11 November 1884, which read:

'Dear Sir, Will you kindly accept the accompanying sword which belonged to my grandfather, as a small mark of a lady sympathiser's interests in your gallant struggle against the oppressors of the people. At present the tyrants rule in Skye and are able to put the machinery of iniquitous laws in force against the people; but if the people are united tyrants shall not very long rule or even live in Skye or in the Highlands. I send you this sword for defence not defiance – in defence of home and family. It is the duty of every Celt to struggle even unto death. God bless your cause and give you all the strength and wisdom in fighting the battle of freedom to live in your beautiful island. All England watches your struggle against tyrant factors and hard-hearted landlords. Good speed the cause,

'Yours sincerely, AN ENGLISH WOMAN.'

Annie was telling the truth this time, though, in denying being the sender. Despite all her aliases and deceptions, the very last thing she would ever call herself was an *English* woman! She was accompanied to Skye by her secretary, Tom Russell, who states quite clearly that 'we visited John Macpherson's house and saw at that time the notable sword, [and] it is untrue to say as the *Times* states that Mrs Gordon Baillie presented it. The statement was made at the time by the Scotch press and contradicted promptly. I saw the letter accompanying the sword and know that it was not Mrs Baillie's.' The matter was finally put to rest by Macpherson himself in an interview with the *Edinburgh Evening Despatch*. He had asked Annie about it when they met, and she denied having sent it but said that she wished she had! He subsequently met the true donor in London, a woman of wealth and respectability, who said the sword had been presented to her grandfather by Wellington after the Battle of Waterloo.

Sometime later, Macpherson had occasion to visit London and invited Mrs Gordon Baillie to his hotel. She arrived, accompanied by two of her daughters, and invited him and his friends to her house to have tea with her. When he enquired as to the master of the house, she replied that he was in Australia. When interviewed about her after her exposure in the press, the Glendale Martyr replied that she would be welcome to share his teapot at any time!

Chapter 17

The Crofters' Friend
(Jan 1885–Apr 1886)

At around the beginning of 1885, Annie's public position was that of an aristocratic lady keen to help the crofters' plight who was engaged in writing a novel to help their cause. Arrangements had been made, she claimed, with publishers in Edinburgh and London, and her first-hand experience of the situation was going to prove invaluable. She was, after all, the first to propose to John Macpherson that his cause might be furthered by airing it in London. There were notices in the press proclaiming the work's forthcoming publication, but no publisher was named. What became of the fabled novel, or if it was ever seriously contemplated, is not known. However, she was still talking about it in New Zealand in March 1885, when she claimed the *Illustrated London News*' special artist in Skye, Henry Paget, was going to illustrate it. This was probably merely a cover story to spy out the land, with a view to collecting money on behalf of the crofters and herself.

Annie's agitation around the crofters' cause soon resulted in her becoming known as 'The Crofters' Friend', but as always there is the question over whether she was genuinely moved by their plight or whether she was playing the long game and her whole campaign was a scam from the start. Tom Russell acted as her secretary from September 1884 until August 1886 – when she was preparing to leave for Australia – and accompanied her to Skye in November 1884. He later said in an interview that she gave £70 to the Highland Crofters Defence Fund as soon as she returned to London and the money was handed to Donald Murray, Honorary Secretary of the Highland Land League, who would also vouch for the fact. For this service, she was presented with an 'address' in September 1885, on the occasion of one of the Skye demonstrations, signed by Fraser Mackintosh MP, Donald Macfarlane MP and the Scottish folklorist and barrister Stuart Glennie, amongst others. 'No doubt she was keen to advertise herself but this is common in politics and she undoubtedly helped the crofter cause,' continued her former secretary.

Writing in March 1888, from the office of the *Dramatic Review*, Russell added that Annie was known throughout Staffordshire for her charities and he could prove the truth of all he said about her in his article. As her secretary for almost two years, and therefore privy to her day-to-day activities, it is interesting that he remained loyal, despite all the later allegations in the press – presumably at some risk to his own reputation.

Annie's early involvement with the crofters led her to support them staying on the island and fighting for better conditions from the landlords, which resulted in a comment piece in the *Yorkshire Post* in February 1885 which stated:

> 'It is a pity that Mrs Gordon Baillie should go to such trouble to discourage the emigration of the Skye crofters. If she can say nothing in favour of the scheme, why hinder others who are trying to benefit the half[-]starving Highlanders and their families? No one outside a lunatic asylum can deny that a crofter would have a better chance of getting on either in New Zealand or Canada than his rocky solitude at home. Canada contains tens of thousands of people descended from emigrants from the Highlands 50 or 60 years ago and who live a comparatively comfortable and prosperous existence, [and] one would like to see any who would return from Canada or the Highlands if they had a chance. Mrs GB is no doubt prepared to do something for the crofters but she is defeating her own objects by opposing the emigration of men who would have starved even if they had small farms of their own.'

She was soon to change her mind on the question, however, although the reasons for this are open to debate, as we shall see.

Percy Frost had travelled to Scotland as both a correspondent of the *Pall Mall Gazette* and a representative of the Land League/SDF, and as we have already seen, during those three weeks away he became very attached to Annie and his attentions were gradually transferred from the public area to the private. As things blossomed in his private life, not all was well on the political front. Perhaps inevitably, a small organization like the SDF, containing such huge and differing personalities, would not hold together for long. Many saw its leader Hyndman as an overbearing dictator whose belief in democracy did not extend to his own party. More than that, the group had divided into two major ideological factions and at the beginning of 1885, William Morris and eight other members resigned from the SDF committee. Annie was present at at least one lecture by Hyndman, and the impression she made was not a favourable one, as he records in his autobiography, *The Record of an Adventurous Life*:

'Frost, another of the Christian Socialist trio, fell under the influence of an extraordinary adventuress who called herself Mrs Gordon Baillie, and unfortunately, owing to her influence, got into all sorts of mischief which ended very badly indeed. I have always partly blamed myself for this ending. Though Mrs Baillie was a very fine-looking woman, I took a great dislike to her from the first, and when she laughed cheerfully at a phrase from a French writer I used in an address I delivered on the French Revolution, to the effect that the Count de Charolais had *ensanglanté la débau*che (had bloodied debauchery), I told Frost she was a very dangerous woman for him to consort with. I had far better have held my tongue. Opposition only made Frost more eager, and off he went with her.'

Personality clashes aside, the Morris faction took a revolutionary Marxist position, while Hyndman, Frost and Champion took the view that change could be achieved by electoral or parliamentary means. With Morris gone, Federation organ *Justice* lost a large part of its financial support and was losing about £10 a week. It was now managed by Champion and Frost, who, being gluttons for punishment, involved themselves in another journal, *To-day, The Monthly Magazine of Scientific Socialism*. Its issue of January 1885 contained a long article by Frost on his trip to the Highlands. Despite his other preoccupations, Frost continued with some activities and on 16 February 1885 he and Hyndman addressed a meeting called by the SDF, of which he was still a council member, from the base of Cleopatra's Needle. They were calling for an eight-hour day and the building of blocks of artisans' cottages, libraries and proper drainage. A procession was formed which marched to the Local Government Board Office, where a deputation was received by G.W. Russell on behalf of Sir Charles Dilke.

Apart from the problems in the Highlands, Annie was experiencing difficulties closer to home. In a formal break with her past, on 25 March 1885 she changed her name by deed poll from Annie Whyte to Annie Gordon Baillie, signifying a final split with Aston, as well as legitimizing a name she had been using for a couple of years, and by which she was becoming increasingly known to the public at large. That same year, Sir Richard King was judged senile by his staff and relatives, who had now seen enough of his fortune slip away and began to consider steps to safeguard their inheritance.

The early stages of the romance between Annie and Frost are not known in detail, but things seem to have moved pretty swiftly, and shortly after their return from Scotland, Frost moved in with her and the children at 4 Bryanston Street, Westminster. This was a magnificent London house owned by two unsuspecting maiden ladies and paid for, in theory, by Sir Richard King. It is not known when, or even if, Frost introduced Annie to Champion, but given the close friendship between the two men she must have at least been discussed at some time during the early stages. Champion was descended from the Scottish aristocracy: his forbears were the Urquharts, one of the oldest families in northern Scotland, and so if he chose to, he could have seen through Annie's pretentions towards that class straight away. Possibly he kept quiet out of respect to his friend, believing no harm would come of it – or possibly he was as taken in as everyone else.

The crofters aside, day-to-day business still had to be attended to. On 7 May 1885, Annie opened an account with the banking company Herries Farquhar & Co. of St James Street, and within the same twenty-four hours she opened another with Percy Frost's bank, Messrs Smith, Payne and Smith, of Lombard Street. Whether these were connected to the deal with Bebro *et al*, which will be considered shortly, or merely her normal run-of-the-mill frauds, is a matter for speculation.

On Tuesday 19 May 1885, the Royal Institute of Painters in Watercolours held a Costume Ball at Prince's Hall, Piccadilly. All guests were requested to appear in period dress, prior to 1837, and Annie attended in Grecian costume as an 'Athenian Lady'. The *Illustrated London News* enjoyed the event very much, reporting that 'it was quite an exceptionally picturesque gathering of gaily and quaintly costumed guests that met the view of their Royal Highnesses the Prince and Princess of Wales when they arrived at the hall … trumpeters blew a blast and the crimson[-]coated company of halberdiers presented arms. The *tableaux vivants* of the Old Masters undeniably merited the general tribute of admiration they at once secured. They were perfect in their way and presented living pictures of the most famous artists of their times prepared with absolute historical accuracy under the sedulous supervision of a number of the most distinguished members of the institute.' Annie must have been in her element, a play within a play, standing amongst the finest artists of the time, with the royal party staying until the small hours; a washerwoman's daughter who hailed from the slums of Peterhead but pretending to be a Scottish aristocrat, dressed in the guise of an Athenian noblewoman.

As was her custom, Annie kept another property at the same time as the house in London, and in June 1885 she spent some 'quiet' time on the Isle of Wight, along with her four children. While there, she was visited by a journalist from *Society* magazine, which in their issue for 6 June 1885 published an article with her portrait and stated that 'the stranger who calls upon Mrs Baillie, either in London or the Isle of Wight cannot fail to be struck by the great womanliness of her nature as she sees her always accompanied by her three pretty girls one of whom has already figured on a Royal Academician's canvas, (Mr Millais)'. This picture, 'Cherry Ripe', was painted in 1879 when her eldest daughter Gabrielle would have been about 2 years old. The child in the painting is much older, possibly about 7, and depicts Edie Ramage, the niece of the editor of *The Graphic* journal. Annie had, of course, heard the comparison made before, but thought it wise to smile sweetly and say nothing. Gabrielle was thought to bear a remarkable likeness to the picture as she grew older.

At the end of July 1885, a legacy of Annie's theatrical adventures came back to haunt her. On the penultimate day of the month, at the Bristol summer assizes, author Rennie Palgrave claimed £50 owed for a manuscript of his play *Shadow and Sunshine*. During the trial, Palgrave claimed that he had been introduced to Mrs Gordon Baillie as the manageress of a London theatrical company via Mr Tait and Mr Poole, and had gone to London in November the previous year to meet her, taking the manuscript with him. He read the script to her, which she enjoyed very much, and they discussed terms. He asked for 100 guineas on delivery of the manuscript and 5 per cent of the takings. Her reply was that she had purchased several other works – some of considerable popularity – for lesser amounts, and so after haggling, Palgrave claimed it had been agreed she would pay £50 for exclusive rights to produce the play plus 2.5 per cent of the gross takings. Annie asked that the contract be drawn up, but that it should omit the agreed price as she did not wish Mr Tait to know what the terms were and have to pay him commission.

In response, Annie claimed that the deal had been for £50 for the rights to produce *Shadow and Sunshine* in the colonies, where her husband – Knight Aston – was performing at the time. When she received the manuscript and contract, she found that Palgrave had included a clause agreeing to pay an additional 2.5 per cent of the takings, totalling 5 per cent, which had not been part of the original deal. She did not sign and the play was not produced. When the two met once more, Palgrave expressed his disappointment at her not accepting the terms and offered her another play instead, but on the same terms. Annie rejected his offer but paid him £10 for his travel expenses. The judge found in Palgrave's favour, without giving his reasons, and the manuscript was returned. As an aside, the playwright himself was no stranger to adopting a pseudonym; indeed Palgrave was one, as writing under his real name of George Rennie Powell he published a history of the Bristol Stage in 1919. He was listed as an 'author and journalist' in the 1901 census, and seems also to have been a Registrar of Births, Marriages and Deaths in Bristol.

On 30 July 1885, The Land Reform League conference ended at Portree with a procession of 3,000 people. Annie was unable to attend, but sent a note explaining that: 'Domestic matters prevent my being at the conference today which I deeply regret. Keep the agitation firm and strong – with one end in view – Liberty for the Highlands – and fear not that the Defence Fund will lack friends.'

There followed a big meeting, held in the local park, during which the speakers, many in Gaelic, put their faith in electing the appropriate candidates to Parliament and praised the efforts of Gladstone in Ireland. Several resolutions were adopted by the meeting: the landlords were charged with oppressing the Highland people with unjust laws and a Royal Commission was called for to enquire into the whole subject of the crofter situation. Meanwhile, the agitation and rent strikes would continue.

Frost was experiencing conflict between his public and increasingly complex personal life. He was now 26 and it can be assumed his experience of the opposite sex was slight, and the effect Annie had had upon him so far must have been immense, with any attempt to juggle the two wildly contradictory aspects of his life doomed to failure. At the annual conference in August, he resigned from the SDF's executive council. Champion too withdrew from full-time involvement; his support for the cause, via its various publications, was taking its toll upon his publishing business and his financial affairs required more attention.

As long anticipated, on 20 February 1886, Sir Richard Duckworth King's relatives met their solicitors, Dawes & Son of Angel Court, and filed a petition of bankruptcy on his behalf. This was undertaken in order to find out the extent of his liabilities. The result astonished everyone, as they consisted almost entirely of bills stretching into the thousands – many drawn by Mrs Gordon Baillie, whom the court now wanted to question. Trustees took charge of the 82-year-old's estate and put him in the care of a doctor. One of Sir Richard's servants, interviewed after his death in November 1887, made the following comments:

'My master was 82[,] hale in body but quite deaf with no memory or mental powers at all. He took a great fancy to White and kept her in Bryanston Street till 1886. During that time, though told all about her and shown pictures of her in prison dress she got nearly £18,000 out of him. At last this large sum greatly alarmed the family and as claims poured in on all sides Sir Richard's estate was put into a receiver's hands, all claims met and Sir Richard put under a doctor's charge who never lost sight of him until he died. He was the kindest master and most respected of men, (as anyone in Mayfair will tell you) who until his brain went and he got amongst this gang, gave two thirds of his money to his numerous poor relatives and the distressed of the district. Then after our bust-up in February things seemed to be looking up. Mrs White moved to a fine house in Upper Brook Street but last year [1887] bills were posted about the sale of furniture so [we] suppose she has left. Nothing more is heard about these 2 ladies till Sir Richard died in October [1887] when White-Gordon Baillie claimed to be left everything absolutely. We have all been many years with Sir Richard, one of us nearly 50, [and] by the proper will we were all well provided for, some left sums down, some annuities; now these harpies have got nearly everything, all the old servants will have to do is starve or go into the workhouse.'

In all probability, the other of the 'two ladies' was Amelia Hill, the estranged wife of John Sylvanus Tanner, at one time Sir Richard's 'confidential agent' and later convicted of fraud. King was the biological father of her child and there were numerous payments into her account in support. Despite this considerable setback, not all were against Annie. An article in the *Court & Society Review* during May of that year overflowed with praise and gave the following details, accompanied by an attractive sketch:

'Mrs Gordon Baillie is a Highlander, a fine daughter of a generous race. She possesses in large proportion the love of country, poetical fervour and warm temper which are her birth right. When things looked black and troubles threatened Skye she visited the crofters in the depths of northern winter and used all her great influence in the cause of order. Although a staunch Tory [she was of course claiming marriage to one of the leaders of the SDF, a socialist revolutionary at this time!], she paid for the defence of the crofters, alleging as reason that the cause of Conservatism and the cause of justice were identical. On the other hand she warmly even bitterly reproached those popular leaders who preached "the cause of the people" in piled inflammatory adjectives. In consequence she is respected by both sides of the quarrel yet never earned that much-dreaded Highland ban, "the curse of neutrality". Moreover in her Midland county as well as in Skye many a one is thankful for the existence of Mrs Gordon Baillie, her appearance is striking, reminding one pleasantly of Sir Walter Scott's Helen Macgregor.

'Her bust and build may be styled Flaxmanesque and her power of dress is amazing. A Highlander not a poet is as rare as an Irishman not a politician. She has not only written much dainty society verse but has largely translated from her favourite Italian literature. Her Scotch lyrics are, however[,] her happiest efforts, some are very quaint, containing the old vigour and heather ascent so noticeable in ballads of the north country. Added to all this, Mrs Baillie has proved herself a competent journalist and even now is a regular "lady correspondent" to many American journals. Had she but the incentive of necessity to spur her on, very fine results might safely be prophesised.'

Before the cash finally ceased to flow, probably early in 1886, Annie managed to persuade King to rent a new country residence for her: Barton Hall at Barton Under Needwood, Trent, in Staffordshire. This was a modest Georgian red brick country house where she lived as Mrs Gordon Baillie and passed as a lady of means. Percy Frost co-habited there, but for most of the time she explained him away as a relative.

According to 'A Country Squire' writing to the *Pall Mall Gazette* in March 1888:

'She kept a full household, a capital stable of horses, entertained the children of the parish on the lawn before the house and spent money most liberally. She then had three beautiful, well behaved children. She spent £200 over the freehold of the house, gave £95 cash down for a horse she fancied and then having thrown away large sums left a number of paltry debts unpaid. At the time Frost was living with her as her "cousin".

'She appears to have a liking for livestock, for there was a chestnut horse named Sultan, a mare called Janet, and a pony Taffy and six others, a goat, four pigs, three turkeys, twenty-eight ducks, and 180 fowls; she used to advertise, as a lady of title, for young ladies fond of hunting and a country life to come and live with her. One essential element in the terms was the payment of £100 in advance—and their stay was quite of a temporary character. Altogether this lady's adventures provide incidents enough to more than make one of the most sensational novels of the day.'

In August 1886 she gave a school picnic to Catholic and Protestant children of the vicinity, entirely at her own expense, while clergymen of both persuasions were constant visitors to the house. As usual, such extravagance was unsustainable, and Barton Hall had to go. Towards the end of September, the furniture and contents were auctioned off in a three-day sale by John L. Knight 'on account of the owner going abroad'. The furniture was described as 'chiefly antique and collected with great taste and care', with many of the carpets coming from Cairo. There were paintings by Sir Peter Lely, Sir Thomas Lawrence, George Moreland, Constable and Correggio, along with an impressive china collection that included Dresden, Lowestoft and Oriental ware, while outside there were horses, ponies, cows, pigs and fine carriages. The house was to be re-let on application to the auctioneer. All the old ladies and gossipmongers of the neighbourhood had left their calling cards seeking invitations, as very few had seen the interior of the house. They now took the opportunity and crowded in to see it taken apart. Despite the claims of the 'Country Squire', it is unlikely that the place was purchased by Sir Richard and it was probably leased. Sir Richard Duckworth King was declared bankrupt on 21 October 1886, but the Court of Bankruptcy soon approved a scheme whereby his bills were met, and the order was shortly after rescinded.

Tom Russell, who had been Annie's secretary during her time at Barton Hall and, as noted earlier, remained loyal to the last, had this to say of his former employer:

'It was untrue that she was unable to write. Her writing was rather illegible and her spelling faulty but it was strong and very characteristic of the woman. People who, accepting what has been written against her think her altogether bad are very wide of the mark. She was in many ways a most generous woman and made few if any enemies – barring creditors. Most people who met her liked her exceedingly, especially domestics. She had great spirit and dash, wonderful nerve and power of resource with the constitution of a Zulu. In some respects she was the canny Lowlander while in others the mad Highlander showed conspicuously. One would say of her that early in life her prospects had been irretrievably blighted by some act or deed perhaps not her own, and despairing of success by legitimate means she made a raid on Society after the old border fashion, dashing for fortune or failure how she could at anyone's expense. If she be a washerwoman's daughter she does not look it, and in respect of her good qualities of spirit and generosity, that washerwoman ought to be proud of her. One likes to believe that she tried to live well but failed, perhaps from hurry, to succeed.'

Meanwhile, Annie had experienced a seismic shift within her ideas for the crofters. Rather than stay and fight the landlords for their cold, miserable and windy crofts, she decided a greater future was possible for them overseas, in the wide-open spaces of New Zealand and Australia. Her fertile brain was hatching a plan which if successful would mean that she, and possibly the crofters, would do very well indeed.

Chapter 18

Percy Frost & the Bebros
(May 1886)

As with her estranged husband Knight Aston, we can never be certain as to just how much Percy Frost knew about Annie's activities, but it is worth a slight diversion to consider his activities during this period. According to the *Pall Mall Gazette* report for 6 March 1886:

'[Frost was] found in connection with persons who were making it their business to pass bills that Mrs Gordon Baillie was getting from Sir Richard King and at the same time posing in the City as a man of wealth and position, and entering into speculations and contracts which required many thousands of pounds to carry out. It has since transpired that he was at the time utterly without means of his own. Nevertheless some well-known bankers of Lombard Street were somehow or other bamboozled into giving him excellent references – and good ones which afforded him the opportunity to float a considerable amount of his own "paper"; and so successful was he that among other gentlemen taken in was a well-known City solicitor, [who] although accounted particularly sharp, one fine morning obliged Frost with a cool £1,000 to be going on with until, "those deuced trustees of mine fork out, you know".'

The 'well-known bankers of Lombard Street' were undoubtedly Smith Payne & Smith, who were not in the least need of being 'bamboozled', as they were the Frost family bank, had known the family 'through a great deal of business transactions' and regarded Percy Frost as an 'honourable young man'. Annie opened her own account with them in May 1885. The *Pall Mall Gazette* report shows him in a totally different light from the naive young idealist fighting for the socialist cause who met Annie in 1884. It is probable that 'naïve' is the key word here, and like so many older and wiser men before him, he was seduced and bewitched by this experienced adventuress. The report had been published as part of the campaign to expose 'Mrs Gordon Baillie' and her frauding ways, and so her 'husband' would have been easily tarred with the same brush. It is surprising that the piece was published in the *Pall*

Mall Gazette though, as it was a campaigning paper under the editorship of the liberal journalist W.T. Stead and the very one that Frost claimed to be working for when he arrived on Skye four years before. Not only that, but he was known to Stead and had written pieces for him previously. It is also interesting that they have his name as Richard rather than Robert.

Very little has been discovered about the precise nature of these business ventures, but it is known that at some point in 1885 or early 1886, Frost and Annie became involved in a scheme to purchase a discount and banking business, along with building projects in Brussels and Antwerp. Indeed, it is in Brussels that Annie claims they were married on 4 May 1886, in a ceremony alleged to have taken place within a schoolroom attached to a Roman Catholic church; as they were not Catholics they could not marry in the church itself and had to marry as 'English visitors'. This is almost certainly false, and it is highly unlikely that they married at all – in all probability Annie was still married to Aston at that time, and would remain so until the summer of 1887. The importance of her claim to be married to Frost is considered in a later chapter. It is about this time that Annie and Frost's daughter, Percy Elizabeth Frost, was conceived.

There were several others involved in the Belgian negotiations, and presumably whatever deal was to be done could be negotiated without actually going there. If they did go to Belgium at all, it must have been as a last-minute attempt to avert looming disaster, as Frost's bankruptcy proceedings over the affair began on 10 May 1886. It does seem to be rather unlikely that a deal negotiated in Brussels at around the time they claimed to marry would be in the bankruptcy court less than a week later. What the real situation was and whether it was a scam from the start is not known, but the *Gazette* states that she was warned against getting involved in the business by the British Consul, 'but not before she had dropped a considerable amount of money'. What is known is that the whole scheme went spectacularly wrong, and in May, as mentioned, Frost petitioned for bankruptcy with totalled debts of £130,378, estimated to equal £6.5 million in today's money.* On 9 June 1886, Robert Percival Bodley Frost of 5 Verulam Buildings, Gray's Inn, and 30 Woburn Place was made the subject of a 'receiving order', as a result of him being 'induced to enter into contracts for the purchase of estates at Dulwich and Tulse Hill, the Ter Elst estate and brickworks in Antwerp, and a banking and discount business at Brussels'. The understanding of the investors, apparently, was that a limited company would be formed to take over and develop the estates. This was not done and the vendors did not carry

---

* National Archives currency converter.

out their part of the bargain, resulting in a massive debt, of which £66,491 14s. 5d. was unsecured, with assets of only £154. Frost was finally adjudged bankrupt on 19 August 1886 and described during the hearings as of 'no occupation, having no capital and never having been involved in the business on a personal level'. He was not the only person to lose money on the Belgian part of the venture. A Mr F.W. Snell put in £12,000 of his own money and raised considerably more on behalf of himself, Bodley Frost and a Marcus Bebro.

Although not named in the hearings, Annie was undoubtedly involved in these schemes, and several writers, perhaps unfairly, interpreted the affair as a test of Frost's suitability to 'join the firm'; one that he failed miserably. Either way, it certainly reduced his usefulness, because as a bankrupt there would be no possibility of him being able to front any future business deals. The small amount we know about the scheme emerged during the trial at the Old Bailey in October 1888. Frost's great friend Henry Champion, who certainly would not have approved of any of this, was able to supply a few details and stated that:

> '[Frost] had £3,000 or £4,000 from his family to go into this business – since then he has had money from his mother; he had some in the early part of the year – he has not been earning any money; it was his share of the family money, I suppose.
>
> 'I heard his bankruptcy was owing to two promoters of public companies inducing him to go into speculations in a bank in Brussels, and a brickfield and buildings – I afterwards came across the son of Bebro, who is in gaol I believe now, and I believe Bebro himself is in gaol – Frost's family invested a few thousands for him, and he became bankrupt for a large sum, not proportionate to the amount he had put in; that was done to protect the rest of the property. The bankruptcy took place in May 1886, and up to 1885 I had seen him almost every day; he had up to then hardly commenced the business – they must have got the money from him in a few months. I know he had £200 or £300 to go to Australia, and in February, 1887, he had £400 or £600. I should say he had roughly £400 or £500 a year.'

Frost would not be discharged from bankruptcy until the tail end of May 1889. Marcus Bebro – the Bebro mentioned in Champion's evidence – was the renowned patentee of a machine which offered 'Improvements in mechanism or apparatus to be employed for numbering and printing tickets, cheques and other similar and like articles, progressively and consecutively.' It seems unlikely that he invented the machine, as his past and future career show no particular aptitude for mechanical devices, and so the probability is that he met the inventor and bought, or otherwise secured, the rights from him. Bebro had initially been in partnership with his brothers in Manchester as 'Job and Fent merchants', or dealers in oddments and offcuts of cloth. For reasons unknown, the partnership was dissolved in 1865 and Marcus carried on trading alone until the business finally failed and was wound up in 1870, when he was around 22 years old. By the following year, he had given up the rag trade and moved to London with a wife, three children and a domestic servant, living in the fashionable Canonbury area. He gave his occupation as 'Patentee', and it seems that the ticket machine was a great success.

By 1881, Bebro was describing himself as a 'printers' financier' and had moved to Hampstead. An advertorial in a local paper gives details of Bebro's business:

> 'The City of London Printing and Stationary Company Limited founded the year before with premises in City Road, capital of £50,000 with "several important contracts for businesses whose stationary requirements are large". Amongst their assents were the rights to the Marcus Bebro Patent Machine for the Printing of Tickets for Tramways, Steamboats, Theatres, Public Entertainments and all purposes for which consecutively numbered tickets are required. This patent and the patent rights connected herewith both at home and abroad have been purchased by the company; tickets can be printed on both sides and perforated in one operation at a rate of 40,000 to 50,000 per hour and rolled into a small compass.'

Despite all these claims and bold advertising, things must not have gone according to plan, as the company was wound up within two years and the rights to the wonderful machine sold at the end of 1881 for £15,000.

Bebro himself was not named as a director of the above company but his name was linked to The Quartz Hill Consolidating Gold Mining Company Limited, registered in 1881. The company received serious derisory comments in the *Mining Journal*, which gave rise to a printed circular put out by a disgruntled shareholder's solicitor, a Mr Alfred Tucker, who offered not to 'molest the company further' on payment of 100 shares or 50 guineas.

Other allegations included various forms of what we would now call 'insider dealing' by Bebro, who seemed to play very much by his own rules. Bebro had nowhere near enough fingers to cover all of the pies before him. Nearly everything he was involved with seemed to end up in the bankruptcy court – either by accident or design – and he accrued debts of thousands, yet walked away unscathed. At a hearing in 1900, it was stated that as many as fifty-eight bankruptcy petitions had been presented against him in his business career. As noted, he would have known Frost, as they were both involved in the Belgian business, and so he would presumably have known Annie. It would be fascinating to know the nature of their relationship; Marcus was about eight years older than her and a consummate businessman, so it would have been unlikely that even she was able to pull the wool over his eyes – as this time he wasn't the one in the bankruptcy court when it all went wrong.

While on the subject of Bebro, it is worth taking another small diversion to consider the career of another member of the family, Joseph Henry Bebro, Marcus's son, who was born in Manchester in 1866 and known to everyone as 'Harry'. It was he who took his father's idea of business to a whole new level, in a life of crime the scale and audacity of which possibly exceeded that of Annie herself.

Harry first made the news at the age of 16 after a night at the theatre with a few pals. They enjoyed the show and drank a good deal of wine, beer and port, but the next thing Harry remembered was waking up in bed with his friend, an articled clerk named Tom, and two young ladies. Having ascertained that they were in Westmoreland Street, off New Cavendish Street, the pair set about getting dressed when one of the girls asked: 'What about our fiver?' Harry and his friend tried to front it out, denying any such agreement had taken place or, indeed, any knowledge of how they got there, but two burly men were swiftly summoned and demanded that the girls be paid. When it became apparent that the sum total of cash on the two friends came to less than two shillings, the 'heavies' took a watch and chain and forced them to write out IOUs, while threatening to throw them from the window. Harry signed his in a false name – a sure sign of things to come – and after a certain amount of unpleasantness, they managed to leave, find a policeman and tell him their sad tale. The case ended up at the Old Bailey, with charges of demanding money with menaces, and one of the girls and one of the henchmen got a few months' hard labour between them.

By 1887, Harry had grown up a little and was in New Zealand, announcing himself as the 'son of the well-known London financier' and promoting his International Cable Company, along with entertaining the locals with his considerable acting and singing ability. The following year, however, he was in court as director of The Great Britain & Colonial Exchange, Chancery Lane, charged with obtaining three tricycles that he had pawned, a diamond, sixteen bottles of wine and several oil paintings. He was acquitted of all charges, but was back in court within two months, this time in Durham and charged with false pretences, conspiracy and passing dud cheques. Bail was granted, but not trusting his luck to the jury a second time, he took off to the United States. In 1889, he married and settled in Brooklyn to run a bogus employment agency. Sometime later he was once more accused of false pretences, but the charges were not proceeded with. He seems to have avoided the law for quite a while, or at least until 1893, when a visit from his mother prompted demands for money from her. The poor woman was so frightened that she called the police and Harry was arrested. He responded by suing her for false arrest, demanding $100,000 in compensation! He was not successful.

Harry eventually moved to Boston, and by 1897 he had half a dozen indictments against him and was convicted of stealing money that his employees had lodged with him as security. He was sentenced to five years in Charlestown penitentiary, where, according to one story, he even managed to borrow money from the warden. Within a few years he was back in New York and started the Bebro Mercantile Agency, advertising in out-of-town papers that he was pursuing bad debts and needed collectors. He amassed a small army of strongarm men and required them to pay $300 apiece as security that they would not run away with any of the collections they were to make. He ran the firm until 1906, when he heard that the authorities in Massachusetts were looking for him. He did the sensible thing – he grabbed all the money, about $100,000, and ran. 'Handsome Harry' or 'The King', as he was known amongst his confederates, headed back to Europe.

Despite the change of continent, it was not very long before he was in trouble again. By now he had adopted the name of Harry Benson and began operating as Feltham's Bank Ltd (using his wife's maiden name), an 'International Securities Corporation'. He issued and sold a number of fake bonds and pocketed the money. The bank was eventually wound up with total liabilities of £15,308, and in October 1909 – despite claims that he was innocent, ill, dying, that others were responsible and that he had become a Rabbi to help prisoners, along with several tearful appeals for the jury's benefit – Harry received five years for larceny and fraud.

It seems that 'Handsome Harry' Benson really was ill with diabetes and Bright's disease, although his appetite for fraud remained undimmed and during his time in Parkhurst he made the most unlikely of useful contacts. Benson became friends with a man convicted of one of the most infamous murders of the time. Stinie Morrison had been found guilty of the robbery and murder of Leon Beron on Clapham Common in 1911. Originally sentenced to death, his sentence was commuted to life imprisonment. Benson explored the possibilities of turning his fellow prisoner's notoriety to his advantage.

Morrison had always claimed to be innocent, and Benson encouraged him to fight for his freedom.

When Harry Benson was released from Parkhurst Prison on licence, on 20 March 1914, he had less than 30 shillings in his pocket. A mere six weeks later, he had 'persuaded' a motor engineer, the proprietor of H. Lee & Co., to turn his business into a limited company and assumed control himself as managing director, despite being an undischarged bankrupt. Harry turned the company into a debt collection agency, Mr Lee 'retired' and all connection to the motor business ceased. Ten accounts with different banks were opened in the company's name, none with a credit balance. Few records were kept, although we know that on 28 July 1914, the company received £2,500 from an Austrian lady, Baroness von Goetz, for the purpose of setting up a newspaper. The benevolent baroness seems to have become obsessed with Morrison and his 'case against injustice', and in August the company started to publish a journal, *Facts*, which concerned itself with matters relating to convict prisons and heavily supported Morrison's case.

On 20 October 1914, von Goetz paid a further £4,500 into one of Harry's accounts, to be used for a new venture called 'Benson's Prisoner's Aid Society' based at Woodgate Farm in Chichester. Shortly after this, Benson sold the newspaper to another of his companies, Facts Limited, for £20,000 in fully paid-up shares, of which 10,000 were allotted to the company and 10,000 to Baroness von Goetz. The sad truth, however, was that Benson's whole organization and publication were nothing more than a ruse to use the Morrison case to extract money from this rather naive Austrian philanthropist, which he did to the tune of about £38,000. He rented a furnished mansion with half a dozen servants and a couple of motor cars, and was known to frequent the most expensive restaurants. He bought Woodgate Farm, which consisted of many acres, and installed several of his old gaolbird acquaintances, in the name of their reformation, while spending money at the rate of £200 a week.

How long he might have continued this magnificent deception will never be known. A visit to his Harley Street doctor informed him he had not long to live, and he was subsequently confined to a nursing home in Merton. Without his constant attention to the minute details of his complex and fraudulent business affairs, questions began to be asked and investigations pursued. It was eventually discovered that 'Her Ladyship' was not the only victim; there were more than 100 men and women who had been swindled by this charming con-man – genuine businessmen, lawyers, merchants and clergymen had all been taken in.

While warrants were being drawn up and witnesses assembled, Joseph Henry Bebro, alias Harry Benson, Handsome Harry and numerous other names, made his final and this time permanent bid for 'freedom': on 22 October 1917, at the age of 51, he died in the nursing home. For Stinie Morrison, his last hope of acquittal died along with his 'great friend' and champion, and he became increasingly depressed and uncontrollable. He starved himself to death in 1921.

Harry Bebro, having been born in 1866, was 18 years younger than Annie and at the time of his father's involvement in the Belgian disaster was aged around 20. It is doubtful they ever worked together, but with so much in common – their love of luxury and theatre, foreign travel, false names and bogus accounts – the two dedicated fraudsters would have made a great team.

Chapter 19

New Zealand
(Nov 1886–Apr 1887)

As the summer of 1886 turned to autumn, Annie experienced a seismic shift in her attitude towards the Highland crofters, which would lead her to embark on the most ambitious scheme of her career. With Sir Richard King's trustees closing in and Toler arrested once more, she decided it was time to make her move. On 5 November 1886, she gathered up her children and, along with her servants, set sail for New Zealand. Why Annie chose to undertake such an arduous voyage while pregnant with Frost's child is not known. King's relatives were certainly at great pains to cut off her income stream and had involved the police in their quest to some extent. According to her secretary, Tom Russell, she was planning the trip as early as August that year and he had left her employ towards the end of that month.

In a later interview, Annie claimed the purpose of the visit was not primarily on behalf of the crofters but for pleasure and recuperation for one of her children, who had recently been ill. She travelled from London in the saloon cabin of the SS *Ionic* in early November as 'Mrs Mathew's Family', a party of eight – four children and four adults – arriving at Lyttleton, New Zealand, on 22 December. Her maid Miss Elliot, governess Miss Heston and housekeeper Mrs Mathews travelled steerage class. Percy Frost did not go with her, despite the fact she was soon to have his child; they were not to meet up again for six months, when he arrived in Tasmania via the *Ionic*'s sister ship, the *Doric*. Later, much was made of the fact the name 'Gordon Baillie' did not appear on the passenger lists, although Annie explained this, quite reasonably, by stating that Mrs Mathews had booked the tickets and had simply used her own name. There would seem to be no reason to doubt this, or indeed any reason for Annie to have travelled under a false name, as upon arrival she went under her adopted and legal name of Mrs Gordon Baillie.

The party booked themselves into the Terminus Hotel, Christchurch, but when the heavily pregnant Annie, her four 'little cherubs' and accompanying servants left, payment of the bill seems to have slipped her mind and required the threat of a summons before she would part with the money.

Moving on from there to house her soon-to-be-expanded brood, she rented a fashionable villa, in Lichfield Street, and added an elderly lady to her 'team', engaged because she was well known and trusted in the town, as well as being familiar with many of the local clergy and gentlefolk. Her ultimate function, therefore, was to provide Annie with introductions to anyone worth knowing or potentially useful. Annie proceeded to fascinate all she met with her 'personal magnetism' and the 'magnificence of her dress', one person later claiming: 'Her fascination was native: it did not depend on education. She was by no means a woman of culture. Her letters are bad in grammar and shaky in spelling; her signature, of which only too [*sic*] specimens are extant in Christchurch, is that of a strong, dashing but illiterate character.'

Annie would rise around noon, and after a 'dainty little champagne lunch' attended to the business of the day, after which she would drive out into the country with her maid. Later, she would take in performances of the *Mikado* or *Iolanthe* – all freely provided by proprietors of the various establishments to whom she would have been known through her association with the famous operatic tenor, and her former husband, Knight Aston. To those closest to her, the story was that she had been married to Aston, a well-known figure in the area, but had divorced him, and married Mr Frost, who was editor of *The Mark Lane Express*, a rather obscure agricultural weekly.

On 29 January 1887, having moved once more with her children and entourage of servants to a house of 'great magnificence', Sumner Lodge in Cashel Street, Christchurch, Annie gave birth to another daughter, Percy Elizabeth Champion Frost.

Despite her claims to an aristocratic heritage and her sociable personality, the local society ladies did not take to her and she was never a social 'success' in the town. It was claimed later by a Mrs Hill of Melbourne – who was described as the 'self-proclaimed correspondent of the *London Morning Post*' and a fountain of society gossip – that this was because they could discover so little about her. There were plenty of Gordons and Baillies in Burke's Peerage, but not a single Gordon Baillie; nor was there, it seemed, such a name among the landed gentry. Above all, they wanted to know who Mr Gordon Baillie was and where exactly he could be found. They did not deny she was beautiful, but there was something about her beauty, mode of living, mission and antecedents they did not trust. Her manners, which had a suggestion, as one of the ladies put it, of the 'unconventionalism of the Parisian' about them, were not calculated to ingratiate her in the favour or affection of '*les dames*'.

Feminine misgivings aside, her story was at first accepted implicitly. She talked with so much real eloquence and pathos about the unfortunate Skye crofters, and her name appeared so frequently in the newspapers in connection with prominent public men, statesmen and divines, that no one dreamt that she could be an impostor. When some of her acquaintances got to know her better and began to see a little behind the scenes, doubts about the genuineness of her philanthropic mission began to set in. It became apparent that her game was to wheedle money out of men, and during her stay she managed to do so very successfully. She was described as having no bashfulness about her, always thoroughly self-possessed, free, off-hand and confident. She looked you straight in the eyes when talking to you, it was said, and was the 'quintessence of frankness and candour'.

Despite all the attractions of a new baby, a new country and a fantastic project to work on (bogus or otherwise), it seems that Annie could not control her self-destructive addiction to small -time fraud, and on 13 April 1887 she was the subject of at least two civil court cases in Christchurch. One case was brought by Warre, Hockley & Co. for £14 17s, and the other by H.B. Lane for £7 12s. 2d. She did not appear, and judgement was entered against her in both cases. According to a report in one of the gossip columns, she ran short of money during this time but was in funds soon after. The writer continued: 'Several names have been mentioned of leading citizens who in all likelihood had the honour of squaring up the lady's accounts but these shall not be repeated by me.'

With creditors now becoming a pest, Annie reasoned that it was time to liquidize some assets and organized a sale of several of her most beautiful and fashionable dresses, including some designed by Charles Worth of Paris and Kate Riley of Dover Street in London. A few paintings and works of art were also sold, but overall the event proved a failure, as the ladies of Christchurch society had taken such a dislike to her that they chose not to buy the dresses at any price. Large supplies of wine and spirits were frequently sent to her house, and rumours abounded of sundry little suppers to which only gentlemen were invited. The lady was undoubtedly very fascinating, beautiful, charming, clever, but socially beyond the pale. For some reason, it suited Annie to represent herself as a Roman Catholic at this time and she became friends with the priest at Christchurch, although not even his influence could assist in her social acceptability.

As she would claim later in interview, the crofters' cause was not her only reason for travelling to the other side of the world; she had not given up on her artistic pretensions. Near the end of her stay in Christchurch she made the acquaintance of James Cassius Williamson, theatre entrepreneur, founder, manager and director of The Royal Comic Opera Company and owner of various rights to the operas of Gilbert & Sullivan – his company was destined to rule Australian opera for five decades. She went to see him to enquire about theatrical employment. Williamson expressed in the politest terms possible the sense of honour her visit and request had conferred upon him, but stated that it was impossible to take her on as he made a rule never to employ anyone cleverer than himself.

Undeterred, Annie fired back: 'But I heard before I left England that you were going to run Phil Robinson.'

'I admit,' replied the wily impresario, 'that he is cleverer than I am, but I am not going to run him.'

She asked what he would advise her to do, and drawing himself up to his full height he gave the following frank and honest judgement:

'In the first place I would advise you to clear out of here as soon as possible. The inhabitants of Christchurch are honest, but simple, not to say stupid. Though you would hardly understand it there are people here moving in good society who would not care to visit a lady who allows herself to be summoned for a milk bill, and who would consider the obtaining of expensive wines without the slightest chance of being able to pay for them as little better than swindling. In Melbourne it is quite different. People there are more liberal and enlightened and would look upon your little peculiarities as mere eccentricities of genius.'

This was possibly the best advice Annie had ever been given, and perhaps realizing that she had at last met her match, after such a masterful putdown, she could do nothing but accept his judgement as sound and asked meekly (and rather optimistically, given the foregoing) whether he would supply her with a few letters of introduction? Williamson replied that he would not, as this was unnecessary because in Melbourne there were always large-hearted souls who were ready at any moment to succour a lovely British female in distress. He handed her a card upon which he had scribbled the names of two cabinet ministers, a bank manager, a lady-killing stockbroker, a reliable auctioneer, the editor of a society magazine and several other potentially 'sympathizing gentlemen', including, for good measure, a leading lawyer.

Williamson was not the only person unwilling to play ball with Annie. Although her visit to New Zealand seemed to consist largely of recreation and nursing baby Percy Elizabeth, she did make some enquiries regarding her crofters' scheme. She was invited to inspect 20,000 acres of land at Dunedin, at the head of Otago Harbour, by a Mr MacAndrew, but thought it unsuitable and so did not follow up on the offer. Meanwhile, Government officials were raising objections to her plans and creating difficulties that affected their viability. Principal amongst them was Sir Julius Vogel, former premier of

New Zealand and the local MP, who dismissed her ideas for a settlement out of hand; without his backing, little could be achieved.

Despite frequent visits to editors of various local newspapers in an attempt to drum up publicity, she was not able to create much enthusiasm for her scheme. Meanwhile, the tradesmen's bills were piling up: the landlord, grocer, butcher and wine merchant began to issue summonses and take steps to recover their money – one was haughtily informed that Mrs Gordon Baillie always paid her bills once a quarter, so he should wait until then. After having judgements recorded against her for trivial amounts in the civil courts, it would only be a matter of time before the word spread and further questions were asked. In what was presumably an attempt to cover her back or head off similar cases, the following notice was placed in two local newspapers:

NOTICE TO TRADESMEN AND OTHERS

All accounts OWING by the Hon. Mrs Gordon Baillie of Sumner Lodge, Cashel Street, Christchurch, are requested to be immediately sent to the undersigned for payment, prior to her departure from the Colony on or about the end of the present month.

Christchurch, April 18th, 1887.

HJ Raphael, Solicitor for the Hon. Mrs Gordon Baillie.

New Zealand was not working. Its inhabitants had not been as kind to her as she had hoped, while its leaders and bureaucracy had not fallen for the scheme as she had planned. Even employment in the theatre, whether it had been serious or not, had been denied to her. It was time to take Williamson's advice and head for Melbourne – probably just before her appeal to tradesmen appeared in print.

Chapter 20

Australia
(May–Jul 1887)

By the middle of May 1887, Annie had arrived in Melbourne, capital of the Australian state of Victoria, with her young daughters, attendants and 4-month-old baby, Percy Elizabeth. She rented a furnished villa at 2 Park Terrace, Toorak Road, which at the time was one of the most fashionable parts of the city and for which the rent was £7 per week.

The city of Melbourne, which doubled as a major port, had only existed since 1835, but in mid-1851, with the discovery of gold, it experienced a rapid growth that saw its population leap from 25,000 to 40,000 within a matter of months. Like its Californian counterpart, which had begun three years earlier, Melbourne's Victorian Gold Rush – as it became known – precipitated a period of exponential growth, and a little more than two decades before Annie's arrival it had overtaken Sydney as Australia's most populous city. With the immense wealth that the gold rush generated, large programmes of civic and residential building were initiated and continued for the rest of the century. As well as public structures such as Parliament House, The Treasury and Melbourne Town Hall, huge inner suburbs were laid out, mainly on a one-mile grid pattern, cut through by wide boulevards, and liberally peppered with parklands surrounding the central city. Terrace and detached houses rubbed shoulders with grander mansions within these areas, and one such part was Toorak Road, where Annie took up residence. Her timing could not have been more fortuitous. The decade had begun for Melbourne with yet another extraordinary period of growth, which saw increased consumer confidence, easy access to credit and steep increases in land prices, which lead to a further and substantial amount of construction. So much so, that during this 'land boom', which would reach its peak the next year, Melbourne reputedly became the richest city in the world and second largest, after London, in the British Empire. In 1885, the visiting English journalist George Augustus Henry Sala coined the phrase 'Marvellous Melbourne', and Annie would soon discover just how true this was.

On Friday 10 June 1887, Annie and her maid Miss Elliot took the express train from Melbourne to Sydney, passing through Albury – around a twelve-hour journey today, and about 500 miles from coast to coast. In all probability the sole purpose of the visit was to meet Knight Aston, who had been living there for some time and was due to open as Fritz in Offenbach's *The Grand Duchess* at The Academy of Music the following evening. Significantly, the children were left in Melbourne, so whether Aston ever saw his daughters again remains in doubt – they certainly stayed with their mother and entourage when she returned to England. This was the first time that Annie and Aston had seen each other for five years, and exactly what took place we will never know, but it was certainly less than cordial. One story is that Aston made an attempt to get access to her apartments when she was in the town, declaring his intention of shooting her with the pistol he carried, and that Miss Elliot was a witness to the incident, but there are no further details. Whether he had been able to follow her more recent career is not known, but she was no longer the little minx and petty fraudster he had left behind in London. Annie was now Mrs Gordon Baillie, an internationally known and respected lady of wealth and breeding, daughter of the Earl of Moray and with strong philanthropic intentions.

While it is not known how aware Aston would have been of his wife's criminal activities, he would have been more familiar with Annie's character than most. Once news of her arrival and activities reached him, he must have read each day's papers in trepidation, waiting for the story of her past and connection to him to appear in print and wondering how much the fallout would affect his career. It could be argued that he had a duty to tell what he knew to protect future victims. He could have exposed her as a fraud, but only at great risk to his own reputation – and of course the effect this would have had on the children would have been intolerable. It is possible to imagine their meeting as a scene of high drama. She, buying his silence by threatening to wreck his career with tales of his involvement in her frauds should she be arrested, denying him access to his children, and taunting him with the new baby and tales of her new love, Percy Frost. He, in turn, would be shouting back about how she had ruined his life and reputation, while threatening to expose her. It was probably during this time that they organized the divorce, though no records have been traced.

Nevertheless, they must have agreed terms of some kind in the face of mutually assured destruction, and he must have decided to keep quiet and hope for the best. He certainly never spoke about her publicly, other than to issue a statement, much later, in order, as he put it, 'to protect his new wife's reputation', by stating that he was divorced from her. Even when Annie's name and activities were the subject of gossip world-wide, there was not a word from him in the press.

Annie remained in Sydney for a week before returning to Melbourne by the same route, while Aston continued with his career, but it wasn't to be long before their names were joined in newspaper headlines and countless gossip columns. Travel records show that Annie and the four children made the trip to Sydney once more on 31 August, while Annie and her maid travelled there in the middle of the following month. Aston appeared at Sydney's Gaiety Theatre on 20 August, but does not appear again in theatrical advertisements until 15 October, when he is back on stage in Melbourne. Quite possibly she took the children to see him, as part of their arrangement, or else she may have timed her visits for when he was away. There is no way of knowing if they ever met again.

Their 'explosive' reunion in Sydney had been less than discrete, and within a fortnight, gossip being what it is, rumours had found their way into the press: 'News comes in to me that Baillie is merely the travelling name assumed by the lady and that she is in reality the wife of a gentleman well known in colonial operatic circles and who preceded her to Australia some 2 or 3 years since.' Sometime later, the society gossip paper *Table Talk*, in its edition of 25 November 1887, gave the opinion that Aston 'had made it his business to trouble her concerning the care of his 3 children. Of the private lives of the parties mentioned very little is known beyond the fact of the lady being a Bohemian of a pronounced type. When the gentleman arrived among us ... five years ago he was understood to have left a wife and family in England of whom he was passionately fond. Some say she, Mrs Gordon Baillie, obtained a divorce.' The genie was emerging from the bottle and there was little Aston could do about it.

Domestic issues aside, it was now time for Annie to focus on her work. In mid-July 1887, the *Gippsland Times*, a paper serving south-eastern Victoria, an area below Melbourne, reported that she had her eye on the coast of Corner Inlet, a 230 square mile bay of mangroves, salt marsh and mudflats, sheltered by a complex of barrier barrier reefs. The scheme was to transport up to 1,000 Skye crofters and have them occupy around 44,000 acres for fourteen years at a low rent. The land would have to be taken in her own name, she claimed, 'to enable her to speak definitively to her people', but it would subsequently be divided into allotments and arrangements would be made for each of the crofters to secure enough land to enable them to make a living from it. She also understood that the government had the power to grant freeholds. Annie was asked to put details of her proposal in writing and was told that the scheme would be given careful consideration by Mr Dow of the Lands Department. The newspaper wished her every success with the scheme: 'We must give the lady credit, for the only motive for her work appears a philanthropic desire for the welfare of her protégés, and while it seems odd that she should prefer the country she has selected for her experiment to New Zealand, it is to be presumed that she would be the best judge.' The land in question had been abandoned by its previous inhabitants because it was poor and scrubby, since when the Land Department had been unable to lease it. Whilst the soil on Skye was neither rich nor fertile, a living could be made from it – but obviously not if the crofters were being continuously harassed by the landowners and their plots constantly reduced in size. The article concluded that the area would be perfect for fishing and curing. Despite these very encouraging signs, her written application never materialized.

Other reports describe the proposed incomers as 'not carpenters, masons or shoemakers, but peasantry of the simplest possible class, who stick to their little cabins and divide their time between fishing and cultivation who would not compete in any way with the existing labour market'. Most reports gave wholehearted support to the scheme. Even the worldly wise editors of *Melbourne Punch* were more than a little impressed with the new arrival:

'Mrs. Gordon Baillie whose portrait we give this week, was born in Argyllshire in 1858 [*sic*]. She is the last of an old and distinguished family; on the Gordon side a descendent of a line of soldiers, on the other of the great Johanna Baillie. She was born Gordon-Baillie and remains Gordon-Baillie, her family legally taking her name on accounts of rights of property. From the whirl and gaiety of the fashionable London world, of which she was a well-known ornament, she went down to Skye during the military occupation to inquire into the cause of the disaffection of the crofters, some of whom were her tenants. She found their poverty and wrongs to be such that she refused to take further rents from her own tenants and became the ardent champion of the crofter cause. By identifying herself with the Liberals she estranged herself from many of her kindred who are strict Conservatives. This lady's defence of the working people and more especially of the Skye crofters has brought her into political notice much more than she anticipated or desired.

'Mrs Gordon Baillie is also well known in London artistic and literary circles. She contributed to various Scotch and English magazines before her twentieth year and is now on a well-known English daily in which she has a personal interest, besides being correspondent to several American papers. Her English and Scotch lyrics and pathetic stories have made her literary name what it is. To quote from "*Society*":

"She stands towards the Highlands as Lady Wilde once did to Ireland. Mrs Baillie possesses a warm and generous temperament, with a keen sense of humour. Her intellect is ever at work and her gift of language lies ever ready to express vividly the ideas and fancies that throng her brain. Her mind seems to have absorbed the strength of her native mountains, with the grace and perfume of her native heather. She is full of interest in schemes for the common welfare, but brings no long drawn countenance of sad melancholy to her work, but an affluence of health, energy and good spirits, which bid fair to achieve success in anything she may undertake, even to the establishment of a settlement of Highland fishers and farmers on Wilson's Promontory.

"Although one of those women who, moving in diplomatic circles keep alive the old days of the Salon, the stranger who calls upon Mrs Baillie either in London or the Isle of Wight cannot fail to be struck by the great womanliness of her nature as he sees her always accompanied by her 3 pretty little girls, one of whom has already figured on a Royal Academician's canvas. To combine a stirring public career with all the beauties of our gentle English home life demands the most of any nature, and that Mrs Baillie has met that demand in its fullness better describes her character than aught else.'"

Despite what on the face of it must have been one of the most interesting and exciting periods of her life, with the possibility of thousands of people dependent upon her and control over assets worth many thousands of pounds – several millions in today's money – along with worldwide fame as a great philanthropist, Annie could not overcome her addiction to petty crime. At the Prahran Police Court on Monday 18 July 1887, judgement was given against her for £4 3s. 3d. in favour of Mr Kyle the milkman. As in Christchurch, it was this failure to pay the humble milkman which was to sow the seeds of her undoing, but despite everything, Annie continued her usual unsustainable extravagance. She hired a carriage and pair from a Charles Willoughby, at £5 per week, from the end of June until mid-August, and ended up in court with an award of £35 plus costs against her. One account claimed that she had six servants plus a private secretary, and that her grocer's bill was the largest of any family in the district. The bill generally included dozens of bottles of 'strong drink', her favourite refreshment, other than champagne, being a brandy and soda. In pursuit of her great scheme, Annie gave an interview during July to the *Melbourne Telegraph*, explaining her plans:

'Some people seem to think that all I have come here for is to settle the crofters, but that is not correct. I intended to come to Australia with one of my children who was delicate and before leaving I saw the men and arranged with them that I would try to arrange for their settlement in this new world. I went to New Zealand first but that would not do, though they offered me free grants of land, just as they have done from Tasmania; but as my protégés are fishermen we want consumers and it is here that I find the market for I believe Melbourne to be the centre of federated Australia –that is if you keep away from Imperial Federation. For goodness sake do not think of that!

'Let me tell you about the crofters and why I am associated with them. I am a land owner in the Highlands. Some of the crofters are on my estates, [but] what did I know of them before the troubles began? I wore fine gowns and all that sort of thing, you know paid for by my rents, and I was dumbfounded when I heard of the riots. I wanted to find out for myself, so I hurried away and went right amongst them. Now before I go any further let me tell you who the crofters are.

'They have rented land for generations, sixty acres was their holding originally. It has come down to five – five acres of hard, barren land which will grow nothing. I soon learnt all about them, and what impressed me more than anything else was the story of an eviction which had taken place the day before I arrived. You know what evictions are of course.

'I must explain, first of all, that the crofters have to go to Peterhead for six or seven months in the year – to earn their living. This is because their holdings will no longer support them at home. By hard toil they succeed in getting together by fishing from £40 to £50. At home their wives are struggling to keep their families together. And let me tell you that if they only go to gather up the sea weed that is thrown up by the waves, they are liable to be imprisoned at once. All they have to live on is, perhaps a little oatmeal. As for beef, they never see it from one year's end to the other; and with mutton it is just the same. The husband, of course, while away has to provide for himself, buy his tackle, clothing, and so on, and he returns home at the end of the fishery with £25 or £30.

'Now for my story. There was at Skye the wife of one of these crofters and his mother was with her. The wife was away gathering peat, they bring it from a long distance carrying home great weights of it on their backs and during her absence the landlord came, turned out the mother and 2 children and burnt the house to the ground. The poor old woman was blind, one of the infants, a boy four years old strayed away and was lost. To this day he has not been found. The wife came home late in the evening, her home was gone and her baby was missing. She went mad.

Two months later her husband returned from the fisheries and saw her in the lunatic asylum. Straight away he went to the landlord and struck him for which he was arrested, but the gaol could not keep him and he died of a broken heart. Can you wonder now that my temper was aroused? I went to the men, spoke with them but they said, "what can this lassie know of us? She is a landowner." Very well I said, I shall make trouble at all events, and I believe I did. I wrote frequently until an immense interest was aroused all over the country, but the men were not pacified. I heard the marines were coming to quell the riots and I went to the party who were prepared to resist them.

"'Now,' I said, "Don't! They are armed and will shoot you down. Think of your wives and children." From their leader I secured a promise that there should be no resistance. "But," I said, "hoist the 'no rent', manifesto. I will be with you in that." For being the owner of some of these places I had decided not to take any rents. Now all this is preliminary. It is just to explain how I am connected with this movement to bring them to Victoria.

'Well here as I said, there is the market, and in the sea there are the fish. Just let me say that I am asking no favour from the government. These are Her Majesty's dominions, and I am a subject and surely I can take up land in the same way as anyone else. I find Wilson's Promontory uninhabited – here is the field for crofters. For twenty, thirty, forty years the land has been going begging. No one would have it, no one thought of it until I made my application. But it is no favour, for I take up this land at £1 per acre as anyone else might do and as some are trying to. Do you think the crofters want charity? They are the most industrious hard working men you could find. Go amongst your unemployed and if you find a Highlander with them I'll eat him. Don't talk to me about philanthropy! I would strike the word out of the English dictionary if I were someone of importance, but being only a little body I can't do it. My interest arises out of real bad temper and nothing else because I have a temper I can assure you.

'If the crofters come they will be a benefit to the colony, they will establish a new industry. What I am asking of the department is that they throw the land open for selection – put it on the Brown I think is the departmental term. It is land hunger with the crofters for they want to stand on their own holding and say, "This is Mine!" You understand the feeling – and I want the whole of the promontory – the scheme would make the place the Brighton of Victoria. It is most lovely, the scenery wonderfully grand and fine.

'Now for the plans. It is intended to bring out about 250 heads of families, a thousand is all nonsense though it might be so bye and bye. By heads of families you will understand men of 50 or so with fine, big sons, fellows inured to deep sea fishing and all the hardships of such a life and in all there would be about 400 of them. They will give you fish here in such abundance that you will be astonished – people of Victoria do not eat fish – I really cannot understand why – and they will let you have it in Melbourne by train three hours before the Gippsland shipments arrive. We will have a train within 25 minutes of what may in the future be the head station.

'That is not all, however, for canning will be a feature in the winter. You know very well that people in the bush never get anything but meat until they are heartily sick of it. They would give anything for it, and we will show them how they can have it. There is a Danish process, known to the crofters by which fish can be dipped, gutted, canned and taken out three months later as fresh as when caught and the system is such that the parcels can be regulated for any period. Now you bring a lot of canned stuff from Canada and pay 10d to 1/6d for a small tin. The crofters, by this process, will make up a 3lb tin and sell it for 4/5d.

'This is not romancing, for I have gone carefully into figures with scientific men who know all about the fish of the colony and we have reduced it down to what I tell you. It is no beggary for the workers either for their profits will be large and I calculate on their holdings of about 50 acres each, for that is all they want, any more would be an encumbrance – they will make between £4–£5 per week. I have given a lot of time to this matter and we are not far wrong. The men will take up the land just as free selectors do, they will be a benefit to the community in many a way and I am sure that everyone will be pleased they are in Victoria.

'As to bringing them out, they will if necessary pay their own passages, they are not paupers, do not run away with that idea. Just here let me remind you that the best men you have in the colony are Highlanders – they are your leaders. The crofters are Highlanders. There are other ways of helping them on the voyage that I cannot discuss at this moment. Should everything work out well – should I be assured that the land will be open to them – you may expect them in 18 months.'

Towards the end of July 1887, the government officials in Victoria were still wrestling with Annie's bold scheme and had decided to put off their decision, pending a professional inspection of the land. The publicity surrounding

Annie's interest in the previously dismissed scrubland had been noticed by others: a Mr James Butters claimed that he had already agreed to purchase 27,300 acres of it the previous year. However, upon meeting Mrs Gordon Baillie and discussing her scheme, he was so impressed that he offered to relinquish his claim for a mere £5,000, so as not to stand in the way of her 'praiseworthy and philanthropic designs', but did want to retain some 340 acres near Wilson's Promontory in order to build a new sanatorium for Victoria. She was offered the donation of three fishing smacks from the leading New South Wales colonists should her plans come to fruition – if not, the boats were to be given to the state of Victoria.

Not everyone was tipsy with joy at the scheme. The fishermen of Queenscliff held a meeting to protest against it, claiming that the sudden influx would take the food from their mouths, despite the fact that fish was almost unobtainable at any price both locally and further afield. One remarked that the colony did not contain a big enough population to support this extra number in the fish trade and that the fishermen already employed were quite sufficient to supply all needs, the speaker seemingly oblivious to the fact that fresh fish in Melbourne, with its 370,000 inhabitants and ocean teeming with fish at their door, was an article of luxury rather than an everyday food amongst all classes of the population. The fishermen declared their intention of forming a co-operative company with a central market to supply Melbourne with fish. They declared they had no objection in principle to the Skye crofters, but asked that the same privileges be extended to 'those who lived in Victoria and had helped build up the colony', it surely being an injustice to bring people thousands of miles by offering special inducements that would result in Victorians being thrown out of work. Not only that, but a railroad was soon to be built to Port Albert which would stimulate the entire fishing industry.

Was it the fishermen's case that turned the authorities' initial enthusiasm for her plans for Wilson's Promontory and Corner Inlet into a more cautious attitude? Had they heard rumours from Christchurch? Or had the publicity given to the area made others realize what value the land held? Did vested business interests turn the tide against Annie with those in power? Three applicants suddenly applied for leases for a total of 86,000 acres covering the area, and presumably they had more than a pretty smile and a clever tongue to back their claims. If Annie achieved nothing else from her visit 'down under', she certainly made its inhabitants more aware of the value of the land they held.

Annie's impact on the Melbourne social scene was certainly felt, if not always in the way she would have wished. Speaking a few months later, a

'Melbourne Gentleman', who knew her during her time there, claimed that she received the same cold shoulder from the society women of the town as she had in New Zealand – due to suspicion, jealousy and snobbery – although, as always, Annie was a great hit with their menfolk:

> 'Like all men, [I was] captivated by her beauty and grace, she was a perfectly beautiful woman. She was a blonde, with lovely features, and the most exquisitely proportioned figure I ever saw. She might have stood for the model of the Venus de Medici. Her voice was one of her chief gifts. It was like the music of a silver bell. There was no resisting its persuasive tones. Like Besant's hero [English novelist Walter Besant], she seemed to throw the glamour of magnetism or some other occult power over nearly everyone who came in contact with her, and whom she desired to make use of, but there was a limit to her influence, [as] her own sex did not, as a rule, fall under it.'

Mrs Hill, a freelance journalist for the *London Morning Post*, who claimed that she had met Annie previously at one of the Duke of Westminster's evening parties, was asked her opinion of the lady and gave an example of her over-familiarity which had so annoyed the wives of the well-connected:

> Before suspicions began to gather round her she obtained the *entree* to several good families in Melbourne. My friend Fritz, who took a paternal interest in her, and who moves in the best circles, introduced her into many select houses. She professed to have an intimate acquaintance with several members of the English aristocracy, and spoke of them in the most familiar terms. She was fond of alluding to the Governors of Victoria and New South Wales as her old friends "Henry Loch" and "Charlie Carrington". According to her story Sir Henry was an old friend of the Gordon Baillie family, and in days gone by had been an intimate chum of her father. She called upon Fritz's home one afternoon, and dumb founded his wife by smilingly looking round the room, and not seeing any one else present, asking with a touch of disappointment in her voice, "Where's Fritz?".'

This forward way of speaking about the lady's husband did not please the wife, and Mrs Gordon Baillie was not invited to repeat her visit. Mrs Hill affirmed that there had been a divorce, although not caused by Mrs Gordon Baillie's misconduct, but quite otherwise, and declared the whole subject 'too painful to dwell upon' – which was probably her way of saying that she didn't know the details. She felt sure, she said pointedly, that all the men who knew her would be sorry she had come to grief. Mrs Hill continued: 'That she was a very clever woman everyone who had met her agreed, and that she was a most fascinating woman was unquestionable.'

Annie failed to get the patronage of Government House, in either Melbourne or Sydney. There was an occasion when Fritz happened to be on a visit to Adelaide, and dining one evening with Sir William Robinson, Governor of South Australia, her name was mentioned in passing. When the latter heard that she was representing herself to be well known to Sir Henry Loch, he doubted the story and subsequently telegraphed the Governor of Victoria. 'What do you know of Mrs Gordon Baillie?' he asked. The answer was laconic. Sir Henry wired back one word: 'Nothing.' When surprise was expressed to Annie that notwithstanding her old friendship with Sir Henry Loch, the door of Government House should be practically closed against her, she 'shrugged her beautiful shoulders and significantly imputed it to Lady Loch's dislike of her'.

The 'Melbourne Gentleman' was asked if she gave the impression of being an educated woman:

'Most certainly. She seemed to me a highly-cultured woman, widely read, and thoroughly pasted up in current affairs. I notice in your paper that in some biographical sketch of her which appeared in a London society journal, it was stated that her favourite pastime was translating from Italian authors. I don't know anything of her linguistic acquirements, as she never paraded them in her conversation. I never heard her make use of a German or French phrase. Her language was terse, picturesque, nervous English, which she spoke without the slightest trace of a Scottish accent. She seemed to have a good knowledge of general literature, and was glibly familiar with art and musical subjects. Her opinions, however, on musical matters in particular, were somewhat eccentric. Her conversational powers were very great, and she could talk prettily and fluently on any topic that happened to be started. She was essentially a woman of the world, clever, well-informed, ready of speech, and unconventional, with her wits sharpened by foreign travel, and made keen by the necessity for their constant use.'

Amongst all the scheming and plotting Annie still had her children to consider. Number 192 Little Collins Street, Melbourne, was home to a small charity for the benefit of the little urchins who sold newspapers on the city streets and on Friday nights they gave concerts so Annie took the girls along for the show. At their appointed time they mounted the platform and one local report claims:

'[They made a] charming picture as they stood singing "Robin" & "The Spider and the Fly" in their sweet childish voices. They were beautiful children, simple and unaffected, and sang their little ditties with surprising precision and power, captivating all who heard them. Mrs Gordon Baillie was, of course, known for her work amongst the poor children of London's East End. It was not only urchins and their sympathisers who were treated to the delightful daughters, Lady Loch and his excellency Sir Henry Brougham Loch, Governor of Victoria, were similarly entertained at the "Exhibition Jubilee Bazaar" on 19 July. "The little Baillies", who must have been respectively eight, six and four years of age, were dressed in frocks of cream serge honeycombed around the neck, fastened at the back of the neck with long loop bows and ends of black velvet ribbon; they all wore open worked black stockings, black mittens and pretty shoes the same colour. They sang in charming style and were warmly encored with Sir Henry dandling two of the little darlings on his knee.'

'It is a remarkable thing,' wrote another, 'that this woman who, it now seems was leading the life of an adventuress, should have been travelling about with four children. But they were useful to her. They lulled suspicion, and were the open sesame to many hearts.' The reporter continued:

'I never saw more beautiful children than those four little girls with flaxen hair and exquisitely chiselled features. They were perfect pictures. Their manners were those of little princesses, and they sang like angels. They were invariably dressed with the nicest care and in admirable taste, and had evidently been brought up in an atmosphere of culture and refinement. Everyone fell in love with them. Even women who detested the mother doted on these charming and innocent darlings, and in their love for them often allowed their feelings towards her whom they called "mamma" to become mollified. What could a woman do when Mrs Gordon Baillie, accompanied by this beautiful quartet, called upon her? She had to be received for the sake of the children. No woman's heart could resist them. Mrs Gordon Baillie could manage the men single-handed; she required the assistance of her pretty children to captivate their wives.'

Nor was the entertainment confined to the younger generation. A correspondent in Melbourne wrote:

'A story is current in the clubs here about that charming impostor, Mrs Gordon Baillie, which I know to be perfectly true. She had invited a select party of gentlemen to sup with her at her rooms one night, among those present being some of our leading merchants. She was profusely hospitable (at the expense, unfortunately, as it now transpires, of our too-confiding tradespeople), and delightfully entertaining. Wines of all descriptions were in liberal supply, and champagne flowed like water. During the evening, or rather the "wee sma' oors ayont the twal," the lady excused herself and retired. After a brief interval, she reappeared, wholly attired in flesh-coloured silk tights, to the no small astonishment of her guests. In this novel costume she continued to grace the festive circle until the party broke up.'

All this entertainment came at a cost, of course. J.H. Knipe, one of Melbourne's smartest auctioneers and a supporter of her ideas for the crofters, had frequent visits from Annie, who noticed that he had a magnificent collection of jewellery entrusted to him for sale. Late one afternoon, after all the employees had left the auction rooms and Mr Knipe was writing letters in his office, Mrs Gordon Baillie drove up in her hired carriage and explained to the auctioneer that she was in a fix. She had an invitation to a dinner at Government House and had not brought her gala jewels to Australia with her; would Mr Knipe therefore possibly oblige her with a 'rig out' for the occasion? Of course she would return the items the following morning. Knipe fell into the trap and decked her out in magnificent diamonds worth £1,000. He never saw her or the jewels again, and of course could not risk the scandal by advertising his loaning of his client's property. He bore the loss himself, as any sensible man of the world would.

Chapter 21

Tasmania and After
(July–Nov 1887)

The tide seemed to be turning against Annie's 'crofter' scheme in Victoria, but she was already looking at other options. On 26 July 1887, she boarded the SS *Flinders* for Launceston in Tasmania, leaving the owner of the house in Toorak Road lamenting her unpaid rent and a bill for the devastation caused by 'drunken orgies'. She caught the express train to the capital, Hobart, and stayed at Hadley's Orient Hotel, where she was joined by Percy Frost, who arrived on the SS *Doric* from England. Her reputation had grown enormously within the previous few months and her visit was discussed at a meeting of the Municipal Council, who suggested a deputation should wait upon her and left the organization in the hands of the Mayor who, in the end, 'didn't have time'. Annie expressed herself as being quite happy at that, as she was averse to her visit being made public and was there partly to visit old friends: Bishop Sandford, with whom she stayed for several days, and the Rev. J.K. McIntyre, the Presbyterian minister at Dunedin, to explain her plans to them. Sandford was known for his liberal and philanthropic views.

Annie made a quick assessment of the available land and considered the Straits Islands to be unsuitable, being too far from the mainland. Tasmania itself was also too small to maintain a healthy demand, although a canning manufactory might be suitable. It was widely reported in the newspapers that the government had offered her the whole of Flinders' Island – 500,000 acres worth – as a settlement for the crofters. They compiled a report especially for her, which described the soil as rich and fertile, well-watered, with vast kelp beds which could provide almost unlimited manure, and swarming with wallaby and kangaroo. It was about as perfect for the project as could be expected. She had a meeting with the Premier, Mr Philip Fysh, who called at her hotel near the end of the month, during which both Spring Bay and Schouten Island were mentioned as possible places for the establishment of the crofter colony. The Premier expressed sympathy with her, but did not think the scheme would meet with the approval of the cabinet; it was a matter on which parliament would have to decide and she was invited to make a formal request to them on the matter in the next few days.

One of those who was less than enthusiastic about the scheme pointed out that a similar proposal had been made in favour of the Danes and Norwegians – the hardy Norsemen who in their own country were regarded as the toilers of the sea, packing and curing fish for the European market and who also farmed the land – but this had come to nothing. What if this latest scheme also failed? The government would find itself responsible for the welfare of numerous helpless families.

On Monday 1 August 1887, Annie was again summonsed to appear before the Prahran police court in Melbourne, this time for a sum of £11 17s. 4d. owed to her grocer, a Mr E. Kempton of Toorak Road, for goods sold and delivered to her. She did not appear and judgement was awarded against her as before, with costs of 5 shillings.

Having done everything she could in Tasmania, Annie boarded the SS *Southern Cross* and returned to Melbourne. At the end of the month, she and her four children took the train once more to Sydney, but what she was doing there is not known; perhaps taking the children to see their father – though it is not certain Knight Aston was in Sydney at this time.

After their initial support for the scale and scope of Annie's scheme, people began to ask serious questions and examine the cold hard facts of the proposal. The fishermen of Melbourne had already made their opposition clear, and now it was pointed out that the laws of the country would not permit such large areas of land to be set aside for such a purpose, unless there was an act of parliament. Colonisers would have to purchase land in the normal way – and there was little chance of such a change, as it would be contrary to the country's immigration policy. Secondly, there has been no clear evidence that around 1,000 Skye families would want to leave their homeland: it was their determination to cling to their native soil that was part of the problem. What they really wanted was to continue to live as they had done for generations without the increasing greed and harassment of the landlords.

On 11 August, a large deputation of Victoria fishermen met Mr Dow, the Minister for Lands, and several members of parliament. The debate became heated, with a Mr Munro MLA* pointing out that the whole question of the crofters' rents had been gone into and the government commission had reduced them by one quarter or less in some cases; the whole affair was a storm in a teacup and would probably be settled very soon. If they did emigrate, however, the cost had been estimated at between £150 and £250

---

* Member of the Legislative Assembly.

per family, and Mrs Baillie was not a woman of great wealth. Mr L.L. Smith MLA countered this argument with the words: 'You're Mad!' To which Munro repeated that a family of five persons could not be brought out for under £250, and asked if the honourable member knew what deep sea fishing was. 'Yes, before you were born,' Smith shot back, showing that the standard of parliamentary debate was as sharp then as it is today. Questions were also asked about the feasibility of mixing agriculture with fishing, it being stated that 'a successful tiller of the soil cannot also be a successful toiler of the sea'.

The fishermen put forward their objections, and Dow expressed his sympathy with them and promised, to their cheers, that 'the interests of the Victorian fishermen would be conserved in every possible way' and that despite speculation in the press, the government had no intention of granting imported fishermen favours that would not apply to existing fishermen. The meeting drew to a close with the minister saying that he was awaiting a report into the whole affair and looking at other possible uses of the land, including a maritime resort for the population of Melbourne or growing timber, promising that Victorian interests would come first. In a very short time, the 'feasibility study' by Reginald Murray, a geological surveyor, was published, which put an end to any hopes of using Wilson's Promontory for the scheme:

> 'Taken as a whole, the feature of the soil of Wilson's Promontory is its forbidding sterility. The pasturage – what little there is of it – is very poor and I also observed a remarkable lack of animal life, as though even wallabies and native bears could not find means of support. It was also stated to me that any cattle pastured on the Promontory were likely to suffer from "coast disease" necessitating speedy change to save their lives. ... to settle a large population on Wilson's Promontory would infallibly end in disappointment and probably in disaster.'

This was the final nail in the coffin of the crofters' scheme. It may well have been inspired by vested interests, but it was accepted by all parties that the scheme could not now proceed.

When Annie returned to Melbourne, she was accompanied by Percy Frost and many were curious as to why she was known as Mrs Gordon Baillie when the gentleman who accompanied her as her husband was named Frost. She explained that Gordon Baillie was her maiden name, and before her marriage she was well known to the public by it, and so on her marriage it had been agreed she was to retain it so long as she was engaged in a public work. This explanation seemed quite natural and was generally accepted. However, the 'Melbourne Gentleman' quoted in the previous chapter certainly had reservations about Frost:

'She lived in grand style, and kept her equipage and coloured footman. One evening she announced that she was going to the theatre, and would be pleased to see any of the assembled company, (there were several gentlemen present) in her box. The party arrived where they found her and her husband, Mr Frost carrying on an animated conversation with those around her, and attracting much attention by speaking in an unusually loud key. Frost was not much liked and was described as shabbily dressed, and had not the appearance or manners of a gentleman. He was, too, very partial to whisky and seemed a particularly shady character. At the close of the performance, she invited two or three of them to sup with her at her house. Her carriage was waiting for her outside.

'The supper was served in excellent style, and there was no limit to the supply of wine, but a little incident happened during the evening which showed the methods she adopted of raising money. She entered the room and told a pathetic story to one of her guests about a poor man who was downstairs, and pleading that she had no gold in her purse begged the loan of a sovereign to cheer the wanderer on his way to his sick wife and desolate home. She got it, and of course stuck to it. As she was posturing in the role of a public philanthropist this extravagant charity did not appear out of keeping with her character, nor did the borrowing of a sovereign seem at the time a matter of much account. I heard afterwards that she raised many a sovereign in a similar fashion, not one of which was ever returned. On another occasion there were thirty gentlemen present and she was the only lady at the table. Many magnums of champagne were drunk that night which, needless to say, has not yet been paid for.

'The milk episode brought her career in Melbourne to an end. She was sued by her milkman for a small amount. After that people began to give her the cold shoulder. When my friend Fritz saw the announcement in the *Argus* he at once waited upon her. Here was a woman whom he had introduced to his wife, to his friends, into the same circle, indeed, in which he himself moved, sued by her milkman! What did it mean? She had professed to be independent, to be a lady of comparative wealth. Was she a fraud? Was she Mrs Gordon Baillie, the crofters' friend, at all? Who was she? He would find out. Perhaps he did. I never heard what transpired at that interview, whether she made a clean breast of it or brazened it out. But from that time he never acknowledged her again. She had blazed across the Melbourne sky, the comet of a season. Now she was to disappear and be seen no more.'

Annie, Frost and her family finished their trip to the colonies by spending time in Sydney. The correspondent of the *New Zealand Herald* wrote of her time there:

'She was living there in the same style as in Melbourne – carriage, coachman, coloured footman, boxes at the opera, and champagne suppers. During the day she was busy interviewing ministers, politicians, and other public men. I fancy, however, she was running short of ready cash. The tradespeople were beginning to be suspicious, and their bills were pouring in, and their importunities were increasing. One morning, in company with a theatrical manager, I met her in George-street. She stopped her equipage and hailed us. "Have you a spare box," she asked my theatrical friend. He had, and was delighted to place it at her disposal. "I shall come to-night and bring some of the big guns with me," she said. But she did not come. That evening she dined with Sir Henry Parkes, the veteran politician, and wrote the manager a little note expressing her regret at not being able to avail herself of the box at his theatre. Next day she and her husband and children sailed for England under assumed names, in the second saloon of an Orient steamer. As their passages had to be paid for, she must have raised the money somewhere. I saw her no more.'

It was time to move on, and at the beginning of November 1887, Mrs Gordon Baillie and family began the fifty-day return trip to London on board the SS *Orizaba* from Sydney to England.

Once the storm broke the following spring, several prominent people were asked to give their opinion of her proposals and time in the colonies. The Reverend Doctor Cameron Lees, the Church of Scotland minister and author, was in Melbourne during the autumn of 1887 and met many of those in society who had made her acquaintance. He stated that her appearance was as though she had suddenly sprung upon Melbourne society with a 'sudden and great flourish of trumpets', and that she had appeared through the medium of the local press as the champion of the Scottish crofters and one who had arrived there for the purchase of land to carry out a great immigration scheme, which she had conceived. Many of the good folks of Melbourne were more than surprised that someone in the position of Mrs Gordon Baillie should be entirely unknown to the Rev. Doctor. In view of what he had heard, Dr Lees thought it advisable to call upon Mr McKinnon, the editor of one of the Melbourne journals, whom he knew to be a Skye man and well acquainted with the names of all the Highland families, to ask what he knew of the Gordon Baillie family. The latter expressed great doubts as to the *bona fides* of the lady, in fact, so much had he doubted her, he had not mentioned her in his journal. Despite this, Annie seemed to have greatly enjoyed her visit, the only hitch having been the dairyman suing her for payment of her milk bill.

As noted above, she also visited Daniel Sandford, Anglican Bishop of St Paul's, while in Hobart, and presented herself as the daughter of an old friend – reminding him of a former meeting they were alleged to have had when she was a girl and the bishop and her family were on visiting terms in Scotland. So convinced was he of her genuineness, that he entertained her for several days as his guest and became enthusiastic about her scheme. When Dr Lees met the bishop her name was mentioned, with the doctor expressing some misgivings about her, but the bishop immediately trotted out the line that he had been fed about her being an old friend of the family in Scotland. This assurance came as a shock to Lees' former scepticism, but he resolved, while not casting any doubts on the lady's character, to give them no assistance by word or deed. Lees had been honoured with a call from Mrs Gordon Baillie since his return to Edinburgh, the article noted, but was not at home to receive her and so they did not meet.

When interviewed about his knowledge of her activities in Melbourne by a representative of the *Edinburgh Evening Despatch*, he gave the following account:

"'I never saw her myself," he said laughingly, "and I fancy she wanted to keep out of my way. One thing which led me to doubt her was being told by a gentleman in Melbourne that she had stood bail for the crofters who were tried in Edinburgh three or four years before. This, of course, I knew she never did."

"'Was she alone in Melbourne?"

"'Oh, no! she had with her a gentleman who was known as Mr Frost. She gave out that he was her husband and stated that Frost was his 'non de plume'. I was told that he signed under that name."

"'Then this was the only person with her?"

"'No, and this I have not seen mentioned anywhere yet. She had along with her two little girls, who during her stay, sang at concerts in Melbourne."

"'And how well did she conduct herself over there?"

"'Well she pushed herself into prominence in every possible way; resided in a fine house and drove about the town. One gentleman told me that she was negotiating with him for the purchase of a large tract of land for crofter settlements, and it is said that she intended acquiring land at a place called Wilson's Promontory. In fact the newspapers were engaged in discussing whether the government should allow her to have it. Another thing, bye the bye, you might like to know," the doctor added with a smile, "was that on the first day of the year I received from her to my surprise a New Year's card, 'With the Compliments of the Season'.'"

Mr Alexander Taylor of 41 Regent Street, Portobello, who was in Melbourne at the start of her visit, seemed to have believed the propaganda and said that she was 'the lioness of the higher circles of wealth and fashion'. He added that she lived in a fashionable house and managed to secure land on a most prolific coast for fishing, near Cape Otway, but the negotiations had brought a storm on the heads of the government from the fishing industry and the entire colony, who feared the competition an influx of crofters would create. Mrs Gordon Baillie had good backers, including the Minister of Lands, and had succeeded, he believed, in securing the land in her own name.

To all intents and purposes, the crofters' scheme was now dead in the water and her trip to the colonies a dismal failure. There was nothing for it but to return home in the hope that her luck would change. She could never have expected how drastic that change would be.

Chapter 22

Familiar Territory
(1888)

Mr and Mrs Frost, their children, baby Percy Elizabeth and all their servants arrived back in England from Sydney in December 1887, having been away for more than a year. The group put up at the Langham Hotel in Portland Place while they looked around for somewhere suitable to live. They soon agreed to rent a house at 32 Eastbourne Terrace, Paddington, for a year at an annual rent of £220, to be paid monthly in instalments. Foolishly, the landlady, Mrs Cox, took neither deposit nor references.

Annie then looked for a driver, and George Fordham of 2 Moor Street, Seymour Place, was interviewed at her new residence. She told him she had been accustomed to ride behind some of the best 'cattle' in London and that she should require him to be very smart on the box. She gave him instructions to get measured for fur capes, cuffs etc., and he was fitted with a hat and gloves at Heath's in Oxford Street. She also sent him to look out for a suitable brougham and stables and he selected a carriage at Coles, of Kensington High Street, but she declined to ride in such a 'rabbit hutch' and shortly afterwards Fordham was discharged.

Annie's long-time benefactor, Sir Richard Duckworth King, had died a few weeks earlier, on 2 November 1887, but the family had cut off her funds via the courts sometime before this. It is estimated that she managed to spend her way through around £18,000 of his money – which, in present-day terms, according to certain estimates, would have been nearly £2 million. This was mainly through 'bills of exchange', which were like cheques but could be sold on to a third party at a discounted rate. King's family and friends had tried to get the police to prosecute her about five years previously, but it seemed that nothing could be done. Upon their return, Annie and Frost had hoped to lay claim to certain of his properties, but by the time the case came to court events had overtaken them, as we shall see. With Sir Richard's death, Annie's glory days were over and she must have become more reliant on her simpler, smaller-scale frauds. This is assuming, of course, that Sir Richard had been her only benefactor – there may have been others, but once her name had started appearing in the papers, they would seek to distance themselves and would certainly not want to brag about any connection.

Similarly, Annie may have been involved with other underworld figures like the famous 'Jim the Penman' of a few years before. There may have been schemes and scams a-plenty which paid off, but again not something which could be bragged about. That August, her old associate and secretary, Henry Toler, had been arrested along with fellow fraudster William Bryant, and the pair were sentenced to five years' imprisonment on 22 November 1887 at the Old Bailey for false pretences. Certain reports claimed that Toler was superseded as Annie's secretary by a man named Matron, who is alleged to have assisted her in perpetrating many frauds, but if true, nothing has been discovered about him.

Despite all evidence to the contrary, several newspapers at home and abroad continued to report that land had been granted to Annie and that the crofters' scheme was still very much alive; its success was simply a matter of raising the funds. Having done all she could in Australia and New Zealand – with pretty negative results – the next thing to do was to muddy the waters, claim victory, continue to publicize the scheme and collect any donations before the truth came out. To this end, Percy Frost went to see his old contact and editor from the *Pall Mall Gazette*, William Stead. He enthused about the incredible schemes of Mrs Gordon Baillie, whom he described as 'rich and philanthropic', brandishing copies of Australian newspapers that had backed her scheme. Frost asked Stead if the newspaper would like him to interview this great lady on their behalf on what was one of the most newsworthy issues of the day. He may not have mentioned that they were living together as man and wife and had a baby daughter together, or maybe neither side thought this relevant. After all, Frost had contributed letters about the crofter issue before and had interviewed the 'Glendale Martyr' in Skye on a previous occasion. Stead readily agreed to the idea, and the interview was published on 23 January 1888, under the heading 'HOW TO HELP THE CROFTERS':

> 'Mrs Gordon Baillie, whose name is so well known in connection with the defence of the Skye crofters in 1883–5 has just returned from a tour through the Australian colonies. She has been travelling as the 'crofters' advocate' with the object of ascertaining the possibility of establishing Scotch village fishing settlements on the coast of one or other of the colonies. Her mission immediately attracted much attention both in the Australian Press and in political circles. She received promises of support from influential landholders both in Victoria and New South

Wales and her success may best be judged by her own words, in an interview which she granted to our representative last week before starting out for the Highlands.

'I found her in her cosy study, the floor of which was strewn with Australian papers while the table was burdened with heavy looking blue-books on the fisheries of different colonies which showed that Mrs Gordon Baillie had not superficially studied the problem which she had set herself to solve. After a few minutes['] general talk on the colonies Mrs Baillie answered the following questions about her scheme:-

"'Do you think it necessary for the crofters to emigrate?" I commenced by asking.

"'I do," she replied, "for the simple reason that any remedies which might be expected from land law reform or Land Acts will be and are likely to be long deferred, while in the meantime the people are dying like dogs from starvation."

"'But I thought in 1884 you expressed yourself publicly as opposed to emigration?"

"'As a Highlander I detest it, but look, even if the crofters did get their land at reduced rents and their holdings enlarged, I see no hope for this generation without capital to till the new lands acquired which are already exhausted by the sheep runs; and for arguments sake give the crofter his present holding rent free, and he would not be able to live. Of course I do not say that with the liberty of the seashore and with the right to sell his fish to any comer, advantages which are now denied him, he might not be able to live, but it would only be existence."

"'You think then, the crofters suitable as immigrants?"

"'Not in individual families, but only in communities, because the Highlander is romantically sensitive and clannish; he will always work better with people of his own race and tongue."

"'What is your scheme for them then?"

"'That we make fishing settlements of 100 to 250 families on the sea coast of Tasmania and Australia, where each head of a family will become proprietor of a 50 acre freehold by a purchase of one shilling an acre. The land is fertile, with plenty of game (and no game laws), and the coast abounds with most excellent fish and is further adapted for deep sea fishing. I have been over a great deal of it personally. I have acquired the pre-emption right of 70,000 acres of land on the Gippsland coast, Victoria and a large quantity of most rich land in Tasmania, which I prefer for this purpose to anything in the colonies."

"'I always understood New Zealand was considered most suitable for the crofters?'"

"'Well the late Mr MacAndrew of Dunedin, wrote me that he had secured 20,000 acres in the Otago District; but I visited it and found it entirely unsuitable. Besides there is no market in New Zealand; the coast is dangerous; the country is burdened with a debt of which every newcomer must bear a share, and it is under great depression, while Sir Julius Vogel's one idea is to borrow money to build railways in which there is no one to ride. To live in New Zealand at present is a luxury only for the wealthy. Now in Victoria I interviewed personally all the fishermen of the colony – they only number 1,500 all told – and I did not find one who did not think he was doing very badly when making £4 per week, and then only a week of four and a half days.'"

"'Look at this contrast,'said Mrs Baillie handing me two photographs, one of a comfortable house of a Victorian fisherman and the other of a wretched crofter's hut in Skye.

"'Well', she continued, "there was a good deal of opposition at first, but that was stirred up by a Melbourne fish salesman who feared that their notorious ring would be broken up, but when I saw the fishermen they came round entirely to my views. The fish ring is a curse to the country. It makes fish a fabulous-priced luxury, so that poor Catholics cannot afford to buy it for their Friday's dinner, and also keeps the money out of the fisherman's pocket; the difference between the price charged to the consumer and that paid to the fisherman being quite 200%, while large quantities of fish are destroyed daily.'"

"'Was the government with you in this scheme?'"

"'I received every courtesy and warm encouragement not only from the government but from all members of Parliament. They not only placed the railways at my disposal, but also gave me an experienced official to assist me in finding out about the fishing industry and the location of lands. Everyone was most anxious for the success of the scheme, and several ladies have promised to provide several boats and tackle.'"

"'Why did you say just now that you preferred Tasmania?'"

"'Because the climate and land are better and the fish are more suitable for curing; the 'Trumpeter' for instance does not exist in other Australian water and the tinning of fish will be a staple industry. There is a great demand in the up-country districts in Australia for tinned fish, and there is no local industry of the kind. The Bishop of Tasmania, a Scotsman, strongly urged in discussion that Tasmania was the only place for the crofters. Here too the government have promised special facilities."

"'How do you intend to carry out your scheme?'"

"'Well my plans on the other side are pretty well cut and dried. The land is arranged and plans taken for dwellings, boats, tackle etc. Money has also, as I have already said, been promised. Here I shall have to arrange for the conveyance of the crofters to their new homes, and the crofters who wish to go will have to be carefully selected. There is sympathy enough to find sufficient money."

"'I mean do you expect assistance from the government?'"

"'It would be premature to discuss that question now as I have only just arrived, but there will be any amount of private assistance."

'Here some more callers appeared so I took my leave. Mrs Gordon Baillie's youth and enthusiasm, together with her indomitable pluck, which has already established so much almost single handed in Australia, are fruitful promises of the success of her cause, especially when the great necessity of something being done for the crofters is urged upon us every day.'

Copies of the *Pall Mall Gazette* were delivered every evening to 32 Eastbourne Terrace, and when the article appeared with her portrait, she showed it to her landlady, Mrs Cox, and remarked, 'However did they get that I wonder!' 'I wonder,' repeated Mrs Cox, in mock surprise, looking her straight in the face. She knew of Frost's connection to the newspaper and had good reason to wonder; she had not received any rent and eventually employed a lawyer who threatened court action unless payment was made. Frost paid the outstanding amount of £54. During their three months there, they employed two maid servants, along with a butler named Gigner, whose main job it seemed was to run errands and to answer the door bell – Annie had him measured for a green suit by Griffith Williams, a tailor of Paddington, which was delivered at a cost of £5 15s. but never paid for. She also rented a stable at 11 Porchester Mews, where she kept her carriage and pair, which she drove everywhere, always on a mission of charity for her 'dear crofters'. Despite what must have been, in reality, the end of her resettlement scheme, Annie continued to work hard at promoting it, still hoping that one day there would be some kind of magnificent pay-off.

A draft prospectus was prepared, in which she named herself as honorary secretary and Henry Leigh Ormsby as paid secretary. Ormsby was a Cambridge graduate and barrister with chambers at 4 King's Bench Walk, who had earlier provided a reference for Frost when he rented Westminster

Chambers and wrote a letter to *The Globe* in support of the emigration scheme: it seems that he was genuinely interested. The Honourable Charles Hamilton Bromby, who had been Attorney General of Tasmania briefly, was described as counsel to the scheme. Bromby was the son of the Bishop of Tasmania, born in England, and after a brief stint in Tasmanian politics, returned there to practice as a barrister. He was quite possibly a cousin to Percy Frost. Both were men of liberal and reformist views, and probably agreed for their names to be used in good faith. The prospectus stated:

> 'A promise has been obtained from the Government of Tasmania by the honorary secretary, of a large tract of land in every way suitable for the crofters in their new home, with comfortable dwellings, all requisite boats and nets and also to establish a canning manufactory to utilise the product of their fishing. Besides the constant demand for such products in Tasmania itself the Australian markets are within easy reach of the proposed settlement. A sum of over £5,000 has already been promised towards this object and it is hoped that the government will be induced to assist in providing the means of transit.'

Annie managed to gain an interview with Secretary of State for Scotland, Lord Lothian, at Dover House in Whitehall, who was in favour of the scheme in principle, although doubted its feasibility. She began letting it be known she had obtained several grants of land for her plan, and due to there being no official statement from Australia to contradict this, several newspapers published her statement as fact. Some, however, realized the bid had failed and were surprised by her statements. 'Could it be,' asked one, 'that the Honourable JL Dow or Mr Fysh have entered into a private arrangement with Mrs Baillie which has been kept from the press? Otherwise one is forced to come to the conclusion that Mrs Baillie's imaginative faculty must be very strong.' They didn't know the half of it!

After being refused a grant of the 70,000 acres on Wilson's Promontory, she applied for a grazing lease there, on the understanding the land would be divided between incoming crofters. The Minister for Lands not only turned down the request, but also questioned whether she had any right to speak for the crofters at all: 'Not a shilling was ever received from her or her husband with regard to the land at Wilson's Promontory and Victoria is under no obligation to supply land to any of her protégés should they make their appearance here.'

Undaunted by these setbacks, Annie continued to swindle and defraud whatever came her way. She carried on with her displays of wealth and extravagance, contracting debts with a large number of tradesmen in the neighbourhood. A jeweller named John Le Cheminant of 32 Craven Road, West London, was one of her victims. According to his account, she first called at his shop in mid-November 1887 and sold him several pieces of jewellery, before returning at a later date to obtain items on approbation. She liked the quality but did not pay him, though he managed to 'get the greater portion of it back'. He says he 'stopped her little game in the area' and thought she shouldn't be too hard to track down, as 'there is a lot of luggage at the Midland railway station cloakroom marked RPBF and they have a manservant who wears a wig'. A dairyman named Chilton seems to have been wiser than most, as he supplied her initially, even though his suspicions were aroused 'the moment she entered the shop', but stopped not long afterwards. Her notepaper at this time was headed with a crest that combined those of the Bruces and the Campbells, along with the motto *Fuimus* (We Have Been). She always used the name Gordon Baillie rather than her husband's name, she explained, when the question arose, because he had once been bankrupt, which was true in part, although she no doubt omitted the part about him still being in that situation.

When interviewed later, landlady Mrs Cox claimed Annie 'assumed the airs and graces of a high born and wealthy lady', but even when her true nature was revealed, still described her as a 'most fascinating woman who had quite won her heart and said that she would have done almost anything for her'. Money still seemed to be coming in from somewhere, and as was their usual practice, the family occupied more than one property. During the early part of 1888, while still living at Eastbourne Terrace, they took a lease under the name of Seymour on the furnished Marine House in Broadstairs at 15s. per week. They retained their existing governess and housekeeper, along with five servants, and lived with all their usual flamboyant extravagance, despite, as one servant later claimed, 'Mrs Gordon Baillie, being unable to write and employs a secretary, [while] when at Broadstairs her letters are written by the governess'.

The resettlement scheme may no longer have been viable, but there was still plenty of activity in the Highlands of Scotland. On 15 December 1887, a group of crofters consisting of around thirty men and women attacked the fence around the newly enclosed farm at Clashmore in Assynt, 10 miles from Lochinver, on the west coast of Scotland. They broke down fences, drove their own sheep and cattle on to the landlord's property and threw stones and mud at his agents. The attackers, it was claimed, wore women's clothes, with shawls over their heads and blackened faces. The ensuing 'riot', as it was called, formed the culmination of a month of similar protests by the locals against the seizure of what had been their grazing land. This was not the first time that this had happened and was merely the most serious occurrence in a long period of local unrest. Despite attempts at disguise, several were easily recognized and arrested, including Hugh Matheson, Mary Kerr and Johan Macleod. Their subsequent trial brought to an end a series of cases against the crofters, held at The High Court of Judiciary in Edinburgh, in front of Lord Craighill. The two women, whom the judge described as 'prominent actors' and said that 'a worse case had not been met with', received nine months each.

Mary Kerr was the wife of Hugh Kerr, one of the crofters' main spokesmen and known as a 'Modern Rob Roy'. He had been on the run since April 1887, after seizing several summonses from a sheriff's officer and burning them. He had been living in caves and sustained by supporters and neighbours, slipping out to address meetings and making the occasional visit home, narrowly evading capture on several occasions. Kerr had had enough and pretty much allowed himself to be captured in the home of a relative. Ironically, the two women prisoners were released at the same time. The trial and imprisonment came like a gift to Annie and could not have been better timed. The sentences were harsh, the cause just and the details were fresh in the mind of every well-meaning and fair-minded Scot. She made plans for a trip north to capitalize on the situation.

On the evening of Tuesday 14 February, Annie arrived at Edinburgh's Caledonian Station via a third-class carriage from London's Euston Station. She was accompanied on her departure by a man 'having outwardly, the appearance of a gentleman', and took a carriage to a fashionable boarding house in Coates Crescent. The house was full, but the respectable-looking lady was referred to No.18 Melville Street, kept by a Miss Paton. Annie arrived and announced herself as Mrs Gordon Baillie, but Miss Paton's suspicions were aroused by the fact that her guest's single piece of luggage bore the name 'Elliot'. Annie explained that the box was her maid's and that she was borrowing it for the trip; the sharp-eyed landlady seemed satisfied. She did, of course, have a maid named Elliot who had accompanied her to New Zealand and Australia. Annie explained to her host that during her stay she should require the use of a carriage and pair, along with the services of a 'steady driver' who, on top of his fee, would receive a good lunch each day at her expense. A carriage was obtained locally and made good use of. One of her first visits was to a servants' register office in Stafford Street to find a well-educated young woman to act as her 'amanuensis' or personal secretary, and Jane Ellen Cameron of Marchmont Street was duly engaged.

One of her other early visits in Edinburgh was to Professor John Blackie, a distinguished classicist and well-respected professor of Greek, as well as an unconventional radical, supporter of the crofters' grievances and a Scottish nationalist. Annie introduced herself as Mrs Gordon Baillie of London, who had a very active interest in the cause of the Highland crofters and was a Highland proprietrix herself with an estate in Ballachulish, Argyllshire. The learned professor seemed quite satisfied of her genuineness and offered to help in any way he could. Her requests were simple; she required, and secured, letters of introduction to the Lord Provost and the Prison Commissioners, as she was anxious to visit and interview the two women in Calton Prison – Joan Macleod and Mary Kerr. She explained to Professor Blackie that her aims were twofold: first, she wished to get up a petition to Lord Lothian, the Secretary of State for Scotland, with the aim of liberating the prisoners; and second, she wanted to set up a scheme of emigration whereby relief would be given to congested parts of the Highlands and Islands, with the lives of those remaining improved and secured. Blackie later described his impressions to a reporter from *The Edinburgh Evening Despatch*, at first protesting he knew nothing much about the lady, but he then asked: 'Well, what's the news?' Upon being informed Mrs Gordon Baillie was the latest sensation, he admitted knowledge of the revelations, but reaffirmed he did not have much to contribute: 'She called upon me as a stranger and I received her politely as I do all strangers.'

'Was there nothing to make you suspicious of her in any way?' the reporter enquired, to which Blackie replied:

'Nothing at all, but [emphatically] I verily believe she would have deceived the devil himself. Her manners were faultless and she gave every appearance of being the Highland proprietrix that she claimed to be, [and I] had never met a woman who talked more sense – good practical sense not mere sentimentalisms. She felt that the islands were overpopulated and she had devised a scheme of her own for bringing about a better state of matters. She spoke as one who had studied the question and who was thoroughly conversant with it. Such an extraordinary combination of head, heart and hand the like of which I have never met.'

Blackie continued that it had been his intention to call on her to discuss the crofters a couple of years previously when he was in London, but something came in the way of him doing so. She had not asked for any money or subscriptions to her scheme, so he had had no immediate need to check her background.

With her simple requests granted, she went first to the Lord Provost's premises in George Street and managed to obtain an audience with the prison commissioners. The result of this was that they gave her an order to visit the two women crofters, which she did on the 17th, along with her scribe Miss Cameron, a Mrs McLaren of Newington House and a Miss Wigham. She found them 'very much dejected' as they had heard nothing from their families, whom they 'had been compelled to leave in the direst distress'. The interview concluded, she was driven to the premises of Mr Henry Erskine, a florist of George Street, where she 'obtained' a handsome bouquet of flowers at the cost of a guinea which she presented to Professor Blackie when she dined with him that evening. The guinea was never paid.

The following day was spent visiting Lady Elizabeth Moore in Grosvenor Street and Mr Murdoch Macleod, both prominent in support of the crofters' cause. At the house of the latter – 3 Argyle Park Terrace, Edinburgh – she overstayed her welcome and her hosts were quite wearied before they could induce her to leave. Mr Macleod was happy to later give details of her visit to the local press:

'Being Treasurer of the Clashmore Crofters Defence & Relief Funds, I am accustomed to receive visits from strangers and when this Lady called upon me – I knew nothing about her previously – I of course received her as I do all my visitors. She had, it appeared, learned from Miss Wigham that I was treasurer of the fund and had come to see me in that capacity. It was 9 o'clock on the Saturday evening when she arrived and not withstanding all our polite hints she did not make her departure until 1 o'clock on Sunday morning. For those four hours she kept the carriage waiting in the street, the door of which the coachman kept opening and shutting with a great noise in his endeavours to attract her attention. When she called there were some ladies with my wife on some other business in connection with the fund and I spoke to Mrs Gordon Baillie in another room. I very soon however showed her in beside the company when the conversation naturally turned on the land question. She referred to her doings in Skye and elsewhere of which I was entirely ignorant.

'During the first two minutes Mrs Gordon Baillie, I must say, made an impression on me as a person of superior manners but during her prolonged visit she disclosed some "traits" I might call them, inconsistent with a lady of her assumed position. From her conversation however she seemed a woman of considerable education. She asked me to account for myself saying that she had not heard of me before in connection with the land question. I explained that I had never taken any active part in the matter. In the course of conversation mention was made of John Macpherson of Glendale and it occurred to me to ask if she was the lady – I had no recollection of any name being given in the newspapers at the time – who had presented him with the sword of her grandfather. No, she replied, I should think not, I have more sense.

'She contradicted herself very often and it was that which made me rather suspicious. One thing that she told me before entering the room she repeated to my wife in [a] different way. She told me for instance that she had got from Lord Craighill a signed statement saying that he was very sorry he had passed such severe sentence on the Clashmore women and that in the next week she intended showing this document to the Home Secretary when he was going to dine or lunch with her in London. How, I asked, did you get his lordship to sign such a document? "Oh," she replied. "I commenced by miscalling the crofters saying that I had not received a penny of rent from my crofter tenants for the last four years, but not telling him that I had myself asked them not to pay any rent to me or anybody in my name until I should ask them for it myself." How incredibly generous! "By this and other such means," she said, "I gained his lordship's sympathies and finished up by ordering him to sign it, and he signed it." To my wife she said that she was still going to get the statement.

'She was going to Clashmore, she said, where she had been when she was 14 years of age. Her mother was a Gordon Cumming while her own name was Gordon Baillie – her husband having adopted her surname so that the Gordon Baillie family might not become extinct. Her mother had died at her birth and she was an only child. She was also the rightful Countess of Moray, a claim that she had made years before, but owing to some "irregular" marriage on the part of one of her predecessors she was debarred from taking her proper position in society. She claimed to have estates in the North and property on the Isle of Skye and added that she had recently visited Australia where she had become the proprietrix of something like 75,000 acres, which she had secured purely in the crofters' interest. She spoke of having property in three different counties including the Isle of Skye but never named any of her estates. Her guardian, she said, had recently left her half a million pounds and I wondered that I have seen nothing about the will in the papers.

'The lady talked enough, and more than enough during the four hours she was here; but then she is a woman and not wishing to be hard on the sex I would not, even if I could, tell you all she said and did. However as you are doing a service to the public in general and to the Highlands in particular, by putting people on their guard against this fair deceiver I will mention a few more incidents of the interview. Mrs Baillie seemed surprised and pleased to find a live lady and gentleman, (Mrs Macleod and myself), from Assynt in Edinburgh outside of Carlton Gaol. She was much interested in the history of the Clashmore grievance and especially in Hugh Kerr on behalf of whom she had taken certain lines of action, which would in my opinion save the government of sending any more naval or military expeditions to Clashmore to arrest him. She asked me to aid her in this manner but I was too old a sparrow to be caught with her chaff and so I believe is Hugh Kerr.

'She gave a sensational colouring to her visit to the Clashmore prisoners. My own quiet interview with the same people a few days previously convinced me that the lady had an eye to dramatic effect. It appears she did not give up to the prison officials her admission order as she offered it to me but not seeing my way to impersonate "Mrs Gordon Baillie" I declined the offer. She seems to know a great deal about the upper classes in the south of Scotland and especially in Edinburgh where she said she was at school and knew a great many important persons as well as Lord Craighill whom she spoke of in disparaging terms but with whom she was on such intimate terms as to invite herself to dine with him on Sunday – even against his own expressed wish!

'Mrs Baillie spoke affectionately of an old and trusty Highland pony she used to have when a girl. It was her pet, she once drove it into a quagmire and had to pay two shillings – the first money she ever had of her own – to get it taken out. She had often passed whole nights in the open air with this pony as her only companion sleeping close beside it to keep herself warm. A most extraordinary proceeding this, I thought, on the part of the only daughter of a Highland proprietor, brother of a[n] Earl and owner of estates in at least three counties! In view of what has since been disclosed about her early life I think that she was giving a romantic version of what was a very prosaic reality – that her favourite Highland pony was identical with the animal that carried the wares of the hawker Sutherland, her step father, and that she may have occasionally slept in the open air as hawkers often do.

'She talked a great deal about Percy, her husband, who was at school with her and was part proprietor of *The Pall Mall Gazette* and other London papers. He is now the happy father of four or five beautiful children whose likeness she was to send Mrs Macleod – if she would accept them. On pointing out that we had no claim to such favours we were told that "all friends of crofters had claims on her". Mrs Baillie also said that she had been trained as a nurse in the Edinburgh Infirmary and used to go in for religion when she was young and foolish but the prospect and enjoyment of her married life with Percy had knocked all these matters out of her head.

'She told the most extraordinary stories about herself. Sheriff Ivory had treated her to a champagne dinner in order that she would not stir up the Skye people too much against his authority. Next day she was at the head of 900 men on the face of a hill; when the sheriff arrived she ordered them to "stand up to a man, off with their hats and give three cheers for the Queen". So the poor sheriff had to depart disappointed at getting no prisoners and at the loss of his champagne dinner. On one occasion in Melbourne she addressed a meeting of 1,500 fishermen brought thither from all parts of Victoria at her expense to discuss her emigration scheme. She was especially severe on the Honourable James Munro of Melbourne[,] a Sutherland man who trained in Edinburgh, [who] has been very successful in business in that city and has made his mark in Victorian politics. Probably the canny Scotsman was too shrewd for her.

'Did she ask you for any money? Well, no; she asked how much I had got and was disappointed at the smallness of the fund. She did not however promise to subscribe, but declared that she would get Lady Elizabeth Moore – whom she styled simply "Miss Moore" to give £300 for the cause; she had demanded £500 and had refused £100 from the Duchess of Sutherland for the same object. She had bearded [confronted] Lady Matheson and had told her that she (Mrs Baillie) would go in a petticoat before she would drink up the life blood of the poor crofters as her ladyship had been doing without right to draw any rent from them. In short, Mrs Baillie's promises, statements and general conduct were so extraordinary that we could account for them only by supposing that her brain was affected. Despite any reservations we had about her – and my wife's were stronger than mine, I considered it a gross breach in proprietary towards people she had never met before to make such a prolonged stay, more especially as my wife is not [in] very good health.

'With reference to her appearance I should say she has a good figure, tall and well-made. I would not describe her face as beautiful but she certainly has the most attractive eyes which are large, black and beautiful, she is one might say of the brunette type. She was richly attired, her chief article of dress being a long fur cloak. In the course of conversation she happened to twist her head energetically to one side and exposed a mole on the neck which I have since learned is one of the marks on Mary Ann Bruce Sutherland. What was the object of her visit to Edinburgh? Well I don't know that, but I think it probable that she intended to get herself interviewed and otherwise noticed by the Scottish press and then to use these notices in England or elsewhere as a lever to "raise the wind". But I have already told you too much, though far short of it all, and hence I must here cease.'

While in Edinburgh she did visit a few tradesmen, but for once none of them appear to have suffered in consequence. She had a valuable collection of furs sent on approval to her apartments, but the salesman became uneasy and got them back, despite Miss Paton trying to allay his fears. At the jewellers Mackay and Cunningham, Annie asked for an expensive gold broach to be made in the form of a crest, which she said was that of the Gordon Baillie family; it was made but never collected. The wording was 'Fuimus', motto of the Bruce family, as she had on her notepaper. Annie was driven back to her apartments in Melville Street, with the coachman left sitting outside for an hour before being informed his services would no longer be required; his bill of £8 15s. was never paid and history does not record whether the promised lunches were forthcoming. Her bill came to £4 12s., including 23s, for 'millinery'. She gave a cheque for £4 10s. and paid 2/- in cash. The cheque was drawn on the London bank of Smith, Payne & Smith, 1 Lombard Street, and was, for once, honoured.

Annie's five days devoted to promoting the crofters' cause in the Scottish capital were drawing to a close, and on the Sunday evening, 18 February 1888, she was visited by a Mr John MacDonald, an insurance clerk of 12 Union Street, who made a little extra money by supplying stories to a few northern newspapers. Annie had met him before and was hoping to use him to get notices, appealing for support for the crofters, inserted in the papers. He accompanied her to the Caledonian Railway Station, along with Miss Cameron, but noticed that she appeared very nervous and anxious not to be seen in his company as she was expecting to 'meet a friend'. Her real reason would seem to be that she was about to travel in a very cheap and uncomfortable third-class carriage – not at all the sort of image she would want portrayed in the newspapers. Giving Miss Cameron a miserly 8/- as part-payment for her four days' dutiful service, Annie explained the cheap carriage was only to Carstairs, where she would change to a more suitable conveyance. According to the railway guard who saw her return, she was again met at Euston by the tall man, presumably Percy Frost.

Once Annie had left, something began nagging in the back of John MacDonald's mind. When he interviewed her for *The Scotsman*, she spoke at length about her Highland estate and her life among the crofters, but the piece had not been published as the editors were very suspicious of her claims and the article had been returned to him. He also forwarded a letter on her behalf, in which she made an appeal to Scottish women in support of the female Clashmore prisoners. MacDonald was not as easily duped as countless others. He had made inquiries and there was no record of a person of that name owning estates in the Highlands, or knowledge of her amongst the crofters he had spoken to. He contacted *The Aberdeen Free Press*, asking them not to publish, but he was too late and the appeal was printed under the headline 'THE IMPRISONED CLASHMORE WOMEN – APPEAL TO THE WOMEN OF SCOTLAND', as the paper thought it deserved publicity in the light of recent events:

'Dear Sir,
'My love of Justice, my love of sex, and my love of fair play are the only reasons I can advance for craving space in your valuable columns.

'I desire to plead the case of the two women who are at present undergoing nine months imprisonment in Edinburgh for the part they took in the recent disturbance in Clashmore. I most strongly condemn the taking of the law into one's own hands, but on the other hand I deeply deplore any miscarriage of justice. In regard to the case I have just mentioned I am convinced that the law was broken but certainly not to the extent that the sentence pronounced would imply.

'The question is one to be considered entirely apart from politics. I myself am a landholder in the Highlands and I have spent a large portion of my life among the crofter population and have given considerable time to what is now commonly called the "Crofter Agitation". There can be no denying the fact that the Highland people as a body have been scandalously treated by their landlords and the outbreaks which have recently taken place are the outcome of a large system of tyranny and oppression on the part of those who should have acted as benefactors of the people.

'Being desirous to see the women, I applied to and received from the Prison Commissioners leave to have a special interview with the prisoners. I found them both bearing the sentence as only Highlanders can, but there can be no concealing the truth that their imprisonment is gradually but surely breaking them down. This is particularly noticeable in Mrs Hugh Kerr, who informed me with tears in her eyes that she feels entirely prostrated and cannot obtain a wink of sleep through thinking of the safety of her husband. She implored me to tell her whether or not he had yet been captured and on my informing her that he still enjoyed his liberty, a great weight seemed to be removed from her mind. Nevertheless I am positive that if she is left much longer in her present position the effects will be most injurious to her mind and body.

'The other woman Mrs Macleod is considerably younger than Mrs Kerr. Her family is not so large and her husband not in the same position as Hugh Kerr. The circumstances tend to make her incarceration fall lighter upon her, but the anxiety she evinced regarding her youngest child was indeed most touching and fully displayed the love which a mother only has for her children.

'My interview was of short duration but the impression it has made upon my memory will never be effaced. Before leaving the women charged me with messages of love to their husbands and families. As I was quitting the cells, each of them embraced me and beseeched me to do my utmost to have them restored as quickly as possible to their homes. As a mother, I therefore appeal to the women of Scotland and more particularly to those women who know what it is to be a mother with a young child at her breast, to do their best to see that the sentence passed on these most unfortunate women, if it cannot be revoked will at least be considerably shortened. The women on whose behalf I plead are not criminals in the ordinary sense of the word. They belong to a class who have long been noted as law abiding and God fearing people.

'I trust my appeal will not be in vain, and should this letter have the effect of stirring up the women of this country to see that justice shall be done to all classes, and especially to their sisters in the Highlands, I shall be amply repaid for any trouble I have taken on behalf of a people whom I dearly love and whom I will do my best at all times to serve,

'I am yours sincerely,

'Gordon Baillie 24/2/88.'

Donations were to be sent to The Caledonian Christian Club, 5 Southampton Street, London. Such a heartfelt appeal was doubtless reinforced by her own memories of having served the same sentence in a Scottish jail many years before. Having achieved what she could, Annie returned to London.

With hindsight, it is hard to think that she ever seriously believed the emigration scheme could still work. It was too blatant a lie, the true facts were easy to find with the minimum of investigation and she now had far too high a profile to slide in under the radar. The more we examine such meagre facts as are available to us about her years of campaigning on behalf of the downtrodden Scots, the more an alternative explanation presents itself. Annie was a lifelong con-artist, a swindler and an adventuress. She was addicted to criminality: no amount was too small to attract her attention, and her craving for the euphoria crime gave her was lifelong and constant. How was money to be earned from this audacious scheme? There was no account set up for her to channel donations, no international appeal for funds, no begging letters to wealthy backers. What would her plan have been had she succeeded in the scheme? She couldn't just sell up, grab the money and run. Where could she go, having made herself famous on three continents? She would have to have gone through with it, exporting crofters to Australia. She could then have just run the scheme and quietly skimmed money off the top of whatever grants and donations came in, although this wasn't really her style. Alternatively, she could have set it up legitimately, taken a good wage and fed her addiction to crime through other channels. Or just possibly she wasn't really bothered whether the plan worked at all – and the true nature of the scam had been missed by almost everybody.

When she and her party set out for New Zealand and Australia, Sir Richard's relatives had put his affairs before the courts and frozen his accounts, her main source of income had been cut off, and yet she continued to live the life of the duchess she professed to be. Her small swindles were in no way enough to support her lifestyle. Whilst abroad she dismissed offers in New Zealand out of hand and even tried to get involved with the theatre once more. She didn't send in the detailed plan outline requested by the Minister for Lands in Melbourne, and spent more time enjoying herself with Frost than getting down to serious business. All this added together points to one thing: she couldn't care less whether the crofters emigrated or not because she had already made her money from those who would benefit most from their evacuation – the Scottish landowners!

Credence to the above supposition is perhaps lent by an unnamed 'crofter representative', who wrote to *The Star* suggesting Annie's success during the latter part of her career was due to her approaching the large landowning proprietors for money, in order to promote the scheme and finance her trips aboard:'They readily rose to the bait, as they naturally gave a warm welcome to any project which held out a prospect of expatriating the men who occupied the room which was required for deer.'

There is no further documentary, or even anecdotal, evidence to support this assertion, but it does make more sense than any other view. Whatever the depths of her deviousness, time was running out. The Metropolitan Police, based at Scotland Yard, had been investigating reports of a prolific lady swindler who had been preying on London shopkeepers and small businesses for some time. As noted, The London Association for the Protection of Trade had been chasing the same phantom since the early part of 1884, as had countless creditors. The London detective branch contacted the Edinburgh police by letter, asking for help, and after some investigation by both parties, they had a clear view of their target. Annie had finally overreached herself – and this time it was to prove fatal.

Part IV

Jan–Dec 1888

Chapter 23

The Net Closes
(Feb–May 1888)

On Wednesday 29 February 1888, the Edinburgh *Evening Despatch*, sister paper to *The Scotsman*, devoted two-and-a-half columns to a report by Edinburgh policemen Detective Inspector McEwan and Detective Frew, entitled 'Report of an inquiry regarding the adventuress who has recently been passing herself in Edinburgh and elsewhere as Mrs Gordon Baillie'. This was a full and comprehensive account of the supposed life and crimes of Mrs Gordon Baillie, the 'Crofter's Friend'. It linked Annie to the offences committed in the name of Mary Ann Bruce Sutherland many years before, as well as details of her impoverished childhood, and caused a sensation. Just about every newspaper in Scotland picked up the story within hours, and it went around the globe within days. Annie's downfall was now inevitable, and took less than a fortnight to bring about. The London Metropolitan Police had been receiving reports, and hearing rumours, of a Scottish female fraudster for some time, and the article in the *Pall Mall Gazette* about her visit to the Clashmore prisoners and her false boasts about her ancestry were brought to their attention. They wanted to know if she was in any way connected to a Mary Sutherland, imprisoned in 1872 for fraud, and immediately contacted the Edinburgh police.

Searching a collection of photographs of prisoners who had been in Perth Prison revealed 'the interesting Miss Sutherland to be possessed of manifold female attractions, and officials who had seen Mrs Gordon Baillie did not hesitate to aver that the photograph bore a striking resemblance to her more matured and beautiful features'. One significant feature was a black mole on her neck, that was otherwise 'as white as a swan's wing', which was common to both women. Now believing themselves to be hot on the trail, Edinburgh detectives went through the files of *The Scotsman* and *The Times* for details of her 1872 trial, contacting the police in Dundee and elsewhere – who were now linking her to a Miss Ogilvie Bruce. The case snowballed, helped in no small part by the reminiscences of a chambermaid from an Edinburgh hotel who had accompanied Annie to have her photograph taken and recognized her straight away.

The police now had a comprehensive file on the mystery woman, but nothing upon which to act, so they offered the file to the press to use as they chose: and they, of course, lapped it up.

There were frantic attempts at damage limitation from several of Annie's circle. Percy Frost, for one, inserted a notice in *The Times*, in its 3 March 1888 edition, threatening legal action:

> 'Mr Percival Frost, Mrs Gordon Baillie's husband requests us to state that she has instigated proceedings against the two Edinburgh papers which have recently published serious allegations concerning her. Mrs Gordon Baillie will be glad if anyone who has ever been asked by her for any monies in connection with the Highland crofters or has ever sent her any would communicate with her solicitors Messrs Kendall, Price & Francis, 62 Carey Street, Lincoln's Inn WC.'

Even this was untrue. The *Pall Mall Gazette* sent a reporter around to the solicitors' office, only to be told that they had received no instructions whatever on the matter and had no intention of acting for Mrs Gordon Baillie or her agent. Henry Champion, anxious to believe his friend as always, pitched in with a claim that solicitor George Lewis had been instructed to commence proceedings against the offending papers immediately. However, Lewis was quick to deny that he had any intention of acting for her, as 'he has known of the woman's doings for years past'.

The *Gazette* sent one of its reporters around to Eastbourne Terrace, but again the birds had flown and they had to make do with Mrs Cox, who said that the family had taken a house at 45 Brook Street, about a month before, presumably hoping to avoid the press and creditors. Frost had also taken rooms at 5 Westminster Chambers off Victoria Street, probably as a bolthole and for similar reasons.

Even as Frost's advert threatening legal action was hitting newsstands, panic had set in at Marine House, the Broadstairs residence. Despite trouble with the landlord, Annie had managed to scrape together enough to secure the place until the next rent due date of Lady Day, 25 March, but there was not enough to pay the staff, who began to leave one by one. The governess went on Friday 24 February, leaving the housekeeper and housemaid with the four children. The gas was cut off, there was no food and tradesmen were again hammering on the door.

On Thursday 1 March, the housekeeper, who had been desperately trying to contact her mistress, discovered that Annie had vacated Eastbourne Terrace, leaving no clue to her whereabouts, so she made tracks herself. According to one newspaper this was Miss Elliot, who had been with her mistress for more than three years and had been part of her party in Australia. She was 'followed to the station', the paper reported, 'by a howling and indignant section of the populace'. The previous Saturday evening (25 February), Annie had booked herself into the nearby Albion Hotel, Broadstairs, to avoid being seen at her house, and collected baby Percy Elizabeth, then about a year old, and her nurse. The following day they took the last train back to London at dusk. In payment of her hotel bill she left her cheque book and promised to send a remittance on the Monday, but of course nothing ever arrived. Frost had written to say that he would be at the house on Friday 2 March, but by seven that evening there was no sign of him, so the governess was picked up by her father and taken back to the family home in Shepherd's Bush. The place was shut up, leaving the four children alone in the house with the last remaining maid and no money. On Saturday 3 March, presumably with great reluctance, the maid informed the relieving officer on duty at the union workhouse in Thanet that there was no food or heating in the house and no sign of the children's parents. The four were immediately admitted under the following names: Gabriel Baillie, born 1878; Ada Mary Baillie, born 1879; Allen Stuart Baillie, born 1880; and Aleck (Alice?) Bruce Baillie, born 1881.

The children's names were wildly inaccurate – presumably the remaining maid had no clear idea of the details of her temporary charges. The following day, Sunday 4 March, Percy Frost finally arrived and, upon finding the house empty, went around to the agent, who told him what had happened. He paid the 'job master' at the workhouse what was owed, and after what must have been an uncomfortable and fearful night for the children, they were entered in the book as 'taken away by father', driven by cab to the railway station and boarded the train for London.

There was, as usual, a good deal of money owed to local tradespeople, and no forwarding address was left at the Post Office. On 4 March, Messrs Flowerdew & Co. of 114a Chancery Lane sent a letter to *The Scotsman* containing the following:

> 'We have read with interest your account of Gordon Baillie in today's issue under the heading of "A Scotch Adventuress" and noticing that you conclude your article with the words "Where is she now?" you may in the interest of the public be glad to give publicity to the fact that we know her various addresses in London and shall be glad to impart our knowledge to any member or the legal profession who may care to apply to us for the same.'

Despite all that was happening, Annie still had a few allies left. Frost's great friend, Henry Hyde Champion, defended her in an interview with the Edinburgh *Evening Despatch*:

'Mr Champion, the socialist said that shortly before she left London for Edinburgh her husband mentioned to him that she was thinking of insuring her life for 6 or 7 thousand. In the course of conversation Mr Champion said that there must be an enormous blunder on the part of the police, as Mrs Gordon Baillie is not the same person as Mary Anne Bruce Sutherland; the crimes of the latter were carried out in 1869 and Mrs Gordon Baillie was at that time only 11 years of age, (ie born in 1858) so she must have been remarkably precocious if she were hiring villas and defrauding tradesmen then, and he knows "beyond doubt" that she was never in Dundee at the time in question. He thinks it is a case of mistaken identity and declared that the lady will obtain sweeping damages for libel.'

Faithful as ever, Champion would only have been repeating what his friend Frost had told him and undoubtedly believed to be true himself. It is quite possible that Frost believed Annie to have been ten years younger than her real age: her eldest daughter was born in about 1877, when Annie was claiming to have been 19, rather than her actual age of 29, so there was certainly no problem there. When did he realize the awful truth? In the dock of the Old Bailey?

It was now time for Annie to defend herself, and the *London Star* carried the following letter from Mrs Gordon Baillie on 7 March, written from her temporary residence, 4 King's Bench Walk:

'Sir, In your issue of yesterday you say that I had not come forward. I have been hitherto taught that it is bad manners to speak while others are talking. When everyone has done I shall know how to answer. I only write now because the name of a dead and esteemed friend, Sir Richard Duckworth King, Bart, has been dragged into this matter, and to say that I am surprised that his relatives and their advisors should let their strong animus against myself go so far as to bring any such disparagement on his name is implied in the vile insinuation of May and September,* more especially as he is not here to answer for himself. I had the honour of his friendship, kindness, and respect during the past 15 or 16 years and had I followed his advice I should probably not have had the honour of writing you this letter. I am Sir, yours obediently, Gordon Baillie.'

---

* 'May–December romance', used when a young, pretty woman is romantically involved with an older man.

Countless rumours spread with increasing speed. *The Scotsman* reported that they had received a letter in which the correspondent told them that Mrs Gordon Baillie was claiming to have married her music teacher, Thomas White, who had run through £70,000 of her money. She had divorced him while she was in Australia, and upon her return had married Mr Frost. Her three children from her first marriage, she said, were in Devonshire. Mr Moss, a well-known Edinburgh showman, had intimated that in the event of Mrs Gordon Baillie's address becoming known, he was prepared to offer her £100 to appear nightly for a week in his Edinburgh Theatre of Varieties.

In response to the letter in the London *Star*, accusing Mrs Gordon Baillie's crofters' scheme of being one big fraud, Frost was most indignant:

> 'I ask anyone, landlord or otherwise, who has ever been asked for or has ever given a penny to Mrs Gordon Baillie for her work to speak up now for the sake of truth and justice ... all monies spent on this matter have been out of her own pocket including the £100 paid to Mr Donald Murray for the defence of the crofters in 1884 which was not "collected". Any debts which she may own or any other grievance anyone may have concerning the crofter matter will be settled through her solicitor and myself if they will kindly forward them to my address, PPB Frost, 4 KBW.'

Frost claimed that by mid-March 1888 he had received bills amounting to no more than £10 in response to his advertisement, which is possibly more a comment on how many people read that paper than anything else.

Try as they might, Annie and Frost could no longer postpone the inevitable, and the final act was now about to begin. Mr Edward Harding, still smarting from the loss of his rent and furniture at Walthamstow seven years before, had been reading a strangely familiar story in the London *Star*. He became an effective private detective and tracked the pair down to their lodgings in King's Bench Walk, before making an appointment at Bow Street Magistrates' Court for the Saturday afternoon. This came to the notice of Frost, who at once appreciated the danger this case posed and sent Harding a telegram: 'Make appointment by writing to Temple when I can see you re the Whyte matter.'

The telegram came after Harding had already gone to Bow Street, only to find that he was too late to make an application for that day. He received Frost's telegram when he returned home, but was determined that he was not be going to be 'humbugged' anymore and continued in his determination to lay his case before magistrate Mr Vaughan. Frost wrote again:

'Sir, I've been talking over with my wife the transactions which you had with Thomas Whyte and she speaks so highly of your courtesy to her while at Stoneydown that I would like to come to some arrangement with you as I have some experience of what it is to be done, and can appreciate your feelings in the matter. If you'll give me an undertaking to sue T. Whyte Aston who was doing well when I left Melbourne and can therefore pay, I will pay the amount though you will understand my unwillingness to pay the debts of another man more especially one who, as you admitted to me, behaved as no man has a right to treat a woman. If you think well of this plan wire me to the Temple what hour you can come and talk it over but not before noon. I'll have the receipts and papers and so there need be little or no delay.'

There is no evidence that Percy Frost and Knight Aston had met at this point, so the wording was probably Annie's. Harding, still not swayed by all the promises contained in the note, kept to his original resolution of going to court. Accordingly, on Monday 12 March he went in front of magistrate Mr Vaughan at Bow Street Police Court and began to tell his sad tale:

Harding: 'I wish Sir, to make an application about a person calling herself Mrs Gordon Baillie, whose name has recently appeared frequently in the newspapers of London & Scotland in connection with large swindling transactions.'

Vaughan: 'But what is it you want to do?'

Harding: 'In 1881 the same person under the name of Ann White in conjunction with a Thomas Whyte, otherwise Knight Aston, defrauded me and my nephew of a houseful of furniture at Walthamstow, valued at about £300 and as I have the names of about 100 other persons at Richmond, Pinner, Watford, Walthamstow and Hackney, who were also swindled out of smaller amounts in the same year by her, I wish to ask you, sir, how can I place the matter before the Public Prosecutor, as she has continued this course ever since 1872 in which year she had nine months' imprisonment?'

Vaughan: 'Well then as I understand it all this happened in Walthamstow?'

Harding: 'Yes.'

Vaughan: 'Would it not be better to make an application in the district where the circumstances occurred?'

Harding: 'Probably it would, I'll take your advice in the matter, but they are now swindling in London, because as recently as a fortnight or three weeks ago this woman, together with a person named Frost, who has letters left for him at 4 King's Bench Walk, Temple, obtained about £80 worth of jewellery at 32 Craven Road, Bayswater, on approbation and the jeweller cannot get either his money or his goods back.'

Mr Vaughan told the applicant the best thing he could do would be to go to the Treasury and swear the facts before the solicitor, who would no doubt take up the matter. Reluctantly, Harding withdrew.

In a bizarre twist, Annie's name was mentioned on the same day in another London police court, less than 2 miles away. At Marlborough Street, William Maitland was summoned to appear before Magistrate Newton by his estranged wife, Jenny Dillon Maitland, to explain why he was not supporting her. Before any formal hearing could take place, their two lawyers seem to have come to an arrangement, the details of which were not reported. However, Mr Abrahams, the wife's solicitor, could not resist a final dig: 'I have now in my possession certain documents which if anything show that the defendant has got off very lightly, indeed ...' Mr Norman, for the husband, butted in here: 'If any speeches are to be made about the matter the offer is withdrawn.'

Mr Abrahams:	'I have come with the intention of handing over to my friend Mr Norman, these documents, and I hope they will enlighten him in respect to what his client is, especially concerning Mrs Gordon Baillie, with whom I find he has been co-habiting ...'
Magistrate, interrupting:	'Really, you ought not to say that.'
Mr Abrahams:	'Very well I will merely hand the papers over.'
Magistrate:	'Yes. What is the use, when you are doing a good act, to ...'
Mr Abrahams:	'Well I have been brought here so many times by Mr Maitland's obstinacy ...'
Mr Norman:	'I could retort that ...'

The magistrate interrupted the bickering solicitors, exclaiming: 'The less said the better.' The matter was dropped, with an order for the payment of 25/- per week by Maitland, which was agreed by both sides.

William Maitland's name first appeared in conjunction with Annie's in an advertisement in the stage newspaper *The Era* in June 1884. His was the address – 52 Regent Street – to which enquiries regarding 'Mrs Gordon Baillie's Provincial and American Tours' had to be sent. He appears again, several years later, during the magistrates' committal hearings where the pair are accused by a Mr Bonham of defrauding him of £150. 'Mrs William Maitland' is also one of the many aliases Annie is alleged to have used during that time. Other reports state that Annie was living at 56 Welbeck Street under the name of Mrs Maitland and was giving elocution lessons in around 1885 – advertising for aspirants to the stage and operating in that regard from 5 Duchess Street.

Emily Soldene, in her memoirs, recalled that Jenny Maitland – originally from Ireland – was 'a charming woman, a bit of a Bohemian and a tremendous smoker of cigars'. It seems possible that William Maitland left his smoke-filled marital home for a while and took Aston's place when he left for Australia, but Mrs Maitland mentions them being married for twenty-three happy years, so as with many other things in Annie's life, their exact relationship must remain a mystery.

William Whyte Maitland had quite an interesting career. He was arrested in 1882 and charged with perjury, having been taken to court by Samuel Stambridge, a sauce and pickle manufacturer, from whom he had rented rooms for some months in 1879 as 'D.J. Wright and Co.' Turf Commission Agents, of Leicester Square. A dispute arose over payment of rent. Maitland signed an affidavit to say that the money was owed by Mr Wright, who had gone to America. Stambridge claimed Maitland was a sole trader who had lied about the existence of Wright, and took him to court for perjury. Maitland was accused of using seven or eight different aliases while operating as a theatrical agent and bookmaker. Further charges of fraud were pending, as it was also alleged that he had accepted sums of between £10 and £100 from young girls and gentlemen with the promise of supplying them with theatrical work. In every case, the prosecution alleged, these theatrical companies were found to be bogus. On this evidence alone, if online dating had been available in 1882, Maitland and Annie would have made a perfect match! Surprisingly, it was discovered that none of the persons who had alleged malpractice in the theatrical line could now be found and those charges had to be dismissed. A little later, it was proved to the court's satisfaction that a Mr Wright did exist and had indeed gone to America, so all charges against Maitland were dismissed.

The history of William's estranged wife, Jennie Maitland, is no less interesting. In 1887, she was arrested for assaulting Mrs Lavinia Stearns, lessee of the Edinburgh Castle public house in Welbeck Street, London. Amongst his many business talents, Mr Maitland appears to have been an expert on finding public houses for prospective tenants, and Stearns desired to increase her portfolio. After a particularly long meeting in Chancery Lane, the pair were returning to his office, along Piccadilly, when the cab was stopped by an irate Mrs Maitland, who attacked them with a stone, threatening to blind Mrs Stearns. After a brief altercation, Stearns told the cab to drive on and left the Maitlands fighting in the street. When she returned to her pub, she found Jennie Maitland had preceded her and smashed the place up. In her defence, Mrs Maitland declared her husband's 'little business transactions' with Stearns had destroyed their marriage after twenty-three happy years. Obviously sympathetic, the magistrate bound her over in the sum of 10 shillings. By 1901, at the age of 53, Jennie was running a boarding house in Kensington.

The continuous and increasingly speculative accusations against Annie within the press generated great interest and prompted the London correspondent of the *Evening Despatch* to track her down and record an interview. She began by denying any knowledge of 'Mary Ann Bruce Sutherland', the Peterhead adventuress with whom police had identified her, and referred to a letter published in the same paper:

'Now I want you to take special note of that point. That letter is dated 1877 when I was in America. It clearly shows that Miss Sutherland was in regular communication of some sort with her temperance mentor. My address – to be seen in the Court Directory – was St James Terrace and I myself was out of the country. Could there be a straighter refutation of the Sutherland allegations?'

She denied that she had been in hiding and continued:

'[N]no one except newspapermen have ever had the slightest difficulty in seeing me. Why should they? Of course it was not everybody who knew where I lived but that was simply because of the enormous correspondence which has resulted from this abominable attack on me. To have my husband's chambers flooded with letters and besieged by press interviewers was quite enough. Why half the papers in London have had representatives after me, [one] kept a man continually trying to make copy out of me. Too ridiculous really! The little man got to know that a cousin of my husband has chambers in the Temple and as he could not extract anything from my husband he just badgered poor Charlie almost out of his wits. It has been dreadful.'

'The first thing that caught my eye as we entered the room in which the interview was to take place,' the reporter observed, 'was a photograph of Professor Blackie prominently exposed on the mantelpiece.'

'You see we have Blackie here in spite of what he said – or rather is reported to have said, for I don't believe the report. If you don't give Blackie's exact words you get a totally wrong meaning.'

(Professor Blackie was reported to have said that she could have 'deceived the Devil', and he received a telegram from Mrs Gordon Baillie at 'The Sanctuary, Westminster' in response, 'I trust you did not say of me that I would cheat the devil himself?' The good professor wired back that 'I said that you were fascinating enough to cheat the devil himself.' His answer was never received, as Mrs Gordon Baillie was 'not known' at the address she had given.)

'He's a dear old man – an eccentric though. Oh! Where is that photo of his with lines on the back and the book *Messis Vitae* which he has just sent me, you must see them, I'll go and find them.'

Reporter: 'And she went only to return in a few minutes to call her husband to assist in the search … It is pleasant room, furnished in excellent taste with low toned carpet and draperies and lighted by candles. Round the walls hang some very choice engravings and etchings which do credit to Mrs Gordon Baillie's artistic perception. On the mantelpiece a photo of Mrs Duncan McLaren (wife of the Scottish Liberal politician) acts as a set off to that of Professor Blackie; and the hostess herself appears in numerous cabinets and panels – sometimes in fancy dress, sometimes with one or other of her very pretty children. The curious thing about her portraits is that not one of the many I have seen could be said to be good. Each catches a little of her but not enough to be recognised at once. She is certainly cast in a generous mould, her conversation is bright, clever, almost entertaining enough to make an interviewer forget his business. She leaves the impression of being a particularly able woman, overflowing with life, kind hearted, clear headed and firm willed; as impulsive as any Highlander, as shrewd as any Lowlander – but shrewd first and impulsive afterwards. Her fleeting expression and general mobility of countenance make it impossible for the photographer to turn out a satisfactory portrait. I was looking at one in which she sits with a little boy in her lap and was marvelling at the bad likeness when she and her husband, whom she had gone to fetch, came back.'

'I suppose you can't recognise it,' she said. 'I've been taken dozens of times and never had a good photo yet. That carte of Blackie has disappeared – can't find it anywhere but these were the lines – "If you love me as I love you" / "You'll send your love and photo too!"

'Dear old man! Here is the *Messis Vitae* though – and just read the inscription.'

The reporter wrote that he had read as follows: '"To Mrs Gordon Baillie with pure human love – John S Blackie" and then came in the original Greek, (and written in villainous characters) the verse, "Not slothful in business; Fervent in spirit; Serving the Lord".'

'Ah well,' Mrs Gordon Baillie laughed, 'no one would misunderstand Blackie when he writes like that. But we will talk about him after. Tell me, for I suppose you have a fair idea – how did this attack upon me arise?'

Reporter: 'Well, the police, as doubtless you read in the *Despatch*, gave the original information.'

'Oh that's rubbish! The police don't raise a hue and cry, do they, when they are after one? And then if the police wanted me why didn't they take me. I'm here. I've been moving about as usual. And what would the police have against me, I should like to know? No, that won't do.'

Reporter: 'How do you yourself account for the scandal?'

'Simply and solely as the outcome of animosity and spite on the part of Sir Richard King's relatives.'

Reporter: 'Indeed?'

'Yes. You see Sir Richard had known me since I was a child and I was a great favourite of his. His relatives were just raging lest he should leave me anything in his will. As a matter of fact he made over to me during his lifetime what he intended for me by deed of gift. And long before he died his greedy friends had detectives watching me, examining my past life to see if there was anything which they could bring forward to induce him to turn against me.'*

Reporter: 'During his lifetime you say?'

'Decidedly. For four years they followed me about. One detective – he used to be employed at Scotland Yard but left under peculiar circumstances – fairly shadowed me. He has even come to my house when Sir Richard had been having tea with my husband and myself. He tried to bribe my servants. Why, he actually tried to bribe me.'

Reporter: 'Bribe you?'

'Yes one evening, when I was going out, he questioned me about Mrs Gordon Baillie and offered me money if I would help him in his

---

* Sir Richard Duckworth King, 3rd Baronet King, of Bellevue, Kent, died on 2 November 1887 at the age of 82.

spying. It's too preposterous. Then finding out about some Miss Bruce Sutherland, or whatever her name is, they try to foist her doings on me'

Reporter: 'Did you belong to Dundee?'

'Oh. No! I was born in the Highlands and educated at Mrs McKechnie's school in Moray Place, Edinburgh. I have the school bills still. But that may be passed over for my mere denial won't affect opinion one way or another. Whichever way one believes now they will believe the same after my denial.'

Reporter: 'Then are you looking for Miss Sutherland?'

'Yes certainly: my husband and I have traced her so far and are confident we shall soon cut the ground from under the feet of the King people in that direction. Of course until we can trace Miss S there's no use in entering the field. Indeed I wasn't inclined to have you interview me just yet; but my husband said that at any rate it wouldn't affect our case – damage it I mean.'

Reporter: 'And can you show that you were elsewhere at the time of Miss S's depredations?'

'Why I was only born in 1858 and so I was 11 years of age or thereabouts when Miss Bruce Sutherland was on evidence first!'

'Oh! and besides that,' said Mr Frost, 'I have ample proof ready concerning Mrs Gordon Baillie's whereabouts at the time.'

'Dear, dear me,' added Mrs Baillie, 'the whole thing is so absurd. Still there is only my word to offer …'

'There is more to it than that,' interrupted Mr Frost.

'Yes, quite so; but until Miss S is completely traced there is no use in giving more than a plain denial. Of course it is very unsatisfactory in the meantime. I have been thoroughly upset. Well you'll know all that; and if it hadn't been for the ludicrous aspect of the charges and the ridiculous things said, I don't know how I should have pulled through. Sense of humour means a lot at times.'

Reporter: 'Just a word more about Miss S. There must be a strong resemblance between you and her.'

'There may be; but you can see for yourself how badly my photos have always been taken. Yet it was from photos that people said they recognised me as Miss Sutherland. All I can say is that Miss Sutherland must be a very "varied" person. One might almost take it that a woman who really was recognised from my photo was anyone but myself. Don't you think so?'

(Reporter: 'I admitted that I did think so – for the thought had occurred to me when looking over the portraits.')

'However,' said Mrs Baillie, 'we had better leave that. Nothing definite can be done until more evidence is gathered.'

Reporter: 'Do you intend to take the matter into court?'

'Undoubtedly. And for the present I have ceased to bother myself on the point. I have not lost a single friend by these so called disclosures – one whom I called a friend previously I mean. More than that hosts of acquaintances have come forward with sympathy. Here's just one example – look at that address presented to me in '85 by the crofters. It seems like bragging to bring it out but the occasion is the excuse. You see the number of signatures. Well! Numbers of the men who signed that have written letters of sympathy to me. I have had altogether over 900 such letters, many of them from Australia. A purification of one's friends is in one way pleasant.'

Reporter: 'When did you return from Australia Mrs Baillie?'

'In November last year by the *Orizaba* from Sydney.'

Reporter: 'What did your party consist of? You know you are said to have gone out under the name of Mathews with some second class male passenger.'

'Supremely ridiculous! I'll tell you how that report got about, and it is a fair specimen of these allegations. I was at Barton for some time before starting and I sent Mrs Mathews, my old house keeper who has been with me for years to book passages. Mr Frost was probably going to be detained in England after I went and so we did not know how many the party would consist of. Mathews booked our tickets and simply took them in her own name. My four children, Miss Heston (my governess), Miss Elliot (my maid), Mrs Mathews and myself eventually sailed together.* My husband followed six months later and joined me in Tasmania. That is the truth of the matter. And some foolish person has added a Mr Mathews to the list.'

Reporter: 'Did you go out on behalf of the crofters?'

'Certainly not. I went out partly on private business, partly on pleasure and merely with the intention of keeping my eyes open about land – so far as the crofters were concerned. The stories of my running away from New Zealand without paying my debts are on the face of them silly in the extreme. Why, my depredators say that I was a sensation all the time I was in in those colonies; they know I had a large party and yet they think it reasonable to suggest that I could run away. It would have been impossible. And as a matter of fact, I always advertised my departure.

---

* Making a party of eight, as stated on the passenger list of the SS Ionic.

Here are some of the advertisements. And that reminds me of what a stumbling block the "Gordon Baillie" has been to some people – my husband's name being Frost.'

Reporter: 'Yes, you might let me know how you came to adopt the name.'

'It was this way. A relative of mine left me some property – worth something among the hundreds per annum – and she stipulated that I should take her name. So as soon as she died I did take the name. That was in '84 shortly before I went to Skye; and in the beginning of '85 I legally became possessed of her name. I think I can find *The Times* with the legal advertisement about it.'

Reporter: 'Then, your name was really Miss Bruce?'

'Certainly my maiden name was. But I was Mrs Whyte when my relative died.'

Reporter: 'About your general indebtedness, then?'

'Bless me, I have lived at the rate of three or four thousand a year ever since I can remember and they accuse me of borrowing single sovereigns! Why, how far do you suppose a sovereign would go with me? It would be no use to me whatever; and as for bringing chickens from Peterhead to London, and such things, not only would I object to pay for them, but I would object to eat them – chickens don't travel from Peterhead to London without feeling it. You can't live as I do on borrowed sovereigns. A sovereign! It's too ridiculous altogether. I assure you I couldn't do it. A sovereign wouldn't go a stone's throw with me.'

(Reporter: 'I said that I believed her.')

'And another thing. I have never been a borrower – the opposite in fact. And if I wanted to borrow money you may take my word that I could do so without the slightest difficulty and not in single sovereigns either.'

Reporter: 'And the debts?'

'The debts!' Why don't those creditors send in their bills? You yourself know that my husband has put notices in the papers asking that all accounts outstanding shall be immediately forwarded to him. And Stead put a paragraph in the *Pall Mall* saying that my creditors had better communicate with him and have the mystery probed to the bottom. Well how much do you suppose the accounts send in amount to? £5.14s. And if I have left debts anywhere all I want to know is what they are. Of course I have always had outstanding accounts – everybody has, and little things may have been overlooked. Just now I owe a couple of hundred pounds perhaps; but not a single one of my tradesmen made the slightest move when I was maligned – not one sent in his bill. Dear me! Who is there in my station who does not run accounts? Spite can make pretty tales indeed. I remember a point which amused me immensely. They say that Miss Sutherland kept a school – in Aberdeen wasn't it? And then they expatiate on the supposed fact that I can't spell and can't write and even "read" books upside down. Delightful!'

Reporter: 'And that mole, Mrs Baillie? If I may mention it.'

'Mention it! Certainly mention it. Here it is quite in view of everybody.'

'Yes,' said Mr Frost, 'after someone remarked the mole on my wife's neck, it was suddenly recollected that Miss Sutherland had one too.'

'Oh, dear,' Mrs Baillie sighed, 'as if I couldn't have had the mole removed had I really been Miss Sutherland! So far from thinking of removing it, I'm vain enough to paint it jet black sometimes.'

In the course of the interview, Annie took up the allegations against herself (as apart from Miss Bruce Sutherland) and denied most of them. She was especially severe on George Stronach, who wrote an account of his acquaintanceship with her in Edinburgh and Dumfries in 1875 as 'The Willing Victim'. Here is an extract regarding him:

'He ate other people's dinners and got into society which he had never approached before – that's all. Nasty little man! Just wait a minute.' (Here Mrs Gordon Baillie went away and returned with a splendid lady's Australian stock whip. She cracked it.) 'That,' she said significantly, 'was sent to me the other day on purpose for Mr. S----. Oh! I know his name of course, so does everybody. There are not many men of such meanness to choose from. It was a colonist who made me a present of this whip. He said I was to use it – energetically – on the shoulders of the Willing Victim. What do you think?'

Annie further said she first visited Inverness in 1873. She is said to have left Perth jail in the autumn of 1873 and remained in Perth only six weeks.

'Now,' she says, 'I left London in July 1873 and travelled to Glasgow, Rothesay, Oban and all those places, and finally reached Inverness. The trip occupied some 3 months. There was a party of us, which varied in size during the journey. When it got to Inverness it consisted of 3 ladies and their servants. I had two retainers with me.'

Discussing the allegations made about her doings in Inverness, Annie got so indignant that Mr Frost had to intervene and remind her there was no use getting into a passion. She remarked that she 'scarcely knew how to contain herself about the foolish things said'.

With regard to statements made by 'an Edinburgh Lady', about her doings in Edinburgh in 1875, Annie said the Edinburgh lady 'is a Mrs. A---, and that her story is false. The fact is, Mrs. A--- was a vain little woman who loved dress and her husband was very close with her in the matter of money'. Annie therefore sold her some dresses which she could not afford to buy first-hand, telling her to pay when she was able to. But Mrs A---, according to Annie, had paid some small amounts but the bulk remained outstanding.

The stories of George Stronach she denounced wholesale:

'About his becoming acquainted with me, there is absolutely no foundation in his story. For his sake I won't say how it happened. As to his story about the play, I never had a play, and never thought of writing one. The infamous fellow! He was telling me one day how he tried to write plays and I, as I had just been reading a lot about the history of Flora Macdonald, suggested that he should base one on that. He was flattered, and I was amused … He used to make frequent calls, and to tell the truth I didn't quite give him the cold shoulder, but I would as soon have thought of going to Roslin with the man in the moon. He was no company except when several people were present to see the fun.'

Then Annie denied the story about her fishing trips and Mr Frost remarked that she would not touch a pistol, adding he would 'wring the neck of that scamp' if it were worth the trouble. She took up the story about the London journalist to whom Stronach was said to have introduced her. She denied that this journalist, Joseph Hatton,* who was easily recognizable as a well-known novelist and once editor of *The Hornet*, introduced her to tradesmen whom she later swindled. She also said that for more than two years she lived near Hatton in St James' Terrace, Regents Park, and instead of the tradesmen complaining that she did not pay, the facts were that some of them complained that they could not get money out of *him*.

Regarding her pursuit of Knight Aston, she admitted that she went to see *Girofle* with Stronach several times, but this was because she was charmed by Catherine Lewis' acting and not because of her fixation with Aston. Mr Aston, she explained, was engaged as her music teacher and she eventually married him, though there is no record of him ever giving lessons. Nearly all the notes and letters that Stronach claimed came from her and had appeared

---

* Joseph Paul Christopher Hatton, 1837–1907.

in the press were forgeries, she claimed, 'charmingly laconic – just ready for printing'. She then talked about the stories of an amorous person who sent up notes in her shoes; she said he was real and that he was a Welshman named Jones. Nearly all her bills were run up by servants with whom she had been over-confident, she claimed: even the cheque for £3,000 signed by Sir Richard King was got up by a servant through a well-prepared tale, and she had been too soft hearted to prosecute.

The story that she took most exception to was the tale that she had disguised herself as a cockney tourist and escaped detection in a kilt: 'A kilt indeed! The *Despatch* is a disgusting paper to let such a thing into its columns.'

The remark was welcomed, as it is the first hint throughout the interview that she was not entirely lost to all sense of decency and right feeling. It was in response to a letter from Mr Frost that the editor of the *Edinburgh Despatch* had cut out some parts of the interview, which gave a one-sided appearance to it. The editor wrote that further intimacy with her only proved more than ever to his mind she is 'a designing and unscrupulous adventuress'.

George Stronach, still hiding behind the name 'Willing Victim' – who had given the touching interview about their activities together in 1875 – had plenty more to say about events. Jumping on the bandwagon of condemnation, he wrote again to the *Despatch*, but his tone had changed significantly since his first reminiscences. He states that he still had the letters he received from her during their acquaintance in 1875, and found himself greatly amused to hear that at that time Mrs Baillie was only 15. He says:

'If any of your readers would like to see this handsome girl of 15 they will have a treat in store for them as the photo taken of her in 1874 is exhibited in the shop of Mr Horsburgh in Princes Street. She owes an account for it yet, but that's nothing for a woman who lives at the rate of "three or four thousand a year" and was educated at Mrs McKechnie's school in Moray Place which is as mythical as her estate in the Highlands ("worth something among the hundreds per annum"), her 900 letters of sympathy or her relationship to Gordon Cummings. From 1858, the date of her birth, according to herself, there has been no Mrs McKechnie in Moray Place, if we are to trust the *Edinburgh Directory*. It is a pity that your interviewer, for the benefit of Edinburgh tradesmen, failed to give Mrs Gordon Baillie's – nee Bruce's or Sutherland's or Frost's or -----'s – address in London. "Why don't the accounts come in?" she says. We shall see.

'Mr Dick a furrier of Frederick Street will be pleased to receive payment of £25 for the sealskin jacket she offered to a friend of mine for £5, a curious proceeding even for the "half-sister to the Earl of Airlie", as she declared herself to be at the time of purchase. Mr Hall, coach driver, will be equally willing to receive a cheque for £8.15 shillings for the use of that coach she sported about in on her last visit to Edinburgh and I don't think he will fail to send a receipt; nor will Mr Cameron of Alva Street for sundry cabs engaged in 1875; nor the two photographers in Princes Street to whom she owes close on £10 for likenesses of her lovely self; nor Messrs Grant & Son of the same street who have an entry against her as Miss Bruce and another as Mrs Gordon Baillie. Among her more recently incurred bills in Edinburgh is one to Messrs E. Pass & Son, hairdressers, Princes Street for a tail of hair, £5.

'I wonder if she plays "nap" better than she did in the old days when in the sweetest way imaginable she would trespass every rule of the game without even turning a hair. She invariably made a single ace trumps, though holding four of another suit in her hand and she never understood why, having gone three on the ace of hearts, the ace of diamonds, the ace of spades and two little clubs, she did wrong to throw the 3 aces on the table and claim the stakes – but seldom receive them. She never thoroughly realised that if you cannot follow suit it is not absolutely necessary to trump the trick and she thought it rather a score to throw down an ace when her partner's king had already taken the trick.'

Stronach showed the paper copies of a number of short letters he received from 'Miss Bruce' in 1875, some of them rather badly spelt, but with nothing particular in them. He also stated that after she left Edinburgh there was some trouble with an amount she owed to Mr Wilson, a jeweller. He also produced copies of letters between him and the London journalist in which the latter complained that Miss Bruce was using his name and victimizing his tradespeople. Stronach adds that he still has some 'trump cards' up his sleeve which he 'reserves for the trial'. Still bitter, it seems, that she rejected him all those years ago, perhaps he should have thought himself lucky that he was to spend his working life in the confines of a library – had their relationship progressed, it could well have been a prison cell.

On 20 February 1888, nine days before the damning report appeared in the Edinburgh *Evening Despatch*, Annie, Frost and Gigner the butler moved to 5 Westminster Chambers, Victoria Street, from where it was alleged they once more 'victimized the neighbourhood'. Despite the fact that Annie was being exposed in nearly every newspaper in the country, she returned to the area and recommenced the system of swindling with which her name had become associated throughout the land. The bulk of the charges that would lead to their downfall occurred subsequent to the disclosures in the newspapers! Perhaps she realized her time would soon be up and wanted to have one final spree. Whatever the truth, after having received the fullest possible warning that her game had been played out, she persisted in it and pretty much forced the police to prosecute. She flitted from Westminster Chambers to Palace Street and practiced the same tricks within the different parts of the locality until 'she had raised the whole neighbourhood against her, and the police had to take notice', as the press reported it. It seems incredible that with her knowledge of the world and the credulity of human nature and skills, honed by twenty years of deception, Annie did not have the acuteness to know when to cut and run. The trio moved to Palmer Lodge, Palace Street, Westminster, on 17 May 1888. This was a furnished house owned by Mr Charles Spencer Smith, described as a burly chap of highly respectable appearance. They took the house for six months and Frost pawned various bits of furniture and several ornaments. They must have been down on their luck, as some of the things they pawned only fetched a few shillings.

Despite the incredible revelations by the Edinburgh press, some still fancied her chances. The Australian daily *The Age* believed that:

'The chance of a newspaper editor against a beauty in distress is an extremely poor one. There seems no reason why she should not continue to have qualified success as philanthropist and injured woman, if she can only contrive to live for a while on ready money. The world only wishes to be deceived and there are scores of persons to whom a woman with doubtful antecedents surrounding her and who puts forward unlimited claims to social rank and influence, is incomparably more interesting than a virtuous woman who pays her way and is commonplace.'

Chapter 24

An Inspector Calls
(Jun 1888)

By 1888, the aristocratic lady swindler had become an obsession for Detective Inspector Henry Marshall of the Metropolitan Police Criminal Investigation Department, and along with his Edinburgh contacts he was determined to put Annie on trial.

Marshall proved a worthy opponent. The son of a gardener from West Farleigh in Kent, he was initially apprenticed as a shoemaker before he joined the Metropolitan Police in 1869, at the age of 20, and rose swiftly through the ranks. Within two years his talents were recognized, and he was singled out for a place in the detective department – soon being promoted to detective sergeant and asked to form his own department attached to 'A' Division, which covered part of Central London. Amongst his more famous cases was that of Esther Pay, who was charged with drowning the 7-year-old – and inconvenient – daughter of her lover in December 1881. Despite some strong circumstantial evidence, Pay was acquitted.

The following year, Marshall was involved in the uncovering of a plot by 'suspicious looking foreigners' in possession of 'infernal machines', whose main aim was to blow up the German Embassy. The alleged perpetrators, William Wolff and Edward Bondurand, were eventually discharged from the Old Bailey when the jury failed to agree on their guilt, despite the pair being found in possession of large amounts of explosives. A few years before, Marshall had played a leading part in the 'Pimlico Poisoning Case', in which Adelaide Bartlett was accused of poisoning her husband with chloroform, but she too had been acquitted.

Despite these setbacks, his dogged pursuance of the Scottish adventuress was beginning to pay off, and stories continued to be leaked to the press in the hope of bringing further witnesses forward. When her story was first published, she laughed it off and intimated that she and her solicitors were going to sue the various newspapers for libel, but the lawyers in question denied having any knowledge of such an arrangement. It was not until June 1888, three months after the devastating press disclosures of March, that

Marshall felt he had enough for her arrest. He had been receiving complaints and information against all three defendants since the early part of May. Her favourite trick, Marshall discovered, was to purchase goods, pay for them with a valueless cheque and receive change in cash. How many times she had done this would never be identified, although nearly eighty cheques were known to have been passed since March.

Marshall's enquiries revealed that the cheques complained of were all in the name of 'Gordon Baillie' and he obtained a warrant for her arrest, along with that of Frost and their servant Gigner, on Saturday 23 June. That evening he went around to Palmer Lodge with a select group of fellow officers. While keeping watch, he saw Frost draw up in a brougham and enter the house. Marshall knocked repeatedly on the door, which was eventually answered by Gigner, who told him that Mr and Mrs Frost were out of town and tried to close the door. Undeterred, Marshall pushed his way in and made for the dining room, which he searched before going upstairs. Returning to the ground floor, he saw Gigner make a dart for the breakfast room and following along he found his prey.

According to one enthusiastic press report:

'Annie was dressed in a ravishing tea gown with just a hint of neat foot and ankle peeping out from beneath the skirt. He bravely shut his eyes to the tea gown and the ankle and exercising almost super human powers contrived to arrest her. She had a curious power of pouring out a flood of brilliant and apparently refined talk for a limited period. Her elocution was perfect and her voice sweet and low but the culture was only skin deep and when she had exhausted her brilliant patter she relapsed into the common woman, the daughter of the Aberdeen farm wench.'

He introduced himself, explained to the trio that they should now consider themselves under arrest and asked the woman if she was Mrs Frost, better known as Mrs Gordon Baillie, to which she replied that she was. Mr Frost confirmed his identity and Gigner the butler gave his first name as James. After reading the warrant, Mrs Gordon Baillie said: 'How can it be conspiracy? Poor James [Gigner] has only done what he was told. He is a servant and a good one. Sit down and explain.'

Marshall replied: 'It is alleged that you have conspired to defraud many people. In Pogson's case [a butcher] Gigner went first and made a small purchase and Mrs Frost followed it up with a letter promising to pay bills weekly.'

Addressing Mrs Gordon Baillie specifically, Marshall accused her of giving the butcher a worthless cheque, which she acknowledged, along with those to a dairyman, a fruiterer and a foreign corn chandler. 'But,' said Mrs Gordon Baillie, 'though there is no money at my bankers they have securities. It's no conspiracy, neither James nor Mr Frost have anything to do with it. It was only a debt.'

After further conversation, during which it is alleged Annie tried in 'the most winning way' to get them all to have lunch and discuss the matter, Marshall called in two other officers, who searched the prisoners and the house. Cheques for £15.10s and £18 signed by Mrs Gordon Baillie were found in Frost's pocketbook, and she acknowledged the signatures were hers. Frost and Gigner were taken at once to the police station, but Annie claimed that she was too ill to be moved.

After remaining with her in the house for about five hours, and calling a doctor, she was conveyed to the station in a cab by Marshall. One of the strange items turned up by the search was a well-thumbed *Bible*, with a bunch of violets, that contained the following in their respective handwriting:

'From this day I say no!' Gordon Baillie
'From this day I say no!' R.P.B. Frost

While Marshall was in the house, a Miss Lloyd came to the door and refused to leave, complaining she had been defrauded of a hat worth a guinea and had been given a worthless cheque for £8, from which she had given change of £6.19s.

Chapter 25

The Police Court
(Jul–Sept 1888)

The Police Court hearings of July 1888 are compiled from reports carried in local and national newspapers, as the original trial transcripts no longer exist. To avoid repetition, events have been described in detail only where they differ substantially from the transcript of the Old Bailey (Central Criminal Court, CCC) hearings, which took place the following October, or when a particular charge was not proceeded with but is worth recording for any light that it might show on Annie's career. Where spellings of names differ from those used in the newspapers, the CCC spellings have been used in both cases.

'The Westminster Police Court', stated one reporter, 'is a small and not very reputable looking building in Rochester Row and somewhat difficult to find. There [is] a small and by no means imposing room with gas lights burning amongst the great unwashed composed mainly of men and women of a very seedy type mainly there from curiosity and for the gossip.' The magistrate was described as a somewhat old fogyish and decrepit-looking gentleman, rubicund in appearance and seemingly feeble: 'His observations on the cases as they went along were only audible with difficulty but so far as I could see he was not wanting in acuteness.'

Day One – Monday 2 July 1888

Mr and Mrs Frost, along with their butler Robert Gigner, made their first appearance in front of Mr D'Eyncourt, the magistrate, at 2.00 pm on Monday 2 July 1888. Reports say that Annie was, as always, 'fashionably attired', and on this occasion our heroine came into court with a dash, tripped into the dock, coolly sat down and put her hand to her head. She wore a black silk and fawn coloured jacket with a lace shawl around her shapely neck, a massive stand-up collar and a large gold broach. Her hat was black with a white bird in front, and she had a waterproof with a tartan lining over her arm. She gave her age as 30 – wide of the mark by a mere ten years, but there was more to this than simple vanity, as we shall see. The verdict of the court was that she was an undeniably pretty woman.

Percy Frost was described as a tall, handsome man with a heavy, dark moustache and an expression to match. He was dressed in a checked tweed suit and a brown felt hat. He gave his age as 29, which was correct. The butler Gigner looked very miserable. He was around 40 years of age, wore a reddish wig and had a few straggling red hairs on his chin. Solicitor Duerdin Dutton appeared for the defence on this occasion, and barrister Mr Rose-Innes was there on behalf of Annie.

Detective Inspector Marshall outlined the charges, remarking with a significant smile: 'There is no knowing when it might finish.' The case, he said, was likely to be one of 'considerable magnitude'. Also present were Inspector Swanson and Detective Ellistrim from Scotland Yard, the latter hugging an immense bundle of letters and documents. Marshall outlined a conspiracy to obtain money by fraud and four cases of obtaining provisions, coal, etc. by means of worthless cheques. Solicitor Mr B. Abrahams said he was instructed to prosecute and there would be more charges of 'considerable magnitude' involving money, property and goods by false pretences, going back several years. Marshall then gave details of their arrest as outlined previously.

The first and only witness of the first day was John Sherris, clerk to bankers Smith, Payne & Smith. He deposed that Mrs Gordon Baillie had opened an account with them in May 1885 with a deposit of £1,290. During 1886, amounts totalling £2,182 had been paid in but since then the account had become dormant. It emerged that Frost's mother had an account with the bank at the present time, that she was a woman of means and position and that Mr Frost was a trustee of the family estate under his father's will. Mr D'Eyncourt expressed surprise that the account was still open, and was told that the bank had written to her that very day asking for it to be closed.

The defence team made an application for bail, on the grounds the amounts were trifling, and previous legal rulings meant that the court had to consider not only the amounts involved but the strength of the evidence, which the defence considered weak. There were suggestions that further charges might be brought, but that should not be a consideration here. Rose-Innes stated that part of the defence case would be that as a married woman, Annie was legally under the control of her husband and therefore the charge of conspiracy could not apply. After some discussion, the court agreed to grant bail on her personal security of £500 and two further sureties of £250; sums that, given her present circumstances, she would find impossible to meet. Had she been anyone else, and had there had not been such a huge press campaign against her – which the judges were bound to have read – the outcome might have been very different. Magistrate D'Eyncourt remanded the prisoners to Holloway Prison, and it was reported that Mrs Gordon Baillie went down to the cells smelling a bouquet of roses, which she had kept in her lap throughout the hearing.

* * *

Day Two – Monday 9 July 1888

The following Monday, the trio – Annie, Frost and Gigner – were transferred from Holloway back to court and the prosecution case continued. The court was full to capacity and, as before, Mrs Gordon Baillie was allowed to be seated. She had a scotch plaid on her arm and a thin veil over her face. Frost stroked his moustache and frowned heavily as usual.

First to take the witness stand was John Ponsonby, a partner in the banking firm of Herries, Farquhar & Company of 16 St James' Street, who told how a letter had been received from a Mrs Gordon Baillie asking to open an account and this was done, despite no references being provided and no money being paid into the account. A cheque book was issued and cheques were presented and dishonoured. 'Mrs Frost' had been written to about a cheque for £15, and a reply received from Mr Frost expressing surprise that money from Scotland had not been credited to the account.

Annie Bassett of 171 Sloane Street, London, a florist, said she knew the prisoner as Mrs Bodley Frost and that she had purchased plants worth £1.7s, which she paid for with a £10, post-dated cheque. As was customary, the florist paid her the difference in cash.Some while later, a gentleman had called and paid the amount owing, taking the cheque away with him.

A butcher, Tom Pogson, told how he had gone to the house to see about his money at the end of the week and found his order book tied to the door knob with a note saying, 'Family out of town, please make up book and post through letterbox', which raised great hilarity in the court. Another laugh was raised when Mr Clarke, who had hired out the brougham, declared that he had no intention of prosecuting Mrs Frost as he fully expected to be paid once the six-month period was up! What was not so funny was that Marshall now brought up the name of Henry Champion and an allegation that Pogson had been approached by Percy Frost's old classmate and best friend, who had offered him money not to turn up. Marshall asked the magistrate to call him, but Mr Dutton quickly cut in: 'Mr Champion is a friend of Mr Frost's mother who is a lady of the highest respectability and standing. He is not a friend of the prisoners themselves. He is here on behalf of the mother watching the interest of the son. It is the mother who instructs me to defend.'

Marshall replied: 'Mr Champion told me himself that he was a great friend of the two prisoners.'

D'Eyncourt asked the inspector if charges were to be brought against Champion, who replied that he wasn't sure yet, but Champion had been 'going about trying to compromise the matter'. He had bought back a dishonoured cheque from Annie Bassett, after the prisoners were in custody, and had also visited George Jones, another creditor, and showed him a lot of money, but did not offer to pay the debt. D'Eyncourt ordered a witness summons to be taken out for Champion's attendance the following week.

Elizabeth Lloyd gave evidence about an unpaid cheque for a hat and was followed by Inspector Marshall, who asked the magistrate if he would like to know how the prisoners obtained the brougham, gained possession of 5 Westminster Chambers and Palmer Lodge. If not, continued the eager policeman, 'I have heaps of other charges.' His worship seemed less than keen and suggested an adjournment, at which point Duerdin Dutton (acting for Annie) made a second attempt at bail. He insisted he had been instructed that his client had never been in custody before, and that the inspector had made a cruel and unjust assertion in saying she had been imprisoned in Scotland and in showing a photograph purporting to be of Mrs Gordon Baillie taken years ago, in prison, under a different name. He hoped Mr Marshall would, in due time, admit his mistake and apologize for it. He also went on to say that he would soon be able to produce facts that would put a completely different complexion on matters. D'Eyncourt declared himself unmoved by that possibility and said that if he did allow bail, it would be two sureties of £100 each.

Inspector Marshall leapt to his feet and exclaimed:

> 'This woman has been convicted before! I shall bring evidence of it! On that ground and on account of the magnitude of the alleged frauds, I ask for substantial bail, otherwise we shall never see her again. This is not an ordinary case. The prisoner is an extraordinary woman, one of the greatest swindlers in the country!'

Now we come to the importance of Annie giving her age as 30, rather than 40. She was desperate to distance herself from one of her former selves; the convicted fraudster and con artist of sixteen years ago, Mary Ann Bruce Sutherland. With extensive police enquiries and press coverage, from John O'Groats in Scotland via London, Paris, the USA, New Zealand and Australia, setting out her past and career in detail for all to read, that separation was essential if she was to avoid a substantial gaol term.

D'Eyncourt asked the extent of the frauds, to which Inspector Marshall replied that it was certainly in the hundreds and probably into the thousands. Holding up a parcel of unpaid bills, he said this was only one lot and there were many more from all parts of the kingdom, Scotland in particular. He was not prepared to say yet how extensive the frauds had been. In one case Mrs Gordon Baillie gained possession of a gentleman's furnished home and mortgaged his furniture. The magistrate asked if the prisoners were really married, and Dutton replied on their behalf that they were not. They had gone through a form of marriage, but it was not possible to enquire further. The question was then put to Frost. Annie whispered to him before he replied, emphatically: 'I beg pardon sir! This is my wife!' The question was put again to Annie, who bowed to the magistrate, motioned deprecatingly to her solicitor, and replied in a low voice that they were indeed married.

Marshall stated that he was about to prefer further charges relating to stolen furniture, at which Dutton became angry and exclaimed that he found the conduct of the police extraordinary and wished to protest strongly. The inspector replied he was only doing his duty to the public.

The prisoners were then taken into the police station, adjoining the court, and further charged with stealing property worth £40 from Westminster United School, owners of Palmer Lodge, which they had taken as furnished at 3½ guineas a week for six months. Mr Spencer Smith, the landlord's agent, had taken an inventory since their arrest and noticed several items, including a clock, curtains and linen, were missing and that pawn tickets relating to a number of the articles had been found at Palmer Lodge and recovered from Mr Sutton, a pawnbroker. They had been pledged in the name of Brotherson. Now that a charge of theft had been preferred, the case had become far more serious and bail was refused.

* * *

Day Three – Monday 16 July 1888

The third day of the case was attended by a reporter who found his surroundings more interesting than the proceedings and gave some interesting insights into the events.

The day opened with the usual procession of drunks and breaches of the peace. Once these were dealt with, the court began to get so full that extra seating was brought in. A host of tradesmen interested in the case began to gather and discuss the eagerly awaited entertainment.

'I saw her age was given as 29 the last day,' said one to another, 'fine joke ain't it!'

'Twenty nine!' rejoined his friend, 'Much nearer sixty.'

'What do you think of the Hatchards case?' the first tradesman asked.

'They won't prosecute, – and did you know she had them before as Miss Bruce?'

'She had them two or three times.'

'She often went back to places,' said the other, 'just stopped away long enough for her hair to change colour.'

The reporter struck up a conversation with another tradesman in the public gallery, who told him:

> 'Well here we are about a score of us poor fellows and we've all been properly fiddled; we come here and waste our time and miss our dinners and I suppose we're in it all for the interests of the public for not a penny of our money will we ever see.
>
> 'I expect they'll call the lady's maid today, the lady's maid who went with her to Australia; Ah! she'll have a story to tell; and Mrs Cox the lodging house keeper.'

The man nodded towards a young-looking clerical gentleman, who was loafing about within the bar, and who he expected was 'one of the clergymen she done'. The clergyman turned out to be Reverend Edmund Mole, whose interference in the affair was to necessitate so much explanation.

'Everybody spoke of "she" or "her", as nobody thought it necessary to give a name,' the reporter continued with his observation, 'and as we waited, time wore on in the hot and stifling court, with stories of how she played the "confidence trick" on this person and how she "done" the other one.' The reporter's new 'friend' told how near 'they' were to escaping, remarking that 'if Frost's mother could ha' got them off they'd have been away the same night'.

There was a general sympathy for 'poor Frost', recalled the reporter, and the tradesmen near him agreed he had been a 'decent fellow'. The reporter continued:

> 'By and by a smart, youngish looking man came into court with papers in his hand and there was a buzz of expectation. This, I was informed, was "Marshall". I had somehow formed the idea of a policeman, or at any rate of an official-looking person, and I was somewhat surprised to find in this gentlemanly and active looking personage, the detective

who had hunted down the Gordon Baillie business. Everyone became very impatient, for all the court were there to see her and my neighbour informed me she had been brought down in the van some time ago and was in the police station adjoining the court room.

'At last D'Eyncourt re-appeared and the police ushered in the three prisoners. They were a curious trio. I sat or stood – for occasionally it was difficult to hear while sitting down – near the end of the dock, just beside Mrs Gordon Baillie and with reporters in front of me and on my right; I therefore had plenty of time to take a deliberate survey of the prisoners.

'Mrs Gordon Baillie looked rather "washed out" and yellow and it was easy to guess that her sojourn in the police cells was not improving her appearance, but one could see she had been a fine woman before Holloway jail began to tell upon her. She wore a very light jacket and light gloves of the description which I believe are called gauntlets. On her hat was a jaunty feather and she wore a neat black scarf around her neck. The "Flaxmanesque bust" was not by any means up to the descriptions of it, but her face and figure altogether were those of a fine voluptuous looking woman. I could not say that I recognised a striking likeness to any of the photographs or portraits of her. When she took her seat in the dock she immediately whispered something to a reporter in front and began a conversation with him, which she kept up until the officer at the other end of the dock leaned along and ordered her to keep silent. For the rest of the time she sat whispering once or twice to Frost, next to her. She made no indication of special interest in the proceedings, but evidently followed them closely. Frost and Gigner stood throughout. The latter, a little oldish man with red whiskers, twinkling eyes and a low brow, certainly did not look very much like a dangerous criminal. Frost did not seem to me quite of the distinguished appearance I had expected, but he was unshaven and looked sleepy about the eyes.'

The proceedings continued and this third day brought a surprise, in the form of Mrs Gordon Baillie being further charged with having 'been concerned' with a Thomas Whyte in fraudulently obtaining by false pretences, on 20 July 1881, the lease of Stoneydown House, Walthamstow, from Edward Harding and John E. Ashcroft, along with livestock to the value of £242.

There was also a change in representation, with Henry Lewis appearing for Mrs Gordon Baillie, while Duerdin Dutton continued to represent the two male prisoners. Dutton made a statement on behalf of Henry Champion, saying that Champion had no intention of interfering with the course of justice; he had merely acted for the mother of the prisoner. Mrs Frost was a widow of 73 years of age and in bad health with heart disease. She had two daughters, but no male person to represent her, and so as an old friend of the family, Henry Champion had adopted that role. With a reverend gentleman named Mole he had called on several of the tradespeople and offered to take up some of the cheques, provided the claims were genuine. Dutton said Champion did not say one word to prevent people coming to court; the sole object was to prevent tradespeople going to Frost's mother's house and making a disturbance.

D'Eyncourt remarked that although Champion may have acted from honest motives, the tendency would be to stop the course of justice, and so he and the other gentleman would be strongly advised to let matters rest, otherwise they may 'get themselves in a scrape'. The Reverend Mole of St Mary's, Soho, and the Clergy House, Charing Cross Road, a young man of the 'pale curate type', produced one of the four cheques he had 'bought back' but was advised, like Champion, not to interfere any further.

A Mr E. Shepherd, manager of Hatchards the publishers, was called. He gave evidence to say that he had first met the female prisoner about ten years before and she was known to him as Miss Bruce. She had called in, now giving the name Mrs Baillie (he presumed her married name) and saying that she wished to pay for two books supplied to her the previous January at Eastbourne Terrace. Shepherd gave her the invoice for £2.1s. Mrs Baillie presented a cheque for £10 and was given the change in cash. When this was returned unpaid, he went around to King's Bench Walk and was directed to a small room on the top floor, with the name Frost on the door. There was no one in and so he sent a telegram to Mrs Baillie. This resulted in a visit from Mr Frost, who said his wife was very annoyed with the bank and had been ill, but would be returning to London soon and could probably be reached care of the Langham Hotel. Shepherd sent in the cheque once more and it was again returned, after which he gave up until Mole turned up and paid him the £10. Henry Lewis, solicitor for Gordon Baillie, asked the witness if he was now satisfied, to which he replied that there was no desire to press charges on behalf of Hatchards.

Evidence was heard from several other creditors and pawnbrokers, which are covered fully in the report of the Old Bailey trial. Towards the end of the day, Inspector Marshall commented:

'The next case, your worship, is a very complicated one which will take some time. On the next occasion the Walthamstow case would be gone into. It is a case which will affect the female prisoner only and I ask your worship to adjourn until Thursday. It is a case in which the female prisoner represented that she was connected with the Earl of Aberdeen and the Hope-Johnstones.'

Mr Lewis countered:

'I do protest against these statements being made by any police officer. Mr Marshall has no right to make them and they are made I say advisedly for the purpose of finding their way into the public press. They cannot be made for the purpose of influencing your worship, for I am sure they would not. Importing gentleman's names of high standing is perfectly monstrous.'

Inspector Marshall responded:

'They are facts sir. This case ranges itself over fifteen years, and is getting too complex for me to take. I am simply a police officer. A warrant was issued against one Kate Miller and one Kate Bruce, for conspiracy to defraud a lady of about £300. The lady is here now. In that case Kate Miller was arrested but the prisoner fled the country and was never arrested. That was in 1877. I shall strongly oppose bail under these circumstances. There is another gentleman here who wishes to prefer a charge against the female prisoner.'

Court observers were now beginning to notice a change in Frost's demeanour towards his 'wife' – as though the position he found himself was at last beginning to sink in and his thoughts were perhaps turning away from Annie's personal fascination towards the possibility of a term of imprisonment.

His Worship remanded the prisoners until Wednesday at noon and gave Inspector Marshall a certificate for legal assistance, as the case was becoming so complicated. Gigner was granted bail on two sureties of £50. The other prisoners were removed to custody.

* * *

Day Four – Wednesday 18 July 1888

Mr Henry J. Lewis, solicitor for Mrs Gordon Baillie, referred to a statement made at the previous hearing concerning a Mr Edward Harding, who desired to prefer a charge against her with regard to his property in Walthamstow. He was present but had brought no documents with him. Magistrate

D'Eyncourt opined that there did not seem to be much of a case without the lease being produced. Marshall said it could be obtained, to which Harding interjected: 'I charge Mrs White with making false representations in taking my house!' D'Eyncourt said he would leave the matter in the hands of the Treasury solicitors.

Also in court was an old gentleman named Bonham, who had attended the hearings every day and who, according to Inspector Marshall, alleged that Mrs Gordon Baillie, and a man named Maitland, had defrauded him of a very large amount several years before; about £150 in 1883 or 1884. Mr Lewis stated that Mr Maitland was prepared to attend court at a moment's notice and defend himself against any charges, but D'Eyncourt replied that he had no interest in speculative investigations and would hear no more about it unless charges were brought.

Harding was referred to Mr St John Wontner, who said that he would refer the case to the Public Prosecutor, but it emerged that Marshall knew all about it and had decided not to bring charges. One newspaper report stated that William Maitland was believed to have an income of something like £360–380 per year, but it was secured under a trust and he could only draw on it at intervals.

After further evidence, the prisoners were remanded until Monday.

* * *

Day Five – Monday 23 July 1888

Day five arrived and our reporter described the scene once more:

> 'Mrs Baillie took her seat in the dock as quietly and as dignifiedly as though she were stepping into her brougham. Mr Frost followed, his lips compressed but quite without any other sign of discomposure. To one who had seen him before it was evident that he is suffering very keenly. "James" otherwise Robert Gigner brought up the rear and taking hold of the rail, appeared to be lost in contemplation of some occult matter connected with the curtain behind the magistrate.'

The proceedings began with the Walthamstow case and it was decided, after a short discussion, not to proceed with it. The prosecuting solicitor, St John Wontner, was persuaded by the magistrate that it was doubtful that any offence had been committed under the terms of the relevant act.

A Mrs Ratcliffe, who hired out horses and carriages, described how the Frosts had been to see her in order to hire a 'Victoria'. When she went to collect her money, after the cheque had been dishonoured, she met Gigner, who said he had just locked Mrs Frost in the house as he was going out. This produced loud laughter in the courtroom, with Mrs Frost joining in. The clerk asked the witness if she had seen Mr Frost, and Mrs Ratcliffe replied he had been locked in as well, which provoked even more laughter.

Mr E. Williams, of 56 Timsbury Street, Brighton, said he had a set of rooms at Westminster Chambers, Victoria Street, which he let to Mr Frost. There had been two references – a Mr Champion and a Mr Ormsby, of 4 Queen's Bench Walk, Temple. They proved satisfactory, and all three prisoners were in occupation for three months.

There followed several other witnesses giving evidence of dishonoured cheques, the details of which are fully described at the later trial.

Mr Julian Thomas, a journalist from *The Age* in Melbourne, who it was said wrote under the name 'The Vagabond', was called. He said that he was a good friend of a man named Knight Aston, a professional vocalist, and had seen him on 29 April that year in Adelaide. He knew the female defendant and Frost by reputation, and had communicated with Inspector Marshall. Knowing so much of Mrs Gordon Baillie's proceedings in the colonies, he wished to see her. He was in Australia when she was there and knew that the story would interest people there. He had seen Mrs Gordon Baillie and Knight Aston together in Australia, and was asked by Mr Lewis if he knew of Mrs Gordon Baillie obtaining a divorce in Australia, but he said he did not. Various friends of Mrs Gordon Baillie were saying that Aston had died and the police were apparently searching files for evidence of 'vitality'.

The question of the Frosts' marital status was an important one. If they were legally married, the charge of conspiracy could not be brought, as a man and wife could not conspire together in law. Wontner said the onus was on the defence to prove that a marriage had taken place, and they had not done so.

Lewis stated: 'It has not been shown at present that this lady was ever married as far as this court is concerned.' At this point, Annie shook her head deprecatingly and remarked: 'Never mind, it is of no consequence.'

D'Eyncourt replied: 'The woman told us that she was married. The man would not say whether he was married or not.'

Lewis: 'I understand that the male prisoner stated that he was married.'

Clerk: 'No, he carefully avoided that. He said "My wife". He was asked if he was married and carefully repeated, "This is my wife!"' D'Eyncourt then looked at Annie and said: 'Annie Frost you told me you were married.'

Annie: 'Yes'.

D'Eyncourt: 'To this man?'

'Yes.'

'Where were you married?'

'It was not in a church but it was by a priest in a schoolroom at Brussels in Belgium on May 4th 1886. It was by a Catholic priest and being non Catholics we had to marry as English visitors outside of the church.'

'What part of Brussels?'

'I cannot tell, I do not remember the name of the street. Mr White was my husband and I divorced him in Australia.'

Frost was asked the same questions and came up with the same answers; he could not remember the name of the street either.

Returning to the witnesses, Mr Griffith Williams, of 20 Spring Street, Paddington, gave evidence that he had known Gigner by sight for fifteen years and knew him to be a gentleman's servant. In December 1887, Gigner asked for his business card, as he was just about to take on a new position with a Mrs Gordon Baillie, a rich lady from Australia who had a large estate in Lancashire. This announcement seemed greatly to amuse Annie, who, as she sat in the dock with a bunch of roses in her lap, buried her face in her hands and laughed loudly.

Mr Wontner said the case for the prosecution was now concluded. Many other matters might be gone into, but to show the present financial position of the female prisoner he might add that he had a score of county court judgements and summonses against her. One, the equivalent to an English county court summons, was issued from a resident's magistrates' court in New Zealand in the name of Annie White, wife of Whyte Aston, otherwise known as Mrs Gordon Baillie. The summonses had been found by the officers when they arrested the prisoners.

The three defendants were then committed for trial to the Central Criminal Court and the question of bail arose once more. Lewis made the first application on behalf of Mrs Frost. He observed Inspector Marshall had stated on previous occasions that he was prepared to bring fifty charges of fraud against Mrs Frost. Now the prosecution case had closed, there were four charges of issuing worthless cheques and nothing else. The total amount involved was £25. Inspector Marshall had also said that he would produce evidence of her previous convictions and this he had not done. In all, continued Lewis, there was no felony, merely charges of misdemeanour.

Wontner replied for the Crown that: 'A warrant had been issued a great many years ago in this court, but she has evaded arrest. The prisoner is a lady of wandering propensities and I am afraid that if you let her out on bail we should not see her again.' There was laughter around the court at this. Bail was refused, and the prisoners were committed to appear at the next sessions of the Old Bailey. The magistrate endorsed the police charge sheet in the following terms: 'Inspector Marshall has shown great energy and ability in collecting the evidence required in this very complicated case and deserves commendation.'

* * *

Somehow a 'special correspondent' from the *Sheffield Daily Telegraph* managed to secure an interview with Annie in the police cells behind the court immediately after this final hearing, which was recorded as follows:

'The lady rose from the bare low bench upon which she had been seated and advancing a step or two to hold out her hand greeted me with a composure which under the circumstances one would have deemed impossible. With the exception of a slight pallor and some little nervousness in her smile she comported herself as though she was in her own drawing room, rather than having just been committed for trial at the Old Bailey. I felt in an uncomfortable position but the charming adventurous had lost not one wit of that *savoir faire* to which so many people can to their sorrow bear striking evidence. She saw my discomfort and at once tried to put me at my ease.

"Well," she said. "It is very horrible isn't it? But just speak quite plainly and frankly as you know I am almost relieved at being committed for trial. It was evident from the clear way in which these infamous charges have been concocted that we should have to go for trial and so of course, I wanted the worrying police court affair over."

"It must have been a trying time for you?"

"Oh dear at first I couldn't realise it – couldn't believe that it was true. But you know, there was nothing for it but to steel oneself against the ignominy. It's that wretched *Edinburgh Despatch* with its cruel, cruel slanders that is to blame for all this. Had it not been for the scandal in March there would never have been a suspicion of fraud in my dealings with people. It was persecution, not prosecution, but there was nothing for it except to try and reconcile ourselves to the position. It can't last long."

"Have you been treated well?"

"'Oh very fairly indeed on the whole. Of course I can have anything in the way of food for which I choose to pay, – that is I could for now that I am committed I suppose it will all be altered. I had my own bedding brought to Holloway."

"'Then you had all your own clothes?"

"No, not at all, they would only let me have one dress, the one I was wearing when Inspector Marshall gave me the surprise of my life. Think of having to wear the same dress all these days! That has been very objectionable. On the whole I can't complain of the treatment hitherto. Why should I have reason to complain? They have to treat me as any other than an innocent person – I have not been condemned."

"'And what about Mr Frost?"

"Poor Frost has had to sleep on a plank bed in an ordinary cell. I have a room to myself; and the greatest source of unhappiness to me has been the fact that he and I have only been allowed to see each other for a few minutes each morning before entering the court. That has been a sad trouble; but come it's no good talking about that."

'Here Mrs Baillie showed as she did several times during the interview, some sign of the fact that in spite of her eminently cool and ladylike bearing in court she was vividly and keenly feeling the horrors of her position. She is losing some of her colour, and in addition to being somewhat pallid she looks worn.

"'Come," she continued, "let us talk of these preposterous allegations. So long as I can keep my mind fixed on them I feel comparatively easy for I know how utterly and completely unfounded they are."

"'Well then, what about the cheques?"

"Oh, first I must say a word as to Inspector Marshall flourishing what he called huge bundles of unpaid bills. It's shameful. Now don't you recollect that when that *Despatch* made the statements about unpaid bills that Mr Frost wrote to the papers on my behalf denying that I owed anything but my current tradesmen's bills and demanding that in fairness all people who said I was owing them money should instantly forward their accounts to him at 4 King's Bench Walk? Well what was the result? Two paltry accounts – one of which was not mine – were all that came in. Then what occurred? Mr Stead put a paragraph in the *Pall Mall Gazette* and it was by no means friendly to me, for it wanted, 'the mystery probed to the bottom'. He asked that that all bills should be sent to him and the only bills that came in were the same two! After that they actually had the unfairness to come and talk the same cruel rubbish about unpaid bills! It is mean. They made unfounded statements of that kind and don't bring forward one jot of evidence to back them up."

"'Of course the cheques were yours, I suppose there is no doubt about that?'"

"'Not the slightest doubt. Of course they were mine. But where does the fraud come in? The true facts of the matter are just these. My bank accounts had run low, several large remittances were coming due and when I believed the money had been paid in – as I had every right to assume – I drew cheques. Well, by some misfortune the money had not been paid in and the cheques were dishonoured and before the arrival of my money permitted me to meet them, the police who have been most impertinently on the lookout ever since the *Despatch* scandal went around some of the more timid and inexperienced of my tradespeople and persuaded them to charge me with fraud. Fraud indeed! Even suppose I had not been sure in my own mind of the days my remittances would come, to say that it is fraudulent on the part of the person of means to pay by means of cheques under the circumstances is … Oh! Why? … no man or woman either who knows anything about money matters would ever dream of imputing an intention to defraud.

"'Why most of my tradespeople indignantly refused to co-operate! Did you not hear that most of the tradespeople brought into court absolutely refused to prosecute! They knew perfectly well there was no fraud. How can anyone call such an affair fraud? A person of ample means drawing cheques under the impression that money had arrived at the bank! It is ridiculous! And as to the money I expected, you know Mr Lewis my solicitor?'"

"'Yes.'"

"'Well you ask him. He knows what I mean and can tell you if he thinks fit – though it won't do of course to anticipate the defence. The main point is that it will be shown that I have sources of income, have means, which place me above suspicion of an attempt to give worthless cheques and so avoid payment. The cheques were not worthless, ultimately.'"

"'Then how about the Walthamstow affair?'"

"'Well, I was surprised to see the serious manner with which you mentioned the word, 'Walthamstow' a few minutes since. You don't mean to tell me that people are thinking there is anything in that charge?'"

"'I must admit that the Walthamstow affair is the one about which there is most talk.'"

"'Good gracious! Even if there were anything in it it's not my affair at all, in the first place it's my late husband Mr White's, he took the lease, and in the second place there is nothing fraudulent in what he did. He took over the lease of the house and bought the furniture that was standing in it. I know that he paid at once the £70, the sum mentioned in the agreement of sale to be paid on signing. Then because he disposed of his own property in some manner or other that pleased him best they call it fraud, forsooth! Supposing for a moment that Mr White did not fully pay up the price of the furniture? Why that is a debt surely, not a piece of fraud. Oh! The whole thing is so preposterous, it's perfectly sickening apart from all the considerations of disgrace."

"'Then you are perfectly convinced, Mrs Baillie, of your power to refute the charges? You must excuse me putting the question in such a direct form, but the public want to know clearly in what light you look at the affair."

"'Certainly I excuse you. You are quite right to put it that way, I asked you to speak plainly, I look at the affair in the light of an innocent person, as an injured woman, a maligned woman. Why when you separate the distinct charges from the clouds of vague, undefined, general accusations which have been made in court what have we? Nothing but the dishonoured cheques and the Walthamstow House! Oh yes and you were in court weren't you, when the magistrate particularly said there was nothing for my solicitor to answer in the Walthamstow House! *Ma foi!* The thing is absurd! It would be positively ludicrous if it were not so sad and painful. I was vexed that Mr D'Eyncourt said what he did at the moment he did. It prevented Mr Lewis cross examining the witnesses. I know the questions he intended to ask and I did want them to be put. Not that it would have mattered much to the case for the charge was practically squashed – but simply because only one side of the ridiculous affair was going before the public. However we shall have it all out sooner or later. I am not going to give way!"

"'But tell me what are people saying?"

"'Well, you give me a very difficult question to answer. Naturally, they are taking a great interest in the case."

"'Ah, yes! I suppose they will all be going against me, and yet one can't blame them. They only have one side, but they'll hear the other when the trial comes on. I'd like now to put before them my refutations in detail, but it wouldn't do to help my accusers by anticipating the defence, you know."

"'No it would be wiser to remain silent on that. How is Mr Frost taking the matter?"

"'Oh he feels it very keenly, of course, but like me after the first few days he had to resign himself to the ordeal. Poor James though! Poor fellow, what a shame to bring my servant into it! Such a good servant too, the best I ever had. I don't know what to do with myself when I think of the horrid shame it is that he should be put into the dock. Why the poor fellow never knew anything of my affairs. I can scarce contain myself when I see him in court absolutely dumbfounded and stupid. He stands there staring blankly before him without a ghost of an idea how it all came about. There is not a single particle of evidence to connect him with any of the allegations and of course he is quite certain to get off but that is not the point. It's a crying injustice I should like ..."

'At that moment the gaoler entered the cell to announce to Mrs Baillie that she must prepare to leave at once for the House of Detention at Holloway. I rose from the bench and left, not without some feeling of pity be it confessed, [for] who, whatever she may or may not be is both brilliantly clever and astonishingly handsome. If all that be said about her be true, she might have been a paragon of all the virtues if she had but been endowed with the command of money. She is intensely ambitious and would have undoubtedly become one of the most prominent women of the century instead of appearing as a notorious adventuress in the dock of a police court.

"'Well, good bye," Annie then said with a constrained smile. "It's a wonder they don't have something against you because you came to interview me last May! I suppose they wouldn't let me have newspapers if you sent them? Perhaps you'll come and see me once or twice. Good bye again.'"

The reporter was ushered out and the cell door clanged behind him.

Annie was taken off to Holloway prison and repeated attempts were made for bail. On Saturday 28 July 1888, there was an application to a judge in chambers, Mr Justice Mainsty, by Mr Rose-Innes for Annie, who made the point that the charges were only those of misdemeanours, and slight ones at that; the total amount being in the region of £6.

Mr Meade, opposing the application, remarked that although she was only committed on three charges, there were eleven sworn to in the depositions and requested that his lordship reflect upon the previous 'career' of the woman. Rose-Innes added that it would take another month to properly prepare the defence, and it was for this period bail was requested. The judge refused on the grounds it was now a matter for consideration by the bench at the Old Bailey.

On Monday 30 July 1888, the three appeared for the first time in front of the Recorder at the Central Criminal Court and again bail was refused, on the usual grounds of Annie's unproven previous convictions, as outlined in the newspapers and enthusiastically described by Inspector Marshall. Her solicitor pointed out she had given her age as 29, and if she was indeed Mary Ann Sutherland, would only have been 13 at the time of her trial in 1872. Meade shot back, amidst much laughter, that prisoners were allowed to give their own ages, but 'ladies sometimes made mistakes'. If all the allegations were true, he remarked, no one wanted to be the person that had let such an adept fraudster escape. Gigner was given bail in the sum of £50 and the trial was adjourned for a month – until the September Sessions – so the defence could prepare its case.

On Monday 6 August 1888, Annie was brought once more before judges Lord Coleridge and Mr Justice Denman, under a writ of Habeas Corpus at the Queen's Bench for one final bail application. She stood in the dock, between a male and a female warder, neatly dressed with a blue Scotch plaid over her arm. She was in custody facing three charges of conspiring with others to defraud three persons of sums of £1/29/9d, £2/3/- and £2/7/6d. The young barrister Rose-Innes patiently explained once more that his client had opened an account with the bankers Smith, Payne & Smith in 1885, and a number of large sums had been deposited between that date and the present time. During the time of the alleged frauds, she had been in Australia and was unaware of the state of her account, and at no time had the bank advised her not to pass more cheques. Any amounts referred to within the charges were small, and despite Inspector Marshall referring to other cases of fraud some of these were mere rumours, while in others the amounts had been paid and the tradesmen were perfectly satisfied.

Meade countered this by citing eleven cases of cheques being dishonoured and pointed out that she would not have needed the bank to urge restraint, as shopkeepers were banging on her door for their bills to be settled. Furthermore, the accounts that had been settled had been done so after the prisoners' arrests! It was also the case that she had not contradicted the allegations of her being the Mary Ann Sutherland sentenced to nine months in 1872, nor to the fact that the warrant of 1877 referred to her.

This time bail was granted, but in the sum of £500 of her own money and two sureties of £250 each, a huge sum. Surprisingly, two sureties were found: the trusting job master who lent Annie the carriage in London's West

End and a tailor in Berkeley Square. The first of them came forward and was accepted, but the tailor drew back at the last minute because, he said, he 'didn't like the look of it'. Had the defence concentrated their efforts on securing the release of Mr Frost, they might have had more success, and he could have been very useful working on the case from the outside.

Annie was again confined to Holloway, and according to newspaper reports her health began to deteriorate. She became an inmate of the infirmary and the medical officer agreed that her case warranted special treatment, with an ample and suitable diet sent in by friends from an adjoining hostelry and approved by the governor. He also allowed her the use of pen and paper, although with the strict proviso that nothing could leave the prison without his authority – not even communications with her solicitor. She now suffered from depression and was said to have altered greatly in appearance. Was all this further manipulation of those around her, or was she beginning to realize the seriousness of her situation? At least part of her old sprit remained, however, as she is reported to have said to a friend who visited her: 'I will not associate with the common people here and take exercise in the prison yard, walking in a circle!'

As in 1872, Annie had two ways to react to prison life. She could maintain the front of a great lady of means and breeding, falsely accused of petty crimes by a vindictive press, or mingle with the common herd, which the daughter of a Dundee washerwoman would surely have found easy enough. She could play either role with ease, but for the present chose the former because, after all, she was not yet convicted.

September arrived, and both sides agreed that they were still not ready and needed a further adjournment to prepare their cases. There were now forty-five counts on the indictment, involving obtaining money by false pretences, by means of cheques. The main plank of the defence remained as before – that a charge of conspiracy could not be made because she was married to Frost and a woman could not legally conspire with her husband. Annie claimed that she had divorced White in Australia, the prosecution had asked her to prove it, but so far she had not done so. Nor could she show any proof she had subsequently married Frost, bigamously or otherwise. She could prove her marriage to White, she said, as well as her divorce – as he had remarried in Australia, he must have been free to do so, but as yet there was no proof either way.

Annie denied in one interview that she would ever have any intention of 'bolting' over so small a sum, if granted bail. And at her trial, she said, she intended to take all the blame for what happened and 'will prove by my bank book to the jury that for the past 5 years, except the one I spent in the colonies, I have paid into my bank more than £2,200 a year on average'. Her six weeks in prison had proved very trying, but she felt very well in health and her spirits had been kept up by the knowledge she would be able to disprove all the 'absurd' charges against her. It was also reported that the young barrister on her defence team, Mr Rose-Innes, was 'throwing himself into her cause with great zeal and intends to make a brilliant effort in her defence'.

A woman who had met her on several occasions gave a pretty full description of her at this time:

'A tall good looking woman of a type which the word elegant seems to fit. Her beauty struck me as the *beaute du diable*, the eyes being rather sly when not full of any other expression, which circumstances might call into them at any moment. A graceful figure clad in a superbly handsome dress worthy of Worth at his best and an undulating grace of movement that might well be considered fascinating by the susceptible sex – by which I do not mean my own. I confess that I envied her dress, a lovely black silk with an exquisite arabesque design in front from waist to feet but her hands were large and thick – one would have considered them clumsy if the face and figure had not taken off one's attention. A rather large mouth and a rather earnest expression also strike me as amongst my recollections of Mrs Gordon Baillie, who I can well believe is a remarkable woman whether the allegations against her are true or the reverse. Her feet were also rather large, so perhaps there is something in the washerwoman story after all – not that a woman need be the worse for that – only washerwomen's daughters are not often clad as gorgeously as she. Her handwriting was bold and masculine but without that indescribable something which we call style.'

Chapter 26

The Reckoning
(Oct 1888)

This transcript is taken largely from the Old Bailey website, with some added detail from newspaper reports of the police court hearings. Where spellings of names differ from those in the magistrates' court, the CCC spellings have been used.

The trial of Mr and Mrs Frost began in the Central Criminal Court at the Old Bailey on 22 October 1888, before the Recorder Sir Thomas Chambers. The prosecutors were Mr Poland and Mr Mead, while Mr Kemp QC and Mr Rose-Innes appeared for Annie Frost, and Mr Besley and Mr Partridge for Robert Frost. The court suffered an embarrassment of barristers on this first day, as the Probate Court was closed due to a sitting of the Parnell Commission (a judicial inquiry into allegations of crimes by Irish politician Charles Parnell), so everyone had piled in to watch the 'show'. Mr Horace Avory, the counsel for Robert Gigner, did not appear as his client had broken his leg whilst on bail and it was agreed he should be tried separately on a future occasion.

Annie appeared fashionably dressed as usual, wearing brown with a handsome mantle of many-coloured plush, a sealskin coat cut to her shapely figure with a high collar and brown silk gloves, but with neither hat nor bonnet. She looked very well, as did Frost, who 'square headed and black haired looked as though the period of regular living had done him good'.

The charges brought against them were that Annie Frost, Robert Percival Bodley Frost and Robert Gigner conspired together to:

1. Obtain by false pretences from Thomas Pogson the sum of £1.19.6d and from other persons their monies in each case with intention to defraud.
2. Obtain from George Jones the sum of £2.7.6d with intent to defraud.
3. Obtain by false pretences the sum of £2.3s from Henry James Hone.
4. Robert Frost was charged alone with stealing a clock and other articles from a dwelling house valued at £40, the goods of Charles Spencer Smith.

To the question 'Guilty or Not Guilty?', Annie at first returned no answer. She leant over and whispered to Frost, and apparently paid no attention to the clerk's question. It was repeated, but again ignored. 'Is she deaf?' exclaimed the clerk, to which 'the fair prisoner' leaned forward and in a polite whisper murmured 'Not Guilty'. Frost repeated these words, although in an offhand manner as though he was used to it.

Mr Poland opened for the prosecution by stating that although he only proposed to go into a few cases, the proceedings of the prisoners had been of such an extensive nature as to make it most remarkable – an elaborate and ingenious system of frauds carried out over a long period of time. He said the woman's real name was Annie Ogilvie Bruce, who on 15 November 1876 had married a music teacher named Thomas White at the Registry Office in Camberwell. At the time she had given her age as 24. (Other than the fact the wedding took place on 1 November and in Marylebone, this was correct, except, of course, Annie had actually knocked four years off her real age – she was 28 at the time of her marriage – and her name wasn't really Bruce at all.) Poland continued that as there was no evidence to the contrary, she was no doubt living in adultery with Frost and her age would now be 36. One of the newspaper men in court reported: 'Mrs Gordon Baillie sat unmoved whilst the advocate talked bluntly about adultery but when the last revelation about her age came she started as if in pain and turned in a excited manner to Frost.' She was in fact 40 years old.

Newspapers reported that the male prisoner was a man of good education, who had once been in a good position and lived with his mother, a woman of considerable means, at the family home in Woburn Place. He represented himself as being the business agent of Mrs Gordon Baillie, who was alleged to be the owner of vast estates in Australia and was arranging for an extensive scheme of emigration from Scotland. She had been living with Frost as his wife, but her correct name was Annie Ogilvie White and her maiden name was Bruce. A great deal of stress was laid upon the marriage question because, as previously noted, a charge of conspiracy could not be sustained if they were married.

Thomas White (Knight Aston) was now living in Australia, it was stated, and the prisoner was with him only the previous year. When she was arrested, letters from him were found in her possession. When Annie and Frost had returned from Australia, the court heard, they lived together as man and wife at 32 Eastbourne Terrace, Paddington, and from December conspired together to carry out a huge system of frauds. They wrote a total of thirty-eight cheques, it was said, amounting to a total of £287, without funds to support them, obtaining goods and valuable property. Frost at times represented himself as the business agent of his wife and signed himself in one letter as 'C.H. Morrison'. When things became too hot for them, they moved to 5 Westminster Chambers, again as Mr and Mrs Frost, paying the first month's rent in advance so as to lead the landlord into thinking they were moneyed people, but ultimately succeeded in cheating him out of future rent amounting to £16.

The court heard their next move was to Palmer Lodge, Pimlico, a furnished house for which they agreed to pay £3.10s per week. To show the dire distress in which they found themselves, it was stated that in order to get some money to live on, they had stolen a number of bed sheets from the house worth £10 and pawned them for £4. Dishonoured cheques were continuously returned from Smith, Payne and Smith's Bank, so they changed bankers. Mrs Frost opened an account with Herries Farquhar & Co. of Charing Cross, saying she wanted it to receive moneys for the crofters of Scotland. Not a penny was paid into this account, but the cheques were used freely as a means of fraud.

The question of Annie's marriage to Frost arose yet again, with Mr Poland asking if the defence still maintained that the 'Frosts' were married. Mr Kemp fudged the issue by stating limply that the parties went through a form of marriage in Australia, but it would be impossible to go the expense of bringing witnesses over to prove it; which is probably just as well, because the couple had stoutly maintained during the police court hearings they had been married in Brussels. As the defence could not prove that they were legally married, it was ruled that the conspiracy charge would be allowed to stand.

Mr Poland then began to call the witnesses for the prosecution. First on the stand was Griffith Williams, who stated:

'I am a tailor at 20 Spring Street, Paddington – last December I knew Gigner, and I knew the female defendant under the name of Mrs Gordon Baillie; she was then living at 32 Eastbourne Terrace. Previous to 28th December, Gigner called and represented himself as an indoor servant; he said he thought he had got a situation with a Mrs Gordon Baillie, and asked me to give him a card, as he wanted to get me to make him the livery – he said she was a rich lady from Australia, with large estates in Lancashire. He afterwards called and said he had got the situation, and I called on the female defendant and took patterns for her to select – she said she wanted a suit for her indoor servant, Gigner – she selected green cloth, and I measured him, made the suit and an extra waistcoat, and charged £5.15s. My account was sent in about a week afterwards. I have never been paid – I have not applied for the money; they had gone and left no address.'

When cross-examined by Mr Kemp, Williams answered: 'My account was sent by post, addressed to Mrs Gordon Baillie, 32 Eastbourne Terrace – I then let the matter rest for about a fortnight – I did not call, she had gone – I only went to the house to take the order.' Upon being asked by Mr Partridge whether he had seen Percy at that time, the tailor replied: 'I did not see Mr Frost.'

The next witness was Thomas Pogson, who said: 'I am a butcher, of 24 Wood Street, Westminster. On 27th March Gigner bought meat off me – he was then living at 5 Westminster Chambers, with Mrs Gordon Baillie, or Mr and Mrs Frost, the defendants – he described himself as their servant – [and] after that be brought me this letter.'

At this juncture, Pogson produced the letter, which was again confirmed as being in Frost's hand by Henry Champion. The letter was signed 'R. Frost', and stated that he had been informed that his servant was getting meat off Pogson, and so he would be glad if Pogson would serve him as well and that the resulting bills would be paid every Monday. Pogson continued:

'I supplied meat at once to Gigner, who brought the letter, and then according to request, sent for orders every day. On 2nd April £1.1s.8d. was due – Gigner brought me for that amount a cheque on Smith, Payne and Smith, drawn by A. Gordon Baillie, which was honoured. On Saturday, 21st, Gigner came and asked me to make the book up, as Mrs Frost was having her banking account made up. The account then due came to £1.0s.3d. Gigner went away, and in about an hour returned with a cheque for about £3.11s. – I cannot recollect what change I gave. Before I heard anything about the cheque Gigner called again and asked me to cash a cheque for £4 upon the same bank, signed "A. Gordon Baillie" – I cashed it. I served some more meat at that time, something under £1. I paid the two cheques away together – they were afterwards returned, each marked "N S".*

'On 26th April I went to 5 Westminster Chambers, and saw Gigner, and told him the cheques were returned. He said he could not account for it, there was plenty of money at the bank, there must be some mistake, he would tell Mrs Frost about it and let me know. I asked him why it was signed by Gordon Baillie, and he said Mrs Frost went by her maiden name, that she was married in America, and signed her cheques in her maiden name – he said perhaps the name was spelt wrong, perhaps it was spelt Gorden instead of Gordon – and next morning, the 27th, I called again and saw Gigner. On the 28th he

---

* Bank shorthand for 'Not Sufficient (Funds)'.

brought me this open cheque for £7 – —the other two were similar
to this in appearance. (This was dated 1st May, on Smith, Payne, and
Smith, to self or bearer, and was signed "Gordon Baillie".)

'On the 1st May I presented it, and it was marked "N S". As I was
going to the Chambers I met Gigner and told him about it, [and] he
said Mr and Mrs Frost had just gone out. He asked me to present it
again, and said it would be all right, [but] I did so with the same result.
About 2nd or 3rd May I went to Westminster Chambers again, but was
not able to see Mr or Mrs Frost. I waited on the stairs till I saw them
coming upstairs. The female defendant said "You are my butcher", I said
"Yes". She said she was very sorry to put me to so much inconvenience;
but she had a large cheque for £200, I think, sent to the bank and it was
signed wrong, and had to be altered and sent back again – I cannot say
whether she said it came from Scotland or America. She promised me
my money that night. I requested her to give me the money, as I was
pressed for money, and she said to Mr Frost, "Edward, give him £2." He
gave me £2 – this was in the afternoon – [and] she promised to let me
have the other in the evening. I did not get it.

'The next morning or the morning after that I went to the house
again, [and] there was a paper on the door with "Family out of town,
will not be back till 12", and my book was hanging on the bell knob
with a paper with the words, "Make up and put in the letter-box". I did
so. About 3 o'clock the same day, from something I heard in a shop, I
went to 5 Westminster Chambers again, [and] I saw Mr Frost. I asked
him to give me another cheque for £5, so that I could present it at the
bank – he said he would do so, but that Mrs Frost was out, and that
he would tell her when she came in. I found after that they had left.
I have lost £3.19s.9d. in cash and meat to the value of £1.14s.5d., it
is nearly £6 Altogether. I communicated with the police then. —My
information was sworn and they were taken into custody.'

Under cross-examination by Mr Partridge, Pogson said: 'The cheque for £7
was given in substitution of the other two – Mr Frost gave me the £2 out of
his own pocket.'

Further witnesses followed. One, Edwin Shepherd, told the court:

'I am manager to the firm of Hatchard, now carried on by the trustees of
the late Mr Hatchard, publishers and booksellers of Piccadilly. I knew
the female prisoner 12 or 14 years ago as Miss Bruce and on April
26th this year she called and gave the name of Mrs Baillie. She said she
was staying at 32 Eastbourne Terrace. She came to pay for some books

she had had earlier in the year – I looked at my book and after some little difficulty, the account having been posted to another person, I discovered £2.1s. was due. She gave me this cheque for £10 dated April 28th on Smith, Payne payable to self or bearer signed "Gordon Baillie". She ordered two or three other books to be sent to 4 King's Bench Walk, to Mrs Baillie. I gave her £7.19s. change. I afterwards received this letter [dated 28 April] ,"Dear Sir, I should be obliged if you would send me, Mr & Mrs Bancroft's *Reminiscences of the Stage* in addition to the books already ordered. Yours truly, A.G. Baillie." [Champion again confirmed, that to the best of his belief, this was in Mr Frost's handwriting.]

'I paid the cheque into my bankers several times – it came back marked "N S". We did not send the additional books. The cheque came back in time to stop the first ones ordered. After I had paid in the cheque I went to 4 King's Bench Walk, Temple. I saw the name of P.B.R. Frost up there. I went upstairs, but did not see Mr Frost, only an office boy. I afterwards sent this letter on May 1st. (This stated that the cheque had been returned by the bankers, no doubt through some error, and requested Mrs Baillie to call.) On May 5th I received a telegram and sometime after Frost called and said Mrs Baillie was very much annoyed that the cheque had been dishonoured, or words to that effect, but that she was coming to town in a day or two and would see to it – I think he named a day. I asked him for her address, and he said she had taken a house, but that at first she would probably be staying at the Langham Hotel. I am not sure whether Frost called once or twice – nothing resulted from the calls. I paid in the cheque three or four times – it was always returned marked "N S". Afterwards we communicated with the Scotland Yard authorities. I got none of my money up to the time of the arrest. After the arrest of the two prisoners on June 30th the Rev Mr Mole, a witness in this case, called on me on July 2nd, the day of the first hearing at the police-court – I did not know him before. I was not aware of their arrest then. Mr Mole gave £10 to our assistant at the shop and the cheque was given up to him—I was not in then.'

Cross-examined by Mr Kemp, the witness stated: 'In January I had supplied books to Mrs Frost to the amount of £2.1s. I was quite willing to trust her. I have made no criminal charge against her – I was satisfied to wait for my money.'

Re-examined, he added:

'After the cheque for £10 had been returned several times I went to Scotland Yard and gave information to the police. We did not identify her at first as Mrs Gordon Baillie – we knew her as Mrs Baillie. I afterwards gave evidence at the police-court.

'I do not think I had seen anything in the newspapers at that time, before I went to Scotland Yard, that some charges were being preferred against her. Some time before I had seen the account about the crofters, and when the cheque was returned I began to question whether it was not the same person I had known 12 years before.'

The next witness, Sarah Franks, said:

'I am a dressmaker, of 23 Mortimer Street, Cavendish Square. In April last Mr and Mrs Frost called on me. Mrs Frost spoke to me in his presence about a dress. She called again and ordered a dress; she called several times. She asked me to change this cheque on Smith Payne to self or bearer, dated 2nd May, for £5, and signed "Gordon Baillie", and endorsed "R.P.B. Frost" – she said she wanted to give the money to a poor woman. I cashed the cheque. [This time Champion stated that the endorsement was like Frost's, but he had no belief as to whether it was his signature or not.]

'I paid the cheque into my bank; it came back, and then I immediately wrote to Mrs Frost. I put the letter in the letter-box in my house, from whence they are posted. I had this telegram in reply. [This, sent by Frost, stated that Mrs Frost was too unwell to see Miss Franks; that she regretted her letter, and would attend to it at once.] I waited a few days, and then wrote a second time to Mrs Frost, 5 Westminster Chambers. I had this letter from Mr Frost. [Champion once more stated that, to the best of his belief, this letter was in Mr. Frost's writing. It requested her to put the cheque through the bank again on Tuesday when his effects would be cleared and matters in order.]

'I received it on May 14th. I put the cheque through my bank again; it was returned on the 15th. I sent it through again on the 17th, and again it was returned. I then put it in the hands of Mr Herbert, my solicitor. I heard that the prisoners were apprehended, and I received the money from my solicitor immediately after the matter appeared in the papers.'

George Jones then told the court:

'I am a dairyman, at 23 Wood Street, Westminster. Mr Williams, who occupied 5 Westminster Chambers, introduced to me Frost, who had become the tenant there, so as to supply him with goods. Afterwards Gigner came and gave me an order – he gave me a cheque on a piece of note-paper for £1; that was paid. I continued to supply goods, and on 2nd May a sum was owing. Gigner brought me a cheque on Smith Payne, dated 3rd May, for £3.3s., payable to Mrs Thomas, and signed "Gordon Baillie". I signed the receipt in my book, and gave Gigner £2.7s.6d. change – I knew him as Mr and Mrs Frost's servant. I paid the cheque to my contractor, and afterwards received it back marked "N S". Then I went several times to 5 Westminster Chambers, and saw Gigner, and ultimately I saw Mr Frost. He said he was sorry about the cheque, and told me to present it again – he said he was in difficulties, but did not say what they were. I presented the cheque again three times. Then I called at Westminster Chambers, and found a notice up, "Family out". After the arrest of the prisoners Mr Champion called on me on the Saturday night. I believe he had money with him. He spoke to me about the defendants, and passed a remark to my wife that he would like to pay the money – he did not pay me; I kept the cheque. Afterwards I gave evidence at the police-court.'

Cross-examined by Kemp, Mr Jones said: 'This cheque was post-dated when it was given to me.' Re-examined, he added: 'It was post-dated seven days. I knew that when I received it; I did not keep it till the date; I paid it away to a customer. It was paid in after 3rd May, when it became due.'

Next to give evidence was Julia Ratcliffe, who stated:

'I live with my husband at Mr Johnson's stables, Wilton Road, Pimlico – he lets carriages. On Saturday, 5th May, the prisoners drove up in a cab, and gave me an order for a Victoria for Sunday to go to Stratford to see their children. I asked for the money, and Mrs Frost said she would not pay me that night, but would give me a cheque on Monday, signed in her or her husband's name. Mr Frost was with her; they were both in the office. I supplied the Victoria. The man that drove then took the bill, 25s., on Monday – he came back without the money. On the following Wednesday, the 9th, Mrs Frost called and left me this cheque for £6.10s. (This cheque was on Smith Payne, to self or bearer, dated 12th May, and signed "Gordon Baillie".) I told her I would send her the change, and in the evening I took the £5.5s. change, and gave it to Mr Frost. Gigner told me that Frost was a member of Parliament. Mr Frost gave me £1.5s. out of the £5. 5s. to pay for a Victoria for the next day, Friday.

'I supplied the Victoria next day. The cheque came back dishonoured. On 15th May Mr Johnson received a telegram, which I opened, "See you this evening, Frost". Before that I had not seen either of the prisoners since the return of the cheque. Frost called in the evening and saw Mr Johnson. Next day I received another telegram, "Kindly present cheque to-morrow afternoon". I paid it in again, and it came back again unpaid. The prisoners were not at 5 Westminster Chambers after that. We do work for the London, Chatham, and Dover Railway – on Saturday, 19th May, I received this order [which was produced], and entered it in my 'bus book, and in consequence sent two omnibuses to Victoria Station to meet Mrs Fraser.'

Cross-examined by Mr Kemp, she added: 'We are sole agents for the Chatham and Dover. Gigner told me in Mr Johnson's office that Frost was member of Parliament for West somewhere – I did not look to see, because I did not believe him. I made no answer to him. I knew the Frosts were living at 5 Westminster Chambers; they told me so. That was all I knew of them.'

Charles Ratcliffe then declared:

'I only saw the Frosts in the office before the cheque was given on 19th May. I received an order from the station master's clerk at Victoria Station, and I took two omnibuses to the station. The prisoners got into our omnibus there, and it was loaded with luggage. They went with the luggage to Palmer Lodge, Palace Street, Pimlico. My man was with us. The female when they saw us said, "Here is Hull and Ratcliffe, too." I was paid for that job at the time. I went one day to Palmer Lodge to see if I could make an arrangement about the £6.10s. cheque – I saw Gigner, and I waited, and saw Mr Frost come home. I asked him about it – he said he was very sorry, and he wrote me not to take it back, and to wait till he could come round, and see Mr Johnson. [A letter of 23 May, from Percival Frost to the witness, was read, asking him not to present the cheque again, as he had been so many times disappointed by his client, and that he would let him have cash for the cheque.] The driver of the omnibus took the money.'

Next on the witness stand was Henry James Hone, who said:

'I am a coal dealer, in Broadway, Westminster. At the end of February I supplied half a ton of coal to 5 Westminster Chambers. I knew Gigner there as servant. He gave me a cheque on Smith Payne for £5.10s., out of which I took £1.14s.6d. due to me for coals supplied to Mr and Mrs Frost, and gave him the change [of] £3.15s.6d. The cheque was returned from the bankers. I went to 5 Westminster Chambers, and saw Gigner there; I told him I had had the cheque returned, [and] he asked me to give it to him. I said "No" – he said, "Will you pay it in again, and it will be met." I paid it in again, and it was met. I continued to supply coals, and then on 9th May a sum was due for them. Gigner gave me this cheque for £4 dated 28th April, signed "Gordon Baillie", and endorsed by "R.P.B. Frost", and I advanced him £1 on it; afterwards the cheque was paid in and returned marked "N S". I kept it for a fortnight or three weeks, and wrote to Mr Frost about it, but got no reply. I never got the money and gave it up as a bad debt but Inspector Marshall called and I gave it to him. I am still owed £2.3s.' [Champion again stated that to the best of his belief the endorsement 'R.P.B. Frost' was in Frost's handwriting.]

Elizabeth Lloyd was the next to give evidence. She stated:

'I am a milliner at 5 Lower Belgrave Street. At the beginning of June the two prisoners came in a brougham on a Saturday afternoon. I supplied Mrs Frost with writing materials; she wrote a letter – she gave me an order for a hat. She said she was Mrs Frost, of Palmer Lodge. I made the hat, and sent it within less than a fortnight by Miss Wells, my assistant, and a bill for 21s. She did not bring the hat back nor the money. The next day Mrs Frost called for her parasol, which she had left. On 7th June, I think, she called again and brought a cheque; she said she had not brought the bill, but she would pay for the hat. [The cheque was for £8, payable to Messrs Durant and Co., or bearer, signed Gordon Baillie; it had been dated 4 April, and that date was altered to 6 June.] I had not sufficient change in the house; I gave £4.10s. to her, and sent the balance in the evening. She said she wanted to pay some poor person, who wanted the money to pay it away. Mr Smith, a neighbour, gave me the money for the cheque, and I handed him the cheque in the evening. About a week after Mr Smith returned the cheque to me marked "N S". I paid him back his money, and kept the cheque. I wrote to Mrs Frost asking for the £8 on Monday. I received this answer. [Champion once more stated that he believed this was in Frost's handwriting; it requested Miss Lloyd to call that evening and bring the cheque with her.]

'I went to Palmer Lodge on the Thursday; I think I saw Mrs Frost then; she asked me if I had the cheque with me. I said "No"; I had it, [but] I would not give it up. She said, "It is alright, I am so very sorry you should have had all this trouble. Tell Mr Smith to pass the cheque through his bankers again, and the money will be paid." I conveyed that message to Mr Smith, who passed it through again, but it was returned to me. Before 30th June I received this letter. [The letter requested Miss Lloyd to call on Mrs Frost next day, and said she need not be anxious – Champion stated this was in Frost's handwriting.]

'I sent Miss Wells several times to try and get the money; I never received any of it. On June 30th I wrote this letter. [This informed Mrs Frost that unless the £8 was paid that day, Miss Lloyd would go to the Magistrate on Monday.] On the evening of 30th June I sent Miss Wells to Palmer Lodge, and she was so long gone that I went and I found Inspector Marshall there.'

Cross-examined by Mr Kemp, Miss Lloyd said:

'I did not see either of the prisoners on the 30th. Inspector Marshall went upstairs, and came down and said I could not see the prisoners. I heard they were in custody. Marshall did not tell me not to take my money, he said he would see me later on; he sent someone – no one advised me not to take the money – they said if I would give up the cheque I should hear about it later on, and then they came for me on Monday to go to Westminster to prosecute.'

Ellen Wells then stated:

'I am in Miss Lloyd's service; I was sent by her to Palmer Lodge to try and get the money for the cheque. I saw Gigner on several occasions and Frost on one – he said he would give me the money, but he had not got it in the house; he said he would let Miss Lloyd know what he would do, and I think he said he would write that evening.'

Cross-examined by Mr Partridge, she added: 'I think he did write that evening.'

John Foster Sherris then gave his evidence, saying:

'I am a clerk in the employment of Messrs Smith, Payne and Smith, of 1 Lombard Street. I had never seen the female prisoner. I knew her by the name of A. Gordon Baillie. Her account was opened on 7th May, 1885 with a deposit of £1,290; this is the signature in which it was opened, "Gordon Baillie". When we closed the account in 1887 there was a small debtor balance of £1.19s.6d. This is a certified copy of the account. The account was reopened on February 10th, 1888, with £200. On 13th February a cheque-book, E 4694, with twenty-four stamped cheques, was given. Some of the cheques that have been produced in this case are from that book; the second one on 5th April, and the third one on 23rd April. There were a number of payments made during April, amounting together to about £57. The last cash payment in was £7.10s. on 26th April. £6 was to the credit of the customer.

'I produce a certified list of returned cheques taken from my town returns book, in which all returned cheques are entered; it is a book kept in the ordinary course of our business, and forms part of our books. There are thirty-eight cheques, representing £287.14s.4d., between 12th March and 30th June – the last cheque that was honoured was on 1st May, for £1. The other cheques that had been drawn but not honoured previous to that were larger than the balance, and could not be met. I know Mrs Gordon Baillie's signature; the cheques in this case are in her writing. The state of the account now is that there is a credit balance of £1.9s.10d. We never held any securities or deeds on her behalf; there was no authority to overdraw. It is not true that a cheque for £200 from Scotland or elsewhere was paid in, and that owing to some informality in the signature it had to be returned.'

Cross-examined by Mr Kemp, he replied:

'On 10th February, 1888, two £100 notes were paid in. When the account was opened £1,290 was paid in on 12th May, 1885; then in July £600; later, another £600; in February, 1886, £400; in May, 1886, £1,700; on October 8, £700; and again in October, £492 10s. In the intervals only small balances were left. From time to time considerable sums were paid in. I knew nothing about Mrs Gordon Baillie except what I found in our books. I found that at times she was in possession of large sums of money. There was no general rule in banks as to sending back cheques: we are guided by the circumstances whether we send back cheques of customers of this kind who have overdrawn their accounts; we judge our customers.'

Cross-examined by Mr Partridge, he responded: 'Frost's family have had a great many business transactions with our bank. He was trustee under his father's will with his sister, and considerable sums passed through the bank. I have always known him as an honourable young man.'

Re-examined, he added:

'I know of a receiving order against him in bankruptcy, I don't know the date. I never heard of, or knew, or saw a Mr Gordon Baillie. The first address of Mrs Gordon Baillie that I had was 4 Bryanston Street, Portland Square. I don't know who was living there ... I know no details of this bankruptcy. I do not know that no single private debt was proved against him.'

Annie Bassett then gave her evidence:

'I am single, and live at Mr Butler's, a florist, of 171 Sloane Street. I know the female prisoner as Mrs Bodley Frost – at the beginning of June she bought some plants of the value of £1.17s. off us, and on 13th June she gave me this cheque for £10, dated 15th June, on Herries Farquhar to self or order, signed and endorsed "A Bodley Frost". She owed £1.17s.; I gave her the difference between that and £10. I paid the cheque into the bank in due course. I received it back marked "Have written for orders". I paid it in again. I wrote and I received this letter. [Champion said he thought this was in Frost's writing. The letter regretted Mr Butler had been put to inconvenience; that he had only returned the previous night, and could not understand how it happened; that he would inquire into it and see Mr Butler on Tuesday at Palmer Lodge.] I wrote again I did not pay the cheque in after a second letter – it remained in my hands unpaid until after the prisoners were in custody; then on 2nd July a gentleman called on me after tea and paid me a £5 note and £5 in gold.' [Champion again stated that he believed the cheque was in Frost's handwriting.]

Cross-examined by Mr Kemp, she said: 'I have been paid this money – nothing is owing to me at the present time.'

William Gatzal then stated:

'I am employed at Mr John Harman's, a hatter, of 422 Strand. On 10th June Frost drove up in a brougham, and selected a silk hat and a felt hat for himself, of the value of £1.11s.6d. He asked that they should be sent to Palmer Lodge, Buckingham Gate. He did not pay for them. I took the hats myself the same night. I saw Gigner; I did not get the money, he said that there was not sufficient change in the house but that Mr Frost would come in and pay for them on the following day. I left the hats on the condition that they were to be paid for the next day – they were not then paid for. On June 26th the female prisoner came in a brougham. She said, "I have called to pay my husband's account, Mr Frost, of Palmer Lodge; I also want a hat for my servant." She gave me the size, and said we could send it on. She produced a cheque for £2.15s. on Herries, Farquhar, and Co., signed "A. Bodley Frost", or "R. Bodley Frost", I could not say which. I gave 16s. change, and paid it into my bank. It was returned dishonoured. On 28th June I went to

Palmer Lodge and saw Gigner. On 2nd July, after the prisoners were in custody, Mr Champion called and gave me £3 in gold, for which I gave a receipt [and] when I asked about the cheque he said, "Destroy it". I could not find it, it had probably found its way into the waste paper basket.'

Next to take the stand was Henry White, who said:

'I am manager to [optician] Mr Henry Lawrence, of 1 Old Bond Street. On 1st June the female prisoner called in a brougham. She had her sight examined, and gave an order for a pair of gold spectacles, value £3.13s.6d. The other prisoner came in while she was there, and they left together. The spectacles were to be made. On 8th June the female prisoner called again, approved of the spectacles, and took them away. She also ordered a pair of glasses with a long handle, at £3.13s.6d., to be made. On 15th June the other things were made and sent. Some time before 30th June she called and complained that the handles of the glasses were not quite long enough. She said, "While I am here I will pay for the gold spectacles", and gave me this cheque for £6.10s. on Herries, Farquhar, and Co., dated 15th June, payable to self or order, and signed and endorsed "A. Bodley Frost". I deducted £3.13s.6d., the price of the spectacles, and gave her £2.16s.6d., the change. The other glasses with the handle were to be returned. Afterwards Frost called and took out some articles to Mrs Frost, who was in the brougham, apologizing for troubling us, and saying she was not well. She ordered a lorgnette to the value of five guineas, which was put in hand as the lenses had to be made.

'On 28th June he called for the glasses that had been ordered, and asked if they were ready; they were not. He wanted a gold monogram or crest put on the handle. I delayed making those. He asked me if I had paid the cheque into the bank; I had not then – he asked me to hold it over for a day or two, as his wife was changing her bankers. I promised to do so. I spoke to Mr Lawrence about it and went to Palmer Lodge, where I saw Gigner, who was dressed as a butler. I asked for Frost; he was not in. I asked Gigner what he was and if Palmer Lodge belonged to him. He said "Yes", [and] he thought his master was a solicitor, as he had offices in Throgmorton Street and High Holborn I believe; nothing was said about an address in the Temple. I returned to my shop and wrote a letter to Mr Frost. [This said that the cheque could not be held over and that it would be paid in tomorrow.] We received no reply and the cheque was paid in on June 30th – it was returned marked "No account". We have lost the gold spectacles and £2.16s. – the ones with the long handles were returned to us. After the prisoners were in custody the Rev Mr Mole called and made inquiries and I returned him the cheque and got cash for it. I did not then know that the prisoners were in custody.'

Cross-examined by Kemp, he told the court: 'The whole of our claim has been paid.'

He was followed by Charles White, who stated:

'I am a chemist of 45 Buckingham Palace Road Gigner came and brought me this order on June 6th for drugs [and] I supplied them. They came to 10s.; he took them away. They were not paid for. He called again and gave me four other orders [also in Frost's writing). I supplied those goods, which came to £1.10s. On June 23rd Gigner called with a note and a cheque for £3.10s. [In the note Mrs Frost requested him to cash the cheque and to send a bottle of peroxide of hydrogen.] I declined to cash the cheque. On June 27th Gigner brought a cheque dated June 27th on Herries Farquhar for £3.10s. signed "A. Bodley Frost". I gave him £2 for it. I paid it into my account and it was returned. I went to Palmer Lodge, I saw Gigner who said that they were out [and] I waited till Mrs Frost came in and told her I wanted £3.10s. for the cheque and should not go until I was paid. I showed it to her. She said there was a mistake in the banking account, she was transferring her banking account and she would pay me. I waited till Mr Frost came in, [but] he knew nothing about it. Mrs Frost admitted writing the cheque. I refused to go unless I was paid. Frost had not the money to give me then, but said he would bring it to me in the morning and I said I would go to Rochester Row police-court if I did not get my money. On Friday morning, June 29th, Mr Frost brought me £3.10s. in gold and I gave the cheque back to him.'

The court then heard from John Ponsonby:

'I am a partner in Messrs Herries, Farquhar and Co., bankers, of 16 St. James' Street. I received this letter. [The letter dated from Palmer Lodge, 4 June 1888, and signed "Annie Bodley Frost" stated that she was desirous of opening an account with them to receive various amounts from Scotland and to keep a current account.] I replied with this of June 6th, that we would have much pleasure in opening an account in her name. On June 8th Mrs Frost called. She referred to the letter she had written on June 4th; she said she wished to open an account. I agreed to let her do so; I took her signature in this book, "A. Bodley Frost". That was the signature to the cheques; I gave her this cheque-book for which she paid half-a-crown. She was alone, [and] she went away taking the cheque-book. No money was ever paid into the account; cheques were presented which were not met. On June 18th I sent this letter [saying a cheque for £15 had been presented for payment, and as they received no remittance to her account, they feared there was some mistake and had returned it for further orders]. I received this answer. [This stated that Mrs Frost had drawn a cheque for £10 as she was advised that money from Scotland had been placed to her account, and that she would see the matter was put right.] On June 27th I wrote this letter [informing her that a cheque for £15 had been presented, and that as no funds had been remitted, they were obliged to return it marked "Refer to drawer"].) We had no securities, no money had been paid in.'

Inspector Marshall informed the court: 'I saw Frost write after I arrested him. I know his writing; the body of these letters of June 4th and 20th to Herries Farquhar are in Frost's writing to the best of my belief. I believe the body of the cheques are in his writing; I have not seen Mrs Frost write.'

Next to be called was Ernest Ebenezer Samuel Williams, who said:

'I live at 56 Finsbury Road, Brighton. I keep a set of chambers at 5 Westminster Chambers, Victoria Street; I know the two prisoners and Gigner, their servant. I let the chambers to Mr Frost at the end of February. He gave as references Mr Champion, of Paternoster Row, and Mr Ormsby, of King's Bench Walk, Temple. I made inquiries and found the references satisfactory and let him the chambers. He paid me in advance £8 by a cheque of Gordon Baillie on Smith Payne; that was honoured. I afterwards saw all three prisoners at the chambers; nothing more was paid. At the end of May I applied for the second amount of rent; I could not get it. I got nothing at the end of the three months. On May 18th they left; £16 was then owing. I put in a distress, but recovered nothing. I knew the female prisoner as Mrs Gordon Baillie.'

Charles Spencer Smith then gave his evidence:

'I let the house, Palmer Lodge, Palace Street, to Mr Frost from 17th of May at a rental of three and a half guineas a week under this agreement; I am the occupier of that house. I took the inventory of the furniture and Front checked it – 14 guineas was paid down on signing the agreement, and 14 guineas was subsequently paid in notes and cash; the rent was payable in advance. The last payment was made about 17th or 18th June. I have been shown a quantity of property produced by pawnbrokers which was in the house at the time I let it.'

Cross-examined by Mr Besley, he continued:

'Mrs Frost came first bringing an order from an agent; and she went over the house, and said her husband was engaged at the Houses of Parliament for some months, and wished to take a house in the neighbourhood; after she had seen it she thought it would suit him, and she said she would bring him later on. I did not know that Frost's mother was a lady of wealth and position. The last payment was about a fortnight before they were taken into custody. My source of knowledge produced a number of pawn tickets. Frost's sister came to me and offered to redeem the things and restore them to me. I did not know there was a formal correspondence with Messrs Wontner, and that they were instructed by Inspector Marshall not to allow it to be done. I made the charge of stealing at the police-court immediately after Mr Champion produced the pawn tickets. The value of the goods missing from my house amounts to £50, the value of the goods referred to at the police-court was £25 perhaps.

'I am not aware that I told Miss Frost that I would not take my goods back; as soon as she knew that the pawnbrokers were liable to have an order made on them by the judge to restore, she said it was not worthwhile to pay for them. I had a letter from Mr Dutton on 24th August, Miss Frost came to see me after that, and the withdrawal of her offer was subsequent to that. I heard of no formal offer to restore the goods. I had no letter from Messrs Wontner. I was not told by Marshall or Messrs Wontner that an offer was made on 17th September and refused. I was no party to the refusal.'

Re-examined, he added: 'They were committed for trial before 17th September. I let my house furnished. After the prisoners were in custody I found a quantity of my goods had been pawned, and then I charged them with stealing. All that Mr Besley has referred to took place since the committal.'

Alfred Oldfield said in evidence:

'I am an assistant to Joseph Raper, a pawnbroker, of 32 Great Queen Street. On 24th May Frost pawned at our shop a quilt, five sheets, four tablecloths [and] twelve table napkins for £1.12s. in the name of Fraser, 19 Sussex Street. On the 25th he pawned a pair of curtains, a quilt, six sheets, ten pillow cases and a toilet cover for £1.10s., in the name of Fraser, 18, Sussex Street. On 18th June he pawned a pair of blankets and a pair of curtains for 16s. in the same name. I have shown those things to Mr Spencer Smith, who has identified some of them. He could not recognise some which were marked "Gordon Baillie".'

Cross-examined by Mr Besley, he stated:

'Frost came in a cab with the parcel carefully packed. The things have been properly taken care of – they are just as valuable as they were. I don't recollect Mr Champion coming. Mr Marshall came twice and produced all the tickets, and we showed him the property. We would have let these pledges be redeemed.'

George White then told the court:

'I am assistant to Mr Sutton, pawnbroker, of 17 Stockbridge Terrace, Pimlico. A French clock and a card tray were pawned with us on 24th May for 25s. by the prisoner Frost in the name of Brockerton, 18 Sussex Street. I showed them to Mr Spencer Smith, who identified them.'

Cross-examined by Mr Besley, he said: 'I had not seen Mr Champion before Mr Spencer Smith came with Marshall. I did not know the tickets had been handed up by Frost. The articles have not been damaged while they have been in my custody.'

He was followed by Thomas Gammon, who said:

'I am a pawnbroker at 44 Wilton Road, Westminster. On 19th May Mrs Gordon Baillie came and pledged nineteen sheets and three tablecloths for £4, in the name of Mrs Ann Fraser, 4 Vauxhall Road. I did not take them in myself, [but] I was present. They have been shown to Mr Spencer Smith, who has identified them. On 23rd June Mr Frost came and pawned a sheet and eighteen pillow cases and a remnant of stuff [which was not identified] for 10s.'

Cross-examined by Mr Kemp, he continued:

'When I said at the police court that Frost had pledged goods, I said nothing about Mrs Frost having pledged some, because I did not know it then. I had seen her at the shop more than once, I can't say how often; I knew her as a customer. I can't say that I have ever taken anything in pledge from her myself. I did not take these sheets and tablecloths from her, [but] I saw her bring them. On closely examining these sheets after I had taken them I found the name Smith. It was in the evening.'

He was also cross-examined by Mr Besley, saying: 'Marshall came and told me Frost had told him about the £4 Pledging. I took the 10s. pledge in myself from Frost. I suppose the value of the goods would be much more than the amount advanced on them. Every care has been taken of them.' Re-examined, he added: 'I did not know Mrs. Ann Fraser by any other name. I was present on 19th May, but did not take in these things from her – William Bateman did, he wrote this ticket for £4.'

William Bateman told the court: 'I was assistant to Mr Gammon on 19th May, when the female prisoner came in a cab with nineteen sheets and four tablecloths, which I took in pledge for £4. I wrote out this ticket I recognise the female prisoner as Mrs Fraser.' Under cross-examination by Mr Kemp, he said: 'I saw her twice in the shop. On the other occasion she pledged something else, I cannot remember what. I have left the service, but the entry would be in our books. I have not been taken to identify her. I did not see her in the police-court. I have not seen her from that day to this [but] I knew whom I was coming to see.' Re-examined, he added: 'I have not the slightest doubt she is the woman who brought these things.'

Charles Spencer Smith was then re-examined, and said: 'These various articles pawned have been shown to me by the different pawnbrokers; their value is £40 to £50; they are household furniture, [a] clock, bed linen. They were all safe in Palmer Lodge when I gave possession of it to Frost on 18th May.'

Cross-examined by Besley, he said:

'Very likely I was in communication with Miss Frost on 13th September. From information she gave to Marshall we knew about the chenille curtains and nineteen sheets at Gammon's. The object of my letter of 13th September was that the things might be traced; she came to see me – that was long after I had made the charge at the police-court. Sometime in August or September she said she would restore any missing goods, and afterwards, when she knew the pawnbrokers would be compelled to give them up, she said she did not see why she should do it.

'No rent was due on 30th June when the prisoners were taken into custody. Frost took the house for twenty-six weeks; he paid me for the eight weeks he was at liberty, so that eighteen weeks are due. I have taken possession, [but] the key was missing; I got in by the servant in the house, and took possession through Mr Champion.'

Re-examined, he added: 'The £40 or £50 includes some goods that were not traced, and are missing; they amount to £4 or £5. I was desirous of getting information where they had gone to.'

Next to provide evidence was Reverend William Edmund Mole, who declared:

'I am a Clerk in Holy Orders. I am a friend of Mrs Frost, Frost's mother. She lives at 20 Woburn Place, and is an elderly lady under medical treatment. She supplied me with money, and I went to Messrs Hatchard and paid £10, and they gave me the cheque on 2nd July after the prisoners were in custody; then I went to Mr Herbert, the solicitor acting for Miss Franks, on 2nd July, and gave his clerk £5, and received the cheque and had a receipt. I also went and paid Lawrence, the optician, £6.10s.'

Under cross-examination by Mr Besley, Rev Mole said:

'I have known the old lady, Mrs Frost, for many years. She has an income of £2,000 or £3,000 a year. She is a widow, Frost is her son; I have known him some time. He has sisters. I was interested on behalf of the family in trying to restore the money – in the three cases I gave money for the full amount of the cheques, which covered the goods and the money. The money was provided by Mrs Frost. I did not go with Mr Champion. I left my name and address at the places I went to, and through that Marshall came to me and insisted on my giving evidence. I can speak highly of Frost's character as an honourable man, that is the reputation he has borne.'

Re-examined, he stated:

'I know he was bankrupt; I do not know the amount of his debts, or if he got his discharge. I had not seen anything of him for 12 or 18 months I should think. I heard he had gone abroad, and I knew he came back to England quite recently. He was not living at home with his mother – I did not know where he was living. I did this out of kindness to the mother. I went before the Magistrate, who told me I had better not interfere further. I was called as a witness to give evidence.'

Questioned by Mr Besley, he added: 'As to the bankruptcy in 1886 I was told there was not a single private debt, and that it was owing to Mr Bebro landing him in speculations as to companies.'

Henry H. Champion, Frost's old friend, was now re-examined, and said:

'I live at 10 Gray's Inn Place. I was at school with Frost; his name is Robert Percival Bodley Frost. I heard of his arrest, and after that saw his mother, and got money to take up these cheques. I took up Butler's cheque for £10., and I paid Harman, the hatter's account, to Gatzal for £10. On the morning of 9th July I found a large number [of], I think eleven, pawn tickets in cupboard in a bedroom at Palmer Lodge, and handed them to Marshall after consulting a solicitor. That was after they had been in custody nine days, I should think. I was acting for the mother, who is an old lady with no male relatives. I went before the Magistrate, who told me I had better not do anything further.

'This letter of 18th January, signed "P.B. Frost", looks like Frost's writing. [This stated he (Frost) had just returned from abroad, and found a summons had been left for Mrs Gordon Baillie; that she had never lived at Woburn Place, though her letters had been received by him, as he transacted business for her prior to her departure for Australia; and that he would communicate with her in the Highlands, where she was staying.]

'During his father's lifetime, after Frost left school, he had occupation in London, but afterwards he was living independently. I know he had some relations with Mrs Gordon Baillie, what they were I don't know. His father died about 1880. This letter of 21st January appears to be in his writing. [This stated he was instructed by Mrs Gordon Baillie to ask for assistance for the distressed crofters, as she was sending out blankets the next week. It was signed "C.H. Morrison, private secretary".] I never knew Frost go by any other name than his own.'

Champion was cross-examined by Mr Kemp, telling the court:

'I think I have heard she had a private secretary of the name of Morrison. I know she did take an interest in the case of the crofters, and that she gave a considerable sum of money to the crofters in Skye in 1884. I heard that she was straitened considerably by what she had expended on the crofters; I do not know it of my own knowledge.'

He was also cross-examined by Mr Besley, saying:

'I was with Frost at Marlborough College from 1872 to 1876, I think. His father died in 1879 or 1880. I was away from England then. The son acted as trustee under his father's will. The estate was better than was expected; it was quite £5,000 a year and £35,000 in cash. There was a marriage settlement on the old lady of £600 or £700 a year – her family was well-to-do. Frost won a scholarship at Marlborough. He was at a shipbroker's in the City for some years before his father died. He left the City because his prospects were so much improved – he has had several large sums of money, and has been in possession of ample funds ever since I knew him, £400 or £500, I should say. In 1880 or 1881 he went with me to America for some months.

'I heard his bankruptcy was due to two promoters of public companies inducing him to go into speculations in a bank in Brussels, and a brickfield and buildings. I afterwards came across the son of Bebro, who is in gaol I believe now, and I believe Bebro himself is in gaol. Frost's family invested a few thousands for him, and he became bankrupt for a large sum, not proportionate to the amount he had put in; that was done to protect the rest of the property. I should have done it myself without dishonour, I should think. I have never heard of any private debts of his.

'I took these cheques up that there should be no loss for the money or the goods. I would have taken up every one of them if it had been permitted. His mother instructed me that she was desirous that no one should lose anything by his having run short, and his debts would have been paid as they have been before. I was acting as I might have done if he had been my brother, he having no brother in London.

'Frost, through me, gave every information as to Mr Smith's goods, so that he might not be a loser. He told me where the tickets were after the detective had failed to find them. There was no rent due on 18th June when the prisoners were taken into custody. I saw Mr Smith first a day or two after the arrest. I assisted in giving him possession of the place. I said to him I had no doubt that Frost and his relatives would be very glad to spare him any inconvenience from the loss of the things, and about the remainder of the agreement and compensation for not leaving the place clean. Every assistance was given by Frost to restore the goods that had been taken from the house.'

Re-examined, he added:

'I saw Mrs Gordon Baillie, on one occasion only; about three years ago at a small public hall. I next saw her about nine months ago, after her return from Australia or New Zealand. I know some of the crofters who were in Skye in 1884; I know their signatures and have seen those signatures to a testimonial thanking her for giving the money. I did not know she was collecting subscriptions.

'From the time Frost left his occupation in the City, from 1880 to 1881, he had an income of £400 or £500 up to 1885 or so; then he had £3,000 or £4,000 from his family to go into this business. Since then he has had money from his mother; he had some in the early part of the year. He has not been earning any money; it was his share of the family money I suppose.'

Replying to a question by Mr Besley, he said:

'The bankruptcy took place in May, 1886, and up to 1885 I had seen him almost every day; he had up to 1885 hardly commenced the business. They must have got the money from him in a few months. I know he had £200 or £300 to go to Australia, and in February 1887, he had £400 or £600. I should say he had roughly £400 or £500 a year.'

Inspector Henry Marshall was then re-examined, and he said:

'In June this year I began to receive complaints with regard to the prisoners. I made inquiries and saw some of these cheques. I applied for a warrant, taking Pogson, Hone and Jones with me. On 30th June I had a warrant for the apprehension of the prisoners and Gigner. [On that day] I was outside Palmer Lodge, and about half-past 4 I saw Frost leave the house and get into a brougham standing at the door. I followed in a hansom cab. He called at two shops and returned to Palmer Lodge and went in.

'I then saw Gigner leave the house. After watching for some time, I placed two men, one at each side of the house, and knocked at the door several times. Gigner opened the door. I said, "Are Mr and Mrs Frost in?" He said, "No, out of town." I said, "I want to see them rather particularly." I put my foot in the doorway and eventually got in. I told Gigner I was an inspector of police from Scotland Yard, and that I wanted to see them. I said, "I know Mr Frost is in, for I saw him enter." When Gigner found I persisted in going over the house he hurriedly ran downstairs into a room. I took him by the collar and put him into the breakfast room, where the prisoners were. I said to them, "I am Inspector Marshall, here is my official card, I hold a warrant for the arrest of all three of you, so consider yourselves in custody." She said, "Oh, Mr Marshall, sit down and tell us all about it."

'I said, "What is your name?", addressing Gigner. He did not reply. Mrs Gordon Baillie said his name was James, and subsequently that it was Gigner, and I said to her then, "I think you are known as Mrs Gordon Baillie." She said, "Yes". I read the warrant, which charged conspiracy against all three. She said when I had read it, "How can it be conspiracy?" Addressing James, she said, "Have not those poor tradesmen been paid?"; and she said "Poor James has only done what he has been told" – that was Gigner. She said he was a servant. She asked me to explain, and I said, "It is alleged you have conspired together to defraud many people. In Pogson's case Gigner first went and got an introduction by making a small purchase, and Mr Frost then took some part."

'I produced a small memorandum about the servant being supplied with meat. Frost said, "That is my writing."—I said to Mrs Baillie, "And you have followed up by drawing cheques that were dishonoured."—I produced the cheque for £7 on Smith Payne, signed "Gordon Baillie". She looked at it and said that was her cheque and signature. I showed her Jones's and Hone's cheques [and] she said those were also in her hand. I said they had been dishonoured. She said to Gigner, "Has not Pogson been paid?" Gigner did not respond. Then she said it was only a debt, as she had paid Pogson £2 on account; she said there were plenty of securities at her bankers, if there was no money. There was a good deal of confusion, and I called in the other officers and told them they would all have to go with me to the police-station. I directed the officers to search Frost and Gigner. Mott handed me a letter-case, which I saw him take from Frost's coat pocket; I found in it these two cheques in the same hand, with the signature "Gordon Baillie". [One of these was dated 18th March, to self or bearer, for £13, and the other was dated 27th April, for £15.10s., to Frost and Co., and endorsed R.P.B. Frost.)

'I told the constables to take Frost and Gigner into custody, and I was about to take Mrs Frost myself, when she said she was unwell, could I not leave her till Monday morning. I sent for a doctor, who pronounced her well enough to go, and I took her in a cab. While I was in the house Miss Lloyd came; one of my officers said she had come; Mrs Frost said, "Let Mr Champion see her." I saw Miss Lloyd, who gave me information, which I communicated briefly to Mrs Gordon Baillie. As I took her to the station I said there were a large number of complaints about her. She said they would all be paid. I returned to the house after they were taken to the station; I made a search and found a quantity of papers, which I have handed over, together with the cheque-book on Herries, Farquhar, found in a desk in the house, to Messrs Wontner and Sons, solicitors for the prosecution.'

Cross-examined by Mr Besley, Inspector Marshall added:

'I saw Frost's sister on 12th September. I have heard they are wealthy people, [but] I don't know it of my own knowledge. I can believe there was earnest anxiety on the part of the mother and sister that no loss should occur to any one; after the prisoners were in custody they were very anxious to compromise the matter. At the time I got the warrant, on 30th June, the only three cases on which I got it were Pogson's, Jones's and Hone's. I also mentioned Miss Lloyd to the prisoners. Mrs Baillie said the old man, Gigner, could not have been guilty of conspiracy, for he had only done what he was told. I cannot say she said that Frost had done nothing at all but at her request. She said, "It is no conspiracy, neither Mr Frost nor James had anything to do with the cheques." I cannot say I was in possession of the apartments for ten days, I put no officers in. I made a pretty good search myself Mr Champion did not bring me these pawnbrokers' pledge notes, I demanded them of him; I knew he had them, not from his information, I had heard he had them in his possession; when I asked him the question he prevaricated. I got them from him after he had consulted Mr Dutton. I knew nothing of a request for me to produce the tickets at the pawnshops, so that the goods might be redeemed, or of Mr Wontner postponing answering the letter till they had consulted me.'

The court then heard from Herbert George Muskett:

'I am a solicitor and a clerk in Messrs Wontner and Sons' office; they are acting for the Director of Public Prosecutions. I have looked through the papers which Inspector Marshall handed to me. I produced three cheque books on Smith, Payne and Smith, in which I find the counterfoils of the cheques that have been given in evidence. I have found the letter of 21st January, signed C.H. Morrison. I found a half sheet of paper on which are a number of specimen signatures, "A. Frost", "A. Bodley Frost", "A. Bodely Frost" [and] "A. Bondly Frost", in Mrs Gordon Baillie's writing, as though she had been practising. I found a summons issuing from the resident magistrate at New Zealand against Annie White, wife of James Ashton White, for £7 due to Mr Weston, of New Zealand; a judgment summons in bankruptcy and a writ dated 16th March, 1888, and a writ against R.P.B. Frost for £30.'

Cross-examined by Mr Kemp, Mr Muskett said: 'The writ of Elliott against Frost has not been paid. This writ for £64.9s. has been paid, I have not referred to that.' He was also cross-examined by Mr Besley, stating: 'The writ of Miss Elliott against Frost, of March, 1888, has not been paid. I have seen Miss Elliott.'

The prosecution was now reaching the conclusion of its case. Mr Poland asked if the prisoners were going to assert that they were husband and wife, as he had evidence of Annie Frost's marriage to Mr White. The defence, in the form of Mr Kemp, reiterated that Annie had been divorced from White and had married Frost. He could not prove it, as to do that would have involved the expense of bringing witnesses from New Zealand, and as she was indicted for conspiracy not only with Frost, but also with Gigner, this was abandoned and the matter would rest as it was.

Two previous witnesses were then briefly re-examined. The first, John Foster Sherris, added to his testimony: 'Of the thirty-eight cheques I have mentioned, some of them were presented over again, and the amounts calculated over again.' In re-examination, Champion stated: 'I was negotiating an advance of £500 for Frost about a fortnight before he was arrested; I had been to his mother in February this year, £350 was put into my hands, and I handed it to him.' This concluded the prosecution case.

Mr Kemp QC then stood up and intimated that there would be no witnesses called for the defence, and launched into his closing speech with the insistence that his client was, according to his instructions, a lady of position and fortune who was, in reality, an object of sympathy, more worthy of pity than blame. He did not dispute the fact she had acted improperly, but that was not the point. The real question was whether she was guilty of fraud, and there was no evidence she had ever made use of any false pretences; if it were not for the interference of the police, the tradesmen would have been paid every farthing owing to them.

As to her adopted name of 'Gordon Baillie', he said there was nothing fraudulent in this; there were many persons who passed in public and private life under different names – actresses, for instance – and there was no evidence to show she had adopted this name with fraudulent intent.

It was not disputed that in 1885 she had large sums of money under her control, and there was nothing to show this source of revenue had dried up or she would not be able to pay the cheques. Mrs Gordon Baillie was perfectly justified in living in the style she did, he avowed, and it was quite clear at one time she possessed an income of £2,000 per year. She had not intended to defraud anyone, and it did not seem to be in dispute that had Mr Frost applied to his mother, she would have at once supplied the required funds. She obtained goods from shops where she was known and others where she was not. She had her orders delivered to her home. Any wrongdoing on her part was merely an attempt to stave off a temporary difficulty, and Mr Kemp claimed there was not a West End milliner who could not prefer a similar charge against a great many of their clients.

Mr Besley spoke on behalf of Percy Frost, who, he informed the jury, was of good character and entirely concurred in the remarks made on behalf of Mrs Frost. There had been no criminal conspiracy, but he was anxious to take his share of responsibility for what had occurred. There was nothing to show Mr Frost believed cheques drawn by Mrs Gordon Baillie were not genuine, and as to pawning of goods from the house they occupied, Mr Besley said if any offence had been committed it would be of illegal pawning and every article would have been replaced long before the term of the tenancy had expired. It would be monstrous to convict under these circumstances, he suggested.

A gentleman named Fowler was called and gave Mr Frost a very high character reference.

The Recorder, Mr Chambers, summed up. He explained to the jury that the specific charge against the defendants was that they had obtained money and goods by false pretences, in that they had given cheques when they were aware there was no money in their bank account to pay them. He said when a cheque was given it was supposed that the party giving it knew that there was enough money available to meet it. The question for them to consider was whether there was an explanation, given by the defendants, that would satisfy them in coming to the conclusion that at the time these cheques were given there was no intention to defraud, and that they had some reasonable explanation at the time they gave the cheques that money would be forthcoming at the bank to meet them.

The jury retired shortly after 3.00 pm to consider their verdict; they returned to the courtroom after only a few minutes, having found both defendants 'Guilty!'.

With the verdict delivered, it was time to move on to the sentencing, but before this could happen the court required details of Mrs Frost's history and any previous convictions. Inspector Marshall was only too happy to be of assistance. Mr James Dow, a sheriff's criminal officer from Dundee, entered the witness box and handed in a document showing that a Mary Ann Sullivan was convicted of fraud in Dundee on 19 December 1872. The woman, the witness stated, was the prisoner, Annie Frost. He could swear positively to her identity, and assured the court that he had had entire charge of the case, and he had arrested the woman himself. He produced a photograph of the woman taken at the time. Despite her continued denials, the warder said that he was quite convinced it was her; she had received a sentence of nine months' hard labour.

In response, Mr Kemp stated that Mrs Frost absolutely denied the statement.

Inspector Marshall stated that he had a long list of frauds committed by her, extending over a period of fifteen years, in various parts of the world, and in as many as forty different names. The last statement created a sensation in the court, and order had to be restored before Marshall could continue with his monologue.

He claimed that although she had given her age as 29, she was in fact 40, having been born in Aberdeenshire in 1848. The police had received countless complaints about her from all over Scotland, along the Clyde from Greenock and Glasgow, and further north to Inverness. There had also been numerous complaints from many parts of England, Belgium, America, Australia and New Zealand. As for the large amounts of money paid into her bank, Marshall said these came from the late Sir Richard King and upon his death her resources were cut off.

She had only been associated with Mr Frost since 1884 or 1885, he continued, but before that she had been associated with several other men. One of these acted as her private secretary and was sentenced to five years' penal servitude; upon his release he went back to live with her. He was succeeded by a man named Matron, who assisted her in perpetrating many frauds and there were many complaints about him. In 1877, Marshall said, she defrauded a Mrs Graham out of £300, but bolted to America before she could be arrested. She had also committed frauds in Paris, Rome and Florence, and he believed she had served a short prison sentence in Turin.

He added that upon her return from New Zealand in November 1887, she went to live with Mr Frost in Broadstairs and swindled tradespeople 'right, left and centre'. She had five children, one by Mr Frost, who were taken care of by a woman who remained unpaid, being owed the sum of around £40. The children had subsequently been taken to the workhouse. A previous conviction for fraud in the name of Mary Ann Appleby Bruce, on 19 December 1882, was also proved.

Although several of Mrs Gordon Baillie's frauds were so palpable that those deceived by them were scarcely deserving of pity, he continued, others were carried out with all the ingenuity and genius of a great imposter. The police were several times put on her track, but either failed to catch her or obtain enough evidence to justify prosecution. On one occasion, she duped a lady named Nelson out of a valuable diamond and emerald necklace, but it was so cleverly done that the magistrate to whom the lady applied for redress felt compelled to refuse a summons.

While Inspector Marshall was detailing her felonious *curriculum vitae*, the newspapers reported that 'Mrs Gordon Baillie appeared very much affected by the recital of her varied experiences and frequently bit her finger nails as though with vexation'.

In sentencing, Recorder Chambers said that after such an account he was confident that the jury's verdict was a correct one and it was unnecessary to use a single syllable of comment on the career of the female prisoner. He sentenced her to five years' penal servitude.

'Mrs Baillie showed no sign of weakness when the sentence was pronounced,' exclaimed the newspapers. 'Although a warder thoughtfully held his arm behind her, she stood firmly and without support. She kissed her hand to the court with charming effrontery and walked down from the dock.'

As for her most recent 'partner in crime', Percy Frost, it was merely stated that he had no convictions and came from a good family. The Recorder addressed him with the words: 'Although your case is not so serious as your fellow prisoner, it is serious enough in itself and you will be imprisoned for eighteen calendar months.'

As for the fate of the butler, Gigner, little is known. His name appears in the 1871 census as a lodger and unemployed day servant or butler in the house of a 66-year old widow, Elizabeth Seaward, of Upper Brook Mews, Paddington. He was recorded as being 36 years old and a widower from Chelsea. He at least appears to have been telling the truth, and after a month in prison on remand he was bailed on 7 August before being found 'Not Guilty' on 10 December 1888.

Recorder Chambers declared that in the opinion of both himself and the committing magistrate, great credit was due to Inspector Marshall for the manner in which he had acted in the case.

He continued that the defence counsel had done the best they could with their clients' instructions, but newspapers and the police had done their homework. Almost a year of gossip and propaganda had the intended effect. That all of it was true was far from the point. During the period of Annie's trial, her name was hardly out of the newspapers, and for column inches she must vie with the other infamous celebrity of that autumn – Jack the Ripper!

Part V

1889–1903

Chapter 27

A Glimpse of Freedom!
(1891)

Despite her calm appearance when sentenced, Annie didn't intend to go quietly. A report from a visiting justice towards the end of October 1888 reported that, once again, 'Mrs Gordon Baillie has resolutely refused to obey the prison rules, objecting to prison dress, and refusing to have her hair cut and has been punished in consequence. Nonetheless her wealth of hair has been materially reduced and the visitor declares that he had difficulty in recognising her as the saucy lady he had seen at the Old Bailey.' Percy Frost, meanwhile, received some good news. In the month after his Central Court appearance, due to 'representations made to the Recorder from influential quarters', his sentence was reduced from eighteen to fifteen months – an excellent example of the importance of coming from a good family and having attended a good school.

The following June (1889), Annie was visited in Millbank Prison by a reporter from *The World* newspaper, who found she seemed to have settled in well:

'As we enter a long gallery of cells the warder whispers to me, "The first cell on the left". The cell door has been thrown open and inside facing us, tall, erect, her head thrown back, stands a most beautiful woman. The strong light from the windows falls on a mass of dark golden hair which seems to rebel openly against the white prison cap. The face with its bright dark eyes is somewhat in shadow and as she stands there in the white cell she looks like some wild falcon that has been trapped and caged for a time only and, who as soon as she regains her liberty, will know how to use her strong pinions as well as her beak and talons just as well as she ever did. And it may be said that she has used them, for this beautiful creature is none other than the notorious Mrs Gordon Baillie, whose brilliant career of fraud came to an abrupt conclusion some months ago when she was sentenced to five years imprisonment by a hard hearted judge who evidently had no feeling for beauty.'

It seems unlikely that Annie spent the first nine months in solitary confinement in Millbank, as was customary, as reports say that she was, for a while, in the Fulham Women's Refuge which had closed completely by 1889. The Refuge was an interesting experiment in the rehabilitation of women prisoners that tried to train them in skills suitable for subsequent employment – cooking, cleaning and laundry – with emphasis on 'softening and civilizing'. Part of the reasoning behind calling it a 'refuge' rather than 'prison' was that potential employers might then be less reluctant to employ women and help them to transition back to respectability. Women were often judged more harshly than men; there was always rough work available for male former prisoners, but women were expected to be of 'good character' for domestic service.

When Fulham closed, the inmates were moved on to Knapp Hill Prison in Woking, which was built to hold 700 prisoners and spread over 10 acres. The prison offered what was called 'an improved form of prison life', which had only recently been introduced. Standing about 2 miles from Woking Junction, it consisted of eighty halls or wards, with the largest containing 150 cells, each of which measured 8ft by 5ft, with floors of blue slate. At night the only light was by gas through a thick pane of glass that allowed only a dim glow to penetrate. Each hall was long and lit by a skylight. A contemporary report described it as 'a colony of wasted lives and dead hopes'.

The women's part of the prison was built in 1870, but by the 1890s most of the site had been turned over to the Army and became Inkerman Barracks, with the female section finally closed for good in 1895. During her time there, Annie and her fellow inmates were involved in making twine, along with sewing post office bags and uniforms. There was a tailor's shop and opportunities for farm work, but the prison was most famous for the creation of mosaics, where women were paid 1s.2d. per day to make the little pieces for marble floors. The prison at that time was intended for inmates who 'are not quite as strong as might be wished and many were aged or feeble', although others were doubtless able to talk their way into a slightly less onerous regime. Other previous occupants had included Constance Kent, who had murdered her step-brother in 1860 in what became known as the Road Hill House case – investigated by Inspector Whicher of the Detective Branch at Scotland Yard – and Madame Rachel, another con-artist who had run a bogus beauty parlour and died in custody several years before. In August 1889, Florence Maybrick was moved to the prison, having had her sentence for the poisoning of her husband commuted from death to life imprisonment; here she began her nine-month probationary period.

Reports from a visit by F.W. Robinson of *The Graphic* in September 1889 noted Annie looking well and in capital spirits. Mrs Baillie and Mrs Maybrick, both reported to be in excellent health, were described as:

'Two of the most noted prisoners of recent years but … entirely different in style and physique; the former being of a very dashing and stalwart nature and the latter is slender and shrinking in demeanour. The prison dress code and method of wearing hair was a great leveller, as both women had hair dressed as laid down in the rules and it seemed the effect was especially apparent on Mrs Gordon Baillie, whose attractions were greatly enhanced by the manner in which she usually wore it. Despite the regulations women who have moved among the upper classes are easily picked out by their bearing.'

There was speculation in the press, via Annie's solicitors Messrs Lewis and Churchman of Chancery Lane, that she would appear in court again, but this time as the plaintiff in a civil case scheduled to take place in early November 1889. Annie was aiming to sue the executors of Sir Richard Duckworth King's estate for possession of his old house in Mayfair, worth in the region of £6,000. The case revolved around a deed which she claimed had assigned the house to her, along with 'certain furniture, goods, carriages etc. bequeathed and given out of King's natural love & affection'. His relatives, in turn, claimed that she had extracted around £60,000 from him during his lifetime, a slightly higher figure than the £18,000 usually bandied about. Rumours of this £6,000 fortune, which she claimed to be close to inheriting, were said to have given her 'additional prestige at Woking'.

There was indeed a case brought against the executors of King's estate in November 1889, but this was by a Captain Charles Barnett, the late baronet's brother-in-law, who claimed that he had been promised £3,000 from the estate of the 'generous and kind hearted man', on condition that he did not pester for money during King's lifetime. John Sylvanus Tanner, who was described as having been Sir Richard's 'confidential agent', was called by Barnett as a witness to the fact that the sum had been promised. Whilst under cross-examination, Tanner was asked to account for various sums being paid out from Sir Richard's bank into that of his former wife, Amelia Louisa Hill. These, it emerged, were in support of a child she had by Sir Richard, who was unknown to Tanner.

Barrett lost his case, but it goes some way to shed light on King's activities. He was a very rich man with time on his hands, who, even though not in the prime of life, still had an eye for a pretty girl. He was very free with his money and affections, and there were plenty to take advantage of his generosity. As to his mental state, we have no independent opinion. He very possibly gave all these sums and goods to Annie and a number of others – even to the point of pledging property and large amounts of cash – all in good faith; but once his heirs and family realized that their inheritance was fast diminishing, they stepped in and pronounced him senile and insolvent, getting him to write a new will that superseded all previous ones and put his estate firmly back in their hands. Tanner seems to have been a bit of a chancer, having once been manager of a Brighton skating rink who had been fined £3 for assaulting a solicitor's clerk trying to serve a summons on him. In 1895, he received three months in prison for fraudulently obtaining money through collecting for non-existent distressed families, having only recently been released from an eighteen-month sentence for an unspecified offence.

Annie had been granted an extension to prepare her case against King's executors, but it was called again in November 1891 by the Lord Chief Justice and, as she failed to appear, being unavoidably detained in Woking, the case was dismissed and costs awarded against her.

Woking seemed to agree with Annie, as a short report in September 1891 found that she was popular with 'her companions in misfortune and officials of all ranks. It is stated that she rather patronises the latter who are impressed by her air of good society and culture doubtless acquired in professional circles in Edinburgh and among the pundits of the new journalism in London.' Mrs Maybrick, continued the report, 'was not doing so well and instead of keeping aloof from the other prisoners and asserting her position as Mrs Baillie does, [she] dreads being left alone and begs to be employed in the midst of them. She has gained a stone in weight whilst in Woking.'

With Annie in prison and Frost now free, but whereabouts unknown, there remained the problem of the five small children. Having been rescued from the Thanet Workhouse a few years before, they were now set adrift once more. On the census return of 5 April 1891, for the Rose Street Mission House at 9 Rose Street in the Strand, London, the following names occur under the care of The Sisters of Mercy:

Gabriella White (12), born New York, USA
Ada White (11), born Edinburgh, Scotland
Alice White (10), born Bushey, Hertfordshire
Percy Elizabeth White (4), born New Zealand

The names and ages do not coincide exactly with those from the Thanet Workhouse, but there is enough to recognize the family. The hostel was for girls only, so there is no record of the whereabouts of little Allen Bruce Whyte, now aged 10, and he has not been traced.

The Sisters of Mercy was a charitable Anglican mission run by the Sisters of St John the Baptist, based in Clewer near Windsor. The home was overseen during this period by Mother Superior Emma Frances Hicks, whose name appears as the rate-payer from 1891 until 1896. At the time of the census, the institution consisted of nine sisters, three servants and fifty-six girls. Its purpose, outlined in an 1883 appeal for funds, was 'essentially a preventive home to rescue orphans and children who have been exposed to evil influence and are on the verge of falling into the worst possible state, and train them for service'. Unfortunately, the admissions register for the years 1888–89 has not survived, and from this point onwards the girls disappear from the record. The home itself moved to Leytonstone in 1899, but their names do not appear there. The little we do know about them is discussed in the final chapter.

On Wednesday 9 March 1892, Annie was released from prison, having served three years and five months of her sentence. Reports at the time claimed that she looked remarkably well and that 'her good looks had not disappeared'. She also intended to write a book about her experiences and expressed a desire to 'settle in the antipodes as the people were so soft hearted out there', while others claimed she was about to move back to her native Scotland: she did none of these things.

In September 1893, and still using the name Annie Frost, she moved into a house at 17 Talbot Road, North Kensington, and began a new round of swindles. She avoided the question of rent through entering lengthy and spurious negotiations with the owners to buy the property. What she had been doing in the eighteen months since her release and how she managed to get back on her feet is not known, but she seemed to have spent at least part of that period in the Isle of Wight, as she had done many years before in the summer of 1885 when she was interviewed by *Society* magazine. Her old nemesis Inspector Marshall was in little doubt that 'since her release she had done nothing but swindling, complaints having reached the police from all over the country'. It was very much business as usual, although the one advantage she lacked this time around was any financial help from Sir Richard King, along with the unthinking loyalty of Percy Frost, who had fled to Australia upon his release, just like Knight Aston before him.

The police were again on Annie's tail, although they were not alone this time: Messrs Maple & Co. were in the process of taking possession of all the furniture in the house for a debt of £29, so it was time to move on once more. She left Talbot Road on 20 March 1894 and took rooms in a high-class lodging house at 11 Park Place, Regents Park, sending a man named Lawrence Taylor, described as her agent, who had also lived at Talbot Road, to secure the place for her. True to form, she paid for the new place with a stolen £5 cheque, for which she received £3 in change; she would hardly have had time to spend it though, as within a couple of days she was behind bars once more.

On 22 March 1894, Mrs Annie Frost, who described herself optimistically as aged 35, and reported as 'tall, fashionably dressed and of no occupation', appeared at Marylebone Police Court charged with stealing from Mr Joyner, a tradesman who had sold her six pictures for £10.17/-. William Taylor, 34, a surveyor and auctioneer of Blandford Road, Bedford Park, and brother to Lawrence, was charged with her. At the end of the initial hearing, when the question of bail arose, Magistrate Plowden asked if anything was 'known' about Taylor. Detective Sergeant Fuller replied in the negative. 'But,' he piped up helpfully, 'I know a great deal about the female prisoner! She is the notorious Mrs Gordon Baillie and I ask for a remand as in all probability there may be other charges against her.' Annie was remanded for a week until 30 March and taken to the cells, while Plowden decided that Taylor had done nothing wrong and he was discharged.

At the next hearing, Annie was charged further that between November 1893 and January 1894 she fraudulently obtained twenty-five books, a picture, a silver crucifix, a silver pyx (a small round container), a gold chain, a set of three oil stocks and various other items, valued together at £33.16s., from Burns & Oates, a Catholic publishers of 28 Orchard Street, Portman Square. The books included the *Works of Cardinal Newman*, Faber's *Poems* and a life of Mary Queen of Scots. She had given her Talbot Road address and that of Culver Lodge, Shanklin, in the Isle of Wight, and taken the books away with her in a cab. She returned to the shop on a few more occasions and asked that an engraving of Cardinal Newman be sent to the newly opened Convent of Jesus and Mary in Willesden, which was done, and the amount added to her account with the other items. Even though Annie had paid 47s. off her account at one point, the firm were suspicious of her and made enquiries to see if she really did live where she said she did. Talbot Road checked out, but letters to the Isle of Wight were returned. Upon hearing this evidence, Annie was heard to mutter, 'Oh Dear, Oh Dear', but whether this was in despair, or in surprise that her letters had not been acknowledged, can only be guessed at. Magistrate Plowden committed her for trial on the pictures case and remanded her in custody until the following week on the other charges.

In the meantime, Detective Sergeant Fuller had made further enquiries and by her next appearance, on 2 April, he had been to Culver Lodge in Shanklin and discovered it to be the home of Lady Elizabeth Cranstoun, who had lived there for the past four years. Mrs Frost had called there many times in the last two years, but had never stayed there and was not particularly welcome. Upon hearing this, Annie was reported to have said from the dock: 'I have been there for two years!' The court heard that Fuller had interviewed Lady

Cranstoun during his visit and she became very indignant at the mention of Annie's claims, declaring:

> 'The house is mine. I bought it four years ago. Mrs Frost has no right here but I have allowed her to call; my daughter, The Hon. Miss Pauline Cranstoun and Mrs Frost are both inclined to spiritualistic ideas and I cannot understand my daughter [the prisoner laughed upon hearing this]. I will come to London and give evidence if you like. Mrs Frost never had anything more with her than she could carry in a piece of brown paper.'

Lady Cranstoun had explained that Annie had been in the habit of visiting them on Saturdays, claiming that she was an American authoress; her last visit was a few days before her arrest on 17 March. The sergeant continued to outline his findings and said that the prisoner was well known to the tradesmen in Ventnor, where she once lived, and they would very much like to see her again, which provoked much laughter in court. Fuller said the assumption here must be that the Hon. Miss Pauline paid handsomely for Annie's spiritual services, but Magistrate Plowden interrupted the detective at this point. He had heard enough, and taking all things into account he decided that the Burns & Oates matter was a civil one, not a matter for the jury, and so dismissed it. Bail was again applied for in the light of the reduced charges, but was refused as Plowden 'felt that he could not shut his eyes to the prisoner's antecedents'. Annie was committed for trial at the Central Criminal Court on the first charge of stealing the pictures.

Chapter 28

Oh Dear! Oh Dear!
(May 1894)

It seemed like history was repeating itself, and on 28 May 1894, five-and-a-half years since her last appearance there, Annie found herself once more in the dock at the Old Bailey. The case was held before the Common Sergeant, and one reporter noted:

'Mrs Gordon Baillie has completely changed since she stood in the dock in 1888; the yellow-dyed locks are a dirty grey and her face is lined and worn. Her manner suggests resignation to cruel and unjust treatment and often she murmurs softly, "Oh Dear, Oh Dear!"'

Annie Frost – who knocked the customary ten to twelve years off her true age and claimed to be 34 – was charged on the first count with stealing six engravings, the property of William Joyner, and on the second count of receiving the same. In a bizarre coincidence, one of the prosecutors – Mr Besley – was the one of those who had the job of defending Frost at the 1888 trial, or at least shared the same name. Alongside him was Mr Heddon, while the defence counsel consisted of Messrs Charles Mathews and Guy Stephenson.

The prosecution began its case with its first witness, William Joyner, who said:

'I carry on business at 47 Old Broad Street, and I have a factory at 100 London Wall, and two other shops in Liverpool Street and Clerkenwell Road. On the 23rd February the prisoner came in, between 3.45 and 3.50 pm; I had never seen her before. She asked the price of a picture in the window. I told her the price. She asked to see some others in a portfolio in the shop. I showed her some. She said, "I cannot stop now; I have to go to my solicitors, in Winchester House; I will be back in a few minutes; they leave at four o'clock; I have had a lot of trouble with some tenants of mine in collecting my rents."

'She came back about 4.20. She looked through the portfolio, and selected six unframed pictures, and two which were framed and hanging on the wall. We bargained about the price, and agreed at £8.7s. for the six unframed pictures, and £2.10s. for the two framed ones. The six unframed were to be framed and glazed – she ordered a black and gold rather expensive moulding for them, with the best glass. The £8.7s. included the frames. The two framed ones had to be cleaned. I said, "Our business is a cash business; none of these goods will be left unless paid for on delivery." She said, "Very well; I will pay for the goods on delivery. Who will bring them; this boy?", pointing to Last, who was in the shop. I said, "Yes; he will bring some of them." She said, "I wish these goods delivered on the 28th, between the hours of three and seven, at 17 Talbot Road, Bayswater." She said she was Mrs Frost, and asked me to cash her a £5 note, which I did.

'Last called a cab for her; she gave him some coppers, and left in the cab. I put the six pictures in hand to be framed, and the other two were cleaned at my London Wall factory. I made out this invoice, stamped and receipted as it is now, and gave it to Last sealed up in an envelope on the 28th, and directed him to go and get the pictures at the factory, and to deliver them to Mrs Frost, but not to part with them without the money. I told him that the receipted bill was in the envelope. I saw him the same evening; he brought back the envelope unopened, just as I gave it to him. He brought back no money, except 1s.2d. for his fare; he said, "The fare has been paid." I had not altered my orders to him at all – I told him not to part with the goods on any account without the money. I gave him no right to use his own mind about it.

'Next morning I learnt that only six pictures had been given to Last to take on the 28th; the other two were sent on 1st March by my manager at London Wall, before I knew of it. I had not been to the factory, and did not know but that the whole of the pictures had been delivered on [the] 28th. I don't know what time the remaining two were sent on 1st March; I learnt after the delivery that they had been sent on. I had given no instructions on the matter. I went to Talbot Road on 1st March, about 7.30 or 8 pm. I rang the bell half-a-dozen times, but could not get in; the house was apparently empty.

'I communicated with the police on March 6th, I think. About 10.30 am on the 8th I applied for a warrant. Detective Sergeant Fuller was with me, and the warrant was entrusted to him. This letter was written on 5th March by my brother, who acts as my clerk, by my direction, to Mrs Frost. Next time I saw it it was produced by the solicitor to Mrs Frost at the Police-court, and handed in by her. This letter read as follows: "Madam, I have placed myself in communication with Messrs

Foster and Sons, solicitors, and shall tell them what information I have in my possession. You have treated me shamefully, but I will find out where my property went to. I am on the cabman's track that took them away, and expect to see him to-morrow. I hope you will send me a cheque, or payment for the goods to save bother."

'I had some information with regard to a cabman removing the goods. I wanted my money, if I could get it. I received no communication, and the warrant was taken out. On 12th March, four days after the Magistrate granted the warrant, I received this letter in this envelope with a crest:

"'Mrs. Frost has been away, and has consequently only just received your letter. She is utterly at a loss to understand your letter; but, as you say you want your pictures back, they will be at once returned."

'On 21st March a young man brought the pictures back. I had previously seen him. I would have nothing to do with them, but referred the matter to the police, and the pictures were taken to the police-station, and the young man was taken into custody for receiving stolen goods. The police still have the pictures. I think the prisoner was taken on the same night, [the] 21st. She and the young man were brought before the magistrate next day, and the case was adjourned till 30th March, when it was completed; the young man was discharged, and the prisoner committed to trial for larceny. I had a writ from the solicitors acting for the prisoner then and now in a civil action against me for malicious prosecution, before this session commenced.'

Joyner, when cross-examined, added:

'That writ was at the suit of the young man whose case was dismissed by the magistrate. He was detained by the police at Moor Lane; he went to the Police-station by his own suggestion to avoid being taken there; he did not want to be seen going through the streets. The pictures were brought into my business premises on [the] 21st, and remained there till the police came afterwards and took them away. I did not send for the police. I should have given the young man into custody if the police had not taken him. On 16th March, five days before, he came to my shop, and he asked me whether I preferred my pictures back, or the money. I told him the matter was out of my hands, and in the hands of the police. He asked me whether there was a warrant issued for Mrs Frost. On the 23rd February the suggestion came from the prisoner that she should see the pictures in the portfolio. She had not given me the name of Annie Frost when she was looking through the portfolio.

'I said before the Magistrate, "On 23rd February last the prisoner called on me, and gave me the name of Annie Frost." She gave me her name after she bought the pictures. I said, "Shall I show you through the portfolio?" She desired to see it. I don't remember her saying "Yes". I did not, when I was examined before the magistrate, say a word about her saying she could not stop at that time, that she had to go to her solicitor, or about her having had trouble with tenants; or about their rents; or about her returning to my shop; I omitted all that. I said nothing about the production of the £5 note, and the asking for change. I am quite confident I used the words, "paid for on delivery". I don't remember saying before the Magistrate that I said, "Our terms are cash, and these goods will not be left unless previously paid for." My deposition was read to me, and I signed it. I thoroughly appreciated its contents, or I should not have signed it.

'I sent Last on the 28th with a receipted bill for the whole eight pictures. I never sent him with six pictures, but he only took six pictures then. I sent him to the factory, in the belief that he would take all the eight pictures; those were my instructions. The factory is 250 or 300 yards off. Last returned between six and seven that evening, and he told me he had been to the house. I said, "Have you got the money?" He said, "No". I said, "Is it a large house?" He said, "Yes, it was a large house." He said, "Mrs Frost has given me the money for my fare, and some money for myself; and she says she knows you very well, and she will come up to-morrow, or the next day, and pay the money." I did not say, "All right"; I am quite clear about that. I said to him, "What did you leave the pictures without the money for?" He said, "I took them down the area steps, and Mrs Frost took them away; I thought she was going to pay for them when she came back with an open purse in her hand." After I had given him a good scolding I said, "All right, you can go about your business." I did not say, "All right" immediately after receiving the message that she would come next day or the day after and pay. My attention has not been called to any of the evidence given before the magistrate, and I have not referred to it in any way. The two pictures were sent on 1st March by my foreman without my knowledge; I thought they had been delivered on the night of the 28th. I said before the Magistrate, "Six were delivered on the 28th, and two the next day." It had come to my knowledge then. I said, "I sent the boy with the two to bring the others back, or the money." That was my evidence in cross-examination on 22nd March. It is not true that

I sent the two pictures on 1st March. I gave the boy the bill to take to Mrs Frost to bring back the money [or the] whole of the pictures.

'I have not referred to my evidence since 22nd March. The question was put to me, "were all these things sent on the 28th?", and I said "No; six were sent on the 28th, and the others on 1st March." It was not true that I sent the boy with the two; I may have thought so at the time; I don't remember saying it. The question was not put to me in the way you put it. I gave the boy instructions overnight to bring back the whole of the pictures, or the money. What I have stated today is correct. I cannot account for my misstatement of fact before the Magistrate, unless I was answering in cross-examination. I have not had any consultation with my solicitor since the matter was before the Magistrate. I have seen him, but not to talk of the case. I gave him instructions. I don't remember my attention being called to the evidence I had given before the Magistrate. I don't remember my solicitor asking any questions about it, or putting any words into my mouth. I don't remember my attention being directed to the fact that it was of very great importance whether I or the foreman sent the boy with the two pictures. My solicitor did not say anything of that to me. By the 1st March I knew from information that all the pictures had been delivered at Talbot Road, and on the 5th I caused this letter to be written. I am responsible for the language in it, as it was written under my instructions. The receipted bill was in my possession.'

Re-examined, he continued:

'I had no solicitor when I was examined [originally]. I had no design in not mentioning about the £5 note being changed; there was nothing extraordinary in changing a £5 note for a customer. The prisoner was represented by a barrister at the Police-court. The question was not put to me in that way, "Sent with the two to bring back the others." I did not read the depositions; they were read to me. I knew on 2nd March, the day I went to Talbot Road, that there had been two separate deliveries of six and two [pictures]. When I wrote this letter I had not seen the police or anybody.'

The court then heard from Edward Last, who stated:

'I am in Mr Joyner's employment. I am not related to him. I am 14. I was in the shop when Mrs Frost came. I heard her speak to Mr Joyner about some pictures, and say she was going round to her solicitors, and something about gathering some rents. I was outside when she came back, and did not hear what passed. I showed her to a cab. On 28th February I saw Mr Joyner write out the invoice, stamp and receipt it, and put it into an envelope, which he gave to me, saying, "Take this over the way and ask Mr Butt to give you the pictures to take down to Mrs Frost, and don't leave them without the money, because this is a receipted bill." I went to London Wall, and Mr Butt gave me two parcels of pictures. Another lad helped me to carry them to Talbot Road; I kept the sealed envelope with the receipt. I got to Talbot Road between five and seven. I went to the front door, and rang the bell – the servant came out of the side door, and called me down there; it was below the street level. I went down the area steps, and said, "Is Mrs Frost in?" The servant said, "Yes". I said, "Can I see her?" She called Mrs Frost who came to the door with her purse in her hand, and I handed the pictures to the servant, because I thought she was going to pay me. The prisoner asked me what my fare was; I told her 1s.2d., and she gave me 2s. and said, "There is 10d. between you." She could see the other lad. I handed her the envelope still sealed up. She said, "Is that receipted?" I said, "Yes". She said, "Oh, you can take that back; I don't want that. Mr Joyner knows me very well. I will call up and pay it to-morrow or the next day, certain." I said, "All right, ma'am."

'I said nothing about the orders I had received from my master. Two of the servants were there and when the pictures were put into the servants' hands, I said, "We must undo them, and see they are right." That was before the conversation with the prisoner. The servant said, "Oh, we can do that", and took the pictures inside, and then the prisoner came to the door and gave me the 2s. It is the usual practice when a picture is taken home to undo it and see if the glass is broken. The servant shut the door, we left and returned to the shop.

'When the prisoner said she would call the next day I said, "All right; you will come up and pay, won't you?" and she gave me no answer, and the door was shut. I rang the bell and waited for three or four minutes, but I got no answer. I saw Mr Joyner that night; I said nothing to him about having only taken six pictures. Next morning Mr Joyner gave me the invoice again, and told me to bring all the pictures back, or get the money. He did not know that the other two pictures had not been delivered. I then went to the London Wall shop, and Mr Butt, the foreman, gave me the two pictures. I went to Talbot Road by myself with the two pictures, and rang the area bell. The servant who had handled the six pictures came. I asked for Mrs Frost but did not see her on that occasion. I stood the pictures down and the servant took them in, and when I asked for Mrs Frost the servant said she was out and shut the door immediately. I did not get any money. I went back and told Mr Joyner I had not got the money, and had not brought back the pictures. I did not tell him I had taken the two that morning.'

Under cross-examination, Last added:

'On 1st March I told Mr Joyner that I had not got the money, and that I had left all the pictures. I knew on 28th February that eight were to be taken; I only got six. I did not tell my master when I came back that I had only left six. I had a talk with him; he was very cross with me for leaving them. He asked me if it was a large house; I said, "Yes". He said, "But Mrs Frost promised to pay on delivery, and she has not done it." I said, "Mrs Frost says she will come up to-morrow or next day certain and pay the money." Mr Joyner did not say, "All right"; I am quite sure of that. He did not make use of those words in the course of the conversation. I have been seen once by the solicitor acting for my master in this case since I gave evidence before the magistrate, and by Detective Fuller. Fuller was at the solicitor's when I was there; Mr Joyner was there, too. I was there about twenty minutes. A statement was written down from what I said by a clerk. The detective and Mr Joyner went out before the clerk started taking my statement down. They were there when I was sent for, but they left before the statement was taken. I do not remember whether my attention was then called to what I had said before the Magistrate. I was asked whether there was something wrong in one statement I made before the magistrate. Mr Carver was there at the time.

'I swore before the Magistrate: "I saw Mr Joyner after I had been there the first time. He said, 'Is it a large house?' I said, 'Yes, sir.' Mr Joyner said, 'Oh, but Mrs Frost promised to pay me on delivery, and she has not done it.' I said, 'Mrs Frost says she will come up to-morrow or next day, and pay the money certain.' Mr. Joyner said, 'All right'." That was true. I don't remember if that was the statement to which my attention was directed when I was at the solicitor's office. I forgot for the moment when I said Mr Joyner did not say "All right". He said, "All right; I will go down there and see for myself."—I don't remember if that was the statement to which my attention was called. I did not tell the Magistrate anything but what was taken down on the depositions and read to me. I do not know why I did not tell the Magistrate that my master was cross with me for having left the pictures without getting the money. I saw him the next morning before I went with the other two pictures. All he said to me was, "Take the bill and get the money, or bring all the pictures back." On my return I told him what I had done; he was not cross then, he remonstrated with me. I did not tell him then that I had left the two pictures that day. I told him I had not got the money. I did not take all the eight on the 28th February, because we could not carry them. I said before the Magistrate that the prisoner said, "Mr Joyner knows me very well, and knows all about it." I don't remember telling the Magistrate that she said, "Mr Joyner knows me very well." I did not say before the Magistrate that when I said, "All right, you will come up and pay, won't you?" that the prisoner said, "Yes".'

Louisa Burgess then told the court:

'I am cook and housekeeper to Mrs Adamson, who keeps a boarding-house at 3 Edinburgh Terrace, Kensington. On the 27th February the prisoner called and said she wanted to come as a boarder. Mrs Adamson showed her a room. She went away, saying she was coming that night to occupy the room; but she did not come. About 7 pm on the 1st March a man arrived in a cab, with two boxes, some parcels and pictures, and left them for Mrs Frost. The pictures were tied up. He said he was Mrs Frost's agent, and "This is Mrs Frost's luggage." He went away. About 9.30 the prisoner came with the man who had brought the pictures. He remained a few minutes in the house, and then went away. She stayed that night. The luggage and pictures were taken to her room. She stayed several nights. The pictures were never unpacked; they remained there until the 3rd, when the prisoner took them away in a hansom cab, saying she was going to send them to her country house at Shanklin. I saw her again that evening; she stayed that night, and on till Tuesday. She went away then, and came back on the following Sunday, I think. On the Friday, I think, she went away. The pictures were not unpacked. I saw they were pictures by their frames, which were black, like these. They were wrapped in brown paper.'

Next to give evidence was Thomas Charles Thompson, who said:

'I am a pawnbroker, at 11 Ladbroke Grove Road, Notting Hill. On 3rd March the prisoner brought eight pictures in a cab. She asked me the price, and said, "I am an artist, and I am in want of money, and so I want to pledge them." I advanced £4, and gave her a ticket. About 16th March she came alone, and took them out, paying me the money advanced and the interest, and said, "I will send for them in the morning", and in the morning someone fetched them. These are the pictures.'

Cross-examined, he added: 'I identify them from the subjects. All the eight brought to me are exactly the same subjects as these eight in Court.'

Edward James Leggatt then stated:

'I am a clerk to Smith and Royden, of 52 Lincoln's Inn Fields, solicitors to Messrs Maple and Co. We acted in an action of which this is the writ. [This, dated 30 January 1894, was between Messrs Maple and Mrs A. Frost for furniture to the amount of £45.10s.3d., with an order for substituted service endorsed on it.] I produce a summons under Order 14. This is the prisoner's affidavit, admitting that £12.6s.9d. was due. There was an order that that money should be brought into Court. In default of that there was judgment for £28.6s.9d. on 26th February, 1894. The man is here who went into possession under a writ of fi fa [a writ after a judgment obtained in a legal action for debt], by our direction. We received the sheriff's cheque for 19s. as the fruit of the judgment.'

When cross-examined, Mr Leggatt added: 'I don't know what the execution realised – we got no goods back. I think the sheriff's charges came out of the results of the execution.'

Albert Withers then told the court:

'I went into possession at the prisoner's house, Talbot Road, on 27th February, under a writ of fi fa, at the suit of Messrs Maple and Co. On 28th February the prisoner said to me, "We have some pictures coming for Mr Taylor; shall you interfere with them?" I said, "No". I levied on her goods. Taylor came to me afterwards, and said, "I have some pictures coming; you will not interfere with them?" Some pictures came; and were taken away on the 28th.'

Under cross-examination, he added: 'I don't know what pictures they were. I was seen twice; but I only made one statement. The first time I was seen I said nothing about the conversation.'

Frederick Stride, Clerk at Marylebone County Court, then said:

'I produce four judgments from that Court against Mrs Frost, of 17 Talbot Road. The first is dated April, 1893, for £7.6s.; one of February 22nd, 1894, for £3.17s.9d. for milk and dairy produce. None of that has been paid. One of 12th June, 1893, £10 was paid into Court, leaving a balance of £23.12s.6d. Nothing has been paid off that since 12th June.

There was an application to examine Annie Frost in February 1894 but the defendant was said to be out of town, and her agent is Mr Robinson. The other judgment is 30th May, 1893, for £21.16s. for coals, nothing has been paid on it.'

Cross-examined, he told the court: 'There is nothing on the documents to show whether or not the parties themselves have been paid.'

The court next heard from Elizabeth Warner, who said:

'I went into the prisoner's service as cook at 17 Talbot Road, on 6th December last, and remained till 20th February, when Withers came in. During the last week I was there people called for money. I told the prisoner about it, and she said, "Say I am not at home", and I did so. Lawrence Taylor lodged in the house. I did not get all my wages.'

Detective Sergeant Robert Fuller then took to the stand to give his evidence:

'I had a communication from Mr Joyner about these pictures on 6th March. I took a statement from him. On 8th March I attended before the magistrate and got this warrant for stealing against the prisoner on a sworn information. I had kept continuous observation on 17 Talbot Road, from about six o'clock on 6th March. I went to a large number of people who knew the prisoner, but could get no information of where she was. I also tried to find Lawrence Taylor, but could not find him. I made further inquiries after the granting of the warrant as to what had become of the pictures. I got information from William Taylor, the brother of Lawrence Taylor, as to what had become of [them]. I did not see them till they were at the police-station. I took the young man, who brought them, into custody. He was discharged on the first hearing.

'I first saw the prisoner about 9 pm on 21st March at Edgware Road Station refreshment room. I said, "Your name is Mrs Frost, I believe?" She said, "No, I am not Mrs Frost, I have only just come from the country today." I said, "I am a police-officer; I am convinced you are Mrs Frost, and I hold a warrant for your arrest for stealing some pictures on the 28th of last month in Talbot Road." After some hesitation she said, "Yes, you are right; I am Mrs Frost." I told her some pictures had been found in the possession of a young man named Taylor, who was now detained. She said, "Yes, I told Mr Taylor to take them back; what he did was under my instructions." I took her to the police-station. She made no reply to the charge.'

He continued, under cross-examination:

'I conveyed the pictures from Joyner's to Paddington Police-station between 4 and 5 pm, on [the] 21st. I have been to the solicitor for the prosecution since it commenced. I did not take Last there, nor did he go with me. To the best of my knowledge he was not there with me; he may have been, because I believe the solicitor sent on the Saturday for two or three people he had not seen. I believe he was in the solicitor's office while I was in the clerk's room. A statement may have been taken from him in my hearing; I am not aware it was. An indictment was preferred against the prisoner for obtaining these same pictures by false pretences, and that indictment was quashed, I have heard.'

When re-examined, he added: 'I went round with the prosecutor and Mr William Taylor for the pictures, and I took Mr William Taylor into custody then.'

Next up was Elizabeth Baker, who stated:

'I keep a lodging-house at 11 Park Place, Regents Park. On Tuesday, 20th March, the prisoner came to live there, occupying the dining-room floor. Mr Taylor took the rooms for her, and brought her there; he only remained a few minutes and she said he was her agent. On [the] 21st she went out, and I saw her at the police-court on the 22nd.'

Mr Mathews, for the defence, then submitted that there was no case to go to the jury, as the prosecutor had parted not only with the possession but with his property in the pictures, and therefore there could be no felony (according to Queen v. Solomons, 17 Cox, p.93).

The Common Sergeant, without calling on Mr Besley, ruled that it was for the jury to decide whether the boy had unlimited discretion and authority to leave the pictures without the money. An indictment against the prisoner for obtaining the pictures by false pretences had on the previous day been quashed by the Recorder.

When the jury returned, like in 1888 after a very short time, it also brought once more a verdict of 'Guilty'.

Annie then admitted to her previous conviction of misdemeanour at the same court in October 1888, when she had been sentenced to five years' penal servitude.

Inspector Marshall then gave further testimony which proved that , in 1872, the prisoner was sentenced to nine months at Dundee under the name of Mary Ann Bruce Sutherland; that she was the notorious Mrs Gordon Baillie, had committed frauds all over the world and had lead such a history as was unrivalled in crime; that she was probably the greatest adventuress of the age; that she came out of prison in 1892, and her ticket had since expired; that since her release she had done nothing but swindling, complaints having reached the police from all over the country; and that she had lived at 17 Talbot Road for eighteen months, evading the payment of rent by being all the time in negotiation for the purchase of the house.

Sergeant Fuller agreed that since Annie's last release she had done nothing but swindling. He had chased her from place to place, all over the country, and complaints followed at every place she stopped. He said she employed 'gentlemen agents' in her frauds.

On 1 June 1894, Annie was sentenced to seven years' penal servitude – a seemingly harsh sentence for a mere £10 worth of pictures that she had offered to return. However, as before, this took into account her previous convictions and every rumour and allegation that had been laid against her by the police and newspapers over the previous twenty-plus years. What became of the complaints that had reached the police from all over the country is a mystery. Annie took the sentence with her usual stoicism and was led away to the cells. She still had the power to mesmerise people, however, as even in what must have been her darkest hour, her old 'victims' still found it hard to condemn her.

Despite what must have been public humiliation several years before, the 86-year-old Professor Blackie still had sympathy for Annie:

'Of course one knows that Mrs Gordon Baillie is a very "bad hat" indeed and I suppose one ought not to sympathise with her at all in the sentence of seven years, but he must have been a stony hearted man who sat at the Old Bailey last Friday and [saw] that singularly pretty, well dressed, lady-like looking woman with the splendid head of fair hair sent to prison for seven long years without feeling a lump in his throat. No doubt had Mrs Baillie been ugly or disagreeable to look at one would have felt no sympathy at all. But as it was one certainly did. Beauty covers a multitude of sins and I am very thankful I am not a judge before whom pretty women are brought for trial.'

One of the regional papers was similarly shocked:

'She was a picture of womanly beauty in the dock and the sentence of 7 years seems a vindictive one. If a woman gets off with 6 years for smashing a man's skull with a poker after robbing him of £10 [see Chapter 29 below], what ought a woman to receive who orders £10 of pictures which she pledges, not paying for them at the time, but who gets them out of pledge and returns them to the owner? Three months would have been amply sufficient on the same scale of punishment ... The truth is we have got 2 civic judges, the Recorder and the Common Sargeant who think it their duty to pass vindictive sentences on offenders and give 10 years for what the Lord Chief Justice would think 6 months amply sufficient to "fit the punishment to the crime".'

Other sections of the press were less forgiving, although their point was a valid one. *The Globe* of 2 June 1894 was of the opinion that:

'To attempt any reclamation of people of this kind is usually utterly futile. Their intelligence is generally above the average rather than below it as in the case of an ordinary criminal and they enjoy the exercise of their predatory instincts as a wild beast enjoys his hunt for game. You can no more persuade them to give up preying on their fellow men than you could persuade a tiger to eat grass.'

Chapter 29

A Sad Ending
(1894–1903)

The long years of prison stretched ahead of Annie again, and were she almost anyone else the case would have been quickly forgotten; but there was one person who was in no mood to forget. Six months after her sentence was passed, in January 1895, William Taylor, the auctioneer and surveyor who carried on his business from Chancery Lane, claimed £1,000 in damages from picture dealer William Joyner for slander, false imprisonment and malicious prosecution.

Taylor's account was that in March 1894, a Mrs Frost asked him to organize a loan of £600 on furniture at her house in Talbot Road. On a visit there to assess the goods, he met an employee of Mr Joyner, who said that his company had supplied Mrs Frost with ten pictures and he was trying unsuccessfully to obtain payment. Taylor advised him not to worry, and said Mrs Frost had put her affairs in his hands and he was arranging to raise money for her. A little later he went around to see Joyner in person at his premises and was told much the same thing, and that payment would not be long in coming. Joyner replied that if it was going to take much longer, he would rather have his pictures back and be done with the matter. Taylor agreed that this might be the best way forward and said that he would see her about it. Joyner then changed tack and stated: 'I have been to the police about this matter and Mr Fuller, a detective, has been to see me about it. You had better see him and tell him that you are about to return the pictures.'

This Taylor did, meeting Sergeant Fuller at Paddington Police Station, who assured him if the items were returned there would be nothing to worry about. So far, the matter was a simple misunderstanding, easily cleared up; but it was not to be quite that easy. Taylor claimed that he wrote to Mrs Frost at the Isle of Wight and that she was willing to have the pictures returned, but as we have seen, letters to her address there were highly unlikely to receive a reply. He claimed that he then took the pictures to Notting Hill Station and placed them in the cloakroom, before going home feeling very ill. On 20 March he was feeling better and went to see Mr Joyner once more, explaining he had been ill but would bring the pictures over the next day. This he did and placed the pictures on the floor of the shop for Joyner to see. Rather than a shaking of hands and an end to the matter, Joyner slammed the door shut, preventing him from leaving, and said to Taylor: 'You have stolen my pictures and I am going to lock you up for it!'

Joyner then asked the shopkeeper next door to call the police and Taylor was taken away and charged with theft. What provoked this seemingly unreasonable behaviour was that Joyner had received an anonymous note telling him that he was being conned and that Mrs Frost was none other than the notorious Mrs Gordon Baillie. He investigated the matter himself and discovered that included in Frost's inner circle was Lawrence Taylor – William's younger brother. The case turned upon whether the jury thought that Joyner had enough cause to believe Taylor guilty of deception. They decided he probably did and the case against Joyner was dismissed.

Future events showed that their verdict may well have been the correct one. Although William soon faded from view, his brother Lawrence, one-time assistant to Annie, made the newspapers again in September 1897. Celebrations for Queen Victoria's Diamond Jubilee were in full swing and Miss Day, a friend of Taylor's, had hired a house in Royal Avenue, Chelsea, to board visitors for the duration. He invited his friends to the house, and they were treated to the best of everything at the table – at the expense of the local traders. Also during this brief period, items to the value of £20, including blankets and a tea pot, disappeared from the house, only to turn up with various local pawnbrokers – a very familiar tale. Lawrence pleaded guilty, possibly to prevent any further investigation, but not before Detective Morgan had informed the court: 'Taylor was connected with some of the cleverest swindlers in the West-End of London and had once been secretary to Mrs Gordon Baillie.' He was sentenced to three months' hard labour in Wormwood Scrubs, and is not heard from again.

In mid-June 1894, Annie, along with an aging Austrian prostitute named Marie Hermann, were received back at Woking Female Convict Prison at Knaphill. Annie accepted her seven years with her customary *sangfroid*, while Hermann was tearful and bemoaning her hard fate. The latter had been found guilty of manslaughter – that of a client – during an argument over money at her room in Grafton Street, Tottenham Court Road. After battering the old man to death, she stuffed his body into a trunk and moved elsewhere, taking the trunk with her. She was eventually traced and arrested while spending her now ex-client's money on clothes and drink. Originally charged with murder, she was eventually convicted of manslaughter and sentenced to six years – one less than Annie's seven for the attempted theft of a few pictures.

The difference between the two sentences is perhaps explained by the fact that Hermann was defended by the rising star of criminal defence, Edward Marshall Hall.

Annie had, of course, been released from Woking only two years earlier and must have recognized many familiar faces amongst the inmates and staff, including Florence Maybrick, the husband poisoner. In August 1895, Woking Prison closed, and Mrs Maybrick and Annie were moved to Aylesbury.

A year later, in August 1896, a party of visitors to Aylesbury Prison were shown around the large red-brick building that was surrounded by elm trees and shrubs. The report of the visit stated that women prisoners there were allowed one hour's association during each day; the kitchen contained a plentiful supply of brown bread, and if in the hospital wing, inmates were allowed anything the doctor thought best: chicken, fish or even brandy. The work was not severe – some involved machines for making string or twine – and the visitors were shown into a large room where several benches were occupied by women of all ages sewing mail bags for the GPO under the supervision of one or two female warders, and here they found Annie, working away with the others. The prison uniform consisted of a kind of violet skirt with a high hat or poke straw bonnet perched on the head in a perpendicular style, which did little to add to the charm of their appearance. Lights were out at 8.00 pm and inmates had to be asleep by 10.00 pm. Florence Maybrick was now an inmate in one of the hospital cells, her health having been greatly affected by her sentence, but she was described as well behaved and often having a calming effect on the other convicts. Whether she and Annie ever conversed or spent any time together is not recorded, but they did spend years in the same institutions, so there is every possibility there was more than just superficial contact.

After her second long spell of imprisonment, Annie Frost was released from Aylesbury Prison on 25 January 1899, and on that cold, grey winter's day her choices were limited. She was 51 years old and internationally known as a notorious swindler and con-artist. Many of her old contacts had moved on or were in prison themselves, her looks were fading, Sir Richard was long gone and she must have been broke. It was time for a new start. Australia had to be ruled out as a place to operate from, as both her ex-husband and former lover were living there, and she was as infamous in that country as she was in Great Britain. New York therefore seemed an obvious choice. She had spent her honeymoon there with her famous husband, her first child was born there and her second conceived. It was a young, rich and growing country, with many opportunities and strong religious communities. Grand schemes were probably beyond her now, but with her bearing, wit and experience, she could still get by. What she did immediately, we do not know, but certainly by the end of 1902, Annie had reverted to her criminal roots.

* * *

'A tall, handsome, slender woman with grey hair, regular features and manners of exquisite refinement' knocked on the door of Mr Roselle Richardson, a prominent member of the Unitarian Church in New York, on 2 October 1902. The female visitor told him she had just left the Presbyterian Hospital, where she had been for several weeks suffering from blood poisoning in one of her feet; she was out of funds and needed help. She also limped and had the aid of a crutch. She continued with her story: she was a member of the Unitarian Church in Lenox Avenue, she told him, and the pastor, the Reverend Dr Wright, had sent her. Upon investigating her story, Richardson found this to be untrue and contacted Agent Forbes of the Charity Organization Society, who held a bulging file containing scores of complaints against the same woman. A warrant was obtained, and Detective Sergeant Hayes of the Central Office arrested Mrs Louise J.F. Baillie at her lodgings at 307 West 117th Street on a charge of vagrancy. The woman the press had referred to as 'Scotch Ellen' was in custody once more.

When questioned, the prisoner wept and pleaded to be released. When that failed, she changed tack and said: 'Then I shall put a curse on you. Do you remember Le Baron Johnson the fire department chaplain who has had so much trouble lately? I put my curse on him two years ago when he was assistant at Grace Church because he said I was an imposter. Now will you let me go?' The sergeant replied he did not feel inclined to do so, which provoked the response: 'Then I pray to God to curse you, waking and sleeping, standing and lying, eating and drinking, as long as you live!' 'If that is all madam,' replied the sergeant politely, 'let's take a little walk and I'll lock you up.'

The prisoner limped for half a block or so until she was quite convinced there was no way to avoid her fate, then gave up the pretence and, swinging the crutch airily from her right hand, marched along without using it again. On Friday 10 October 1902, Annie – for Mrs Louise J.F. Baillie was just her latest alias – was brought before Magistrate Zeller in the Harlem Police Court, by which time she was limping and using the crutch once more.

'Ah, Your Honour,' she exclaimed from the dock, 'how sad I should be arraigned here, a prisoner before you, when we have mutual friends. The Rev Mr Collier, your friend, is also a friend of mine. He will vouch for me and I can give many ...'

The magistrate cut Annie off in mid-speech, perhaps fearful of what she might say next, but then said: 'I shall postpone the hearing and have an investigation.' Agent Forbes immediately leapt to his feet, exclaiming 'One moment your honour', and hastily produced scores of written complaints against the woman, fearful that if released on bail she would simply disappear.

'Oh, I see,' said Zeller, after realizing the truth of who was standing before him. 'This being the case Mrs Baillie, I sentence you to six months' confinement in the workhouse on Blackwell's Island.' In all honesty, it was not much in the way of a trial!

The 'elderly woman' prisoner, who had given her age as 38 (although by now nudging 55), hobbled away on her crutch, although by the time she reached Harlem Prison (City Prison) it had been discarded once more and was carried under her arm on the journey to Blackwell's Island. The workhouse was a massive granite building built in 1852, which contained 221 cells arranged in tiers along three storeys, and functioned as an institution for the punishment of petty violators. Many of its inmates were classified as habitual 'drunks and disorderlies', including several who had become permanent residents, even though a normal 'stay' was counted in days. Most workhouse inmates were assigned labour either in the workhouse shops or at other island institutions. It was closed and demolished in 1936.

When Annie was searched upon arrival, she was found to have fifty pawn tickets and a list of prominent persons, including many clergymen, in her pockets. Agent Forbes did some research and subsequently issued a statement:

'Scotch Ellen is one of the finest fakers we have ever discovered. Her career is one of the most romantic in the annals of beggary and swindling. She was originally Mary Ann Sutherland, child of a Dundee labourer, but by long association with people of refinement she acquired an air of distinction and a splendid manner. With her patter about noble descent and present bad luck, her patrician speech and air as well as earnest protestations of religion the woman has gathered money wherever she went.

'She was once married to Captain John Hill of the British Royal Engineers, now a retired General, but was divorced. She married again in 1882 at St George's, Hanover Square, to a Scottish solicitor, Allen William Cam, who was afterwards stricken from the rolls for breach of trust. Mrs Baillie claimed that the couple came to New York in 1884 with funds of about £75 and when this ran out they applied to the St George's Society and are said to have received $562 from them. She also claimed a third marriage to Viscount Hamilton.

'Her career in Britain and Australia was meteoric. She was sentenced in London to five years imprisonment in 1888 and her trial was the sensation of the hour. Upon moving to the US, Mrs Baillie had continued her lifetime of fraud and had obtained 5 and 10 dollar bills from many New York and Brooklyn clergymen in the last year. When the Rev Dr George R. Van De Water, rector of St Andrew's Church in Harlem, returned from Europe a few weeks ago she got 10 dollars from him. She then worked her way down through the deaconesses and charity agents of the church.

"Dear Dr Van De Water has been so kind to me," she told them. "After the coronation he visited my father the Earl of Dundonald and was entertained by him. The kind rector was deeply affected as he told me how my father wept as he spoke of his poor estranged daughter Gladys alone and friendless in far-off America duped and despoiled by the heartless wretch who persuaded her to marry him but then stripped her of her riches. But all's well that ends well. My noble father is sending me ample funds to return to our ancient home."'

In the meantime, Forbes added, the high-born lady would be much obliged for a few trifling loans, and she got them. Who could deny a few paltry dollars to a noble earl's child in distress?

Agent Forbes had come up with a bizarre mixture of fact and fantasy. There was indeed a solicitor named Alan William Cam and he did get married at St George's, Hanover Square, but in July 1881 and to a Louisa Florence Catherine Hill, of Buckland's Hotel, Brook Street. She claimed on the register that her father was Thomas Barnes Cochrane, a 'gentleman' and the Eleventh Earl of Dundonald. Research revealed that the family tree did not contain a daughter named Louisa Florence, and that in reality she was the widow of a Captain T. Cowper, who had died some time before 1875, when she married another captain – John Hill of the Royal Engineers. After their marriage they lived in various rented places in England; his wife now calling herself Lady Louisa Hill, despite her husband asking her not to. In January 1877, Hill was called away to his regiment in Burma and she followed him that October, but the camp living arrangements were not everything a lady required, so she returned in May 1878, saying she had urgent business to attend to in the Court of Chancery – and that she was expecting a child.

On the journey back to England, via Calcutta, she began an affair with James Roderick Duff McGrigor – otherwise known as Lord Glengarry – who returned to England with her. She booked into the St James Hotel, Piccadilly, where their affair continued. Once she had run up a suitably large bill, she left without paying and moved to a succession of rented apartments – and a succession of lovers – all the time writing back to her beloved husband in Burma that the baby was a beautiful child and so like its father. During all this time she was running up massive bills, and the family solicitor became so concerned that he contacted Captain Hill, who returned to England in October 1879.

It didn't take Hill long to work out what had been going on. The 'baby' had consisted of a large pillow, there was no Chancery case, Louisa was hundreds of pounds in debt and had had a string of lovers. The divorce was granted in December 1880, with the three named respondents ordered to pay the costs.

Seven months later she married Alan Cam. Cam wasn't from Scotland but from Bedford, in Bedfordshire, the son of a businessman who had obtained his degree at Oxford. On census night in April 1881 he was living in the St Paul's district of Birmingham, aged 27, with his 29-year-old wife, Florence L.I.C.C. Cam, born in Florence, Italy – entered as the daughter of a peer! A couple of weeks later, his partnership with fellow solicitor George Wright, operating from 325 Broad Street Corner, Birmingham, was dissolved, and in early December of that year, he was still in practice, advertising on behalf of an auctioneer seeking a partner. In April, another partnership was dissolved, one between himself and Paul M. James, trading from 40 King Street, Cheapside, London, and by May 1883 he was £3,500 in debt and petitioned for bankruptcy, giving his London office address as 6 King Street, Cheapside.

The following February, Lady Florence Cam of Cromwell Road, Teddington, took one of her ex-employees to court for 'misconducting herself in a manner tending to cause a breach of the peace'. It seems her maid, Emily Herring, believed she was owed money and turned up with a couple of friends on her former employers' doorstep, continued to ring the doorbell and refused to leave. The magnanimous Lady Cam didn't want her punished, she told the court, just made to go away. Herring was about to explain the circumstances to the magistrate when he cut her short and told her she could get a month's imprisonment for this sort of thing, but in view of what Lady Cam had said, he was going to bind her over to keep the peace for six months.

The Cams are next heard of in December 1888, in Glasgow, having returned from New York the previous September. An 'elegantly dressed and pretty young lady', giving the name of Mrs Florence Hill or Cam, appeared in front of the Sheriff, charged with stealing a sealskin jacket from a fur warehouse in Buchanan Street. Despite living in 'excellent style' at lodgings in Bath Street, the pair were short of money and being pressed by the landlady for the rent. To raise funds, they appealed to various charities, with

Mrs Cam claiming she was born in Florence and was the daughter of the Earl of Selkirk. Investigations by one of the charities had discovered the late earl had died childless, help was refused.

Mrs Cam was more successful in an appeal to Dr Underwood, the American Consul, who not only handed over £2 but found her a job in the warehouse, from which she stole the jacket worth £40 and subsequently pawned it for £4.10s. Further enquiries revealed other furs were also missing. In January 1889, she pleaded guilty to theft of goods worth £59 and was sent to prison for three months, and from there her life seemed to deteriorate quite quickly. She appeared at the Old Bailey in November 1891, as Louisa Florence Hill, aged 36, charged with several petty thefts, to which she pleaded guilty and received six months in Holloway. One of the counts was for stealing £7 in rent money from the landlady of her lodgings in Lillie Road, Kensington, under the pretence of taking over the lease of the house and buying the furniture. She used the name Lady Louisa Hill, and stated that her husband had left her and that she was working at The German Exhibition for 30s. per week. After that nothing more is heard of her, concluded Agent Forbes, and her fate was as mysterious as her origins.

The similarities between the two women are uncanny: the delusions of nobility, connections to Scotland, the debts, deception, even down to their physical attractiveness and fondness for sealskin jackets! But for the fact that we know exactly where Annie was at key points, like New York in 1877, rather than Burma, and in prison from 1888–91, we could almost be as convinced that it was her as Agent Forbes was when he reported his findings to the New York courtroom. How the confusion arose is one more mystery in this amazing story. It is extremely unlikely Annie would have claimed the activities of another swindler and serial adulteress – how would that have helped her? The most likely explanation is that Forbes took his stories from the English press and got the accounts mixed up, and by the time the tale was told in court, Annie had no opportunity to refute it and was probably past caring anyway.

Annie was due to be released from the workhouse in March 1903, by which time she would have been 55 years old. The chances of her circumstances improving were slim, and were fast diminishing; her petty swindles were now increasingly transparent and her stories more preposterous, while her mind had become increasingly delusional. Her life as an operative adventuress had been effectively over since her arrest in 1888. Her five-year prison term was swiftly followed by another of even longer length, and the move to New York, where she was reduced to begging for coins and clothing from the clergy, was reminiscent of how she had started out in her teenage years. Unless she had a stroke of good fortune, her most probable fate was to die in obscurity within a workhouse or homeless shelter; a very sad but almost certainly inevitable end to an amazing criminal career. As with other key episodes in her life, any official documentation seems to be missing … what a story she could have told.

Chapter 30

Afterword

Whatever happened to …

KNIGHT ASTON: On Saturday 2 September 1882, within three weeks of stepping off the SS *John Elder*, Knight Aston opened in a new opera, *Boccaccio*, by Austrian composer Franz von Suppe, at the Opera House in Melbourne. It was an immediate success and his part was well received. Aston had made the break from Annie, and whatever his emotional state after parting from her, he was able to face an audience with confidence and build an impressive career. His picture, in full costume, appeared in *The Illustrated Australian News* the following day. The opera ran for sixty-six nights and was succeeded by *The King's Dragoons* and other short runs. In February 1883, however, as the troupe was about to open in Adelaide, the two promoters, Dunning and Wallace, had a furious row, causing the company to split in two. John Wallace and Aston stayed behind in Melbourne, while the others went on as planned. Their loss, it was reported, was severely felt, with replacements having to be found at very short notice.

Dunning was the treasurer and business manager of the company, while Wallace had been stage manager, as well as an accomplished comedian. Within a few days of the split, Wallace and Aston announced 'an entirely new and original entertainment' with which they intended to tour the colonies. Aston took part in a couple of single concerts, including one standing in for a sick tenor in Mendelssohn's oratorio *Elijah*. Not the sort of role he was used to, he still received reasonable reviews given the circumstances.

By April the show was ready and *Mixed Pickles*, an 'original *Tragico*, *Farcico*, and *Dramatico* Entertainment to include Comicalities, Amusing Jokes, and Funny Dances' was let loose upon the public at the Oddfellows Hall, Kilmore, for one night only. On 24 April, they gratuitously gave their talents at the lunatic asylum in Beechworth, and then toured the provinces for a couple of months, although Aston was back in Melbourne by July with the Royal Comic Opera Company, starring as Ralph Rackstraw in Gilbert and Sullivan's *HMS Pinafore*, followed by *Manteaux Noirs* at the Sydney Opera House in August. Wallace, meanwhile, had teamed up with Miss Minnie

Hope and was doing bit parts at the Theatre Royal, before being engaged as the stage manager at the Princess Theatre in Melbourne. There is nothing in the gossip columns about the two falling out, so it seems likely the audience just wasn't there to support their unlikely sounding venture.

Having made their livings independently for a while, Aston and Dunning reunited in March 1884 under the banner of the Dunning Opera Company. Aston travelled in various guises, spending the rest of the year on a brief tour of New Zealand, Tasmania and Adelaide, putting in his first performance in that city at the Theatre Royal in a familiar role in *Boccaccio*. Things were going well; he was singled out for praise wherever he appeared, and was constantly in work, but trouble wasn't far away.

When in Brisbane in May of the following year, there was a benefit concert for Aston, but shortly after that the company got into financial difficulties. For a while Dunning had been paying the players half salaries 'on account', as business was 'dull'. He claimed to have lost £1,000 in Sydney and more than £200 in Brisbane, and stated that the troupe was £10,000 in debt and no more could be paid out in wages. The case went to court, with the players claiming that business was good and that they had played to packed houses and enthusiastic reviews. Aston's name does not appear in the case; possibly he made sure he was paid on time, having learned from Dunning's falling out with his previous partner – he would after all have known more about the details than most, having been in close partnership with Wallace himself.

Aston was now without a patron, so he linked up with Charles Huenerbein and tried once more to be his own boss. From early summer 1885 he began to advertise himself as a 'Professor of Music', based in Sydney, and contactable through Huenerbein. This continued for the rest of the year and into the next, with the occasional concert laid on by Huenerbein. In early June he was engaged at the Sydney Academy of Music in Offenbach's *The Grand Duchess*. Life must have seemed pretty good, his reputation was growing and he had all the work he needed.

Sadly, his past was about to catch up with him. As we have seen, it was around this time that Annie arrived in Sydney, and it was no flying visit. She stayed a week in the town, and it was time for some straight talking. This was probably when the divorce was organized.

On 15 October he opened in Offenbach's *La Fille du Tambour Major* at Melbourne's Princess Theatre and was reunited with his old friend John Wallace, then on 27 November he was married for a third time, to Miss Margaret Johnstone, a fellow opera singer, in Carlton, Melbourne.

On 3 March 1888, Aston was back at the Princess Theatre, playing Valentine in a production of Gounod's *Faust*, when a series of events, worthy of scenes from one of their own comic operas, occurred. Frederick Federici (aka Frederick Baker), an English-born Italian opera singer best known for his roles in Gilbert and Sullivan productions, was playing Mephistopheles and, in the last scene, having spoken his final lines and as he was descending to Hell with Faust, his bright red cloak wrapped around his victim. Amid smoke and flames, he had a heart attack as the trap sank below the level of the stage and was quickly rushed to the 'green room', surrounded by fellow actors still in costume, like a scene from Hell. Despite the application of a galvanic battery and the efforts of doctors for over an hour, he did not recover and died at the age of 37. The audience were unaware of his death – in fact, many in the audience that night claimed to have seen him take a bow with the others at the end. His funeral took place a couple of days later, with Aston as one of the pall bearers. The processional route passed the theatre and into Melbourne General Cemetery. To top all this, the Reverend Godwin, who was conducting the service, collapsed as the coffin was being lowered and had to be carried unconscious from the scene, leaving one of the pall bearers to complete the service.

A month later, Aston himself almost met death. While being driven in a Melbourne cab in heavy rain, the horse's hooves slipped, pulling the cab into the path of an oncoming tram, whose driver only averted disaster by throwing the whole weight of his body on the gripper, which stopped the tram within an inch of the cab.

Meanwhile, Aston continued to be dogged by the world's fascination with his former wife. Two days before Federici's death, *The Scotsman* published the detailed police investigation into Mrs Gordon Baillie. Aston continued to perform on stage while details of his previous life were repeated daily in every newspaper, mixed in with reviews of his current performances in *Dorothy* at the Theatre Royal. Not only did speculation include him in the affair of the pawned furniture from Walthamstow, but many wondered if Aston and Frost were not the same person, pushing him even further into the realm of criminal conspiracy. He had until this time maintained a dignified silence about his estranged wife and her criminality, but continued press speculation about involvement by him in criminal activities provoked a response in the *Tasmanian News* of 20 April 1888:

'To the editor, Mrs Gordon Baillie – Mr Knight Aston in Explanation
'Sir, As my name has been mentioned in your issue of today in connection with the above lady, I wish to say that I was divorced from her some years ago and that she is now (I understand) the wife of a Mr Percy Bromby Frost. I would not have troubled you with this but in justice to

my present wife. By inserting in your next issue you will confer a great favour.'

Whatever knowledge he had of her activities or what his thoughts were as the tale dramatically unfolded, we will never know. This letter was one of only two public comments he made concerning her, the other being a statement to the press saying he had been in the colonies for six years and knew nothing of Mrs Gordon Baillie's deeds; which was really a case of dodging the issue, as the alleged furniture incident happened in 1881, the year before he left.

As we know, Annie and Frost were committed for trial at the Central Criminal Court on 23 July 1888, and in an interview with a journalist shortly after, Annie defended Aston against any wrongdoing, although of course she was also defending her own position:

'Mr White took the lease, and there is nothing fraudulent in what he did. He took over the lease of the house and bought the furniture that was standing in it. I know that he paid at once the £70, the sum mentioned in the agreement of sale to be paid on signing. Then because he disposed of his own property in some manner or other that pleased him best they call it fraud, forsooth! Supposing for a moment that Mr White did not fully pay up the price of the furniture? Why that is a debt surely, not a piece of fraud. Oh! The whole thing is so preposterous, it's perfectly sickening apart from all the considerations of disgrace.'

Aston continued to perform well in Offenbach's *La Fille du Tambour Major*, but the thought that he might be charged over the Walthamstow affair must have caused some anxiety. No decision on the matter had been reached at the end of committals and charges could still have been brought when the case reached the Old Bailey, but in the end were not proceeded with. Possibly the strain had an effect on his health, as in August 1888 he missed two nights while playing in Gilbert and Sullivan's *Princess Ida* due to 'a cold', and as Poo Bah in *The Mikado* at the Theatre Royal, Adelaide, he was off for a while in September and described as 'very unwell'; his complaint is not specified, though he was known to suffer seriously from gout.

In March 1889, Aston made yet another attempt to form his own operatic company, which was to be called the Knight Aston Opera Company, formed and financed by Walter Alden, an American who was to also be its promoter and general manager. Aston's current wife, Maggie, was to supervise costumes, and Aston himself had apparently secured the rights to several new operas. The troupe opened on 21 March at Rockhampton, Queensland, for six nights, and the plan was to move on to Ceylon, India and Japan, followed by the US, at which point several American celebrities would be engaged and the company expanded. Alden had placed £3,000 on account and Aston was to be paid £20 per week, a very high figure for a touring company. The contracts were for an initial two years.

They opened with Lecocq's *Manola* at the School of Arts and the reviews were good; one paper saying the costumes and scenery were exceptional and the whole performance superior to anything seen there before. Everything seemed to be going well and the company was booked on the boat to Batavia en route to China, but things didn't work out as planned. The trip was abandoned, and they returned to Melbourne. What went wrong is not exactly clear, but it seems likely they just ran out of money. In July, Alden was in court for performing plays without a licence and in the following month he claimed £500 in damages against two members of the company for refusing to perform, which was a breach of their contracts. The case was dropped, but obviously all was not well.

Not one to be down or out of work for long, Knight Aston was soon back on stage in Sydney as part of Solomon & Bracy's Opera Company in *The Sultan of Mocha*. Reviews again found him in excellent voice and 'looking 20 years younger' than his last appearance there. Knowing that Annie was safely out of the way was probably a contributing factor. The next few years passed in much the same manner, with him taking the occasional tour and residency, building his reputation and being well reviewed. He gave an interview by telephone to a journalist on *Quiz* magazine in the early part of 1890, in which he outlined his stage career and declared that: 'In the colonies my health has been better than it ever was in England and I don't think I could stand the English climate after this.' In the same interview he describes how he was in Louisville, Kentucky, once when the rain came down so heavily that he was forced to take cover in a church. A black preacher was giving a sermon on how black and white people were the same apart from skin colour, and somehow recognizing Aston as from England he got him to agree that in that country a black man could attend the same church as a white man and even travel on the same buses. Finally the preacher quoted Shakespeare as supporting equality when he wrote: 'A man's a man for all that.' Aston said: 'This was too much for me and I walked out.' This was a pretty amazing response, even given the prejudices of the time, and offers some idea of the nature of the man.

In the summer of 1892 he was reunited briefly with his old friend and former manager Emily Soldene when he appeared in Sydney in *La Fille de Madame Angot*, followed by a spell in Clara Merivale's English Comic Opera Company back in Melbourne, playing the King of Portugal in Johann Strauss's *The Queen's Lace Handkerchief*.

Annie was released from her five-year sentence in October 1893, which might have caused Aston some anxiety, but not for long, as she was back inside within months. Towards the end of 1894, Aston decided to settle permanently in Melbourne. He put an advert in the local papers once more, as a voice coach, before announcing in January 1896 he had now retired from the stage to teach full-time. It was seemingly a premature announcement on both counts, as he was in a concert in Bendigo in February 1896 and stated that he would move there, 'given sufficient inducement'! The pull of the stage (or lack of pupils) was obviously too strong for him, as in February 1897 he signed with promotor Henry Bracy for his old part of in *The Beggar Student* in Sydney, but unfortunately was unable to take the role initially, due to illness. What this was isn't specified, but it was likely a recurrence of gout and he was off for some weeks.

In January 1898, Mr and Mrs Aston sailed for San Francisco to appear at the Orpheum Theatre, along with such wonders as Professor Gallando the lightning clay modeller, The Knaben-Kapelle, a 40-strong troupe from the Hungarian Boys' Imperial Military Band, and Rice and Elmer, comedy athletes. He must have really needed the money. There was a proposed 'tour of the East' that didn't happen, so he was on the boat back home after a few weeks. Retirement was still eluding him, although his work schedule had been greatly reduced. In the summer of 1899, he made his way to The Temperance Hall in Hobart, Tasmania, billed as 'one of the best known artists in the colonies, in fact, in the Old World also, and the original principal in many of the French comic operas in London'. After a few concerts here he returned to Melbourne, but seldom troubled the critics.

In May 1902, he boarded the RMS *Rome* in Adelaide and returned to London after exactly twenty years away. He appeared in fine health and spirits, and had several songs with him that he hoped to get published. He professed himself amazed at the changes which had occurred since he had left. He gave an interesting interview to *The Era* newspaper, along with a portrait, but did not reveal anything about his intentions or personal circumstances. He 'bumped into' Emily Soldene in Southampton Row, and the pair 'exchanged confidences'. He also had his appendix removed while back in England, but apart from that, he is not mentioned again until July 1906, when he is back in Melbourne at The Gaiety Theatre, along with a showing of the 'Instantaneous and Emphatic Furore Caused by our New Biograph Film SAN FRANCISCO DISASTER. The only genuine picture in Melbourne! Portraying the People of America Light-Hearted and Happy – then the awful Catastrophe followed by Rout Ruin and Desolation'. Aston's songs were followed by Shaw and Gilbert, 'End Men & Patter Comedians'. It really must have seemed like the end of the road this time – and it was.

Knight Aston became ill and finally retired. The nature of this illness is not known, but Melbourne newspaper *The Argus* reported the following in its deaths columns in its 11 March 1916 edition:

'ASTON: On 6 March at his residence 96 Brunswick Street, Fitzroy, Thomas Knight Aston beloved husband of Maggie Aston father of Nell, Snowie, Paddie, and Allan after 10 years suffering. Private Internment Melbourne Cemetery.'

He was aged 72.

* * *

PERCY FROST and **HENRY CHAMPION:** Percy Frost's sentence of eighteen months at the Old Bailey in October 1888 was, as we have seen, reduced by three months almost immediately. The details of his time inside have not emerged, but with some remission he would have been freed towards the end of 1889; he was released from bankruptcy on 29 May the same year. He was now free to try to rebuild what must have been the wreckage of his life. His aging mother was still at Woburn Square, and this is probably where he spent the next few months, aided as always by his good friend Henry Champion. There is no record of him ever resuming contact with his daughter or step-children. Annie was, of course, still in prison and it is unlikely he had anything further to do with her, accepting the wiser counsel of Champion and doubtless still reeling from the shock and embarrassment of the revelations at the Old Bailey. As an ex-prisoner and former bankrupt, any reasonable line of employment would have seemed closed to him.

Champion's life was becoming ever more complex. He had been seriously involved with Ben Tillett in the fight for the 'Dockers' Tanner' during the London dock strike of 1889 and emerged with much credit, but he had made powerful enemies within the labour movement, who suspected the motives of the aristocrat in the top hat and frock coat who claimed to support their cause but would take money from the Tories if he thought it would help the movement. His business and the radical paper he published, the *Labour Elector*, was forced to close through lack of support. He was now broke, in danger of being sued for libel by a factory owner he had insulted, in poor health and probably in love with a woman who thought that he was only after her money. These were reasons enough for a change of scenery, and so on 5 July 1890, Percy Frost and Henry Champion sailed saloon-class to Australia on the RMS *Oruba*.

News of Champion's success with the London dock strike had preceded him, and upon arrival in Melbourne he walked straight into involvement with the Maritime Strike of 1890. Presumably Frost was at his side, but his lack of political activity during the 'Gordon Baillie' period and time in prison meant that he retained little public credibility and kept off the stage for the time being. It is probable that he was able to provide financial support for his friend, as his family were still wealthy back in England, and he received the odd amount from them. He was almost certainly near to being a broken man upon his arrival in Australia. In a letter to a mutual friend years later, Champion recalled: 'Frost went to the deuce here completely, he was left a few thousands and drank himself almost to death.'

The maritime strike ended in defeat and there were several who blamed Champion. Even within the socialist world he was a square peg in a round hole, and the general mistrust of his motives followed him across the seas; the idea of an aristocratic socialist went down even less well in Australia than in England. There were brief reports in the press that he and Aston were 'touring Australia' during December, but by June 1891, Champion had returned to London and then to Scotland, where he tried his hand again at leadership of the labour movement, while trying to answer his critics and avoid the scandal of an affair with a married woman.

Little is known of Frost's activities during his first years in Australia, although in August 1894 there is lodged a less-than-enthralling account of the butter export trade compiled by Frost, as an employee of the shipping company McIlwraith, McEacharn & Co. and published in *The Age*. McEacharn had begun his own shipbroking business in 1873, aged 21, and two years later he went into partnership with Andrew McIlwraith in London. The company became very successful carrying goods and immigrants between Britain and Australia.

Frost is reported to have shared a house for several years with Rev Ernest Selwyn Hughes, a Christian Socialist and engaging character, who was vicar of St Peter's Church, Eastern Hill, until 1926. Frost became his sacristan, and his time during this period seems to have been taken up with promoting the increasing Anglo-Catholicism of this church and its rituals rather than the radical political ideology of his former years.

On 5 April 1894, Champion, the human boomerang, returned once more to Melbourne, having had his political aims crushed yet again. In 1895, he became a member of The Wallaby Club, an exclusive walking club for professional, likeminded and 'thinking men': by a bizarre twist, Knight Aston was given honorary membership of the same club. If he and Frost ever met, the conversation must have been fascinating. Champion soon became honorary secretary, while a Mr E.W. Carey became treasurer. Carey was also secretary of the Northern District Starr-Bowkett Building Society and was introduced to Percy Frost. Frost became great friends with Carey, and the pair helped Champion set up in The Champion Printing & Publishing Company with, inevitably, a newspaper of the same name – *The Champion* – that they registered with a capital of £2,500. The directors were listed as Mr E.W. Carey (Queen's Walk), Herbert Brookes (St Kilda Road) and Percy Frost (31 George Street, Fitzroy, Melbourne).

Despite Frost helping with a substantial sum from his inheritance, the paper failed, and Champion was now in poor health, depressed and largely disillusioned with his personal and political life. He tried twice to share a house with Frost and four others, but gave up on that idea, having decided he was 'quite unfit for human companionship, gloomy, dyspeptic and non-gregarious'. His ongoing affair with a married woman, Adelaide Hogg, was the talk of the labour movement and prevented him from standing for any meaningful political position until she went back to her husband and England, never to return.

Despite all the gloom, things were about to take a turn for the better for both he and Frost. In July 1898, Champion became engaged to Elsie Belle Goldstein, second daughter of a good friend of his. Then, only weeks later, Frost married his nurse, Violet Lyle Jessie Richardson, at St Peter's Eastern Hill, Melbourne, and that same year he became superintendent of the large Sunday school there and ran a literary class for young men. Violet was ten years his junior and is credited with nursing Frost through his bouts of excessive drinking. According to Champion, years later, 'He had the DTs pretty badly and then married his nurse and became a completely reformed character.'

The Frosts spent their honeymoon early in 1899 on a tour of Europe, including England, where Violet was introduced to Frost's mother. He continued with his Christian Socialist mission, running a well-attended series of lectures on the subject at St Peter's between 1900 and 1903, and on 15 April 1902 he gave a lecture on 'Housing & Female Labour' on behalf of The Christian Social Union, of which he was honorary acting lay secretary. His role in the church was that of sacristan, looking after the day-to-day care of the church and its contents, as well as parish clerk. The only known photograph of him shows him in the role of server, looking very drawn and solemn in his robes.

Meanwhile, Champion continued to be heavily involved in the promotion of his own brand of socialism through pamphlets, journalism and publishing. In 1899, he and Elsie established The Book Lovers Library, with, of course, a literary journal of the same name. This was, for a while, a great success and he was able to pay off some debts. He suffered a stroke in 1901, which affrected his speech and left him semi-paralyzed, with a limp, as well as being unable to use his right hand for typing.

Frost was employed for a time by a financial agency, before taking charge of it, along with his new friend Carey. This may well have been the Starr-Bowkett Building Society, though Frost's name has not been found in connection with it. Carey had been secretary for many years before fleeing to America with his mistress, and £7,000 of the society's money, in the early part of 1905. Shortly before Carey's defection, on 16 July 1904, Mr and Mrs Frost were on the passenger list for the RMS *Ortona* to London. Accompanying them were Sir Malcolm and Lady McEacharn, the former mayor of Melbourne and founder of the shipping company. McEacharn had lost the mayoral election earlier that year, and left Australia to return to London, taking Frost with him as his secretary. Whether he and Champion kept in touch is not known, but it is likely they saw less of each other now they were both married, although neither produced a family.

Still in Melbourne, where he was to live out the rest of his days, Champion became friends during the First World War with cartoonist David Low, who would later record:

'Who in 1915 would have identified the mild old gentleman, editor of a tiny literary monthly, walking tremulously with the aid of two sticks in the Melbourne sunshine, with the determined young ex-artillery officer H.H. Champion of the 1880s ... No one, I wager. Illness, disappointment and age had long since withdrawn Champion from politics to books. But he retained an interest in justice and right.'

Champion suffered more strokes and the indignity of the bankruptcy court, before he died on 30 April 1928, with Elsie at his side.

There seems to have been no repercussions for Frost over the Carey affair, and his time back in England seems uneventful. Apart from details of a lecture he gave in Croydon before the Church Institute in December 1905, nothing further has been found. His talk on 'Commercial Morality' was well attended, and Frost was described as 'late of the Christian Social Union Council, Melbourne'. In another radical career change, he was offered the post of Professor of English at the university in Perugia, Italy, which he accepted 'for his health', but even here trouble followed him around. In

February 1908, he was with the Melbourne vicar Rev Snodgrass and whilst the pair were admiring some church architecture they were arrested by Italian detectives and taken off to jail, then being dragged before the magistrates to face an extradition warrant. It seems they resembled suspects in a large London jewel robbery and had been followed for two days. Luckily, they were able to prove their whereabouts at the time of the robbery and were released.

Robert Percival Bodley Frost died at the age of 77 on 21 November 1936. There are conflicting reports as to whether it was in Italy or Australia, but either way, Percy Frost was now gone. His wife Violet died eight years later, on 17 March 1944, at the age of 73, at Via Siepe 4, Perugia, Italy. She left her entire estate, valued at £15,908, to Percy and Annie's daughter, Percy Elizabeth Champion Frost.

* * *

DETECTIVE INSPECTOR HENRY MARSHALL: While the case of Annie and Frost was making its way through the courts in 1888, terrible events occurred elsewhere in London, causing the latter months of that year to become known as the 'Autumn of Terror'. A murderous psychopath forever known to history as Jack the Ripper was murdering women in the Whitechapel area of London, and although Marshall was not directly involved in the case, the whole city was on heightened alert.

On 3 October 1888, a case which the press dubbed 'The Whitehall Mystery' was entering its initial stages. The dismembered and badly decayed torso of a young woman was discovered on the site of the new police headquarters on the Thames Embankment. It was found to be a match to an arm found in the Thames at Pimlico sometime previously. As the search progressed, a crane and engine weighing several tons fell from about 60ft and crashed through the concrete floor and into the vaults below. Fortunately the search party heard it coming and were able to jump aside, but only just; it missed them by just a couple of feet.

Shortly afterwards there was a report of a dismembered leg having been found near the railway line in Guildford, and Marshall went out to investigate. He was greeted upon arrival with a brown paper parcel containing what the police doctor claimed to be a right foot and part of a left leg from the knee down to the ankle. The remains, which appeared to have been boiled or roasted, were conveyed back to London. Had it been part of the woman's body its location and condition would have been bizarre enough, but the doctor's conclusion was even more of a surprize – the remains were not human at all but those of a bear! At the same time, the area in which the body was found was thoroughly searched but revealed nothing else, and the police had very little to go on. Press reports of the case ran alongside those of the Whitechapel Jack the Ripper murders, with the possibility that the two were connected. To add to the mystery and embarrassment of the police, a member of the public was, after some trouble, given permission to search the area with his dog, which 'had a nose for this sort of thing'. Within minutes the dog had turned up the lower part of a woman's leg, which had been buried in a few inches of soil within a mere 4ft of the original find! An inquest was heard, the jury returned an open verdict of 'found dead' and the remains were buried at Woking on 30 October. The mystery of the woman's identity remains to this day.

After the conviction of Annie and Frost, Inspector Marshall appeared in many other high-profile cases. One of these concerned a pair of enterprising American con-men, Louis Perlman and Edward Webber, who moved to London in October 1895 and began to advertise a scheme called 'Cash for Brains'. The newspaper adverts asked people to complete a simple word puzzle and send it in to them. Correct entries would receive a £4 reward – but first they would be invited to send 10s.6d. for a tin of Oxyzone, which would arrive with the reward money. The pair received so many replies – an amazing three or four thousand per day! – that they employed nine women to attend to the mail at their office in High Holborn. The wonderful Oxyzone was not mentioned in the advertisement, which merely stated that the exercise was 'an original method of securing a favourable introduction for something more surprising to follow, and for that introduction we are willing to pay'.

Each winning punter, claimed the organizers, would have received their tin of Oxyzone – some 400 had already been sent out, along with the promised £4 reward. If only Marshall hadn't interfered and arrested them before the transactions could be completed! Further details of the scam emerged at the magistrates' court. Oxyzone was said to guarantee to 'keep absolutely pure anything on the face of the earth!'. One firm applied it to many thousands of eggs, which it was able to resell at a vast profit, claimed the advertising. Strange that a tin containing equal measures of charcoal and sulphur and costing only about two pence could have such an effect, but there you are! The enterprising pair were remanded in custody several times, with Marshall constantly opposing bail on the grounds that they would flee. They were committed for trial at the Old Bailey in April, whereupon bail was granted in the huge sum of £2,000 and they were released. According to the American press, their scheme had raked in close to $175,000. On the night of their release, they held a huge banquet for their closest friends, gave each a valuable gift and then scarpered off back to the United States – never to be seen again!

In 1896, two labourers from Notting Hill broke into the house of 79-year-old Henry Smith in Muswell Hill, believing that he kept a lot of money there. Albert Milsome and Henry Fowler were disturbed by Smith as they gained entry and bashed him over the head, causing his death. The pair got away with very little and were tracked down to an address in Bath. On 12 February 1896, Marshall and other officers crept up on the house, obtained entry and despite knowing the pair were armed with revolvers, rushed into the room shouting, 'Hands up, we are the police!' Fowler put up serious resistance – he had been a circus strongman – and it took Marshall and several others to subdue him. During the struggle Marshall was forced to smack him across the head with the butt of his pistol a few times before they could get the cuffs on.

At the trial each blamed the other, and after much histrionics in the dock, with Fowler trying to strangle Milsome, they were sentenced to death. Such was the hatred of the former for his partner in crime that even on the gallows, in June, another condemned man, William Seaman, had to be placed between them, prompting him to comment that it was the first time he had been a peacemaker – an authentic example of gallows humour!

The following year saw the case that Marshall always regarded as his biggest disappointment. When looking back over his career upon his retirement in May 1898 after twenty-nine years in the service, Chief Detective Inspector Henry Marshall stated that his one serious regret was his failure to catch the murderer of Elizabeth Camp.

On 11 February 1897, the 8.35 pm train from Feltham pulled into Waterloo Station and as the cleaner walked through the carriage, he noticed a pair of legs protruding from beneath a seat. These belonged to Miss Camp, a housekeeper at The Good Intent pub in Walworth, South London, who had been on her way to see her fiancé after visiting her two sisters. During the journey she had been beaten around the head with a pestle, which was found on the line with her blood and hair on it. She had fought her killer after the first blow had been struck, but the second one had fractured her skull and killed her. Blood was found in various parts of the carriage and her clothes were torn, indicating a struggle. Unfortunately, the body was taken to hospital and the carriage cleaned before anyone thought to inform the police.

The sole object of the murder seemed to have been robbery. As she worked in a busy pub, her private affairs were well known. She was about to be married, it was said, and her employer had given her a valuable watch. It was also rumoured that she had a fairly large sum of money. There were numerous sightings of 'suspicious looking persons', and the investigation turned up an ex-boyfriend, a 'man who bought a pestle', a wild character at the Elephant and Castle pub at Vauxhall, who trembled so much he could hardly hold his drink, and another at the Alma in Wandsworth with blood down his front, who had hastily downed two brandies and jumped into a cab.

Although robbery was considered the motive, Inspector Marshall's investigations revealed that when she had visited her sister in Hounslow, she mentioned that she had only three shillings on her, while her watch was later discovered in her room in the pub. The miscreant who boarded the train with a pestle in his pocket must have been intent upon robbery or murder. If it was the former, then he got very little for his pains, but if the object of the assault was murder, for some unknown motive, then the perpetrator achieved the perfect crime and a place in the history books. Beyond that we cannot go, as the trail was cold by the time Marshall arrived – the case was never solved.

Marshall retired to the coast – Hove in Sussex – with his second wife of five years, Florence, twenty years his junior, and one servant. He had many years to enjoy his retirement, dying at the age of 88 in 1936. No children have been traced, and it is a great shame he did not write his memoirs after such a long and fascinating career.

* * *

THOMAS HENRY LEE TOLER: As Toler was led down the steps from the dock at the Old Bailey, the future must have looked bleak indeed. He was 52 years old and facing a tough prison regime for up to five years. He and his accomplice William Barrett were taken initially to Newgate, and then on 13 May to Pentonville, to begin their sentences. On 4 March 1880, Toler was moved to Parkhurst to serve out his time.

Records show Barrett was released on licence on 4 April 1883, and unless he had seriously misbehaved it can be assumed that Toler was freed at about the same time. Nothing more is heard of him until April 1885, by which time he was calling himself Tasker Toler and renting a warehouse and basement at 50 Bartholomew Close, near Smithfield, which he occupied until the end of the year. He set up as a wholesale provision merchant and used the place to store various goods, including barrels of butter that he had ordered from Castlereagh in Ireland and was hawking around the local shops. He never paid any rent, and although he claimed to be trading as Tasker Toler & Co., no name board was ever put up. The landlord stated: 'I watched the place to find him and at last found him in a very ragged condition for which he apologized.'

Toler had obviously fallen on hard times, and this may well have been the period during which Annie claimed he came begging to her. Since the spring of 1885 he had been living in lodgings at 60 Sussex Street, Belgravia, supplementing whatever income he had by passing false cheques. In this he was joined by old friend William Rowland Bryant, who had worked with him as general superintendent at New Bridge Street but had not been arrested with the others at the time. Described as of 'good education', Bryant had spent a large part of his adult life in prison for frauds of various kinds, including a term of five years for deception that corresponded roughly with Toler's own incarceration.

In a bizarre twist, Toler decided to put himself forward in the General Election campaign of July 1886 as a parliamentary candidate, standing against Prime Minister William Gladstone for the seat of Leith Burghs. He presented himself as a passionate Unionist in 'violent opposition' to Gladstone's Home Rule policy. His somewhat strange proclamation stated: 'The present time admits of no wavering, no halting between two opinions. The whole ministerial programme is mysterious. Union or separation is a question to be solved and nothing else is before the people.' This, it seems, was only a throwing of his hat into the ring and was to be followed by a full explanation of his political views and creed, but nothing further was heard from him.

Gladstone eventually decided to stand for Midlothian constituency, which must have wrong-footed Toler somewhat and left the Leith Burghs constituency with three Unionist contenders. As one London paper put it:

'First there is Tasker Toler who issues an address which some think will be the end, as it is the beginning, of his candidature; then Mr Donald McGregor a gentlemen commanding much local influence has issued his address as a Unionist candidate also. But meanwhile many Liberal unionists in the Burghs who knowing nothing of Mr Tasker Toler and knowing much about Mr. Donald McGregor favour of the candidature of neither and still hanker after a statesman.'

To no one's surprise, Toler was not selected as a candidate, though some said they would have preferred the 'low comedian of the piece' who had not even shown his face in the Burgh. The result was a resounding victory for the Gladstonian candidate. Whether Toler ever had any serious hopes of being selected or just wanted to vent his views and maybe pocket a bit of campaign money we will never know, but his political career did not last long – and nor did his liberty.

In March 1888, the Edinburgh *Evening Despatch* speculated on his motives:

'It seems to have been an impudent attempt, and presumably a successful one, to promote his interests in the fraudulent acts in which he was then engaged. He was engaged in obtaining money from various persons by false pretences by means of worthless cheques and as part of one or two of these little transactions he might possibly produce a copy of the *Scotsman* or *Evening Despatch* containing his election address as proof of his respectability and good standing.'

On 29 September 1886, Tasker Toler, aged 59, was arrested in Sussex Street on a charge of passing fraudulent cheques. Police Sergeant Cousens said upon finding him: 'I have a warrant for your arrest for this case which we were investigating in the spring. I will read it to you.'

Toler was alleged to have replied: 'You need not do that, if you take me out of this bedroom tonight you will endanger my life!' The policeman responded: 'It's no good mincing matters you'll have to come.' This evoked the response: 'Well if I do I shall destroy some of these papers before I go.' The 'papers' Toler was referring to were on the table, but the sergeant prevented him from destroying them.

Also arrested was long-term associate William Rowland Bryant, who was already serving four months for false pretences in Reading Gaol and thus quite easy to find. Bryant was 45 years old and described as a collector for a trade agency. They were committed for trial at the Old Bailey, and on 22 November 1886, after a short trial, sentenced to five years each. After an initial time in Pentonville, Toler was moved once more to Parkhurst in August 1887.

Toler has not been traced any further, but Bryant continued in his chosen career and was sentenced to seven years in 1893 for false pretences and various small terms after that. Barrett also spent a large part of his remaining years in prison, receiving ten years for forgery in 1894.

* * *

THE CHILDREN: Undoubtedly, one of the most difficult pieces of research for this biography has been trying to trace Annie's children. There are five in total, and the little that we have uncovered is presented in chronological order.

1. Eleanor Mabel Aston was born in about 1873 in London, the result of Knight Aston's first marriage to Mabel Brent. Her name appears on the 1881 census as living with her father in a lodging house at 7 Gower

Street, Finsbury. Aston is described as a vocal artiste, married and aged 31. Eleanor is recorded as being aged 8 years old and born in London. She would have been about a year old when her mother died in March 1874, and about 3 when Annie and Frost met.

Knight Aston does not appear in any theatrical notices between June and October 1881 and no record of the child's birth has been found under Aston, Whyte or White, nor any trace discovered about her after the 1881 census, by which time Aston had, of course, been married to Annie for five years and produced two further daughters. Presumably Eleanor became Annie's stepdaughter upon their marriage. References to Aston having been a good father to Nell, Snowie, Paddie and Alan in his death notice of 1916 is the only other possible reference; Nell was a common diminutive for Eleanor, although this is not proof that she ever went to Australia. If she remained in England, it is likely that she stayed with a relative or at a boarding school. She does not appear with Annie after Aston left the country.

2. Gabrielle Whyte was born in New York in 1877, Annie's first child. The discovery of her pregnancy was possibly the reason for the hurried marriage before Aston left for America. No record of her birth has been found as this was before New York kept such details. The first mention of her by name occurs in March 1888, when she was placed with her siblings for the night in the Thanet Workhouse. Her name was recorded as Gabriel Baillie, born in 1878. Nothing further is known until the census of April 1891, when she is recorded as aged 12, born in New York and living with her sisters in the Rose Street Mission House in the Strand, London. She is probably the girl known as 'Snowie' in Knight Aston's obituary mentioned above.

3. Ada Mary Ogilvie-Whyte was born on 22 November 1878 in a house named Ferndell at Clynder, in the parish of Roseneath, Dumbarton, Scotland. This time there is a birth certificate, which records her father as Thomas Ogilvie-Whyte, a 'merchant', and her mother as Annie Ogilvie-Whyte, formerly Miss Ogilvie. The circumstances of her birth are mentioned in a previous chapter, and she was also listed, under the name of Ada Mary Baillie, at the Thanet Workhouse, although said incorrectly to have been born in 1879. She is recorded in the census for 1891 as Ada White and born in Edinburgh in 1878. Annie wrote a poem about her in 1885, and she is most likely the 'Paddy' mentioned in the 1916 obituary. No further details are known.

Aberdeen Evening Express 1888-03-08.

'A year or two ago there appeared in a number of the 'Railway and Tramway Express' the following verses with the double signature Gordon Baillie (Ayrd Whyte):-

MY PADDY

Wee bonay, happy, prattling' thing'
      An' art thou there,
Wi' a' thy playmates in a ring
      Aroun' thy chair?
Wha' seem tae ma a fairy ban',
Direct from some Elysian lan',
An' thou as fittin' in comman',
      My Paddy.

This twarie weeks they've missed thee sair
      in ilka play.
An' noo they're wonnerin' what for
      Thou look'st sae wae.
But little, little dae they know
Thou hast been wrestlin' wi' a foe
Wha'll some day lay the stoutest low
      My Paddy

Thou'st scarcely learned in life's frail cage
      To pipe a tune,
Ere that fell kite wi' envious rage,
      Pounced on my boon.
But in thy ear why should I mourn?
Why tell thee of my bosom torn?
Though know'st not how such ills are born,
      My Paddy

May Heaven spare thee, bonnie flower,
      Long, long tae bloom,
An' scent the sweet domestic bower
      Wi' love's perfume
An' when thou'st grown a maiden fair,
An' time's snows tinge thy mither's hair,
Her old age frailties be thy care,
      My Paddy.

'These versus were stated to be written about one of her children just recovered from a dangerous illness.'

4. Allen Bruce Whyte was born on 10 September, 1881, at Stoneydown House, West Ham. His birth certificate describes his parents as Thomas Whyte, an artist, and Annie Whyte, formerly Annie O. Bruce. Even less has been discovered about Allen. He was listed as being in the workhouse with the others as Allen Stuart Baillie, born 1881, but does not seem to have been included in the trip to Australia of 1887 nor in the 1891 census for the Rose Street Mission, as this was a women-only hostel. He is mentioned in Aston's obituary, but simply as 'Allen', and was the last child of Annie and Knight Aston.

5. Percy Elizabeth Champion Frost was born on 29 January, 1887, in Cashel Street, Christchurch, New Zealand. Percy Elizabeth appears with some of her half-siblings in the 1891 census, aged 4, as Elizabeth 'White', a pupil at the Rose Street Mission House. Presumably she was entered in the records under the name of White for convenience, as the others were the children of Annie's husband, Thomas White, and Elizabeth's mother probably didn't want to upset the nuns by having children with different surnames. It is also possible that Annie was still married to White at this time, although on the child's birth certificate she gives her name as 'Annie Gordon Frost', with her birth name as Baillie and birthplace as Oban, Scotland.

Understandably, the daughter was not happy with having been given a boy's first name and soon used her middle name, Elizabeth; in some press reports, Annie is described as having two sons. She disappears from the record until the 1911 census, when she is aged 23 and living with maiden aunt Margaret Hannah Frost, aged 62, in Park Avenue, Cricklewood, a pleasant road of large red-bricked semis. She is unmarried and described as of 'no occupation'. Hannah is described as a 'Guardian of the Poor', and appeared on the census of 1901 and electoral role of 1907 as Matron of Willesden Cottage Hospital. The 1911 household also contains Hannah's adopted son, a lad of 13 named Edward Creamer, and Sarah Evans, a servant and cook.

With her parents having gone their separate ways long before, her father with a new wife in Australia and Annie probably in the USA, Elizabeth died a spinster in Canonbury, North London, in 1956, at the age of 69, after what must have been a rather lonely life with no family or occupation. She left the substantial sum of £24,000, a goodly portion of which came from her father's widow, Violet, who had died in 1944. The money went to the Treasury, as by the time of her death she had no known relatives and died intestate.

The most obvious problem with tracing the three children that Annie had with Knight Aston is the constant changing of names. Neither could be found in the census of 1901, and if they were still living in England, Ada, the younger of the two girls, would have been 23 and Gabrielle 24 – both could easily have been married by then. Other possibilities are that they changed their names – or had them changed to avoid any notoriety – or one or both may have fallen prey to the many epidemics prevalent in London at that time. On the rare occasions that Annie is mentioned in connection with her children, their names are not given and they are referred to as either her two or three 'beautiful children'; but does this include Aston's daughter, Eleanor, or was she put somewhere else entirely, away from the mayhem? It is the fond hope of the authors that the publication of this research will produce some information about their eventual fate and maybe even some descendants.

*   *   *

There were many unrecognized victims of Annie's long career. A correspondent wrote to the *Star* from Broadstairs to say:

'It is very hard for Sir Richard King's servants but what of the poor servants Mrs G.B. engaged itself, many with long and good characters. Now because they cannot live with the woman she has turned out to be they lose wages and character both. One I know who is quite respectable went to see a lady the other day respecting a situation and was in every way suitable. When the said lady was told with whom she had been living she would not think of engaging her and expressed surprise that the girl should apply for the situation. This girl had not known anything about Mrs Gordon Baillie's previous character. This is only one case of many. There is one worse still. A poor washerwoman at Broadstairs with a large family who cannot get any money is in very bad circumstances.'

*   *   *

And of Annie herself? This poem was reprinted in the *Aberdeen Free Press* of 13 March 1888, without provenance or comment other than to say that it was 'written in a rather questionable feminine hand'. Presumably it was sent to the paper anonymously; could it be Annie explaining herself at last?

A GENTLE REMONSTRANCE

Here's a scandalous fuss! Here's a hue and cry!
In the chase of a poor fluttering frail butterfly;
Here's a grinding and gnashing of molar's in rage –
Sure we live in a carping, censorious age!
But go slow, friendly critics; I'm bound to protest
That it's time to be giving a woman a rest,
For all that your rumpus and riot's about
Is the sin I've committed of being found out.

> And I marvel your censures so savage should be
> On a beautiful cadger of noble degree.

It is true that I've begged and I've borrowed where'er
I discovered a Juggins with shekels to spare.
That my 'sweet pensive face' and my 'deep earnest eyes'
Were the baits to which wealthy old grudgeons would rise;
But why should your moral in *my* case be sought
When you've lords and MPs in the Bankruptcy Court?
As to punishment – pooh! Keep this fact in your head
That our jails are for beggars who beg for more bread;

> Not for gentlemen born who go 'broke on the spree'
> Nor a sweet lady cadger of noble degree.

But begging? What nonsense! – subscription's the word;
And to question the object were quite too absurd,
When a lady drives up to your door in her chaise,
And the graceful young darling your sympathy prays
For African blacks, Jewish perverts at home,
Scotch crofters, or Protestant converts in Rome,
When you know – or you think –she's got wealth of her own,
Then you sign a fat cheque for your sins to atone,

> While you pleasantly mention how grateful you be
> To the dashing young cadger of noble degree.

Yes, I'd rattle the box, in my sweet winsome way,
And merchants and brokers – e'en lawyers would pay,
In the free-handed style of each sinner who tries
To purchase a mansion of bliss in the skies.
How simple it seemed, by vicarious aid,

To wipe out the record of lies told in trade;
Of smart overreaching's by sharp versus flat,
By pitching a cheque into Charity's hat;

>And Charity's cloak fitted warmly round *me*
>The rakish young cadger of noble degree.

Perhaps as you say, people failed to get news
From the crofters, the Romans, the niggers and Jews,
Of the poor I had succoured, the sick brought to health –
It was clearly my practice to do good by stealth!
Yet my maxim was simple, by all understood,
'For the greatest of numbers the greatest of good.'
And the Inference plain, controverted by none,
Is the greatest of numbers is great Number One!

>Yes, that was the figure most precious to me
>To the beautiful cadger of noble degree!

But turn on your limelight; I prithee look round,
And say if alone of my tribe I am found;
Some queer little dodges I think you'll recall,
If you'd worked the May meetings at Exeter Hall.
Is there never a mission that comes to your mind,
Whose officers sleek in a palace you'll find.
When they shift through a ladder the gifts of the good
And the Blacks get the pieces that stick to the wood?

>Where Pecksniff presides as the secreta-ree
>O'er an army of cadgers of noble degree?

If the devil was casting his net, have you thought
What crowds of big fish up in town would be caught
Where they pray and they preach and they pass round the hat
For promotion of this and prevention of that?
If the meshes were tightened, each fraud to contain,
Would the Salvation Army slip through them like rain?
Ah! beggars imprisoned for vagrancy's crime
Must grin as they think, while they are 'doing their time'

>Of the coin that was cadged for the Queen's Jubilee
>By fine lady cadgers of noble degree!

So sharpen you blades, noble knights of the Press,
And slash at your quarry, sans mercy *****

In brief, spicy, sections my story relate –
How I plundered the pious and nobbled the great,
How I moved in Society's innermost 'set',
How I bilked all my tradesman and paid ne'er a debt,
But if *that* is your heaviest charge to be brought,
With bankers and baronets still I'll consort;

> And remember I pray, when you're slating poor me
> Other feminine cadgers of noble degree.

Index